Preventing Reading Difficulties in Young Children

Catherine E. Snow, M. Susan Burns,
and Peg Griffin, *Editors*

Committee on the Prevention of Reading Difficulties
in Young Children

Commission on Behavioral and
Social Sciences and Education

National Research Council

NATIONAL ACADEMY PRESS
Washington, DC   1998

NATIONAL ACADEMY PRESS   2101 Constitution Avenue, N.W.   Washington, D.C. 20418

NOTICE: The project that is the subject of this report was approved by the Governing Board of the National Research Council, whose members are drawn from the councils of the National Academy of Sciences, the National Academy of Engineering, and the Institute of Medicine. The members of the committee responsible for the report were chosen for their special competences and with regard for appropriate balance.

The study was supported by Grant No. H023S50001 between the National Academy of Sciences and the U.S. Department of Education. Any opinions, findings, conclusions, or recommendations expressed in this publication are those of the author(s) and do not necessarily reflect the views of the organizations or agencies that provided support for this project.

Library of Congress Cataloging-in-Publication Data

Committee on the Prevention of Reading Difficulties in Young Children.
    Preventing reading difficulties in young children / Committee on the Prevention of Reading Difficulties in Young Children ; Catherine E. Snow, M. Susan Burns, and Peg Griffin, editors.
        p. cm.
    Includes bibliographical references and index.

    ISBN 0-309-06418-X (cloth)
    1. Reading (Primary)—United States. 2. Reading disability—United States. 3. Reading—Remedial teaching—United States. 4. Reading comprehension—United States. 5. Word recognition. I. Snow, Catherine E. II. Burns, M. Susan (Marie Susan) III. Griffin, Peg. IV. Title.
    LB1525.76 .C66 1998
    372.4—ddc21
                                                                        98-9031

Additional copies of this report are available from National Academy Press, 2101 Constitution Avenue, N.W., Lockbox 285, Washington, D.C. 20055.
Call (800) 624-6242 or (202) 334-3313 (in the Washington metropolitan area).
This report is also available online at http://www.nap.edu

First Printing, June 1998
Second Printing, September 1998
Third Printing, January 1999
Fourth Printing, May 1999
Fifth Printing, October 1999

COMMITTEE ON THE PREVENTION OF READING DIFFICULTIES IN YOUNG CHILDREN

The National Academy of Sciences is a private, nonprofit, self-perpetuating society of distinguished scholars engaged in scientific and engineering research, dedicated to the further-ance of science and technology and to their use for the general welfare. Upon the authority of the charter granted to it by the Congress in 1863, the Academy has a mandate that requires it to advise the federal government on scientific and technical matters. Dr. Bruce M. Alberts is president of the National Academy of Sciences.

The National Academy of Engineering was established in 1964, under the charter of the National Academy of Sciences, as a parallel organization of outstanding engineers. It is autonomous in its administration and in the selection of its members, sharing with the Na-tional Academy of Sciences the responsibility for advising the federal government. The Na-tional Academy of Engineering also sponsors engineering programs aimed at meeting national needs, encourages education and research, and recognizes the superior achievements of engi-neers. Dr. William A. Wulf is president of the National Academy of Engineering.

The Institute of Medicine was established in 1970 by the National Academy of Sciences to secure the services of eminent members of appropriate professions in the examination of policy matters pertaining to the health of the public. The Institute acts under the responsibility given to the National Academy of Sciences by its congressional charter to be an adviser to the federal government and, upon its own initiative, to identify issues of medical care, research, and education. Dr. Kenneth I. Shine is president of the Institute of Medicine.

The National Research Council was organized by the National Academy of Sciences in 1916 to associate the broad community of science and technology with the Academy's pur-poses of furthering knowledge and advising the federal government. Functioning in accor-dance with general policies determined by the Academy, the Council has become the principal operating agency of both the National Academy of Sciences and the National Academy of Engineering in providing services to the government, the public, and the scientific and engi-neering communities. The Council is administered jointly by both Academies and the Institute of Medicine. Dr. Bruce M. Alberts and Dr. William A. Wulf are chairman and vice chairman, respectively, of the National Research Council.

Preface

"Few things in life are less efficient than a group of people trying to write a sentence" (Scott Adams, *The Dilbert Principle*, 1996). The decision that a group of people should write a report of this size clearly was not motivated by the goal of efficiency; it was motivated by the goals of comprehensiveness and accuracy and made feasible by the expectation of compromise and consensus. The field of reading is one that has long been marked by controversies and disagreements. Indeed, the term "reading wars" has been part of the debate over reading research for the past 25 years. The unpleasantness of the conflicts among reading researchers was moderated, if not eliminated, by the realization that all the participants are primarily interested in ensuring the well-being of young children and in promoting optimal literacy instruction.

The study reported in this volume was undertaken with the assumption that empirical work in the field of reading had advanced sufficiently to allow substantial agreed-upon results and conclusions that could form a basis for breaching the differences among the warring parties. The process of doing the study revealed the correctness of the assumption that this has been an appropriate time to undertake a synthesis of the research on early reading development. The knowledge base is now large enough that the controversies that have dominated discussions of reading development and reading instruction have given way to a widely honored *pax lectura*, the conditions of which include a shared focus on the needs and rights of all children to learn to read. Under the treaties that have recently been entered into, furthermore, the focus of attention has shifted from the researchers' theories and data back to the teacher, alone in her classroom with a heterogeneous group of children, all awaiting their passports to literacy.

From the perspective of the teacher, our task can be conceptualized as cutting through the detail of partially convergent, sometimes discrepant research findings to provide an integrated picture of how reading develops and how reading instruction should proceed. It may come as a surprise to the reader to find that consensus in achieving that integrated picture, among the members of this diverse committee, was not difficult to reach. All members agreed that reading should be defined as a process of getting meaning from print, using knowledge about the written alphabet and about the sound structure of oral language for purposes of achieving understanding. All thus also agreed that early reading instruction should include direct teaching of information about sound-symbol relationships to children who do not know about them and that it must also maintain a focus on the communicative purposes and personal value of reading.

In this report, the committee makes recommendations for practice, as well as recommendations for further research that needs to be undertaken. Our discussions also explored how people need to start thinking about reading and reading instruction. This turned out to be harder to formulate, because it evokes the often frustrating and familiarly academic position that "this is an incredibly complicated phenomenon." Although we can see the readers' eyes rolling at the predictability of this claim, we nonetheless persist in the contention that much of the difficulty in seeking real reforms in reading instruction and intervention derives from simplistic beliefs about these issues, and so one step in improving matters involves making the complexities known.

Not only the first-grade teacher, but also the parent, the pediatrician, the school administrator, the curriculum consultant, the textbook publisher, the state legislator, and the secretary of education need to understand both what is truly hard about learning to read and how wide-ranging and varied the experiences are that support and facilitate reading acquisition. All these people need to understand as well that many factors that correlate with reading fail to explain it, that many experiences contribute to reading development without being prerequisite to it, and that there are many prerequisites, so no single one can be considered sufficient.

The focus of this report is prevention. We thus try to sketch a picture of the conditions under which reading is most likely to develop easily—conditions that include stimulating preschool environments, excellent reading instruction, and the absence of any of a wide array of risk factors. Our focus on trying to provide optimal conditions does not mean that we think that children experiencing less than optimal conditions are in any sense doomed to failure in reading; many children from poor and uneducated families learn to read well, even without excellent preschool classroom experience or superb early reading instruction. Nonetheless, with an eye to reducing risk and preventing failure, we focus on mechanisms for providing the best possible situation for every child.

We submit this report with high hopes that it may indeed mark the end of the reading wars and that it will contribute to the successful reading development of many children. It is the collective product of the entire committee, and it could not have been produced without the selfless contributions of time, thought, and hard work of all members, or without their willingness to confront with integrity and resolve with grace their many productive disagreements with one another.

> Catherine Snow, *Chair*
> Susan Burns, *Study Director*
> Committee on the Prevention of Reading
> Difficulties in Young Children

Addition to the Preface, Third Printing

Since its release in March 1998, *Preventing Reading Difficulties in Young Children* has captured considerable attention. While it is, of course, gratifying to have the work of the committee validated, the carefully crafted message of the book has sometimes been represented in a way that is somewhat simplified or even, in some cases, distorted. Thus we take this opportunity to restate with emphasis what we see as the core message concerning reading instruction: that reading instruction *integrate* attention to the alphabetic principle with attention to the construction of meaning and opportunities to develop fluency.

The committee's position has often been presented as one endorsing "balance" or "some phonics and some whole language." "Balance" is not the right metaphor to carry our message, and we certainly did not suggest an approach that involved "a little of this and a little of that." "Balance" could mean splitting one's time evenly across activities designed to practice the alphabetic principle and activities designed to support comprehension. "Integration" means precisely that the opportunities to learn these two aspects of skilled reading should be going on at the same time, in the context of the same activities, and that the choice of instructional activities should be part of an overall, coherent approach to supporting literacy development, not a haphazard selection from unrelated, though varied, activities.

A list of developmental accomplishments typical of children at various ages was included in the report, with some diffidence. We cautioned that these were "neither exhaustive nor incontestable" and that "the timing of these accomplishments will to some extent depend on maturational and experiential differences between children." Thus, finding some of these developmental accomplishments written into the Head Start reauthorization bill as bases for judging the adequacy of Head Start classrooms was somewhat surprising; we can only hope that the net effect is to improve the consistency of attention to genuinely enriching language and literacy experiences in Head Start, and not to penalize programs or children who fail to meet the expectations.

The value of a report like this one is that it represents a solid platform of consensus across a wide array of perspectives, from which collaborative efforts at educational improvement can be undertaken. The consensus achieved is not permanent; research will continue to refine our views of how skilled readers function, of what factors contribute to skilled reading and constitute risks to its easy development, and of the features of excellent reading instruction. Nonetheless, the consensus achieved has already been taken advantage of in national and several state-level efforts at reading reform, and as such has proved its value in deflecting attention from conflicts about reading methods to a concerted effort to prevent reading difficulties.

Still, the report outlines important challenges. Although it concludes that a knowledge base for greatly improving reading outcomes already exists, it also suggests that substantial improvement in the preparation, support, and ongoing professional development of early childhood and primary educators is needed. We argue in the report that teacher education needs to be rethought and redesigned in quite radical ways, if the goal of minimizing the incidence of reading difficulties is to be achieved. Members of the committee have been energetic in bringing the message of the report to professional organizations, to school districts, and to sites for professional development of classroom teachers, but structural changes that go far beyond these efforts are clearly needed. We welcome this third printing as evidence that interest in preventing reading difficulties is widespread among American educators.

December 1998

Acknowledgments

Many people contributed in many different ways to the completion of this report, and we are most grateful for their efforts. First, the committee and staff would like to acknowledge Ellen Schiller (U.S. Department of Education), Naomi Karp (U.S. Department of Education), and Reid Lyon (National Institutes of Health) for assistance given during the project. Judith Heumann, Tom Hehir, and Louis Danielson of the Office of Special Education (U.S. Department of Education) and Duane Alexander of the National Institutes of Health provided support and encouragement. Our thanks to Rebecca Fitch (U.S. Department of Education) and Fritz Mosher (Carnegie Corporation) for their help in developing plans for liaison activities.

During the information-gathering phase of our work, a number of people made presentations to the committee on programs that focused on the prevention of reading difficulties: Steve Barnett (moderator); Elizabeth Segal (Beginning with Books); Marcia Invernizzi (Book Buddies); Andrew Hayes (Comprehensive Family Literacy Program); John Guthrie (Concept-Oriented Reading Instruction); Bob Stark (Early ID: Reading Early Identification and Intervention); Barbara Taylor (Early Intervention in Reading); Jerry Zimmerman and Carolyn Brown (Breakthrough to Literacy); Sabra Gelfond (HAILO); Annette Dove (Home Instruction Program for Preschool Youngsters—HIPPY); Pia Rebello (Home Instruction Program for Preschool Youngsters—HIPPY); Darcy Vogel (Intergenerational Tutoring Program); Ethna Reid (Keyboarding, Reading, Spelling); Bob Lemire and Kathy Hook (Phonics-Based Reading); George Farkas (Reading One-One); M. Trika Smith-Burke (Reading Recovery); James Wendorf, Linda Gambrell, and Suzanne Kealey (RIF's Running Start Program); John Nunnary (Success For All); Marilyn Howard (Auditory Discrimination in Depth).

In addition, materials and advice were provided by various programs and professional and advocacy groups. The program materials include: 4 H Family; Books Aloud; Books and Beyond; Children's Television Workshop/Sesame Street; Class-Wide Peer Tutoring; Cornell Cooperative Extension; Dyslexia Training Program; Expeditionary Learning Outward Bound; First Book; Four Blocks; Four Remedial Reading Programs; Friend/Non-Friend; Getting Books in Children's Hands; Ladders to Literacy: Kindergarten; Ladders to Literacy: Preschool; Listening Comprehension; Little Planet Publishing; National Reading Research Center-Georgia; National Speech Language Therapy Center; New Chance; Open Court; Project Read Program; Project Seed; Reach Out and Read; Readnet: Pathways to Literacy Readnet Foundation; Stony Brook Reading and Language; Sound Partners; Waterford Early Reading Program; Wiggle Works; and Youth Opportunities Unlimited.

The professional associations and other groups include the American Association of Colleges for Teacher Education; American Humane Association; American Library Association; American Psychological Association, Division 37; Child, Youth and Family Services; American Public Welfare Association; Big Brothers/Big Sisters of America; Child Welfare League of America; Families, 4-H and Nutrition; Home and School Institute; Initiatives for Children; Institute for Educational Leadership; International Reading Association; Learning Disabilities Association; National 4-H Council; National Association for Bilingual Education; National Association of Elementary School Principals; National Association of School Psychologists; National Association of State Boards of Education; National Center for Education in Maternal and Child Health; National Center for Family Literacy; National Center for Immigrant Students; National Education Association; National School Boards Association; Save the Children International; and School-Age Child Care Project.

The panel was assisted in its deliberations by a number of people who wrote background papers: Steven Barnett, "The Effects of Preschool Programs on Reading Achievement"; Lynn Fuchs, "Monitoring Student Progress Toward the Development of Reading Competence: Classroom-Based Assessment Methods"; Stanley Herr, "Special Education Law and Young Children with Reading Disabilities or at Risk of Such Disabilities"; Laura Klenk, "Review of Selected Remediation and Early Intervention Programs"; James McClelland, "The Basis and Remediation of Language Impairments in Children"; Kevin S. McGrew, "The Measurement of Reading Achievement by Different Individually Administered Standardized Reading Tests: Apples and Apples, or Apples and Oranges?"; Robert Needlman, "Pediatric Interventions to Prevent Reading Problems in Young Children"; Carol Padden, "Reading and Deafness"; Bennett A. Shaywitz, "The Neurobiology of Reading and Reading Disability"; Margaret J. Snowling, "A Review of the Literature on Reading, Informed by PDP Models, with Special Regard to Children Between Birth and Age 8, Who May Be at Risk of Not Learning to Read."

Numerous researchers also shared their work with the committee, including Catherine Dorsey-Gaines (Kean College of New Jersey); Vivian L. Gadsden (University of Pennsylvania); Russell Gersten (University of Oregon); Robert Rueda (University of Southern California); Rune J. Simeonsson (University of North Carolina); Frank R. Vellutino (State University of New York, Albany); and special education project directors present at our information-gathering meeting in July 1996.

This report has been reviewed by individuals chosen for their diverse perspectives and technical expertise, in accordance with procedures approved by the National Research Council's Report Review Committee. The purpose of this independent review is to provide candid and critical comments that will assist the authors and the National Research Council in making the published report as sound as possible and to ensure that the report meets institutional standards for objectivity, evidence, and responsiveness to the study charge. The content of the review comments and draft manuscript remain confidential to protect the integrity of the deliberative process.

We wish to thank the following individuals for their participation in the review of this report: Benita A. Blachman, School of Education, Syracuse University; Peter Bryant, Department of Experimental Psychology, University of Oxford; Courtney Cazden, Graduate School of Education, Harvard University; Britton Chance, Departments of Biochemistry and Biophysics (emeritus), University of Pennsylvania; Ruth Fielding-Barnsley, Psychology Department, University of New England, New South Wales, Australia; John Guthrie, College of Education, University of Maryland, College Park; Eileen Kowler, Department of Psychology, Rutgers University; Frank Manis, Department of Psychology, University of Southern California; Luis Moll, Division of Language, Reading, and Culture, University of Arizona; P. David Pearson, College of Education, Michigan State University; W. Charles Read, School of Education, University of Wisconsin, Madison; Patrick Suppes, Center for the Study of Language and Information (emeritus), Stanford University; Richard Wagner, Department of Psychology, Florida State University; and Grover J. Whitehurst, Department of Psychology, State University of New York, Stony Brook.

While the individuals listed above have provided many constructive comments and suggestions, responsibility for the final content of this report rests solely with the authoring committee and the National Research Council.

Throughout the research, conceptualization, and writing phase of this work, our coeditor, Peg Griffin, was an invaluable colleague—a strong-minded collaborator, a tireless writer, and a reliably good-natured colleague. Alexandra Wigdor, director of the Division on Education, Labor, and Human Performance, and Janet Hansen, also of the division, provided guidance and support throughout the project. This final product has benefited enormously from the editorial attention of Christine McShane. Marie Suizzo, Marilyn Dabady, Roger Butts, and Sharon Vandivere ably assisted the committee at different stages. The committee extends its sincere thanks and appreciation to all those who assisted us in our work.

Catherine Snow, *Chair*
Susan Burns, *Study Director*
Committee on the Prevention of Reading
Difficulties in Young Children

Contents

Preventing
Reading
Difficulties
in Young
Children

Executive Summary

Reading is essential to success in our society. The ability to read is highly valued and important for social and economic advancement. Of course, most children learn to read fairly well. In this report, we are most concerned with the large numbers of children in America whose educational careers are imperiled because they do not read well enough to ensure understanding and to meet the demands of an increasingly competitive economy. Current difficulties in reading largely originate from rising demands for literacy, not from declining absolute levels of literacy. In a technological society, the demands for higher literacy are ever increasing, creating more grievous consequences for those who fall short.

The importance of this problem led the U.S. Department of Education and the U.S. Department of Health and Human Services to ask the National Academy of Sciences to establish a committee to examine the prevention of reading difficulties. Our committee was charged with conducting a study of the effectiveness of interventions for young children who are at risk of having problems learning to read. The goals of the project were three: (1) to comprehend a rich but diverse research base; (2) to translate the research findings into advice and guidance for parents, educators, publishers, and others involved in the care and instruction of the young; and (3) to convey this advice to the targeted audiences through a variety of publications, conferences, and other outreach activities.

THE COMMITTEE'S APPROACH

The committee reviewed research on normal reading development and instruction; on risk factors useful in identifying groups and individuals at risk of reading failure; and on prevention, intervention, and instructional approaches to ensuring optimal reading outcomes.

We found many informative literatures to draw on and have aimed in this report to weave together the insights of many research traditions into clear guidelines for helping children become successful readers. In doing so, we also considered the current state of affairs in education for teachers and others working with young children; policies of federal, state, and local governments impinging on young children's education; the pressures on publishers of curriculum materials, texts, and tests; programs addressed to parents and to community action; and media activities.

Our main emphasis has been on the development of reading and on factors that relate to reading outcomes. We conceptualized our task as cutting through the detail of mostly convergent, but sometimes discrepant, research findings to provide an integrated picture of how reading develops and how its development can be promoted.

Our recommendations extend to all children. Granted, we have focused our lens on children at risk for learning to read. But much of the instructional research we have reviewed encompasses, for a variety of reasons, populations of students with varying degrees of risk. Good instruction seems to transcend characterizations of children's vulnerability for failure; the same good early literacy environment and patterns of effective instruction are required for children who might fail for different reasons.

Does this mean that the identical mix of instructional materials and strategies will work for each and every child? Of course not. If we have learned anything from this effort, it is that effective teachers are able to craft a special mix of instructional ingredients for every child they work with. But it does mean that there is a common menu of materials, strategies, and environments from which effective teachers make choices. This in turn means that, as a society, our most important challenge is to make sure that our teachers have access to those tools and the knowledge required to use them well. In other words, there is little evidence that children experiencing difficulties learning to read, even those with identifiable learning disabilities, need radically different sorts of supports than children at low risk, although they may need much more intensive support. Childhood environments that support early literacy development and excellent instruction are important for all children. Excellent instruction is the best intervention for children who demonstrate problems learning to read.

CONCEPTUALIZING READING AND READING INSTRUCTION

Effective reading instruction is built on a foundation that recognizes that reading ability is determined by multiple factors: many factors that correlate with reading fail to explain it; many experiences contribute to reading development without being prerequisite to it; and although there are many prerequisites, none by itself is considered sufficient.

Adequate initial reading instruction requires that children:

- use reading to obtain meaning from print,
- have frequent and intensive opportunities to read,
- be exposed to frequent, regular spelling-sound relationships,
- learn about the nature of the alphabetic writing system, and
- understand the structure of spoken words.

Adequate progress in learning to read English (or any alphabetic language) beyond the initial level depends on:

- having a working understanding of how sounds are represented alphabetically,

- sufficient practice in reading to achieve fluency with different kinds of texts,
- sufficient background knowledge and vocabulary to render written texts meaningful and interesting,
- control over procedures for monitoring comprehension and repairing misunderstandings, and
- continued interest and motivation to read for a variety of purposes.

Reading skill is acquired in a relatively predictable way by children who have normal or above-average language skills; have had experiences in early childhood that fostered motivation and provided exposure to literacy in use; get information about the nature of print through opportunities to learn letters and to recognize the internal structure of spoken words, as well as explanations about the contrasting nature of spoken and written language; and attend schools that provide effective reading instruction and opportunities to practice reading.

Disruption of any of these developments increases the possibility that reading will be delayed or impeded. The association of poor reading outcomes with poverty and minority status no doubt reflects the accumulated effects of several of these risk factors, including lack of access to literacy-stimulating preschool experiences and to excellent, coherent reading instruction. In addition, a number of children without any obvious risk factors also develop reading difficulties. These children may require intensive efforts at intervention and extra help in reading and accommodations for their disability throughout their lives.

There are three potential stumbling blocks that are known to throw children off course on the journey to skilled reading. The first obstacle, which arises at the outset of reading acquisition, is difficulty understanding and using the alphabetic principle—the idea that written spellings systematically represent spoken words. It is hard to comprehend connected text if word recognition is inaccurate or laborious. The second obstacle is a failure to transfer the comprehension skills of spoken language to reading and to acquire new strategies that may be specifically needed for reading. The third obstacle to reading will magnify the first two: the absence or loss of an initial motivation to read or failure to develop a mature appreciation of the rewards of reading.

As in every domain of learning, motivation is crucial. Although most children begin school with positive attitudes and expectations for success, by the end of the primary grades and increasingly thereafter, some children become disaffected. The majority of reading problems faced by today's adolescents and adults are the result of problems that might have been avoided or resolved in their early childhood years. It is imperative that steps be taken to ensure that children overcome these obstacles during the primary grades.

Reducing the number of children who enter school with inadequate literacy-related knowledge and skill is an important primary step toward preventing reading difficulties. Although not a panacea, this would serve to reduce considerably the magnitude of the problem currently facing schools. Children who are particularly likely to have difficulty with learning to read in the primary grades are those who begin school with less prior knowledge and skill in relevant domains, most notably general verbal abilities, the ability to attend to the sounds of language as distinct from its meaning, familiarity with the basic purposes and mechanisms of reading, and letter knowledge. Children from poor neighborhoods, children with limited proficiency in English, children with hearing impairments, children with preschool language impairments, and children whose parents had difficulty learning to read are particularly at risk of arriving at school with weaknesses in these areas and hence of falling behind from the outset.

RECOMMENDATIONS

The critical importance of providing excellent reading instruction to all children is at the heart of the committee's recommendations. Accordingly, our central recommendation characterizes the nature of good primary reading instruction. We also recognize that excellent instruction is most effective when children arrive in first grade motivated for literacy and with the necessary linguistic, cognitive, and early literacy skills. We therefore recommend attention to ensuring high-quality preschool and kindergarten environments as well. We acknowledge that excellent instruction in the primary grades and optimal environments in preschool and kindergarten require teachers who are well prepared, highly knowledgeable, and receiving ongoing support. Excellent instruction may be possible only if schools are organized in optimal ways; if facilities, curriculum materials, and support services function adequately; and if children's home languages are taken into account in designing instruction. We therefore make recommendations addressing these issues. (The complete text of all the committee's recommendations appears in Chapter 10.)

Literacy Instruction in First Through Third Grades

Given the centrality of excellent instruction to the prevention of reading difficulties, the committee strongly recommends attention in every primary-grade classroom to the full array of early reading accomplishments: the alphabetic principle, reading sight words, reading words by mapping speech sounds to parts of words, achieving fluency, and comprehension. Getting started in alphabetic reading depends critically on mapping the letters and spellings of words onto the speech units that they represent; failure to master word recognition can impede text comprehension. Explicit instruction that directs children's attention to the sound structure of oral language and to the connections between speech sounds and spellings assists children who have not grasped the alphabetic principle or who do not apply it productively when they encounter unfamiliar printed words.

Comprehension difficulties can be prevented by actively building comprehension skills as well as linguistic and conceptual knowledge, beginning in the earliest grades. Comprehension can be enhanced through instruction focused on concept and vocabulary growth and background knowledge, instruction about the syntax and rhetorical structures of written language, and direct instruction about comprehension strategies such as summarizing, predicting, and monitoring. Comprehension also takes practice, which is gained by reading independently, by reading in pairs or groups, and by being read aloud to.

We recommend that first through third grade curricula include the following components:

- Beginning readers need explicit instruction and practice that lead to an appreciation that spoken words are made up of smaller units of sounds, familiarity with spelling-sound correspondences and common spelling conventions and their use in identifying printed words, "sight" recognition of frequent words, and independent reading, including reading aloud. Fluency should be promoted through practice with a wide variety of well-written and engaging texts at the child's own comfortable reading level.

- Children who have started to read independently, typically second graders and above, should be encouraged to sound out and confirm the identities of visually unfamiliar words they encounter in the course of reading meaningful texts, recognizing words primarily through attention to their letter-sound relationships. Although context and pictures can be used as a tool to monitor word recognition, children should not be taught to use them to substitute for information provided by the letters in the word.

- Because the ability to obtain meaning from print depends so strongly on the development of word recognition accuracy and reading fluency, both of the latter should be regularly assessed in the classroom, permitting timely and effective instructional response when difficulty or delay is apparent.

- Beginning in the earliest grades, instruction should promote comprehension by actively building linguistic and conceptual knowledge in a rich variety of domains, as well as through direct instruction about comprehension strategies such as summarizing the main idea, predicting events and outcomes of upcoming text, drawing inferences, and monitoring for coherence and misunderstandings. This instruction can take place while adults read to students or when students read themselves.

- Once children learn some letters, they should be encouraged to write them, to use them to begin writing words or parts of words, and to use words to begin writing sentences. Instruction should be designed with the understanding that the use of invented spelling is not in conflict with teaching correct spelling. Beginning writing with invented spelling can be helpful for developing understanding of the identity and segmentation of speech sounds and sound-spelling relationships. Conventionally correct spelling should be developed through focused instruction and practice. Primary-grade children should be expected to spell previously studied words and spelling patterns correctly in their final writing products. Writing should take place regularly and frequently to encourage children to become more comfortable and familiar with it.

• Throughout the early grades, time, materials, and resources should be provided with two goals: (a) to support daily independent reading of texts selected to be of particular interest for the individual student, and beneath the individual student's frustration level, in order to consolidate the student's capacity for independent reading and (b) to support daily assisted or supported reading and rereading of texts that are slightly more difficult in wording or in linguistic, rhetorical, or conceptual structure in order to promote advances in the student's capabilities.

• Throughout the early grades, schools should promote independent reading outside school by such means as daily at-home reading assignments and expectations, summer reading lists, encouraging parent involvement, and by working with community groups, including public librarians, who share this goal.

Promoting Literacy Development in Preschool and Kindergarten

It is clear from the research that the process of learning to read is a lengthy one that begins very early in life. Given the importance identified in the research literature of starting school motivated to read and with the prerequisite language and early literacy skills, the committee recommends that all children, especially those at risk for reading difficulties, should have access to early childhood environments that promote language and literacy growth and that address a variety of skills that have been identified as predictors of later reading achievement. Preschools and other group care settings for young children often provide relatively impoverished language and literacy environments, in particular those available to families with limited economic resources. As ever more young children are entering group care settings pursuant to expectations that their mothers will join the work force, it becomes critical that the preschool opportunities available to lower-income families be designed in ways that support language and literacy development.

Preschool programs, even those designed specifically as interventions for children at risk of reading difficulties, should be designed to provide optimal support for cognitive, language, and social development, within this broad focus. However, ample attention should be paid to skills that are known to predict future reading achievement, especially those for which a causal role has been demonstrated. Similarly, and for the same reasons, kindergarten instruction should be designed to stimulate verbal interaction; to enrich children's vocabularies; to encourage talk about books; to provide practice with the sound structure of words; to develop knowledge about print, including the production and recognition of letters; and to generate familiarity with the basic purposes and mechanisms of reading.

Children who will probably need additional support for early language and literacy development should receive it as early as possible. Pediatricians, social workers, speech-language therapists, and other preschool practitioners should receive research-based guidelines to assist them to be alert for signs that children are having difficulties acquiring early language and literacy skills. Parents, relatives, neighbors, and friends can also play a role in identifying children who need assistance. Through adult education programs, public service media, instructional videos provided by pediatricians, and other means, parents can be informed about what skills and knowledge children should be acquiring at young ages, and about what to do and where to turn if there is concern that a child's development may be lagging behind in some respects.

Education and Professional Development for All Involved in Literacy Instruction

The critical importance of the teacher in the prevention of reading difficulties must be recognized, and efforts should be made to provide all teachers with adequate knowledge about reading and the knowledge and skill to teach reading or its developmental precursors. It is imperative that teachers at all grade levels understand the course of literacy development and the role of instruction in optimizing literacy development.

Preschool teachers represent an important, and largely underutilized, resource in promoting literacy by supporting rich language and emergent literacy skills. Early childhood educators should not try to replicate the formal reading instruction provided in schools.

The preschool and primary school teacher's knowledge and experience, as well as the support provided to the teacher, are central to achieving the goal of primary prevention of reading difficulties. Each of these may vary according to where the teacher is in his or her professional development. A critical component in the preparation of pre-service teachers is supervised, relevant, clinical experience providing ongoing guidance and feedback, so they develop the ability to integrate and apply their knowledge in practice.

Teachers need to be knowledgeable about the research foundations of reading. Collaborative support by the teacher preparation institution and the field placement is essential. A critical component for novice teachers is the support of mentors who have demonstrated records of success in teaching reading.

Professional development should not be conceived as something that ends with graduation from a teacher preparation program, nor as something that happens primarily in graduate classrooms or even during in-service activities. Rather, ongoing support from colleagues and specialists, as well as regular opportunities for self-examination and reflection, are critical components of the career-long development of excellent teachers.

Teaching Reading to Speakers of Other Languages

Schools have the responsibility to accommodate the linguistic needs of students with limited proficiency in English. Precisely how to do this is difficult to prescribe, because students' abilities and needs vary greatly, as do the capacities of different communities to support their literacy development. The committee recommends the following guidelines for decision making:

- If language-minority children arrive at school with no proficiency in English but speaking a language for which there are instructional guides, learning materials, and locally available proficient teachers, these children should be taught how to read in their native language while acquiring proficiency in spoken English and then subsequently taught to extend their skills to reading in English.

- If language-minority children arrive at school with no proficiency in English but speak a language for which the above conditions cannot be met and for which there are insufficient numbers of children to justify the development of the local capacity to meet such conditions, the instructional priority should be to develop the children's proficiency in spoken English. Although print materials may be used to develop understanding of English speech sounds, vocabulary, and syntax, the postponement of formal reading instruction is appropriate until an adequate level of proficiency in spoken English has been achieved.

Ensuring Adequate Resources to Meet Children's Needs

To be effective, schools with large numbers of children at risk for reading difficulties need rich resources—manageable class sizes and student-teacher ratios, high-quality instructional materials in sufficient quantity, good school libraries, and pleasant physical environments. Achieving this may require extra resources for schools that serve a disproportionate number of high-risk children.

Even in schools in which a large percentage of the students are not achieving at a satisfactory level, a well-designed classroom reading program, delivered by an experienced and competent teacher, may be successful in bringing most students to grade level or above during the primary grades. However, achieving and sustaining radical gains is often difficult when improvements are introduced on a classroom-by-classroom basis. In a situation of school-wide poor performance, school restructuring should be considered as a vehicle for preventing reading difficulties. Ongoing professional development for teachers is typically a component of successful school restructuring efforts.

Addressing the Needs of Children with
Persistent Reading Difficulties

Even with excellent instruction in the early grades, some children fail to make satisfactory progress in reading. Such children will require supplementary services, ideally from a reading specialist who provides individual or small-group intensive instruction that is coordinated with high-quality instruction from the classroom teacher. Children who are having difficulty learning to read do not, as a rule, require qualitatively different instruction from children who are "getting it." Instead, they more often need application of the same principles by someone who can apply them expertly to individual children who are having difficulty for one reason or another.

Schools that lack or have abandoned reading specialist positions need to reexamine their needs for such specialists to ensure that well-trained staff are available for intervention with children and for ongoing support to classroom teachers. Reading specialists and other specialist roles need to be defined so that two-way communication is required between specialists and classroom teachers about the needs of all children at risk of or experiencing reading difficulties. Coordination is needed at the instructional level so that intervention from specialists coordinates with and supports classroom instruction. Schools that have reading specialists as well as special educators need to coordinate the roles of these specialists. Schools need to ensure that all the specialists engaged in child study or individualized educational program (IEP) meetings for special education placement, early childhood intervention, out-of-classroom interventions, or in-classroom support are well informed about research in reading development and the prevention of reading difficulties.

Although volunteer tutors can provide valuable practice and motivational support for children learning to read, they should not be expected either to provide primary reading instruction or to instruct children with serious reading problems.

CONCLUSION

Most reading difficulties can be prevented. There is much work to be done, however, that requires the aggressive deployment of the information currently available, which is distilled in this report. In addition, many questions remain unanswered concerning reading development, some of which we address in our recommendations for research. While science continues to discover more about how children learn to read and how teachers and others can help them, the knowledge currently available can equip our society to promote higher levels of literacy for large numbers of American schoolchildren. The committee's hope is that the recommendations contained in this report will provide direction for the first important steps.

PART I

Introduction to Reading

Reading is a complex developmental challenge that we know to be intertwined with many other developmental accomplishments: attention, memory, language, and motivation, for example. Reading is not only a cognitive psycholinguistic activity but also a social activity.

Being a good reader in English means that a child has gained a functional knowledge of the principles of the English alphabetic writing system. Young children gain functional knowledge of the parts, products, and uses of the writing system from their ability to attend to and analyze the external sound structure of spoken words. Understanding the basic alphabetic principle requires an awareness that spoken language can be analyzed into strings of separable words, and words, in turn, into sequences of syllables and phonemes within syllables.

Beyond knowledge about how the English writing system works, though, there is a point in a child's growth when we expect "real reading" to start. Children are expected, without help, to read some unfamiliar texts, relying on the print and drawing meaning from it. There are many reasons why children have difficulty learning to read. These issues and problems led to the initiation of this study.

Even though quite accurate estimates can be made on the basis of known risk factors, it is still difficult to predict precisely which young children will have difficulty learning to read. We therefore propose that prevention efforts must reach all children. To wait to initiate treatment until the child has been diagnosed with a specific disability is too late. However, we can begin treatment of conditions associated with reading problems, for example, hearing impairments.

Ensuring success in reading requires different levels of effort for different segments of the population. The prevention and intervention efforts described in this report can be thought of in terms of three levels (Caplan and Grunebaum, 1967, cited in Simeonsson, 1994; Pianta, 1990; and Needlman, 1997). *Primary prevention* is concerned with reducing the number of new cases (incidence) of an identified condition or problem in the population, such as ensuring that all children attend schools in which instruction is coherent and competent.

Secondary prevention is concerned with reducing the number of existing cases (prevalence) of an identified condition or problem in the population. Secondary prevention likewise involves the promotion of compensatory skills and behaviors. Children who are growing up in poverty, for example, may need excellent, enriched preschool environments or schools that address their particular learning needs with highly effective and focused instruction. The extra effort is focused on children at higher risk of developing reading difficulties but before any serious, long-term deficit has emerged.

Tertiary prevention is concerned with reducing the complications associated with identified problem, or conditions. Programs, strategies, and interventions at this level have an explicit remedial or rehabilitative focus. If children demonstrate inadequate progress under secondary prevention conditions, they may need instruction that is specially designed and supplemental—special education, tutoring from a reading specialist—to their current instruction.

1

Introduction

Reading is essential to success in our society. The ability to read is highly valued and important for social and economic advancement. Of course, most children learn to read fairly well. In fact, a small number learn it on their own, with no formal instruction, before school entry (Anbar, 1986; Backman, 1983; Bissex, 1980; Jackson, 1991; Jackson et al., 1988). A larger percentage learn it easily, quickly, and efficiently once exposed to formal instruction.

SOCIETAL CHALLENGES

Parents, educators, community leaders, and researchers identify clear and specific worries concerning how well children are learning to read in this country. The issues they raise are the focus of this report:

1. Large numbers of school-age children, including children from all social classes, have significant difficulties in learning to read.

2. Failure to learn to read adequately for continued school success is much more likely among poor children, among nonwhite

children, and among nonnative speakers of English. Achieving educational equality requires an understanding of why these disparities exist and efforts to redress them.

3. An increasing proportion of children in American schools, particularly in certain school systems, are learning disabled, with most of the children identified as such because of difficulties in learning to read.

4. Even as federal and state governments and local communities invest at higher levels in early childhood education for children with special needs and for those from families living in poverty, these investments are often made without specific planning to address early literacy needs and sustain the investment.

5. A significant federal investment in providing bilingual education programs for nonnative speakers of English has not been matched by attention to the best methods for teaching reading in English to nonnative speakers or to native speakers of nonstandard dialects.

6. The passage of the Americans with Disabilities Act (ADA) provides accommodations to children and to workers who have reading disabilities. In order to provide full access for the individuals involved, these accommodations should reflect scientific knowledge about the acquisition of reading and the effects of having a reading difficulty.

7. The debate about reading development and reading instruction has been persistent and heated, often obscuring the very real gains in knowledge of the reading process that have occurred.

In this report, we are most concerned with the children in this country whose educational careers are imperiled because they do not read well enough to ensure understanding and to meet the demands of an increasingly competitive economy. Current difficulties in reading largely originate from rising demands for literacy, not from declining absolute levels of literacy (Stedman and Kaestle, 1987). In a technological society, the demands for higher literacy are constantly increasing, creating ever more grievous consequences for those who fall short and contributing to the widening economic disparities in our society (Bronfenbrenner et al., 1996). These economic disparities often translate into disparities in educational resources, which then have the self-reinforcing effect of further exacerbating economic disparities. Although the gap in reading performance between educational haves and have-nots has shrunk over the last 50 years, it is still unacceptably large, and in recent years it has not shrunk further (National Academy of Education, 1996). These rich-get-richer and poor-get-poorer economic effects compound the difficulties facing educational policy makers, and they must be addressed if we are to confront the full scope of inadequate literacy attainment (see Bronfenbrenner et al., 1996).

Despite the many ways in which American schools have progressed and improved over the last half century (see, for example, Berliner and Biddle, 1995), there is little reason for complacency. Clear and worrisome problems have to do specifically with children's success in learning to read and our ability to teach reading to them. There are many reasons for these educational problems—none of which is simple. These issues and problems led to the initiation of this study and are the focus of this report.

The many children who succeed in reading are in classrooms that display a wide range of possible approaches to instruction. In making recommendations about instruction, one of the challenges facing the committee is the difficult-to-deal-with fact that many children will learn to read in almost any classroom, with almost any instructional emphasis. Nonetheless, some children, in particular children from poor, minority, or non-English-speaking families and children who have innate predispositions for reading difficulties, need the support of high-quality preschool and school environments and of excellent primary instruction to be sure of reading success. We attempt to identify the characteristics of the preschool and school environments that will be effective for such children.

The Challenge of a Technological Society

Although children have been taught to read for many centuries, only in this century—and until recently only in some countries—has there been widespread expectation that literacy skills should be universal. Under current conditions, in many "literate" societies, 40 to

60 percent of the population have achieved literacy; today in the United States, we expect 100 percent of the population to be literate. Furthermore, the definition of full-fledged literacy has shifted over the last century with increased distribution of technology, with the development of communication across distances, and with the proliferation of large-scale economic enterprises (Kaestle, 1991; Miller, 1988; Weber, 1993). To be employable in the modern economy, high school graduates need to be more than merely literate. They must be able to read challenging material, to perform sophisticated calculations, and to solve problems independently (Murnane and Levy, 1993). The demands are far greater than those placed on the vast majority of schooled literate individuals a quarter-century ago.

Data from the National Education Longitudinal Study and High School and Beyond, the two most comprehensive longitudinal assessments of U.S. students' attitudes and achievements, indicate that, from 1972 through 1994 (the earliest and most recently available data), high school students most often identified two life values as "very important" (see National Center for Educational Statistics, 1995:403). "Finding steady work" was consistently highly valued by over 80 percent of male and female seniors over the 20 years of measurement and was seen as "very important" by nearly 90 percent of the 1992 seniors—the highest scores on this measure in its 20-year history. "Being successful in work" was also consistently valued as very important by over 80 percent of seniors over the 20-year period and approached 90 percent in 1992.

The pragmatic goals stated by students amount to "get and hold a good job." Who is able to do that? In 1993, the percentage of U.S. citizens age 25 and older who were college graduates and unemployed was 2.6 percent (U.S. Department of Labor, Office of Employment and Unemployment Statistics, quoted in National Center for Education Statistics, 1995:401). By contrast, the unemployment rate for high school graduates with no college was twice as high, 5.4 percent, and for persons with less than a high school education the unemployment rate was 9.8 percent, over three times higher. An October 1994 survey of 1993-1994 high school graduates and dropouts found that fewer than 50 percent of the dropouts were holding jobs (U.S. Department of Labor, 1995; quoted in National Center for Education Statistics, 1995:401).

One researcher found that, controlling for inflation, the mean income of U.S. male high school dropouts ages 25 to 34 has decreased by over 50 percent between 1973 and 1995 (Stringfield, 1995, 1997). By contrast, the mean incomes of young male high school graduates dropped by about one-third, and those of college graduates by 20 percent in the 1970s and then stabilized. Among the six major demographic groups (males and females who are black, white, or Hispanic), the lowest average income among college graduates was higher than the highest group of high school graduates.

Academic success, as defined by high school graduation, can be predicted with reasonable accuracy by knowing someone's reading skill at the end of grade 3 (for reviews, see Slavin et al., 1994). A person who is not at least a modestly skilled reader by the end of third grade is quite unlikely to graduate from high school. Only a generation ago, this did not matter so much, because the long-term economic effects of not becoming a good reader and not graduating from high school were less severe. Perhaps not surprisingly, when teachers are asked about the most important goal for education, over half of elementary school teachers chose "building basic literacy skills" (National Center for Education Statistics Schools and Staffing Survey, 1990-1991, quoted in National Center for Education Statistics, 1995:31).

The Special Challenge of Learning to Read English

Learning to read poses real challenges, even to children who will eventually become good readers. Furthermore, although every writing system has its own complexities, English presents a relatively large challenge, even among alphabetic languages. Learning the principles of a syllabic system, like the Japanese *katakana*, is quite straightforward, since the units represented—syllables—are pronounceable and psychologically real, even to young children. Such systems are, however, feasible only in languages with few possible syllable types; the *hiragana* syllabary represents spoken Japanese with 46 characters, supplemented with a set of diacritics (Daniels and Bright, 1996). Spoken English has approximately 5,000 different possible syllables; instead of representing each one with a symbol in the writing system, written English relies on an alphabetic system that represents the parts that make up a spoken syllable, rather than representing the syllable as a unit.

An alphabetic system poses a challenge to the beginning reader, because the units represented graphically by letters of the alphabet are referentially meaningless and phonologically abstract. For example, there are three sounds represented by three letters in the word "but," but each sound alone does not refer to anything, and only the middle sound can really be pronounced in isolation; when we try to say the first or last consonant of the word all by itself, we have to add a vowel to make it a pronounceable entity (see Box 1-1).

Once the learner of written English gets the basic idea that letters represent the small sound units within spoken and heard words, called phonemes, the system has many advantages: a much more limited set of graphemic symbols is needed than in either syllabic (like Japanese) or morphosyllabic (like Chinese) systems; strategies

---

BOX 1-1
Some Definitions

What is morphology?
The study of the structure and form of words in language or a language, including inflection, derivation, and the formation of compounds.

What is orthography?
A method of representing spoken language by letters and diacritics; spelling.

What is phonology?
The study of speech structure in language (or a particular language) that includes both the patterns of basic speech units (phonemes) and the tacit rules of pronunciation.

What is a syllable?
A unit of spoken language that can be spoken. In English, a syllable can consist of a vowel sound alone or a vowel sound with one or more consonant sounds preceding and following.

for sounding out unfamiliar strings and spelling novel words are available; and subsequences, such as prefixes and suffixes, are encountered with enough frequency for the reader to recognize them automatically.

Alphabetic systems of writing vary in the degree to which they are designed to represent the surface sounds of words. Some languages, such as Spanish, spell all words as they sound, even though this can cause two closely related words to be spelled very differently. Writing systems that compromise phonological representations in order to reflect morphological information are referred to as deep orthographies. In English, rather than preserving one-letter-to-one-sound correspondences, we preserve the spelling, even if that means a particular letter spells several different sounds. For example, the last letter pronounced "k" in the written word "electric" represents quite different sounds in the words "electricity" and "electrician," indicating the morphological relation among the words but making the sound-symbol relationships more difficult to fathom.

The deep orthography of English is further complicated by the retention of many historical spellings, despite changes in pronunciation that render the spellings opaque. The "gh" in "night" and "neighborhood" represents a consonant that has long since disappeared from spoken English. The "ph" in "morphology" and "philosophy" is useful in signaling the Greek etymology of those words but represents a complication of the pattern of sound-symbol correspondences that has been abandoned in Spanish, German, and many other languages that also retain Greek-origin vocabulary items. English can present a challenge for a learner who expects to find each letter always linked to just one sound.

SOURCES OF READING DIFFICULTIES

Reading problems are found among every group and in every primary classroom, although some children with certain demographic characteristics are at greater risk of reading difficulties than others. Precisely how and why this happens has not been fully understood. In some cases, the sources of these reading difficulties are relatively clear, such as biological deficits that make the processing of sound-symbol relationships difficult; in other cases, the source is experiential such as poor reading instruction.

Biological Deficits

Neuroscience research on reading has expanded understanding of the reading process (Shaywitz, 1996). For example, researchers have now been able to establish a tentative architecture for the component processes of reading (Shaywitz et al., 1998; Shaywitz, 1996). All reading difficulties, whatever their primary etiology, must express themselves through alterations of the brain systems responsible for word identification and comprehension. Even in disadvantaged or other high-risk populations, many children do learn to read, some easily and others with great difficulty. This suggests that, in all populations, reading ability occurs along a continuum, and biological factors are influenced by, and interact with, a reader's experiences. The findings of an anomalous brain system say little about the possibility for change, for remediation, or for response to treatment. It is well known that, particularly in children, neural systems are plastic and responsive to changed input.

Cognitive studies of reading have identified phonological processing as crucial to skillful reading, and so it seems logical to suspect that poor readers may have phonological processing problems. One line of research has looked at phonological processing problems that can be attributed to the underdevelopment or disruption of specific brain systems.

Genetic factors have also been implicated in some reading disabilities, in studies both of family occurrence (Pennington, 1989; Scarborough, 1989) and of twins (Olson et al., 1994). Differences in brain function and behavior associated with reading difficulty may arise from environmental and/or genetic factors. The relative contributions of these two factors to a deficit in reading (children below the local 10th percentile) have been assessed in readers with normal-range intelligence (above 90 on verbal or performance IQ) and apparent educational opportunity (their first language was English and they had regularly attended schools that were at or above national norms in reading). This research has provided evidence for strong genetic influences on many of these children's deficits in reading (DeFries and Alarcon, 1996) and in related phonological processes (Olson et al., 1989). Recent DNA studies have found evidence for a link between some cases of reading disability and inheritance of a gene or genes on the short arm of chromosome 6 (Cardon et al., 1994; Grigorenko et al., 1997).

It is important to emphasize that evidence for genetic influence on reading difficulty in the selected population described above does not imply genetic influences on reading differences between groups for which there are confounding environmental differences. Such group differences may include socioeconomic status, English as a second language, and other cultural factors. It is also important to emphasize that evidence for genetic influence and anomalous brain development does not mean that a child is condemned to failure in reading. Brain and behavioral development are always based on the interaction between genetic and environmental influences. The genetic and neurobiological evidence does suggest why learning to read may be particularly difficult for some children and why they may require extraordinary instructional support in reading and related phonological processes.

Instructional Influences

A large number of students who should be capable of reading ably given adequate instruction are not doing so, suggesting that the instruction available to them is not appropriate. As Carroll (1963) noted more than three decades ago, if the instruction provided by a school is ineffective or insufficient, many children will have difficulty learning to read (unless additional instruction is provided in the home or elsewhere).

Reading difficulties that arise when the design of regular classroom curriculum, or its delivery, is flawed are sometimes termed "curriculum casualties" (Gickling and Thompson, 1985; Simmons and Kame'enui, in press). Consider an example from a first-grade classroom in the early part of the school year. Worksheets were being used to practice segmentation and blending of words to facilitate word recognition. Each worksheet had a key word, with one part of it designated the "chunk" that was alleged to have the same spelling-sound pattern in other words; these other words were listed on the sheet. One worksheet had the word "love" and the chunk "ove." Among the other words listed on the sheet, some did indicate the pattern ("glove," "above," "dove"), but others simply do not work as the sheet suggests they should ("Rover," "stove," and "woven"). In lesson plans and instructional activities, such mistakes occur in the accuracy and clarity of the information being taught.

When this occurs consistently, a substantial proportion of students in the classroom are likely to exhibit low achievement (although some students are likely to progress adequately in spite of the impoverished learning situation). If low-quality instruction is confined to one particular teacher, children's progress may be impeded for the year spent in that classroom, but they may overcome this setback when exposed to more adequate teaching in subsequent years. There is evidence, however, that poor instruction in first grade may have long-term effects. Children who have poor instruction in the first year are more seriously harmed by the bad early learning experience and tend to do poorly in schooling across the years (Pianta, 1990).

In some schools, however, the problem is more pervasive, such that low student achievement is schoolwide and persistent. Sometimes the instructional deficiency can be traced to lack of an appropriate curriculum. More often, a host of conditions occur together to contribute to the risk imposed by poor schooling: low expectations for success on the part of the faculty and administration of the school, which may translate into a slow-paced, undemanding curriculum; teachers who are poorly trained in effective methods for teaching beginning readers; the unavailability of books and other materials; noisy and crowded classrooms; and so forth.

It is regrettable that schools with these detrimental characteristics continue to exist anywhere in the United States; since these schools often exist in low-income areas, where resources for children's out-of-school learning are limited, the effects can be very detrimental to students' probabilities of becoming skilled readers (Kozol, 1991; Puma et al., 1997; Natriello et al., 1990). Attending a school in which low achievement is pervasive and chronic, in and of itself, clearly places a child at risk for reading difficulty. Even within a school that serves most of its students well, an instructional basis for poor reading achievement is possible. This is almost never considered, however, when a child is referred for evaluation of a suspected reading difficulty. Evidence from case study evaluations of children referred for special education indicate that instructional histories of the children are not seriously considered (Klenk and Palincsar, 1996). Rather, when teachers refer students for special services, the "search for pathology" begins and assessment focused on the child continues until some explanatory factor is unearthed that could account for the observed difficulty in reading (Sarason and Doris, 1979).

In sum, a variety of detrimental school practices may place children at risk for poorer achievement in reading than they might otherwise attain. Interventions geared at improving beginning reading instruction, rehabilitating substandard schools, and ensuring adequate teacher preparation are discussed in subsequent chapters.

DEMOGRAPHICS OF READING DIFFICULTIES

A major source of urgency in addressing reading difficulties derives from their distribution in our society. Children from poor families, children of African American and Hispanic descent, and children attending urban schools are at much greater risk of poor reading outcomes than are middle-class, European-American, and suburban children. Studying these demographic disparities can help us identify groups that should be targeted for special prevention efforts. Furthermore, examining the literacy development of children in these higher-risk groups can help us understand something about the course of literacy development and the array of conditions that must be in place to ensure that it proceeds well.

One characteristic of minority populations that has been offered as an explanation for their higher risk of reading difficulties is the use of nonstandard varieties of English or limited proficiency in English. Speaking a nonstandard variety of English can impede the easy acquisition of English literacy by introducing greater deviations in the representation of sounds, making it hard to develop sound-symbol links. Learning English spelling is challenging enough for speakers of standard mainstream English; these challenges are heightened for some children by a number of phonological and grammatical features of social dialects that make the relation of sound to spelling even more indirect (see Chapter 6).

The number of children who speak other languages and have limited proficiency in English in U.S. schools has risen dramatically over the past two decades and continues to grow. Although the size of the general school population has increased only slightly, the number of students acquiring English as a second language grew by 85 percent nationwide between 1985 and 1992, from fewer than 1.5 million to almost 2.7 million (Goldenberg, 1996). These students now make up approximately 5.5 percent of the population of public school students in the United States; over half (53 percent) of these students are concentrated in grades K-4. Eight percent of kindergarten children speak a native language other than English and are English-language learners (August and Hakuta, 1997).

Non-English-speaking students, like nonstandard dialect speakers, tend to come from low socioeconomic backgrounds and to attend schools with disproportionately high numbers of children in poverty, both of which are known risk factors (see Chapter 4). Hispanic students in the United States, who constitute the largest group of limited-English-proficient students by far, are particularly at risk for reading difficulties. Despite the group's progress in achievement over the past 15 to 20 years, they are about twice as likely as non-Hispanic whites to be reading below average for their age. Achievement gaps in all academic areas between whites and Hispanics, whether they are U.S. or foreign born, appear early and persist throughout their school careers (Kao and Tienda, 1995).

One obvious reason for these achievement differences is the language difference itself. Being taught and tested in English would, of course, put students with limited English proficiency at a disadvantage. These children might not have any reading difficulty at all if they were taught and tested in the language in which they are proficient. Indeed, there is evidence from research in bilingual education that learning to read in one's native language—thus offsetting the obstacle presented by limited proficiency in English—can lead to superior achievement (Legarreta, 1979; Ramirez et al., 1991). This field is highly contentious and politicized, however, and there is a lack of clear consensus about the advantages and disadvantages of academic instruction in the primary language in contrast to early and intensive exposure to English (August and Hakuta, 1997; Rossell and Baker, 1996).

In any event, limited proficiency in English does not, in and of itself, appear to be entirely responsible for the low reading achievement of these students. Even when taught and tested in Spanish, as the theory and practice of bilingual education dictates, many Spanish-speaking Hispanic students in the United States still demonstrate low levels of reading attainment (Escamilla, 1994; Gersten and Woodward, 1995; Goldenberg and Gallimore, 1991; Slavin and Madden, 1995). This suggests that factors other than lack of English proficiency may also contribute to these children's reading difficulties.

One such factor is cultural differences, that is, the mismatch between the schools and the families in definitions of literacy, in teaching practices, and in defined roles for parents versus teachers (e.g., Jacob and Jordan, 1987; Tharp, 1989); these differences can create obstacles to children's learning to read in school. Others contend that primary cultural differences matter far less than do "secondary cultural discontinuities," such as low motivation and low educational aspirations that are the result of discrimination and limited social and economic opportunities for certain minority groups (Ogbu, 1974, 1982). Still others claim that high motivation and educational aspirations can and do coexist with low achievement (e.g., Labov et al., 1968, working in the African American community; Goldenberg and Gallimore, 1995, in the Hispanic community) and that other factors must therefore explain the differential achievement of culturally diverse groups.

Literacy is positively valued by adults in minority communities, and the positive views are often brought to school by young children (Nettles, 1997). Nonetheless, the ways that reading is used by adults and children varies across families from different cultural groups in ways that may influence children's participation in literacy activities in school, as Heath (1983) found. And adults in some communities may see very few functional roles for literacy, so that they will be unlikely to provide conditions in the home that are conducive to children's acquisition of reading and writing skills (Purcell-Gates, 1991, 1996). The implications of these various views for prevention and intervention efforts are discussed in Part III of this volume.

It is difficult to distinguish the risk associated with minority status and not speaking English from the risk associated with lower socioeconomic status (SES). Studying the differential experiences of children in middle- and lower-class families can illuminate the factors that affect the development of literacy and thus contribute to the design of prevention and intervention efforts.

The most extensive studies of SES differences have been conducted in Britain. Stubbs (1980) found a much lower percentage of poor readers with higher (7.5 percent) than with lower SES (26.9 percent). Some have suggested that SES differences in reading achievement are actually a result of differences in the quality of schooling; that is, lower-SES children tend to go to inferior schools, and therefore their achievement is lower because of inferior educational opportunities (Cook, 1991). However, a recent study by Alexander and Entwisle (1996) appears to demonstrate that it is during nonschool time—before they start and during the summer months—that low-SES children fall academically behind their higher-SES peers and get progressively further behind. During the school months (at least through elementary school) the rate of progress is virtually identical for high- and low-SES children.

Regardless of the specific explanation, differences in literacy achievement among children as a result of socioeconomic status are pronounced. Thirty years ago Coleman et al. (1966) and Moynihan (1965) reported that the educational deficit of children from low-income families was present at school entry and increased with each year they stayed in school. Evidence of SES differences in reading achievement has continued to accumulate (National Assessment of Educational Progress, 1981, 1995). Reading achievement of children in affluent suburban schools is significantly and consistently higher than that of children in "disadvantaged" urban schools (e.g.,

NAEP, 1994, 1995; White, 1982; Hart and Risley, 1995). An important conceptual distinction was made by White (1982) in a groundbreaking meta-analysis. White discovered that, at the *individual level*, SES is related to achievement only very modestly. However, at the *aggregate level*, that is, when measured as a school or community characteristic, the effects of SES are much more pronounced. A low-SES child in a generally moderate or higher-SES school or community is far less at risk than an entire school or community of low-SES children.

The existence of SES differences in reading outcomes offers by itself little information about the specific experiences or activities that influence literacy development at home. Indeed, a look at socioeconomic factors alone can do no more than nominate the elements that differ between middle-class and lower-class homes. Researchers have tried to identify the specific familial interactions that can account for social class differences, as well as describe those interactions around literacy that do occur in low-income homes. For example, Baker et al. (1995) compared opportunities for informal literacy learning among preschoolers in the homes of middle-income and low-income urban families. They found that children from middle-income homes had greater opportunities for informal literacy learning than children of low-income homes. Low-income parents, particularly African-American parents, reported more reading skills practice and homework (e.g., flash cards, letter practice) with their kindergarten-age children than did middle-income parents. Middle-income parents reported only slightly more joint book reading with their children than did low-income families. But these middle-income parents reported more play with print and more independent reading by children. Among the middle-class families in this study, 90 percent reported that their child visited the library at least once a month, whereas only 43 percent of the low-income families reported such visits. The findings of Baker et al. that low-income homes typically do offer opportunities for literacy practice, though perhaps of a different nature from middle-class homes, have been confirmed in ethnographic work by researchers such as Teale (1986), Taylor and Dorsey-Gaines (1988), Taylor and Strickland (1986), Gadsden (1993), Delgado-Gaitan (1990), and Goldenberg et al. (1992).

ABOUT THIS REPORT

Charge to the Committee

The Committee on the Prevention of Reading Difficulties in Young Children has conducted a study of the effectiveness of interventions for young children who are at risk of having problems in learning to read. It was carried out at the request of the U.S. Department of Education's Office of Special Education Programs and its Office of Educational Research and Improvement (Early Childhood Institute) and the National Institute on Child Health and Human Development (Human Learning and Behavior Branch). The sponsors requested that the study address young children who are at -risk for reading difficulties, within the context of reading acquisition for all children. The scope included children from birth through grade 3, in special and regular education settings. The project had three goals: (1) to comprehend a rich research base; (2) to translate the research findings into advice and guidance for parents, educators, publishers, and others involved in the care and instruction of the young; and (3) to convey this advice to the targeted audiences through a variety of publications, conferences, and other outreach activities. In making its recommendations, the committee has highlighted key research findings that should be integrated into existing and future program interventions to enhance the reading abilities of young children, particularly instruction at the preschool and early elementary levels.

The Committee's Perspective

Our recommendations extend to all children. Of course, we are most worried about children at high risk of developing reading difficulties. However, there is little evidence that children experiencing difficulties learning to read, even those with identifiable learning disabilities, need radically different sorts of supports than children at low risk, although they may need much more intensive support. Childhood environments that support early literacy development and excellent instruction are important for all children. Excellent instruction is the best intervention for children who demonstrate problems learning to read.

Knowledge about reading derives from work conducted in several disciplines, in laboratory settings as well as in homes, classrooms, and schools, and from a range of methodological perspectives. Reading is studied by ethnographers, sociologists, historians, child developmentalists, neurobiologists, and psycholinguists. Reading has been approached as a matter of cognition, culture, socialization, instruction, and language. The committee that wrote this report embraces all these perspectives—but we acknowledge the difficulty of integrating them into a coherent picture.

The committee agrees that reading is inextricably embedded in educational, social, historical, cultural, and biological realities. These realities determine the meaning of terms like *literate* as well as limits on access to literacy and its acquisition. Literacy is also essentially developmental, and appropriate forms of participation, instruction, and assessment in literacy for preschoolers differ from those for first graders and also from those for sophisticated critical readers.

Reading as a cognitive and psycholinguistic activity requires the use of form (the written code) to obtain meaning (the message to be understood), within the context of the reader's purpose (for learning, for enjoyment, for insight). In children, one can see a developmental oscillation between these foci: the preschool child who can pretend to read a story she has heard many times is demonstrating an understanding that reading is about content or meaning; the same child as a first grader, having been taught some grapheme-phoneme correspondences, may read the same storybook haltingly, disfluently, by sounding out the words she had earlier memorized, demonstrating an extreme focus on form. The mature, fluent, practiced reader shows more rapid oscillations between form-focused and meaning-focused reading: she can rely on automatic processing of form and focus on meaning until she encounters an unfamiliar pharmaceutical term or a Russian surname, whereupon the processing of meaning is disrupted while the form is decoded.

Groups define the nature as well as the value of literacy in culturally specific ways as well. A full picture of literacy from a cultural and historical perspective would require an analysis of the distribution of literacy skills, values, and uses across classes and genders as well as religious and social groups; it would require a discussion of the connections between professional, religious, and leisure practices and literacy as defined by those practices. Such a discussion would go far beyond the scope of this report, which focuses on reading and reading difficulties as defined by mainstream opinions in the United States, in particular by U.S. educational institutions at the end of the twentieth century. In that context, employability, citizenship, and participation in the culture require high levels of literacy achievement.

Nature of the Evidence

Our review and summary of the literature are framed by some very basic principles of evidence evaluation. These principles derive from our commitment to the scientific method, which we view not as a strict set of rules but instead as a broad framework defined by some general guidelines. Some of the most important are that (1) science aims for knowledge that is publicly verifiable, (2) science seeks testable theories—not unquestioned edicts, (3) science employs methods of systematic empiricism (see Box 1-2). Science renders knowledge public by such procedures as peer review and such mechanisms as systematic replication (see Box 1-3). Testable theories are those that are potentially falsifiable—that is, defined in such a way that empirical evidence inconsistent with them can in principle be accumulated. It is the willingness to give up or alter a theory in the face of evidence that is one of the most central defining features of the scientific method. All of the conclusions reached in this report

---

BOX 1-2
Dictionary Definition of "Empirical"

1.a. Relying on or derived from observation or experiment. b. Verifiable or provable by means of observation or experiment.

BOX 1-3
Systematic Replication

Systematic replication allows researchers to repeat systematically the conditions and variables that a particular study, program of research, or researcher has reported as worthy of classroom application.

Systematic replication allows researchers to rely on an empirical test of the results of a study instead of a researcher's testimony or report.

are provisional in this important sense: they have empirical consequences that, if proven incorrect, should lead to their alteration.

The methods of systematic empiricism employed in the study of reading difficulties are many and varied. They include case studies, correlational studies, experimental studies, narrative analyses, quasi-experimental studies, interviews and surveys, epidemiological studies, ethnographies, and many others. It is important to understand how the results from studies employing these methods have been used in synthesizing the conclusions of this report.

First, we have utilized the principle of converging evidence. Scientists and those who apply scientific knowledge must often make a judgment about where the preponderance of evidence points. When this is the case, the principle of converging evidence is an important tool, both for evaluating the state of the research evidence and also for deciding how future experiments should be designed. Most areas of science contain competing theories. The extent to which one particular theory can be viewed as uniquely supported by a particular study depends on the extent to which other competing explanations have been ruled out. A particular experimental result is never equally relevant to all competing theoretical explanations. A given experiment may be a very strong test of one or two alternative theories but a weak test of others. Thus, research is highly convergent when a series of experiments consistently support a given theory while collectively eliminating the most important competing explanations. Although no single experiment can rule out all alternative explanations, taken collectively, a series of partially diagnostic studies can lead to a strong conclusion if the data converge. This aspect of the convergence principle implies that we should expect to see many different methods employed in all areas of educational research. A relative balance among the methodologies used to arrive at a given conclusion is desirable because the various classes of research techniques have different strengths and weaknesses.

Another important context for understanding the present synthesis of research is provided by the concept of synergism between descriptive and hypothesis-testing research methods. Research on a particular problem often proceeds from more exploratory methods (ones unlikely to yield a causal explanation) to methods that allow stronger causal inferences. For example, interest in a particular hypothesis may originally stem from a case study of an unusually successful teacher. Alternately, correlational studies may suggest hypotheses about the characteristics of teachers who are successful. Subsequently, researchers may attempt experiments in which variables identified in the case study or correlation are manipulated in order to isolate a causal relationship. These are common progressions in areas of research in which developing causal models of a phenomenon is the paramount goal. They reflect the basic principle of experimental design that the more a study controls extraneous variables the stronger is the causal inference. A true experiment in controlling all extraneous variables is thus the strongest inferential tool.

Qualitative methods, including case studies of individual learners or teachers, classroom ethnographies, collections of introspective interview data, and so on, are also valuable in producing complementary data when carrying out correlational or experimental studies. Teaching and learning are complex phenomena that can be enhanced or impeded by many factors. Experimental manipulation in the teaching/learning context typically is less "complete" than in other contexts; in medical research, for example, treatments can be delivered through injections or pills, such that neither the patient nor the clinician knows who gets which treatment, and in ways that do not require that the clinician be specifically skilled in or committed to the success of a particular treatment.

Educational treatments are often delivered by teachers who may enhance or undermine the difference between treatments and controls; thus, having qualitative data on the authenticity of treatment and on the attitudes of the teachers involved is indispensable. Delivering effective instruction occurs in the context of many other factors—the student-teacher relationship, the teacher's capability at maintaining order, the expectations of the students and their parents—that can neither be ignored nor controlled. Accordingly, data about them must be made available. In addition, since even programs that are documented to be effective will be impossible to implement on a wider scale if teachers dislike them, data on teacher beliefs and attitudes will be useful after demonstration of treatment effects as well (see discussion below of external validity).

Furthermore, the notion of a comparison between a treatment group and an untreated control is often a myth when dealing with social treatments. Families who are assigned not to receive some intervention for their children (e.g., Head Start placement, one-on-one tutoring) often seek out alternatives for themselves that approximate or improve on the treatment features. Understanding the dynamic by which they do so, through collecting observational and interview data, can prevent misguided conclusions from studies designed as experiments. Thus, although experimental studies represent the most powerful design for drawing causal inferences, their limitations must be recognized.

Another important distinction in research on reading is that between retrospective and prospective studies. On one hand, retrospective studies start from observed cases of reading difficulties and attempt to generate explanations for the problem. Such studies may involve a comparison group of normal readers, but of course inference from the finding of differences between two groups, one of whom has already developed reading difficulties and one of whom has not, can never be very strong. Studies that involve matching children with reading problems to others at the same level of reading skill (rather than to age mates) address some of these problems but at the cost of introducing other sources of difficulty—comparing two groups of different ages, with different school histories, and different levels of perceived success in school.

Prospective studies, on the other hand, are quite expensive and time consuming, particularly if they include enough participants to ensure a sizable group of children with reading difficulties. They do, however, enable the researcher to trace developmental pathways for participants who are not systematically different from one another at recruitment and thus to draw stronger conclusions about the likely directionality of cause-effect relationships.

As part of the methodological context for this report, we wish to address explicitly a misconception that some readers may have derived from our emphasis on the logic of an experiment as the most powerful justification for a causal conclusion. By such an emphasis, we do not mean to imply that only studies employing true experimental logic are to be used in drawing conclusions. To the contrary, as mentioned previously in our discussion of converging evidence, the results from many different types of investigations are usually weighed to derive a general conclusion, and the basis for the conclusion rests on the convergence observed from the variety of methods used. This is particularly true in the domains of classroom and curriculum research.

For example, it is often (but not always) the case that experimental investigations are high in internal validity but limited in external validity, whereas correlational studies are often high in external validity but low in internal validity. Internal validity concerns whether we can infer a causal effect for a particular variable. The more a study approximates the logic of a true experiment (i.e., includes manipulation, control, and randomization), the more we can make a strong causal inference. The internal validity of qualitative research studies depends, of course, on their capacity to reflect reality adequately and accurately. Procedures for ensuring adequacy of qualitative data include triangulation (comparison of findings from different research perspectives), cross-case analyses, negative case analysis, and so forth. Just as for quantitative studies, our review of qualitative studies has been selective and our conclusions took into account the methodological rigor of each study within its own paradigm.

External validity concerns the generalizability of the conclusion to the population and setting of interest. Internal validity and external validity are often traded off across different methodologies. Experimental laboratory investigations are high in internal validity but may not fully address concerns about external validity. Field classroom investigations are often quite high in external validity but, because of the logistical difficulties involved in carrying out such investigations, are often quite low in internal validity. Hence, there is a need to look for a convergence of results—not just consistency across studies conducted with one method. Convergence across different methods increases confidence that the conclusions have both internal and external validity.

A not uncommon misconception is that correlational (i.e., nonexperimental) studies cannot contribute to knowledge. This is false for a number of reasons. First, many scientific hypotheses are stated in terms of correlation or lack of correlation, so that such studies are directly relevant to these hypotheses. Second, although correlation does not imply causation, causation *does* imply correlation. That is, although a correlational study cannot definitively prove a causal hypothesis, it may rule one out. Third, correlational studies are more useful than they used to be because some of the recently developed complex correlational designs allow for limited causal inferences. The technique of partial correlation, widely used in studies cited in this report, provides a case in point. It makes possible a test of whether a particular third variable is accounting for a relationship.

Perhaps the most important argument for quasi-experimental studies, however, is that some variables (for instance, human malnutrition, physical disabilities) simply cannot be manipulated for ethical reasons. Other variables, such as birth order, sex, and age, are inherently correlational because they cannot be manipulated, and therefore the scientific knowledge concerning them must be based on correlational evidence. Finally, logistical difficulties in carrying out classroom and curriculum research often render impossible the logic of the true experiment. However, this circumstance is not unique to educational or psychological research. Astronomers obviously cannot manipulate the variables affecting the objects they study, yet they are able to arrive at scientifically founded conclusions.

Outline of the Report

In Chapter 2 we present a picture of typical skilled reading and the process by which it develops. We see this as crucial background information for understanding reading difficulties and their prevention.

Part II presents a fuller picture of the children we are addressing in this report. We survey the population of children with reading difficulties in Chapter 3. In Chapter 4 we discuss risk factors that may help identify children who will have problems learning to read.

Part III presents our analysis of preventions and interventions, including instruction. Chapter 5 focuses on the preschool years. Chapter 6 discusses prevention and literacy instruction delivered in classrooms in kindergarten and the primary grades. Chapter 7 presents our analysis of organizational factors, at the classroom, school, or district level, that contribute to prevention and intervention for grades 1 through 3. Chapter 8 continues discussion of grades 1 through 3, presenting more targeted intervention efforts to help children who are having reading difficulties.

Part IV presents our discussion of how the information reviewed in the report should be used to change practice. Chapter 9 discusses a variety of domains in which action is needed and obstacles to change in those domains. Chapter 10 presents our recommendations for practice, policy, and research.

2

The Process of Learning to Read

In this chapter, we review research on the process of reading and what happens as children become readers. First, we outline how children develop language and literacy skills before they begin formal reading instruction. We then describe skilled reading as it is engaged in by adults and continue by describing how children develop to become readers.

READING AND LITERACY

In focusing in this report on preventing reading difficulties among young children in the United States, we take a limited view of reading, putting aside many issues and concerns that would belong to a full consideration of literacy in various societies inside and outside the United States. Acts of literacy vary a great deal—for example, reading a listing in a phone book, reading a Shakespearean play, and reading a dissertation on electromagnetic force. As different as these are, there are commonalities among them. For most texts in most situations, understanding what the text means is, if not the end goal of the reader, at least an important intermediate step. If someone has difficulty understanding, the problem could be a matter of limited knowledge; in the case of the physics dissertation, for example, limited knowledge of physics could be the downfall, rather than a reading difficulty per se. Having learned to read without difficulty may not suffice to be literate with respect to that dissertation.

In our sense, literacy is both broader and more specific than reading. Literate behaviors include writing and other creative or analytical acts and at the same time invoke very particular bits of knowledge and skill in specific subject matter domains (e.g., history, physics, mathematics, etc.) (Anderson and Pearson, 1984). The reading difficulties that we are considering are those that impede what virtually all literacy activities have in common—the use of the products and principles of the writing system to get at the meaning of a written text.

We recognize that reading-related development can start in infancy or with toddlers. Many very young children are surrounded by written language products and are exposed to the importance and functions of reading in society. A child's reading-related development is interwoven and continuous with development that will lead to expertise in other spheres of life.

There is, however, a point in a child's growth when we expect what many, including young children, often refer to as "real reading" to start. Children are expected, without help, to read some unfamiliar texts, relying on the print and drawing meaning from it. What starts at this point is referred to in a variety of ways in the literature: independent reading (Holdaway, 1979), the alphabetic principle (Ferreiro and Teberosky, 1982), the alphabetic stage (Frith, 1985), the cipher stage (Gough and Hillinger, 1980), fully or truly productive reading (Perfetti, 1985), and conventional reading (Sulzby, 1994). We use the term *conventional reading* to encompass the common meanings of these different terms.

Moving toward being a good reader means that a child has gained a functional knowledge of the principles of the culture's writing system—the English alphabetic writing system for children in the United States—and details of its orthography. But the foundations start earlier. Prior to real reading, young children gain functional knowledge of the parts, products, and uses of the writing system and the ways in which reading and oral language activities complement each other and diverge from each other.

DEVELOPMENT BEFORE KINDERGARTEN: THE FIRST FIVE YEARS

Learning to read and write begins long before the school years, as the biological, cognitive, and social precursors are put into place. One of the most important preconditions for literacy is the integrity of a child's health and sensory organs, since the window for the establishment of such skills as language is relatively brief. The child's intelligence, as long as it is in the normal range, does not have much of an impact on the ease of learning to read (Stanovich et al., 1984). The capacity to learn to read and write is related to children's age-related developmental timetables, although there is no clear agreement on the precise chronological or mental age nor on a particular developmental level that children must reach before they are "ready" to learn to read and write.

Children gain an increasingly complex and decontextualized understanding of the world as their brains develop during their first years of life. As they grow and gain experience, new neural connections are established at irregular rates, with spurts and plateaus (Peterson, 1994). Although this process is orderly, it is variable among individual children due to differences in both biological and experiential influences.

Children who become successful readers tend to exhibit age-appropriate sensory, perceptual, cognitive, and social skills as they progress through the preschool years. Through the interaction of maturation and experience, they become increasingly adept at mastering physical dexterity and locomotion, at categorizing and constructing relationships between physical objects, at remembering facts and events over time, at engaging in imaginative play, at forming social relationships, and so forth.

Of course, many factors in an infant's life can affect development, ranging from maternal mental and physical health to conditions of housing, temperament, nutrition, and emotional stress and support. Although all these can have an impact on later literacy development via their impact on general development, we focus in this chapter on factors that differentially affect reading. Counting, number concepts, letter names and shapes, phonological awareness, interest in literacy, and cooperation with peers are some of the preschool accomplishments that are of particular relevance to later academic challenges.

For instance, children grasp the notion that one object or event may stand for another quite young (Marzolf and DeLoache, 1994). Learning that the alphabet is a symbol system for sounds fits into this stream of development. The ability to use symbols is gradually acquired during the first years of life as children interpret and create first iconic and then graphic representations. At age 3, most children in the United States recognize that golden arches "stand for" MacDonald's. But the fact that most 3-year-olds are able to use symbols in one context or domain does not mean that they can apply this ability across all contexts and domains without specific practice. Young children also begin to learn how symbols work, for instance, using both hash marks and numerals to represent numerical information, noting the differences between numerals and letters, comparing the way letters work in their own and their friends' written names, and understanding that letters symbolize sound segments within words.

Children's concepts about literacy are formed from the earliest years by observing and interacting with readers and writers as well as through their own attempts to read and write (Sulzby and Teale, 1991). In each situation they encounter, their understanding is both increased and constrained by their existing models of written language. In other words, while these existing models mediate and enable understanding, the knowledge and beliefs of which these models are composed are modified with use as the child explores language, text, and meaning. Beyond incremental learning, certain changes in perspective and reorganizations of concept are also necessary. In this way, the breadth, depth, and nature of children's engagement with text determines a great deal of literacy learning.

The interplay between elaboration and reorganization of children's mental models has been well documented in the domain of orthographic development (Ehri, 1991; Gough and Juel, 1991). Visual word recognition can flourish only when children displace the belief that print is like pictures with the insight that written words are comprised of letters that, in turn, map to speech sounds. Even as children begin to learn about spellings, they must also develop more sophisticated understandings of the forces beyond pictures and individual words that direct text meaning. These include, for example, the nature of word, sentence, paragraph, and text structures and the sorts of thinking and devices that hold them all together. Whereas each such type of learning depends on experience and exploration, it must also depend on certain conceptual insights.

For the child, Downing (1979:27) suggests, language is not an object of awareness in itself but is "seemingly like a glass, through which the child looks at the surrounding world, . . . not [initially] suspecting that it has its own existence, its own aspects of construction." To become a mature reader and writer, charged with constructing and corroborating the message of an author, this perception must change. Moreover, each such change must be guided by the metalinguistic insight that language invites inspection and reflection. Indeed, literacy growth, at every level, depends on learning to treat language as an object of thought, in and of itself (Halliday, 1982; Olson, 1995). See Box 2-1 for definitions of *metacognition* and *metalinguistic*.

For most children, growing up to be a reader is a lengthy process that begins long before formal instruction is provided in school or elsewhere. The following sections offer a brief sketch of what is

BOX 2-1
More Definitions

"Metacognition" refers to thoughts about thinking (cognition); for example, thinking about how to understand a passage.

"Metalinguistic" refers to language or thought about language; for example, noting that the word "snake" refers to a long skinny thing all in one piece but that the word itself is neither long nor skinny and has four parts when spoken and five parts when written.

learned, when it is learned, and in what kinds of situations learning takes place during the course of successful language and literacy development in early childhood.

Language Development

Children with intact neurological systems, raised by caring adults in a speech community, fairly effortlessly acquire the spoken language of that community, exhibiting abilities within the domains of phonology, morphology, syntax, semantics, pragmatics, and lexicon or vocabulary (see Box 2-2).

Knowing a language, however, does not require a conscious awareness of the various systems involved in that language, nor does it necessitate an ability to articulate the underlying principles or components of the systems. Metalinguistic insights about some language domains typically emerge in the preschool years, however, as discussed later in this section.

Practically from birth, infants are able to distinguish all the sounds of any human language, and within a short time their perceptual abilities become tuned to their native language, even though their productive repertoire remains limited to nonspeech sounds and babbling for much of the first year of life (e.g., Werker and Lalonde, 1988). Phonological development continues well beyond the first

---

BOX 2-2
Key Definitions of the Components of Language

"Phonology" refers to the way sounds of the language operate.

"Morphology" refers to the way words are formed and are related to each other.

"Semantics" refers to the ways that language conveys meaning.

"Pragmatics" refers to the ways the members of the speech community achieve their goals using language.

"Lexicon" or vocabulary refers to stored information about the meanings and pronunciation of words.

year and probably continues to be refined even in the early school years (e.g., Nittrouer, 1992; Gerken et al., 1994; Fowler, 1991).

It has been argued that children's perception of speech undergoes a shift from holistic (based on overall prosodic or acoustic shapes of syllables and words) to truly segmental (based on small phonemic units) during the late preschool period (Jusczyk et al., 1993; Studdert-Kennedy, 1986; and other studies reviewed in Gerken et al., 1994). This issue could be important for alphabetic reading, in which the letters correspond roughly to phonemes, especially if, as has been suggested by some speech researchers (Walley, 1993), it is not until the early school years that a child's lexicon becomes large enough to force the shift from holistic to segment-based strategies. It also points to one possible basis for the well-documented link between vocabulary size and early reading ability: the development of fine within-word discrimination ability (phonemic representation) may be contingent on vocabulary size rather than age or general developmental level. The potential immaturity of some children's phonological encoding/representation systems at the time formal reading instruction begins may impede their achieving a level of phonemic awareness for spoken words related to fluent decoding of written words.

Comprehension of words emerges somewhat before the ability to produce words, at around the time of a child's first birthday (Huttenlocher and Smiley, 1987; Nelson, 1973), and many children exhibit a sharp increase in the size of their working vocabularies during the second year of life (Bates et al., 1988). Vocabulary growth is rapid throughout the preschool and school years, and it is highly variable among individual children. Although there have been many attempts to estimate the size of children's vocabularies, problems arise because of definitions (e.g., what it means to know a word) and differences in the procedures used to estimate vocabulary size (Beck and McKeown, 1991; Nagy and Anderson, 1984). Despite this imprecision, individual differences have been shown to be reliably related to demographics; for example, one study found that first graders from higher-income backgrounds had about double the vocabulary size of those from lower-income ones (Graves and Slater, 1987).

Vocabulary size continues to increase with schooling and beyond. It is estimated that students acquire around seven words per day (2,700-3,000 words per year) during the elementary through high school years (Just and Carpenter, 1987; Nagy and Herman, 1987; Smith, 1941). A review of this research points out that it may be more correct to say that children become aware of seven words per day but that a longer learning process is necessary for these words to affect the child's comprehension and use of language (Beck and McKeown, 1991).

Another perspective on vocabulary growth stresses that new words are not simply added in a serial fashion to a static and established vocabulary. Rather, the exposure to new words alters and refines the semantic representations of words already in the child's vocabulary and the relationships among them (Landauer and Dumais, 1997). Word counts, then, may be a very imprecise measure of vocabulary development.

Research on grammatical development in young children suggests a very rapid acquisition of the basic syntactic structures of the native language (e.g., Brown, 1973; Pinker, 1984; other studies reviewed in Bloom et al., 1994). For example, children under two years of age show the kind of knowledge of word order in English that allows them to appreciate that "Big Bird is tickling Cookie Monster" means something different from "Cookie Monster is tickling Big Bird" (Hirsh-Pasek et al., 1987; see Golinkoff and Hirsch-Pasek, 1995, for a review). Some time after they are able to comprehend simple sentences, children begin to combine words so as to express some structural and/or syntactic relationship between them. The child's sentences grow in length and complexity from two to three to four or more words, on average, over the remainder of the preschool period. By the time of school entry, most children produce and comprehend a wide range of grammatical forms, although some structures are still developing.

Children's increasing linguistic sophistication allows them to use language as a means of engaging in more complex information exchanges with adults and older children. During book sharing with an adult, for instance, children progress from just focusing on the names of objects in the pictures to asking questions about the content of the text. The child's ability to produce and comprehend complex sentences (with appropriate vocabulary and accurate pronunciation) then enables him or her to discuss abstract ideas ("What if . . . ?"), absent objects, and past events. This decreased reliance on immediate context as a support for communication is a developmental accomplishment that may ease the transition to school, where decontextualized language is highly valued.

Throughout the preschool period and well into adulthood, individuals learn the pragmatics of their language, that is, how to use language appropriately and effectively in social contexts (see Ninio and Snow, 1996, for a review). During the preschool years, the development of these abilities occurs in three domains: (1) production of conventional speech acts, such as requesting, attention getting, and describing (Dore, 1974, 1975, 1976; Snow et al., 1996); (2) use of conversational skills, including turn taking, topic contingency, and topic development (Bloom et al., 1976; Dorval and Eckerman, 1984; Schley and Snow, 1992; Snow, 1977); and (3) production of extended autonomous discourse such as narratives, explanations, definitions, and other socially defined genres (Donaldson, 1986; Peterson and McCabe, 1983; Snow, 1990).

Much of the work in the field of pragmatics describes how children learn the rules for using language in specific situations, such as book reading (Ninio and Bruner, 1978; Snow and Ninio, 1986; Snow and Goldfield, 1983), sharing time (Michaels, 1991), and dinner table talk (Beals, 1993; Blum-Kulka, 1993). One avenue for introducing and refining new pragmatic functions is through experience with books and other literacy activities. For instance, in time, children begin to appreciate stories in which characters use language to deceive or pretend, to understand the point of fables and other texts that include metaphors and other figurative devices, and to grasp the differences between narrative, expository, poetic, and other varieties of texts that books can contain.

As proficiency in the forms and functions of language grows, children also gain "metalinguistic" skills. These involve the ability not just to use language but to think about it, play with it, talk about it, analyze it componentially, and make judgments about acceptable versus incorrect forms (e.g., Pratt et al., 1984). Metalinguistic insights are applied in all language domains (phonology, syntax, semantics, pragmatics), such that pronunciation, word usage, and sentence and text forms can all be thought about in this new way by the child. It was originally thought that this aspect of language development did not begin to emerge until about school age, but more recent research has demonstrated that some children exhibit rudimentary metalinguistic skills by age 3 or even younger and that many children acquire a considerable degree of metalinguistic insight about sentences, words, and speech sounds by age 4 to 5 years, before they enter school. It is also clear that metalinguistic skills continue to improve throughout the school years.

One interesting metalinguistic development is the child's growing appreciation of what a word is. Although even very young children understand the idea that things have "names," the more abstract concept of words as the building blocks of phrases and sentences, and as linguistic units whose sounds are arbitrarily related to their meanings, is only gradually attained during the preschool years (e.g., Tunmer et al., 1984; Chaney, 1989; Papandropoulou and Sinclair, 1974). These studies revealed that young children initially are unable to make a distinction between the word itself and the object or action it refers to and cannot break sentences into their component words. When asked to judge the length of words, for instance, "snake" is typically deemed to be a "long" word, and "caterpillar" a "short" one, until the child begins to understand words as distinct from their referents. Likewise, when asked to segment sentences (e.g., on the pretext of saying it slowly enough for the examiner to write it down), young children rarely isolate single words but instead break the sentence into phrases (e.g., The little girl / was eating / an ice cream cone.) Gradually, nouns, then verbs and modifiers, and finally function words (such as articles, conjunctions, and prepositions) come to be understood as individual linguistic units, even though the boundaries between them may sometimes be mistaken (e.g., "a / nambulance" rather than "an / ambulance").

Another aspect of metalinguistic development is the child's ability to attend to and analyze the internal phonological structure of spoken words.

Phonological Awareness

This sketch of language development and of initial metalinguistic accomplishments applies quite universally to all children learning to read. For children learning an alphabetic language, like English, there is an important additional ingredient: *phonological awareness* and, in particular, *phonemic awareness*. As discussed in Chapter 1, in English, the printed symbols (letters or graphemes) systematically represent the component sounds of the language. Understanding the basic alphabetic principle requires an awareness that spoken language can be analyzed into strings of separable words and words, in turn, into sequences of syllables and phonemes within syllables (see Box 2-3).

The assessment of phonemic awareness typically involves tasks that require the student to isolate or segment one or more of the phonemes of a spoken word, to blend or combine a sequence of separate phonemes into a word, or to manipulate the phonemes within a word (e.g., adding, subtracting, or rearranging phonemes of one word to make a different word).

Spoken words can be phonologically subdivided at several different levels of analysis. These include the *syllable* (in the word *protect*, /pro/ and /tEkt/); the *onset* and *rime* within the syllable (/pr/ and /o/, and /t/ and /Ekt/, respectively); and the individual *phonemes* themselves (/p/, /r/, /o/, /t/, /E/, /k/, and /t/). The term *phonological awareness* refers to a general appreciation of the sounds of speech as distinct from their meaning. When that insight includes an understanding that words can be divided into a sequence of phonemes, this finer-grained sensitivity is termed *phonemic awareness*.

For most children, an awareness of the phonological structure of speech generally develops gradually over the preschool years. Among the first signs of awareness that spoken words contain smaller components are monitoring and correcting speech errors and "playing" with sounds (e.g., "pancakes, cancakes, canpakes"), both of which even 2- to 3-year-olds have been observed to do occasionally in naturalistic conversational settings. Appreciating rhymes (for instance, that *light* rhymes with *kite)* has also been noted in young preschoolers. The entry to phonemic awareness typically begins with

BOX 2-3
Key Definitions of Some Terms
That Are Often Confused

The terms *phonology* and *phonological* refer to the sound structure of speech and, in particular, to the perception, representation, and production of speech sounds. As such, the phonological aspects of language include its prosodic dimensions—intonation, stress, and timing—as well as its articulatory units, including words, syllables, and *phonemes*.

Phonemes are the speech phonological units that make a difference to meaning. Thus, the spoken word *rope* is comprised of three phonemes: /r/, /o/, and /p/. It differs by only one phoneme from each of the spoken words, *soap, rode*, and *rip*.

Phonemic awareness is the insight that every spoken word can be conceived as a sequence of phonemes. Because phonemes are the units of sound that are represented by the letters of an alphabet, an awareness of phonemes is key to understanding the logic of the alphabetic principle and thus to the learnability of phonics and spelling.

Phonological awareness is a more inclusive term than phonemic awareness and refers to the general ability to attend to the sounds of language as distinct from its meaning. Phonemic awareness generally develops through other, less subtle levels of phonological awareness. Noticing similarities between words in their sounds, enjoying rhymes, counting syllables, and so forth are indications of such "metaphonological" skill.

Speech discrimination, including *phonemic discrimination*, is distinguished from phonemic awareness because the ability to detect or discriminate even slight differences between two spoken words does not necessarily indicate an awareness of the nature of that difference. Moreover, the study of the phonetics indicates that, both within and between speakers, there are many variations in the acoustic and articulatory properties of speech, including phonemes, that are not functionally significant to meaning.

The term *phonics* refers to instructional practices that emphasize how spellings are related to speech sounds in systematic ways.

The term *phonological decoding* or, more simply, *decoding*, refers to the aspect of the reading process that involves deriving a pronunciation for a printed sequence of letters based on knowledge of spelling-sound correspondences.

an appreciation of alliteration, for instance, that *boy* and *butterfly* begin with /b/. Even so, many children initially find it difficult to separate the component phonemes of a complex onset, reporting for example that the first sound of *play* is /pl/ rather than /p/ or failing to represent both sounds of such initial blends in their independent spelling. Many books geared toward this age group appropriately include rhyming and alliterative texts, and this may be one avenue by which children's attention is drawn to the sounds of speech (Bryant et al., 1990). In a sample of 3- and 4-year-olds, Chaney (1992) found that 91 percent of the children could judge correctly whether a "Martian" puppet said English words correctly, 37 percent could be induced by the examiner to engage in sound play, and 26 percent could reliably identify rhyming words. Identifying words that began with a particular phoneme, however, was accomplished only by 14 percent of the children, and we know from other studies that not until age 5 or 6 are such segmentation skills exhibited by a majority of children (e.g., Calfee et al., 1973; Liberman et al., 1974). Hence, phonological awareness is correlated with age (Chaney, 1992; Hakes, 1980; Smith and Tager-Flusberg, 1982).

Chaney (1992) also observed that performance on phonological awareness tasks by preschoolers was highly correlated with general language ability. Moreover, it was measures of semantic and syntactic skills, rather than speech discrimination and articulation, that predicted phonological awareness differences. Correlations between metalinguistic and more basic language abilities have similarly been reported by others (e.g., Bryant et al., 1990; Bryant, 1974; Smith and Tager-Flusberg, 1982). These findings indicate that the development of phonological awareness (and other metalinguistic skills) is closely intertwined with growth in basic language proficiency during the preschool years.

True phonemic awareness extends beyond an appreciation of rhyme or alliteration, as it corresponds to the insight that every word can be conceived of as a sequence of phonemes. Children with phonemic awareness are able to discern that *camp* and *soap* end with the same sound, that *blood* and *brown* begin with the same sound, or, more advanced still, that removing the /m/ from *smell* leaves *sell*.

Because of the physical and psychological nature of phonemes as well as the nature of human attention, few children acquire phonemic awareness spontaneously (Adams et al., 1998). Rather, attaining phonemic awareness is difficult for most children and far more difficult for some than others. Still, because phonemes are the units of sound that are represented by the letters of an alphabet, an awareness of phonemes is key to understanding the logic of the alphabetic principle. Unless and until children have a basic awareness of the phonemic structure of language, asking them for the first sound in the word *boy*, or expecting them to understand that *cap* has three sounds while *camp* has four, is to little avail.

In terms of acoustics, the syllable is an indivisible entity. By extension, unless and until children have come to conceive of syllables in terms of the underlying sequence of elementary speech sounds of which they are comprised, their only option for learning to read or spell words is by rote memorization.

The theoretical and practical importance of phonological awareness for the beginning reader relies not only on logic but also on the results of several decades of empirical research. Early studies showed a strong association between a child's ability to read and the ability to segment words into phonemes (Liberman et al., 1974). Dozens of subsequent studies have confirmed that there is a close relationship between phonemic awareness and reading ability, not just in the early grades (e.g., Ehri and Wilce, 1980, 1985; Perfetti et al., 1987) but throughout the school years (Calfee et al., 1973; Shankweiler et al., 1995). Furthermore, as we discuss in Chapter 4, even prior to formal reading instruction, the performance of kindergartners on tests of phonological awareness is a strong predictor of their future reading achievement (Juel, 1991; Scarborough, 1989; Stanovich, 1986; Wagner et al., 1994).

Phonological and phonemic awareness should not be confused with speech perception, per se. Speech perception is the natural ability to detect and discriminate the sounds of one's language, for instance, to be able to tell the difference between spoken stimuli that have many elements in common, such as *mail* and *nail*, *back* and *bag*. (The term *auditory discrimination* is sometimes incorrectly applied to this skill, but that broader label also encompasses the ability to perceive other nonspeech sounds, such as tones, environmental noises, music, and so forth.)

Because speech perception involves some of the same sensory and neural circuits as are used for hearing generally, children with hearing impairments generally also have poor speech discrimination. Other children have intact hearing but are selectively impaired in making discriminations among speech sounds. Not surprisingly, children who, for whatever reason, possess poor speech discrimination skills are likely to have difficulty acquiring phonological awareness. Nevertheless, many young children who perform satisfactorily on tests of speech discrimination exhibit weak phonological awareness.

Furthermore, whereas good phonological awareness in young children is a strong predictor of reading success, good performance on speech discrimination measures is not (see Chapter 4). In short, when administering a test of phonological awareness, it is always prudent to assess also the accuracy of the child's perception of the stimuli (e.g., by having the child repeat items aloud before performing the desired manipulation of the sounds). The research is clear, however, in showing that phonological awareness is different from and much more closely related to reading than speech perception itself.

It is also important to clarify the difference between phonological awareness and phonics. *Phonics* is the term that has long been used among educators to refer to instruction in how the sounds of speech are represented by letters and spellings, for instance, that the letter *M* represents the phoneme /m/ and the various conventions by which the long sounds of vowels are signaled. Phonics, in short, presumes a working awareness of the phonemic composition of words. In conventional phonics programs, however, such awareness was generally taken for granted, and therein lies the force of the research on phonemic awareness. To the extent that children lack such phonemic awareness, they are unable to internalize usefully their phonics lessons. The resulting symptoms include difficulties in sounding and blending new words, in retaining words from one encounter to the next, and in learning to spell. In contrast, research repeatedly demonstrates that, when steps are taken to ensure an adequate awareness of phonemes, the reading and spelling growth of the group as a whole is accelerated and the incidence of reading failure is diminished. These results have been obtained with normal as well as various at-risk populations (see Chapter 5).

Despite some confusion in the media and in some educational circles, phonemic awareness and phonological awareness are not just new terms for speech discrimination or for traditional phonics instruction. Instead, they are terms that emphasize the importance of sensitive and informed early literacy support and assessment that take account of the cognitive elusiveness of the insights and observations on which learning an alphabetic script depend. In addition, they are terms that serve to remind us of the fact that, no less than for higher-order dimensions of literacy growth, productive learning about decoding and spelling necessarily builds on prior understanding.

One of the most interesting findings from research on the development of phonological awareness is that its relationship to learning to read appears to be bidirectional, involving reciprocal causation (Ehri and Wilce, 1980, 1986; Perfetti et al., 1987). In other words, on one hand, some basic appreciation of the phonological structure of spoken words appears to be necessary for the child to discover the alphabetic principle that print represents the sounds of the language. Moreover, as we discuss in later chapters of this report, numerous studies have shown that learning to read can be facilitated by providing explicit instruction that directs children's attention to the phonological structure of words, indicating that phonological awareness plays a causal role in learning to read (see Chapter 6). On the other hand, instruction in alphabetic literacy, particularly regarding the correspondences between letters and phonemes, in turn appears to facilitate further growth in phonological (especially phonemic) awareness. That is why adults from nonliterate societies and students who learn to read nonalphabetic languages exhibit much weaker levels of phonological awareness than do readers of alphabetic languages (Morais et al., 1986; Read et al., 1986).

Not surprisingly, therefore, the correlation between reading and phonological awareness, which is already substantial by the start of school, becomes stronger during the early grades. This strong correlation appears to be strengthened by the association between phonemic awareness and children's ability to sound out (or phonologically decode) pronounceable nonwords and unfamiliar printed words. Theorists such as Share (1995) have argued that becoming skilled in phonological decoding provides the child with a self-teaching mechanism that, along with oral vocabulary knowledge and context, is useful for learning to read words that they have not previously encountered. After a few such correct decodings, these words can be recognized quite automatically. In thinking about the process of learning to read and about how best to frame early reading instruction, it is important to bear in mind these powerful reciprocal influences of reading skill and phonological awareness on each other.

Literacy Development

Children live in homes that support literacy development to differing degrees. Optimal development occurs through interactions that are physically, emotionally, socially, and cognitively suited to the changing needs of the infant through toddler years. Late in the first year, when babies begin to purposely grasp and manipulate various objects, books and writing implements enter their exploratory worlds. Parents negotiate with children about how books are to be handled (Snow and Ninio, 1986; Bus and van IJzendoorn, 1995, 1997). Infants between about 8 and 12 months who are read to by their parents typically show monthly progress from grabbing and mouthing books, to "hinging" the covers, to turning the pages. Much of this reading-like behavior is accompanied by babbling.

In years two and three, children advance from babbling to producing understandable speech in response to books and to markings that they themselves create. Late in the second year or early in the third, many children produce reading-like as well as drawing-like scribbles and recognizable letters or letter-like forms (see Box 2-4). Two- and three-year-olds are often introduced by adults to models of letters and related sounds, drawing attention to sources such as *Sesame Street* on television. Many of these children are also in child care settings where teachers and caregivers expose them to models of reading and writing.

> **BOX 2-4**
> *Goodnight Moon*
>
> "*Goodnight Moon,* by Margaret Wise Brown," proclaims a three-year old girl, who pretends to read the cover page and author's name. With great relish, she opens the book and faithfully recites each word from memory.
> The mother knows that the girl is not really reading but encourages her just the same. Intuitively, she suspects what has been found by research to be true: that children who pretend to read at this early age are more likely to become successful later.
> " . . . and a picture of the cow jumping over the moon," continues the girl. She lifts the book close to her eyes and scrutinizes the print on the page.
> "A-B-A-B-Z," she recites. while pointing to the word *cow.* This is an important connection. Already, she knows that words are made of letters that can be named.
> She resumes the story word for word, turning pages slowly. "Goodnight noises everywhere," she whispers, and then pronounces, "The end," proudly snapping the book shut.

Parents assist in their children's literacy development with sensitivity to culturally specific social routines in book reading[1] (Snow and Goldfield, 1982; Snow and Ninio, 1986; Teale and Sulzby, 1986; 1987; Kaderavek and Sulzby, 1998a, 1998b; Sulzby and Kaderavek, 1996). Research conducted by Taylor and Dorsey-Gaines (1988) and Gadsden (1994) reveals that literacy resources are available in the homes of even very poor and stressed families, although different in quantity and variety than in moderate- or higher-income families (Baker et al., 1997). It is clear that during this period children develop expectations that certain kinds of intonations and wording are used with books and other written materials. Those who are read to frequently and enjoy such reading begin to recite key phrases or longer stretches of words specific to certain books.

---

[1]Routines with cultural significance as powerful as that of book reading do not appear to be widespread in the area of writing, although this may be due to lack of relevant research (Burns and Casbergue, 1992; Anderson and Stokes, 1984; Teale, 1986).

Late in this period, many children label and comment about pictured items, describe pictured actions, and engage in some question-and-answer dialogue and/or create voices for characters in pictures (Kaderavek and Sulzby, 1998a, 1998b; Sulzby and Kaderavek, 1996; Sulzby and Teale, 1987; Whitehurst et al., 1988).

Between the ages of 3 and 4, children show rapid growth in literacy (as in other domains), as they experiment with writing by forming scribbles, random strings of letters, and letter-like forms. Some children begin to identify salient sounds within words, and some 4-year-olds are even able to demonstrate this knowledge in their writing by beginning to use invented spelling, at least with initial consonants (in English, many Spanish-speaking children tend to use vowels first). These children may spend time with toys and manipulatives that include letters, numerals, and playful representations of letter sounds and other symbol systems. More and more such toys contain mechanisms that "say" letters or words in response to a child's action. *Sesame Street* on television and CD-ROMs also provide meaningful stimuli at the letter, sound, word, and text level, and children at this age often control the repeatability of these stimuli using VCRs and computers.

Children who are frequently read to will then "read" their favorite books by themselves by engaging in oral language-like and written language-like routines (Sulzby and Teale, 1987, 1991). For most children at this age, emergent reading routines include attending to pictures and occasionally to salient print, such as that found in illustrations or labels. A few begin to attend to the print in the main body of the text, and a few make the transition into conventional reading with their favorite books (Anbar, 1986; Backman, 1983; Bissex, 1980; Jackson, 1991; Jackson et al., 1988; Lass, 1982, 1983; Sulzby, 1985a).

During this time, children tend to create many and varied texts and display different kinds of writing systems. Clay's (1975) title, "What did I write?", came from a child query to a parent and captures part of children's writing development during this period. Clay examined children's early nonconventional writings and found that, even with scribble and nonphonetic letter strings, children appear to be exploring features that they abstract about print, such as its linearity and use of recursive features. Read (1971) and Chomsky (1975) were among the first to examine the writing of children whose untutored spellings reflected phonetic and phonological analysis of speech. Read (1975) demonstrated that children at these ages have already developed conceptual categories for consonant and vowel sounds in spoken English and that these categories, which were linguistically sound, appeared to underlie the invented spellings found in the children's writing.

Although it appears that children are hard at work as scholars of language, observations of children engaging in literacy activities in homes and preschools depict them as playful and exploratory in most of these activities.

Table 2-1 shows a set of particular accomplishments that the successful learner is likely to exhibit during the preschool years. This list is neither exhaustive nor incontestable, but it does capture many highlights of the course of literacy acquisition that have been revealed through several decades of research. Needless to say, the timing of these accomplishments will to some extent depend on maturational and experiential differences between children.

CHARACTERISTICS OF SKILLED READING

Skilled readers can be compared with less skilled readers on their comprehension (meanings of words, basic meaning of text, making inferences from text) and on the accuracy and speed of their identification of strings of letters as words (decoding familiar, unfamiliar, and pseudo-words). The same set of cognitive skills distinguishes skilled from unskilled readers at the adult level as at the middle grade level (Bell and Perfetti, 1994; Bruck, 1990; Daneman and Carpenter, 1980; Haenggi and Perfetti, 1992; Jackson and McClelland, 1979; Palmer et al., 1985; Cunningham et al., 1990). We present an overview of the capacities of the skilled reader in comprehension and in word decoding.

TABLE 2-1 Developmental Accomplishments of Literacy Acquisition

Birth to Three-Year-Old Accomplishments
- Recognizes specific books by cover.
- Pretends to read books.
- Understands that books are handled in particular ways.
- Enters into a book-sharing routine with primary caregivers.
- Vocalization play in crib gives way to enjoyment of rhyming language, nonsense word play, etc.
- Labels objects in books.
- Comments on characters in books.
- Looks at picture in book and realizes it is a symbol for real object.
- Listens to stories.
- Requests/commands adult to read or write.
- May begin attending to specific print such as letters in names.
- Uses increasingly purposive scribbling.
- Occasionally seems to distinguish between drawing and writing.
- Produces some letter-like forms and scribbles with some features of English writing.

Three- and Four-Year-Old Accomplishments
- Knows that alphabet letters are a special category of visual graphics that can be individually named.
- Recognizes local environmental print.
- Knows that it is the print that is read in stories.
- Understands that different text forms are used for different functions of print (e.g., list for groceries).
- Pays attention to separable and repeating sounds in language (e.g., Peter, Peter, Pumpkin Eater, Peter Eater).
- Uses new vocabulary and grammatical constructions in own speech.
- Understands and follows oral directions.
- Is sensitive to some sequences of events in stories.
- Shows an interest in books and reading.
- When being read a story, connects information and events to life experiences.
- Questions and comments demonstrate understanding of literal meaning of story being told.
- Displays reading and writing attempts, calling attention to self: "Look at my story."
- Can identify 10 alphabet letters, especially those from own name.
- "Writes" (scribbles) message as part of playful activity.
- May begin to attend to beginning or rhyming sound in salient words.

Comprehension

Skilled readers are good comprehenders. They differ from unskilled readers in their use of general world knowledge to comprehend text literally as well as to draw valid inferences from texts, in their comprehension of words, and in their use of comprehension-monitoring and repair strategies.

Comprehension research has demonstrated clearly the importance of the reader's background knowledge for understanding texts (Anderson and Pearson, 1984; Anderson et al., 1977; Bransford and Johnson, 1972). Knowledge of the content addressed by a text plays an important role in the reader's formation of the text's main ideas (Afflerbach, 1990) and can be traded off to some extent against weak word recognition skills (Adams et al., 1996; Recht and Leslie, 1988). When studies have assessed the role of both basic processes and stores of relevant knowledge at a sufficiently fine grain, the two seem to make separable contributions to comprehension (Haenggi and Perfetti, 1994).

Recent research accommodates the role of world knowledge in a comprehensive account of text comprehension that focuses on encoding the basic meaning of the text sentences (Kintsch, 1988; Mannes and St. George, 1996). Both the basic comprehension of literal text meanings and the use of knowledge necessary to go beyond the literal (propositional meaning) are accounted for. In combining the importance of the linguistic forms of the text with the importance of the reader's background knowledge, the research makes a distinction between the reader's understanding of what the text says, the *text base*, and what the text is about, the *situation model* (van Dijk and Kintsch, 1983). In fact, text research has increasingly focused on the fact that a reader may understand several levels of text information, including information about text genre and communication contexts, as well as the text itself and the referential situation (Graesser et al., 1997). To consider just one level for illustration, understanding the situation described in storylike texts typically requires understanding the narrative and the temporal-causal structures, even when the causal relations between text elements are only implicit (Trabasso and van den Broek, 1985; van den Broek, 1994). Because texts cannot be fully explicit, situation models require the use of knowledge and inferences (see Fletcher et al., 1994, for a review).

An important part of comprehension is concept development and knowledge of word meanings. Vocabulary knowledge has long been known to be a major correlate of comprehension ability, as measured by standardized tests (e.g., Davis, 1944, 1968). Research has found that comprehension is diminished by lack of relevant word knowledge (Anderson and Freebody, 1983; Kame'enui et al., 1982; Marks et al., 1974). Mezynski (1983) and Stahl and Fairbanks (1986) reviewed a series of studies that trained subjects for word/concept development to improve comprehension scores and found that, when certain conditions of instruction were met, the gain in comprehension was attained.

Of course, some comprehension of passages is possible, even when a few of the words are unknown to the reader (Anderson and Freebody, 1983; Kame'enui et al., 1982). Reading itself can provide one with meanings for unfamiliar words, although readers also fail to learn much about most of the unfamiliar words they encounter (Jenkins et al., 1984; Nagy et al., 1985; Shu et al., 1995; Stahl et al., 1989).

Comprehension monitoring is the ability to accurately assess one's own comprehension (Baker and Anderson, 1982; Garner, 1980; Otero and Kintsch, 1992; Vosniadou et al., 1988). To study this, an inconsistency is introduced into a short text, to see whether the reader detects it either during recall or when explicitly questioned. A typical result is that some readers do and some do not detect these inconsistencies, and those who do tend to be either older readers (compared with younger readers) or more skilled (compared with less skilled) readers. A less skilled reader may fail to detect the contradictions in texts because they have misconceptions about high-level reading goals (Myers and Paris, 1978). An alternate explanation is that less skilled readers have difficulties with the component processes of representing a text (i.e., word identification and basic comprehension) and that this difficulty rather than an independent failure to employ a monitoring strategy is the source of the problem.

There is some evidence supporting the latter explanation (Kintsch, 1992; Vosniadou et al., 1988). Whatever the explanation, however, training in metacognitive skills has been shown to be effective for improving comprehension (Brown et al., 1984; Paris et al., 1984; Gambrell and Bales, 1986; Palincsar and Brown, 1984).

Many basic cognitive processes are shared during reading and listening. Syntactic and inferential processes as well as background and word knowledge play a role in both. The correlations between listening comprehension and reading comprehension are high for adult populations (Gernsbacher et al., 1990; Sticht and James, 1984) and for older children (Carlisle, 1989). A large number of studies have compared listening to a text and reading one at different grade levels (Sticht et al., 1974; Sticht and James, 1984). The correlation between reading and listening across these studies rose from grades 1 through 6 and tended not to show further increases. Sticht et al. (1974) further noted that studies tended to find reading comprehension to exceed listening comprehension for college-age students but not younger students. Using their analysis as an approximation, "mature" reading comprehension might be said to begin when the advantage of listening over written comprehension disappears, in seventh or eighth grade.

Three observations are important in interpreting data on the relationship between listening and reading comprehension. First, such data come from studies that control message content across listening and reading. They do not address the question of whether fundamental differences between typical speech exchanges and typical written texts might play a significant role in comprehension. We know there are differences between written and oral language in terms of their social processes. The differences and similarities between written and oral language have been discussed by numerous researchers (Kamhi and Catts, 1989; D.R. Olson, 1977; Tannen, 1982; Sulzby, 1985a, 1987; Perfetti, 1985; Rubin, 1980; Galda et al., 1997).

Second, the high correlations between reading and listening comprehension occur after the child has learned how to decode. Third, correlations inform us about variability across a population, not within specific individuals. Thus, on the basis of the correlations among adults, the shared variance between listening and reading comprehension may be as much as 80 percent. For children, the shared variance may be somewhat smaller, for example, around 50 percent in fifth grade, approaching adult levels subsequently. This does not mean that a given individual reads as well as he or she listens. The gap between one's listening and reading comprehension can in fact be quite large, even when the correlation between the two is quite strong.

Word Identification

The identification of printed words has long been treated as a skill that is essential for novice readers, yet it remains important in skilled adult reading as well and is a necessary (but not sufficient) factor for comprehension. By "word identification," we mean that the reader can pronounce a word, not whether he or she knows what it means.

For a skilled reader, the identification of a printed word begins with a *visual process* that operates on the visual forms of letters that make up a word. The visual process is constrained by the sensitivity of the retina, such that visual forms are perceived sufficiently for identification only within a relatively narrow region (the fovea). Studies of eye movements suggest that readers can correctly perceive only 5 to 10 letters to the right of the fixation point (McConkie and Rayner, 1975; Rayner and Pollatsek, 1987). The effect of this limitation is that readers' eyes must come to rest (fixate) on many words.

Visual processes initiate word identification and immediately trigger other processes that complete it, including, most importantly, *phonological decoding processes*, which concern the correspondences between printed letters and the sounds of the language, especially phonemes, the small sound units within spoken and heard words. The research on reading in alphabetic writing systems has developed an important consensus that phonological decoding is a routine part of skilled word identification. How the phonological and visual-orthographic information gets combined for the identification of individual words has been the focus of much research, fueled in recent years by theoretical debates about how to conceptualize the cognitive mechanisms of word identification (Besner, 1990, in press; Coltheart et al., 1993; Paap and Noel, 1991; Plaut et al., 1996; Seidenberg and McClelland, 1989). The various models, although they appear dramatically different, can explain many of the same facts about reading and about reading failure (Plaut et al., 1996). Generally speaking, what we know about word identification and its development is based more on the common ground of these models than on their differences.

One thing that is especially clear from the research that underpins the models is that skilled readers develop both a knowledge of how spelling patterns correspond to possible word pronunciations and a sensitivity, based on experience, to the relative frequency of printed word and subword forms. The only issue is the extent to which sublexical phonology (pronouncing portions of words based on a string of letters within the word) actually plays a role in the retrieval of word meaning from memory. Some work suggests there is substantial phonological mediation (Berent and Perfetti, 1995; Lesch and Pollatsek, 1993; Lukatela and Turvey, 1990; van Orden et al., 1990); other paradigms generate findings suggesting that phonological mediation occurs only some of the time (Besner, 1990; Coltheart et al., 1991; Paap and Noel, 1991; Waters and Seidenberg, 1985). Even results suggesting that some word retrieval can occur without phonological mediation are consistent with the assumptions that (a) phonology is automatically activated during the identification process and (b) phonological word forms are retrieved along with meanings.[2] In addition to supporting word identification, phonological processing during reading supports comprehension and memory for recently read text (Slowiaczek and Clifton, 1980; Perfetti and McCutchen, 1982).

Word identification research has provided information about how words are understood as well as how their phonological form is initially identified from print. Word meanings and sometimes their pronunciations are necessarily context dependent; for example,

---

[2]Indeed, it is becoming clear that, even in nonalphabetic systems, simple word identification brings about an activation of the phonology of the word form, even if the reader's task is to determine meaning (Perfetti and Zhang, 1995).

"spring" can refer to a season of the year or a coiled piece of metal, and "read" can be pronounced like "reed" or "red." Context is important in interpreting the meaning of a word in a sentence, and skilled readers do this more efficiently than less skilled readers (Gernsbacher, 1993). However, it is equally important to note the limits of context. Skilled readers do not skip many words when they read texts (Rayner and Pollatsek, 1989), despite the potential that context might provide for doing so. Indeed the percentage of words in texts that skilled readers look directly at is quite high, ranging from above 50 percent to 80 percent across a range of reading situations (Rayner and Pollatsek, 1989). The benefits of context seem to be mainly on the amount of time a reader spends on a given word— the duration of fixation—with only slight effects on the probability of a word fixation. And, although skilled readers are very good at using context to figure out the meaning of a word, it is less skilled readers who attempt to make the greater use of context to identify a word (Stanovich et al., 1981; Perfetti et al., 1979).

Finally, experience builds automaticity at word identification, and it appears to establish an important lexical-orthographic source of knowledge for reading (Stanovich and West, 1989). This lexical-orthographic knowledge centers on the letters that form the printed word and is tapped by tasks that assess spelling knowledge, as opposed to tasks that tap mainly phonological knowledge. It can be most easily indexed by the amount of reading a person has done (Stanovich and West, 1989). The phonological decoding and lexical-orthographic abilities are correlated, but each makes unique contributions to reading achievement. There are two complementary but overlapping kinds of knowledge that support the identification of words: one is grounded in knowledge of the phonological structure of spoken words and knowledge of how orthographic units represent these structures. The other develops with the experience (made possible by the first) of reading printed word forms. These two types of knowledge may derive from related kinds of learning, however, since theories of word identification include both single-process and dual-process accounts of how a reader can come to know both individual word forms and general procedures for converting letter strings into phonological forms.

BEGINNING TO READ

Emerging Literacy in the Transition to School

When children go to school, they find a social, emotional, and intellectual structure different from the one at home. They join a group in which they have new rights and new responsibilities. There are over 20 others who are somewhat like them, with whom they can be compared for better or worse. There are routines and structures. There is only one adult, and there is talk that is separated from familiar routines. There are expectations—from the child, the child's family, the teacher, and the curriculum. In light of these many challenges, it is not surprising that the experience a child has during the first year of schooling has lasting impact on school performance (Alexander and Entwisle, 1996; Pianta and McCoy, 1997).

The acquisition of "real" reading typically begins at about age 5 to 7, after the child has entered kindergarten. Schools with greater concentrations of urban minority students may send approximately half of their students to second grade not yet reading conventionally, although these students may be memorizing and then recognizing some words as whole units (i.e., sight words).

The transition to real reading involves changes not only in the composition of skills but also in concepts about the nature of literacy (Chall, 1983). Adjusting to formal instruction in a school setting is mediated by the child's broadening of his or her concept of literacy, extending it to the new school culture. The purposes and practices of literacy and language in classrooms necessarily differ from those in any home, and all children entering school must adjust to the culture of the school if they are to become successful achievers in that milieu (Heath, 1983). This transition is likely to be less difficult for a child whose home literacy experiences and verbal interactions more closely resemble what goes on in the classroom than for a child whose prior conceptualization of the role of literacy has been attained through experiences of a much different sort. Gradually the curriculum emphasis shifts, and students find they are engaged in a wide range of literacy activities and are responsible for doing them well, all involving the common core of the reading on which they begin work in the early grades.

Most 5-year-olds from supportive literacy backgrounds continue to make rapid growth in literacy skills. Children who are, as Hiebert (1994) puts it, dependent on schooling for literacy, or who have spent four or more years without rich support for literacy, will tend to show patterns more like younger children. However, when such children are asked or enticed into doing tasks such as "reading your own way" or "writing your own way," they do respond in interpretable ways rather than showing no knowledge.

Children during this period will "read" from books that have been read to them frequently, increasingly showing the intonation and wording patterns of written language in their pretend readings (Purcell-Gates, 1991). Initially, they act as if pictures are what one looks at when reading aloud from familiar stories (Sulzby, 1985b, 1994). When watching an adult read silently, they may insist that something be said for reading to take place (Ferreiro and Teberosky (1982), but five-year-olds increasingly engage in intensive scrutiny of the pictures in a page-by-page fashion, as if reading silently before they begin to "read to" another aloud in an emergent fashion. Some of these emergent readings will focus on pictures as the source of the text, but increasing numbers will begin to attend to the print.

Print-focused emergent readings are significant in a number of ways. Children may temporarily refuse to read, saying that it is the print that is read and they do not know how to do that. Or they may temporarily read by focusing solely on an isolated feature of reading, such as sounding out real words or nonsense strings with signs of great satisfaction, picking out isolated strings of sight vocabulary words, or tracking the print while reciting text parts that do not match the print. These reading behaviors appear to indicate a period during which the child is bringing together to the text bits and pieces of knowledge about how print works from other contexts, such as play, writing, and environmental print (Sulzby, 1985b, 1994).

Children's writing also takes great strides forward during this period. Children appear to move across various forms of writing even up to grade 1, using scribble, nonphonetic letter strings, and drawing as forms of writing from which they subsequently read.

They plan their compositions to various degrees and respond to adults who ask them what they plan to write. They tend to hold to a plan and then read back consistent with that plan at this age, even though the writing cannot be read by another conventionally. As children become more proficient writers, they also often go through a period or periods of insisting on "writing it the right way," asking for conventional spellings. Others simply show their growing aware-ness of the difference between invented and conventional spelling by the growing numbers and/or categories of words that they spell con-ventionally (Sulzby, 1996).

During this period, writing tends to become an active arena in which children practice their increasing ability to read convention-ally, albeit from familiar texts. Children identify letters and learn letter-sound correspondences. Invented spelling signals an impor-tant breakthrough. The knowledge of letters, sounds, and words that has been developing from the earliest years appears to begin to make some conventional sense to children. During kindergarten and first grade, many, if not all children who are allowed to, begin to write using phonetically based invented or creative spelling (Read, 1971; Chomsky, 1970, 1972; Henderson, 1981; Sulzby et al., 1989; Clay, 1975, 1979; Bissex, 1980). An interesting phenomenon ap-pears to take place: children seem to first encode phonetically in early invented spelling; then there is a lag, during which time they reread their own text without making use of their phonetic encod-ing. Soon, however, they begin to decode phonetically as well (Kamberelis and Sulzby, 1988). Children's early writing shows the abstractions they are making about the writing systems of their cul-ture—and reveals how children form new understandings and solve problems creatively in the process of becoming real readers.

Learning to Identify Words in Print

Beginning

Some research has demonstrated that 5-year-old children associ-ate features of print with spoken word names without any indication that they are using the orthography of the word (Gough, 1993;

Gough and Juel, 1991). Children learned, in one experiment, to "recognize" a word by use of a thumbprint placed on a card containing a printed word. When the thumbprint was absent, so was recognition. In another experiment, children were found to use selective parts of the printed word to associate to the spoken word. In fact, children who could "recognize" the word when only the first letters were presented were unable to recognize the word when only the final letters were presented, and vice versa. This study suggests that attending to all the letters of a word is not something that all children do at the beginning, at least when only selective attention is necessary for the task. The study does not imply that the child cannot use letter forms and associated speech forms at that age. It merely shows that, in the absence of reading instruction and knowledge of letter-sound correspondences, children can approach a reading task by solving the problem of memorizing words but without learning how the system works. Moving to productive reading requires more than this attempt to memorize on the basis of nonproductive associations between parts of printed words and their spoken equivalents.

Becoming Productive

Addressing the early stages of learning to read, researchers argue that children move from a prereading stage, marked by "reading" environmental print (logos, for example, such as MacDonald's or Pepsi), into true reading through an intermediate stage, referred to as phonetic cue reading (Ehri, 1980, 1991; Ehri and Wilce, 1985, 1987). In this intermediate stage, the child begins to use the phonetic values of the names of letters as a representation of the word. For example, children can learn to read the word "jail" by picking out the salient first and last letters, j and l, and associating the letter names, "jay" and "ell" with sounds heard when the word "jail" is pronounced. This kind of reading is viewed as a primitive form of decoding (or what Gough and Hillinger, 1980, called "deciphering")—decoding because it uses systematic relationships between letters and speech segments in words, and primitive because it is a strategy that ignores some of the letters and also because it maps letter names rather than the phoneme values of the letters. In the full decoding or deciphering stage, children begin to attend to all letters and to map them to phonemes. Although these phonemes are not always the right ones, the child is then in the stage of full productive reading, because he or she is applying the alphabetic principle very generally across encounters with words.

Frith (1985) has proposed a stage model that provided framework for both reading and spelling development. In this model, children first read and write "logographically," using images of whole words; they then adopt an alphabetic stance to both reading and spelling, using letter-to-sound correspondence in reading and sound-to-letter correspondence in spelling. Finally, they adopt an orthographic stance, recognizing that spellings often do not reflect pronunciations directly and that reading requires attention to word-specific orthographic information. Perhaps most important in Frith's framework is the idea that a stage change in reading drives a corresponding stage change in spelling and vice versa. Ellis (1997) has recently concluded that longitudinal research provides some support for the predictions of this model.

These early connections between print and speech forms can drive a rapid transition to real reading. Indeed, the combination of these print-sound connections along with phonological sensitivity are critical factors in reading acquisition (Bradley and Bryant, 1983; Ehri and Sweet, 1991; Juel et al., 1986; Share, 1995; Tunmer et al., 1988). Studies by Stuart and Coltheart (1988) and Stuart (1990) illustrate the importance of these early phonologically based approaches to reading. The extent to which children made phonological errors (e.g., "big" for "beg") in word reading early in the first grade predicted end-of-year reading achievement. Nonphonological errors—including errors that shared letters but not in-position phonemes (e.g., "like" for "milk")—were associated with low end-of-year achievement. The point at which phonologically similar errors became more common than nonphonological errors coincided with the child's attainment of functional phonological skill, measured by knowledge of at least half the alphabet and of success in at least some tests of phonological sensitivity. Stuart (1990) added to these results by finding that the level of a child's phonological sensitivity corresponded in some detail to the level of achievement in word reading.

The idea that errors can be useful in diagnosing a child's reading strategies as well as his or her skills is one developed by Goodman and Burke (1972) in pioneering work with children reading texts aloud. In miscue analysis, a child's omissions, substitutions, and additions and self-corrections in oral reading provide a window on the extent to which children are monitoring for meaning, attending to spelling-sound correspondences, etc. The pattern of miscues can be informative to teachers and researchers.

Becoming Fully Productive

Truly productive reading, the ability to read novel words, comes only from an increase in orthographic representations that include phonology. This requires attention to letter strings and the context-sensitive association of phoneme sequences to these letter strings. This is where phonological sensitivity should play its most important role. Children who have attained this level of reading can read pronounceable nonwords, and their errors in word reading show a high degree of phonological plausibility.

An important aspect of learning to identify words may be sensitivity to morphology. The morphological structure of English allows systematic changes in word forms to be associated with systematic changes in word meanings. For example, "dislike" is related to "like," and "undo" is related to "do." Most of the time, phonology (pronunciation) reflects spellings, so words that are morphologically related share spellings and pronunciations, as in the examples in the preceding sentence. Other times, however, the pronunciations change systematically with morphological changes, and the underlying morphology is preserved through spelling. For example, "national" preserves the root spelling of "nation" while altering the first vowel sound. Certainly readers, like speakers and listeners, develop some sensitivity to a wide range of morphological relations.

The research on word identification has explored whether words are identified based on their morphological structure, that is, whether some kind of morphological decomposition process accompanies printed word identification. One view is that words are represented as full forms without reference to their morphological constituents (Butterworth, 1983; Osgood and Hoosain, 1974). An alternative view, more widely held, is that morphemes contribute to word reading. Whether words are decomposed into morphological components before or after word recognition is a further question (e.g., Fowler et al., 1985; Feldman, 1994; Taft and Forster, 1975; Taft, 1992). Whether the morpheme is a unit of processing and mental organization is the question, and this question has proved difficult to answer in a simple manner.

How morphology is actually used in skilled word identification is probably less important for learning to read than the awareness of morphology that a child can use to support learning words. Along with syntax (the structure of sentences), morphology (the structure of words within a sentence) provides a grammatical foundation for linking forms and meanings in a systematic way. For reading words, morphology is especially important because it connects word form and meaning within the structure of sentences. For example, children learn that events that have already occurred are marked by morphological inflections such as -ed. For children, sensitivity to morphology may be an important support for skill in reading and spelling. Research by Nunes et al. (1997) has identified a series of stages that characterize the development of children's spelling of simple inflectional morphology, such as the -ed that signals past tense of regular English verbs. For words like "kiss" and "kissed," for example, children appear to progress from phonetic spelling of the past tense (kist) to a morphological spelling (kissed). Notice that phonetically, "kissed" and "soft" have identical endings. Children may learn the -ed spelling and overgeneralize it to produce "sofed" as well as "kissed," before learning to use ed specifically for regular past tenses. The key development here may be an increased sensitivity to parts of speech, a "morphosyntactic awareness" that allows fuller use of the linguistic system in spelling (Nunes et al., 1997). Thus, although phonological sensitivity is critical for the discovery of the alphabetic principle (and is reflected in very early spellings), a fuller sensitivity to the syntactic system may be critical to a full mastery of English spelling.

Progress in Fluency and Automaticity

Gaining fluency in reading entails developing rapid and perhaps automatic word identification processes (LaBerge and Samuels, 1974). The main mechanism for gains in automaticity is, in some form or another, practice at consistent input-output mappings (Schneider and Shiffrin, 1977). In reading, automaticity entails "practice" at word identification, such as frequent retrievals of word forms and meanings from print. On a word-based account of reading acquisition, automaticity is a characteristic of words, not readers. Words move from the functional lexicon to the autonomous lexicon in this perspective (Perfetti, 1992). These gains from experience normally come from accumulating normal reading activity centered on reading text of increasingly greater complexity.

Progress in Understanding

For children learning to read, comprehension can take advantage of skills they have been using in their oral language: the shared basic language components (lexical, syntactic, and interpretive processes), cognitive mechanisms (working memory), and conceptual knowledge (vocabulary, topic knowledge). As mentioned earlier, reading comprehension skills are at first limited by unskilled decoding; later, comprehension when reading and when listening to a text are highly correlated; still later, the advantage of listening over reading disappears and, in some cases, for some kinds of texts and purposes, reverses (Curtis, 1980). But in the beginning, many tricks of the trade that children have as native speakers will help a great deal. Moreover, early books can be well designed to support the child's engagement and curiosity and keep the process going.

Theories of individual differences among both younger and older readers have emphasized, in one way or another, the dependence of higher levels of comprehension on high levels of skill in elementary word identification processes (Perfetti, 1985) and processes required to manage limitations in functional working memory (Just and Carpenter, 1992; Gernsbacher, 1993; Perfetti, 1985; Shankweiler and Crain, 1986). Of course, systematic differences between oral language and written language may produce some difficulties for learning to comprehend what one reads, and limits on background knowledge or a lean conceptual vocabulary can affect some text passages and not others. It is not clear that limits on inferencing processes for reading- and comprehension-monitoring strategies can be viewed as independent of the powerful effect of knowledge—background and word knowledge as well as knowledge of the features of written language that are not in the child's oral language repertoire.

Research on what young good comprehenders do is not as far along as research on children's word processing. Studies that contrast skilled and less skilled comprehenders have shown that skilled comprehenders are better at decoding (e.g., Perfetti, 1985), have superior global language comprehension (Smiley et al., 1977), and have superior metacognitive skills (Paris and Myers, 1981). As Stothard and Hulme (1996:95) note, though, many studies use measures of comprehension that "confound decoding and comprehension difficulties" and are less useful for identifying the crucial features of skilled comprehension in children. Few studies have been completely successful, however, in avoiding this confound. Some studies have matched subjects on decoding measured in oral reading by counting errors.

In a series of studies of 7- and 8-year-olds in English schools, Yuill and Oakhill (1991) compared children matched for chronological age and for reading accuracy but who differed significantly in reading comprehension on a standardized norm-referenced test that measures the two aspects of reading separately. The skilled comprehenders (at or slightly above the level expected for their chronological age in comprehension) were notable for the work they did with the words and sentences they encountered in texts. For example, they understood pronoun references, made proper inferences about the text from particular words, drew more global inferences from elements of the text that were not adjacent, detected inconsistencies in texts, applied background knowledge, and monitored their comprehension.

Stothard and Hulme (1996) compared similarly identified skilled and less-skilled comprehenders but included a comprehension age match for the less skilled as well and found an additional feature:

skilled comprehenders (and the comprehension-age-matched children) had strong verbal semantic skills, whereas the less skilled comprehenders were better at performance IQ than verbal. Stothard and Hulme suggest that high verbal abilities facilitate vocabulary learning from context, so that children with high verbal ability know more words to begin with, can read them, and when they encounter unknown words in their reading can also learn from them.

Cain (1996), also comparing 7- and 8-year-olds who differed in comprehension while being matched on word errors in context, added comprehension age match in studying story knowledge in reading comprehension. In a study of story production, skilled comprehenders and the comprehension-age-matched children told stories with the events more integrated when the prompt was simply a title. When the prompt for the story was a sequence of pictures that provided an integrating structure, the less skilled comprehenders performed better and the difference between them and their comprehension-age matches disappeared. Cain also interviewed the children about the parts of stories that they encounter in reading. Skilled comprehenders had more formed ideas of the information that can be gleaned from a title and definite expectations that the beginning of a story will provide information needed to understand characters, setting, and plot.

Up to and including third grade, children are learning to monitor their comprehension. It is clear that these skills can improve with training (e.g., Elliott-Faust and Pressley, 1986; Miller, 1985; Palincsar and Brown, 1984; Paris et al., 1984). Baker (1996) showed that providing information and examples about what kinds of difficulties might be encountered in a passage helped children to identify them, but that children in grade 3 worked with a smaller range of types of difficulty than did children in grade 5.

Tracing the development of reading comprehension to show the necessary and sufficient conditions to prevent reading difficulty is not as well researched as other aspects of reading growth. In fact, as Cain (1996) notes, "because early reading instruction emphasizes word recognition rather than comprehension, the less skilled comprehenders' difficulties generally go unnoticed by their classroom teachers." It may well be that relieving the bottleneck from poor word recognition skills will reveal, for some children, stoppages in other areas that create comprehension problems; more research is called for on factors related to comprehension growth from birth to age 8 that may produce problems as children read to learn in elementary school.

The "fourth-grade slump" is a term used to describe a widely encountered disappointment when examining scores of fourth graders in comparison with younger children (see Chall et al., 1990). Whether looking at test scores or other performance indicators, there is sometimes a decline in the rate of progress or a decrease in the number of children achieving at good levels reported for fourth graders. It is not clear what the explanation is or even if there is a unitary explanation. The most obvious but probably least likely explanation would be that some children simply stop growing in reading at fourth grade.

Two other explanations are more likely. One possibility is that the slump is an artifact; that is, the tasks in school and the tasks in assessment instruments may change so much between third and fourth grade that it is not sensible to compare progress and success on such different tasks and measures. It may be that the true next stage of what is measured in third grade is not represented in the fourth-grade data and that the true precedents for the fourth-grade data are not represented in the third-grade data.

A second possibility is that it is not so much a fourth-grade slump as a "primary-grade streak," that is, that some children have problems in the earlier years that are hidden while so much else is being learned, in the same way that a tendency to make errors in the outfield does not bother a ball club while the pitching staff is having a streak of strikeouts. Previously "unimportant" reading difficulties may appear for the first time in fourth grade when the children are dealing more frequently, deeply, and widely with nonfiction materials in a variety of school subjects and when these are represented in assessment instruments. It may be that there had been less call for certain knowledge and abilities until fourth grade and a failure to thrive in those areas might not be noticed until then. It is, of course, this latter possibility that is important for preventing reading difficulties, and more attention needs to be paid to research on the fourth-grade slump.

CONCLUSION

Table 2-2 shows a set of particular accomplishments that the successful learner is likely to exhibit during the early school years. This list is neither exhaustive nor incontestable, but it does capture many highlights of the course of reading acquisition that have been revealed through several decades of research. Needless to say, the timing of these accomplishments will to some extent depend on the particular curriculum provided by a school. For example, in many areas of the country, the kindergarten year is not mandatory and little formal reading instruction is provided until the start of first grade. The summary sketch provided by the table of the typical accomplishments related to reading over the first years of a child's schooling presupposes, of course, appropriate familial support and access to effective educational resources. At the same time, there are enormous individual differences in children's progression from playing with refrigerator letters to reading independently, and many pathways that can be followed successfully.

Ideally, the child comes to reading instruction with well-developed language abilities, a foundation for reading acquisition, and varied experiences with emergent literacy. The achievement of real reading requires knowledge of the phonological structures of language and how the written units connect with the spoken units. Phonological sensitivity at the subword level is important in this achievement. Very early, children who turn out to be successful in learning to read use phonological connection to letters, including letter names, to establish context-dependent phonological connections, which allow productive reading. An important mechanism for this is phonological recoding, which helps the child acquire high-quality word representations. Gains in fluency (automaticity) come with increased experience, as does increased lexical knowledge that supports word identification.

Briefly put, we can say that children need simultaneous access to some knowledge of letter-sound relationships, some sight vocabu-

TABLE 2-2 Accomplishments in Reading

Kindergarten Accomplishments
- Knows the parts of a book and their functions.
- Begins to track print when listening to a familiar text being read or when rereading own writing.
- "Reads" familiar texts emergently, i.e., not necessarily verbatim from the print alone.
- Recognizes and can name all uppercase and lowercase letters.
- Understands that the sequence of letters in a written word represents the sequence of sounds (phonemes) in a spoken word (alphabetic principle).
- Learns many, thought not all, one-to-one letter sound correspondences.
- Recognizes some words by sight, including a few very common ones (a, the, I, my, you, is, are).
- Uses new vocabulary and grammatical constructions in own speech.
- Makes appropriate switches from oral to written language situations.
- Notices when simple sentences fail to make sense.
- Connects information and events in texts to life and life to text experiences.
- Retells, reenacts, or dramatizes stories or parts of stories.
- Listens attentively to books teacher reads to class.
- Can name some book titles and authors.
- Demonstrates familiarity with a number of types or genres of text (e.g., storybooks, expository texts, poems, newspapers, and everyday print such as signs, notices, labels).
- Correctly answers questions about stories read aloud.
- Makes predictions based on illustrations or portions of stories.
- Demonstrates understanding that spoken words consist of a sequences of phonemes.
- Given spoken sets like "dan, dan, den" can identify the first two as being the same and the third as different.
- Given spoken sets like "dak, pat, zen" can identify the first two as sharing a same sound.
- Given spoken segments can merge them into a meaningful target word.
- Given a spoken word can produce another word that rhymes with it.
- Independently writes many uppercase and lowercase letters.
- Uses phonemic awareness and letter knowledge to spell independently (invented or creative spelling).
- Writes (unconventionally) to express own meaning.
- Builds a repertoire of some conventionally spelled words.
- Shows awareness of distinction between "kid writing" and conventional orthography.
- Writes own name (first and last) and the first names of some friends or classmates.
- Can write most letters and some words when they are dictated.

TABLE 2-2 Continued

First-Grade Accomplishments
- Makes a transition from emergent to "real" reading.
- Reads aloud with accuracy and comprehension any text that is appropriately designed for the first half of grade 1.
- Accurately decodes orthographically regular, one-syllable words and nonsense words (e.g., sit, zot), using print-sound mappings to sound out unknown words.
- Uses letter-sound correspondence knowledge to sound out unknown words when reading text.
- Recognizes common, irregularly spelled words by sight (have, said, where, two).
- Has a reading vocabulary of 300 to 500 words, sight words and easily sounded out words.
- Monitors own reading and self-corrects when an incorrectly identified word does not fit with cues provided by the letters in the word or the context surrounding the word.
- Reads and comprehends both fiction and nonfiction that is appropriately designed for grade level.
- Shows evidence of expanding language repertory, including increasing appropriate use of standard more formal language registers.
- Creates own written texts for others to read.
- Notices when difficulties are encountered in understanding text.
- Reads and understands simple written instructions.
- Predicts and justifies what will happen next in stories.
- Discusses prior knowledge of topics in expository texts.
- Discusses how, why, and what-if questions in sharing nonfiction texts.
- Describes new information gained from texts in own words.
- Distinguishes whether simple sentences are incomplete or fail to make sense; notices when simple texts fail to make sense.
- Can answer simple written comprehension questions based on material read.
- Can count the number of syllables in a word.
- Can blend or segment the phonemes of most one-syllable words.
- Spells correctly three- and four-letter short vowel words.
- Composes fairly readable first drafts using appropriate parts of the writing process (some attention to planning, drafting, rereading for meaning, and some self-correction).
- Uses invented spelling/phonics-based knowledge to spell independently, when necessary.
- Shows spelling consciousness or sensitivity to conventional spelling.
- Uses basic punctuation and capitalization.
- Produces a variety of types of compositions (e.g., stories, descriptions, journal entries), showing appropriate relationships between printed text, illustrations, and other graphics.
- Engages in a variety of literary activities voluntarily (e.g., choosing books and stories to read, writing a note to a friend).

TABLE 2-2 Continued

Second-Grade Accomplishments
- Reads and comprehends both fiction and nonfiction that is appropriately designed for grade level.
- Accurately decodes orthographically regular multisyllable words and nonsense words (e.g., capital, Kalamazoo).
- Uses knowledge of print-sound mappings to sound out unknown words.
- Accurately reads many irregularly spelled words and such spelling patterns as diphthongs, special vowel spellings, and common word endings.
- Reads and comprehends both fiction and nonfiction that is appropriately designed for grade level.
- Shows evidence of expanding language repertory, including increasing use of more formal language registers.
- Reads voluntarily for interest and own purposes.
- Rereads sentences when meaning is not clear.
- Interprets information from diagrams, charts, and graphs.
- Recalls facts and details of texts.
- Reads nonfiction materials for answers to specific questions or for specific purposes.
- Takes part in creative responses to texts such as dramatizations, oral presentations, fantasy play, etc.
- Discusses similarities in characters and events across stories.
- Connects and compares information across nonfiction selections.
- Poses possible answers to how, why, and what-if questions.
- Correctly spells previously studied words and spelling patterns in own writing.
- Represents the complete sound of a word when spelling independently.
- Shows sensitivity to using formal language patterns in place of oral language patterns at appropriate spots in own writing (e.g., decontextualizing sentences, conventions for quoted speech, literary language forms, proper verb forms).
- Makes reasonable judgments about what to include in written products.
- Productively discusses ways to clarify and refine writing of own and others.
- With assistance, adds use of conferencing, revision, and editing processes to clarify and refine own writing to the steps of the expected parts of the writing process.
- Given organizational help, writes informative well-structured reports.
- Attends to spelling, mechanics, and presentation for final products.
- Produces a variety of types of compositions (e.g., stories, reports, correspondence).

TABLE 2-2 Continued

Third-Grade Accomplishments
- Reads aloud with fluency and comprehension any text that is appropriately designed for grade level.
- Uses letter-sound correspondence knowledge and structural analysis to decode words.
- Reads and comprehends both fiction and nonfiction that is appropriately designed for grade level.
- Reads longer fictional selections and chapter books independently.
- Takes part in creative responses to texts such as dramatizations, oral presentations, fantasy play, etc.
- Can point to or clearly identify specific words or wordings that are causing comprehension difficulties.
- Summarizes major points from fiction and nonfiction texts.
- In interpreting fiction, discusses underlying theme or message.
- Asks how, why, and what-if questions in interpreting nonfiction texts.
- In interpreting nonfiction, distinguishes cause and effect, fact and opinion, main idea and supporting details.
- Uses information and reasoning to examine bases of hypotheses and opinions.
- Infers word meanings from taught roots, prefixes, and suffixes.
- Correctly spells previously studied words and spelling patterns in own writing.
- Begins to incorporate literacy words and language patterns in own writing (e.g., elaborates descriptions, uses figurative wording).
- With some guidance, uses all aspects of the writing process in producing own compositions and reports.
- Combines information from multiple sources in writing reports.
- With assistance, suggests and implements editing and revision to clarify and refine own writing.
- Presents and discusses own writing with other students and responds helpfully to other students' compositions.
- Independently reviews work for spelling, mechanics, and presentation.
- Produces a variety of written works (e.g., literature responses, reports, "published" books, semantic maps) in a variety of formats, including multimedia forms.

lary, and some comprehension strategies. In each case, "some" indicates that exhaustive knowledge of these aspects is not needed to get the child reading conventionally; rather, each child seems to need varying amounts of knowledge to get started, but then he or she needs to build up the kind of inclusive and automatic knowledge that will let the fact that reading is being done fade into the background while the reasons for reading are fulfilled.

PART II

Who Are We Talking About?

Who has reading difficulties and what are the factors present in early childhood that predict failure and success in reading? Part II addresses these questions.

Large numbers of school-age children, including children from all social classes, have significant difficulties in learning to read. To clarify this statement, we outline a number of conceptual issues in identifying and measuring reading difficulties in young children. Categorical and dimensional approaches to estimating reading difficulties are presented, as are prevalence figures.

In a study on preventing reading difficulties, however, it is not enough to assess actual reading difficulties. Ideally, we want to know which children or groups of children will have problems learning to read when they are in school and given reading instruction. Effective preventions are necessary for children to receive in their preschool years, in some cases even starting in infancy—for example, for children with hearing impairments. Thus, there is a need to know what factors predict success and failure in learning to read. We consider predictors that are:

- intrinsic to the individual and would be identified by assessing the child;
- identified in the family environment; and
- associated with the larger environment of the child—the neighborhood, school, and community in which the child lives.

3

Who Has Reading Difficulties?

Among the reasons public attention has turned to the need for systematic prevention of reading difficulties are the patterns of reading difficulty cited in the first chapter: failure to learn to read adequately is present among children of low social risk who attend well-funded schools and is much more likely among poor children, among nonwhite children, and among nonnative speakers of English. To begin our consideration of who is likely to have reading difficulties and how many children we are talking about, we outline a number of conceptual issues in identifying and measuring reading difficulties in young children.

MODELS OF READING DIFFICULTIES

The major sources of evidence pertaining to these conceptual issues are several large-scale epidemiological studies in which population-representative samples of children have been examined to determine the incidence, prevalence, characteristics, persistence, and academic outcomes of individuals who have been identified (by various criteria) as having reading difficulties. Prospective longitudinal studies of sample surveys and general populations allow us to determine the natural history of a disorder over time, to determine whether the problem is transient or chronic, and how various risk factors relate to outcomes. Earlier studies of representative school-age children are those by Rutter and Yule (1975) in the important Isle of Wight and London studies and, later, studies by Rodgers (1983) in Great Britain and Northern Ireland and by Silva et al. (1985) in Dunedin, New Zealand.

More recently, Shaywitz et al. (1990, 1992) have reported on the results of a sample survey of Connecticut schoolchildren followed longitudinally from kindergarten through high school, and Catts et al. (1997) have reported on reading difficulties in a representative sample of children in Iowa. Together, these studies provide the strongest basis for estimating the prevalence of reading difficulties in childhood. It is also of interest, of course, to compare estimates of reading problems from studies like the National Assessment of Educational Progress (NAEP) and the Prospects Study to those from prospective sample surveys.

Categorical Approach to Estimating Reading Difficulties

In identifying, studying, and treating reading problems, two main kinds of reading difficulties have traditionally been distinguished. Reading disability, also called "dyslexia" and "specific reading retardation," was at first considered to be a qualitatively and etiologically distinct condition that an individual either had or did not have. The condition was viewed as having a biological and perhaps genetic basis, as being invariant over time, and as affecting a small group of children, primarily boys.

A key criterion for identifying dyslexia was the existence of a substantial discrepancy between the child's aptitude (operationalized as IQ) and his or her achievement, reflecting the assumption that the reading problems of a bright and otherwise capable youngster are different in nature from those of a child who is generally less able to cope with schoolwork. In this traditional conceptual model, poor readers who do not meet the criteria for a reading disability are characterized instead as having garden-variety reading problems (or "general reading backwardness"), arising from such causes as poor instruction, low intelligence, and weak motivation. This model is called a "categorical" one, in that reading disability is viewed as a separate diagnostic category, distinct from "normal" reading and from other reading problems. This categorical approach is typically followed in educational classifications, in which a variety of separate diagnostic labels are applied to children who are assumed to have different kinds of reading problems.

A categorical model is still reflected in current education policies for the provision of services to learning-disabled children, affecting in particular those with reading disability. Special education services or programs, for example, require children to qualify for services in specific disability categories, such as mental retardation, specific learning disabilities, speech or language impairment, serious emotional disturbance, multiple disabilities, hearing impairment, visual impairment, deafness-blindness, and other health impairments. Special education services are required by federal and state law and are provided at no cost to parents.

The U.S. Department of Education is mandated by Congress to report annually on the number of disabled children who are receiving assistance through special education programs. According to the most recent data (from the *18th Annual Report to Congress on the Implementation of the Individuals with Disabilities Education Act* of the U.S. Department of Education for the 1994-1995 school year), 2,560,121 school-age children ages 6 to 21 with specific learning disabilities are receiving special education services under the Individuals with Disabilities Education Act, Part B and Chapter I. This group of children represents 4.43 percent of the total estimated population of 57,803,809 schoolchildren in this age group. The U.S. Department of Education does not specify the nature of the learning disability, but the generally accepted estimate that reading disability accounts for about 80 percent of all learning disabilities indicates that 3.54 percent of all schoolchildren in the United States (or 2,046,254 children) are ostensibly receiving services for a reading disability (Lerner, 1989).

Of course, these data reflect school-based decisions, using arbitrary cutoffs, subject to local personnel and financial constraints; they clearly underestimate the number of children having difficulties in reading by ignoring those who are just on the other side of an arbitrary categorical boundary (Shaywitz et al., 1992).

In prospective epidemiological studies, the rates of specific reading retardation in Yule et al.'s sample was 3.5 percent of 10-year-olds and 4.5 percent of 14-year-olds on the Isle of Wight and 6 percent of the 10-year-olds in London; the criterion was scores that were two standard deviations (SD) from the mean (Yule et al., 1974). In contrast, Silva et al. (1985) found only 1.2 percent of a sample of New Zealand schoolchildren met the same SD criterion. Similarly, Rodgers (1983), examining populations in Great Britain and Northern Ireland, reported that 2.29 percent of children had scores falling two SD below the mean for reading achievement.

The Connecticut longitudinal study, using a less stringent discrepancy criterion of a 1.5 SD discrepancy between predicted and actual reading achievement based on a regression equation or on a criterion of low achievement in reading, found 17.5 percent of the population of schoolchildren in primary and middle school to have reading difficulties (Shaywitz and Shaywitz, 1996). Other available prevalence data are limited either by the population base or by definitional concerns. For example, in Canada, a privately appointed multidisciplinary committee, the Commission on Emotional and Learning Disorders in Children (1970), estimated that between 10 and 16 percent of school-age children required diagnostic and remedial help in learning. This finding is consistent with findings in U.S. studies that 14.8 percent of students in grades 3 and 4 (Mykelbust and Boshes, 1969) and 14 percent of students in grades 7-11 (Meier, 1971) met criteria for underachievement.

Reviewing both population-based studies and numbers of school-age children receiving special education services, the Interagency Committee on Learning Disabilities (1987), in a report to Congress, estimated the prevalence of learning disabilities as ranging from 5 to 10 percent. The vast majority of children identified as having learning disabilities, and therefore reading difficulties, are identified by grade 4. Standard measures of reading are often inappropriate for identifying reading difficulties in older individuals, particularly those who can identify words accurately but not automatically. Prevalence estimates based only on children in grade 4 or below will inevitably underestimate reading problems.

Dimensional Approach to Reading Skills

In recent research, strong challenges to the traditional categorical model have been raised. For instance, evidence for qualitative differences between dyslexics and other poor readers has been shown to be sparse, and genetic influences appear to be equivalent for the two categories. Also, for many years it was thought that reading difficulties were much more common in boys than girls. Even today the ratio of boys to girls in samples of students identified by schools or clinics as reading disabled typically ranges from 2:1 to 5:1 or higher (e.g., Critchley, 1970; Finucci and Childs, 1981). When more population-representative samples have been examined, however, much smaller sex ratios have been observed, sometimes approaching unity (e.g., Flynn and Rahbar, 1994; Naiden, 1976; Shaywitz et al., 1990; Wadsworth et al., 1992).

As a result of this research, the categorical distinction between these two kinds of reading difficulties is no longer as widely accepted. A "dimensional" model of individual differences in reading achievement, described below, has been embraced by most researchers, although not yet by a majority of educators (Shaywitz et al., 1992).

Dimensional models are appropriate when human abilities, such as reading skill, are distributed in a statistically normal way along a continuous dimension. From this perspective, reading difficulties form the lower tail of a bell-shaped distribution that shades gradually into normal and superior ranges of reading abilities. The population distribution is bell shaped because relatively fewer individuals have extremely high or extremely low reading scores, and relatively more individuals have intermediate scores. The same factors—biological, cognitive, instructional—are assumed to influence differences in reading skill at all points along the continuum. Therefore, deciding on the precise point on the dimension at which to distinguish normal reading from reading disability is quite arbitrary. In this sense, reading difficulties are analogous to many dimensional disorders in nature, such as hypertension (high blood pressure) and obesity. Blood pressure, like most physiological parameters (e.g., heart rate, temperature), varies from individual to individual along a continuum. Somewhere along the gradient from low to high values, a cut-point is imposed to distinguish hypertension from normal blood pressure (see Box 3-1).

Evidence supporting the hypothesis that reading disability represents the lower tail of a normally distributed ability comes from several sources. First, the results of most epidemiological studies support a normal distributional model of reading ability (e.g., Rodgers, 1983; Shaywitz et al., 1992; Silva et al., 1985; Share et al., 1987; van der Wissel and Zegers, 1985), whereas only Stevenson's (1988) research has been consistent with Rutter and Yule's (1975) original findings. Second, data from research in behavioral genetics employing a range of models and techniques (including admixture, segregation, linkage, and twin studies) have also converged to support the conclusion that reading disability is neither distributionally

---

BOX 3-1
Reading and Hypertension

There is considerable evidence to show that reading difficulties represent not a discrete entity but instead a graded continuum (Shaywitz et al., 1992). However, the fact that the distribution is a graded continuum does not render the concept of reading difficulty scientifically useless, as many critics would like to argue.

Years ago, Ellis (1985) argued that the proper analogy for reading difficulty is a condition like hypertension (high blood pressure). Hypertension is a good analogy because no one doubts that it is a very real health problem, despite the fact that it is operationally defined in a somewhat arbitrary way by choosing a criterion in a continuous distribution.

One's blood pressure is located on an uninterrupted continuum from low to dangerously high. Although the line between "normal" and "hypertensive" is drawn somewhat arbitrarily, hypertension is a real and worrisome condition. The question of how prevalent reading difficulty is in a particular population is as meaningful as the question of how prevalent hypertension is. The prevalence of both is dependent on the choice of a cut-point in a continuous distribution.

nor etiologically distinct from other types of reading problems (Gilger et al., 1996). Third, many studies that have compared groups of poor readers, who would be assigned to different categories according to the traditional categorical model, have generally found few meaningful differences between them (e.g., Fletcher et al., 1994; Stanovich and Siegel, 1994).

When reading difficulties are understood from a dimensional perspective, it becomes clear that using a dimensionally distributed measure to assign children to categorical groupings (such as special education classifications) can be problematic due to the arbitrariness of the choice of a cut-point for distinguishing normal reading from reading disability. For instance, children who do not quite meet the arbitrary cutoff score have very similar abilities and needs as those of children whose reading levels are just on the other side of the cut-point. In the blood pressure analogy, individuals with values just below the cut-point, although not labeled as hypertensive, share many physical traits and vulnerabilities with those who do meet the arbitrary clinical criterion for hypertension. Also, when reading ability (or blood pressure) is measured, we know that the results can vary somewhat from one test to another. These fluctuations in scores within individuals may shift a child from one side of the cut-point to the other, leading to the erroneous conclusion that a change in reading status has occurred (Shaywitz et al., 1992). To serve children with reading difficulties effectively, it is essential that the dimensional nature of reading ability be understood and taken into account in making educational decisions—just as in treating hypertension a range of therapies are instituted to benefit those "border-line" as well as those with severe hypertension.

Assessing Reading Difficulties

In terms of the dimensional model, we have defined reading difficulties as the lower tail of a normal distribution of reading ability in the population. In other words, individuals with reading difficulties are those whose achievement levels are lower than those of the rest of the people in the distribution. In general, it is most reasonable to consider as the population of interest the people who have had the same amount of formal reading instruction. That is, there is a distribution of first graders, a distribution of second graders, and so on, and the children at the low end of each are said to have reading difficulties.

A nationally standardized reading test is one that provides information about where a particular test taker's score falls within the distribution that is typical for all children from around the country who are in the same school grade. When using a nationally standardized reading test, therefore, the cut-point for identifying reading difficulties can be set at a particular agreed-on level (e.g., the 25th percentile). The location of the cut-point necessarily determines the incidence and prevalence of reading difficulties in the population.

The situation is complicated, however, by the fact that two sorts of children who have traditionally been viewed as having legitimate reading problems and in need of special help would often fail to qualify for additional assistance if a national norm criterion is the only one used. First, it is well known that the distributions of reading scores in some schools (typically schools with affluent families) are consistently much higher than those for the nation as a whole. In other words, the second-grade distribution in these schools actually resembles, say, the fourth-grade distribution for a school that is more typical of the national average. Many of the poorer readers (relative to their classmates) at such a school will not earn scores that are below a cut-point (such as the 25th percentile) based on national averages. Nevertheless, their teachers, parents, and communities consider these children to have real reading difficulties because their achievement is considerably lower than that of their classmates, despite equivalent schooling.

Second, a key criterion for assignment to the category of reading disability has been a large discrepancy between achievement and aptitude (IQ). This notion of an IQ-achievement discrepancy criterion has been incorporated into many states' guidelines for classifying learning disabilities in schools. Studies have shown that about 75 percent of children who meet an IQ-achievement discrepancy criterion are poor enough readers that they would also be considered to have reading difficulties even if only their reading levels were considered, ignoring IQ (Shaywitz et al., 1992). The other 25 percent would not, however, because these children have very high IQs but only average, or slightly below average, reading scores for their grade.

Should these two subgroups—those whose reading levels are low relative to their classmates but not relative to national norms, and those whose reading levels are discrepant from their aptitude but not low in relation to national (or even local) norms—be considered to have reading difficulties? The committee's affirmative answer to this question is based on research findings that (1) the way these children read (i.e., the aspects of the process that are most difficult for them to learn, the kinds of errors they make, and so forth) is very similar to that of children who are poor readers by other criteria (see, e.g., Francis et al., 1996; Fletcher et al., 1994; Shaywitz et al., 1992; Stanovich and Siegel, 1994) and (2) they are at risk for the same kinds of negative educational and occupational outcomes, discussed below, as are other poor readers (Fowler and Scarborough, 1993).

In endorsing an inclusive approach to the identification of reading problems, however, we emphasize that no claim is being made for any distinct qualitative categorical differences between these children and others. Instead, we are simply suggesting that in interpreting reading test scores it is sometimes appropriate to use criteria other than the national distribution to represent the expectations for achievement for some children.

So far, we have considered only how well a child reads relative to an appropriate comparison population—a "norm-referenced" basis for identifying reading difficulties (i.e., norms). This approach presumes that the population distribution matches expectations about how well children at a given grade "ought" to be reading. Another approach, called "criterion-referenced" assessment, offers a means of addressing this issue. Briefly, this approach requires that standards be established regarding what achievements children should attain at successive points in their educational careers. In principle, such standards can be stated in very narrow terms (e.g., by grade 2, the "silent e" convention should be mastered in reading and spelling) or much more broadly (e.g., by grade 4, all children should be able to read and understand the literal meaning of texts; by grade 11, the reader should be able to "understand complicated information" through reading). Assessments are then designed to determine whether or not children have reached the standards for their grade. The National Assessment of Educational Progress (NAEP) is an important national program that takes this approach.

Based on criterion-referenced assessments, any child who does not demonstrate mastery of the expected skills and knowledge, despite having received instruction in a curriculum that covered the requisite material, would be considered to be having difficulty learning to read. Note that, when this approach is taken, the prevalence of reading difficulties will depend on how challenging the standards are. If higher standards are expected to be met than are currently aimed at, large numbers of children will fail to attain them. If the standards are less challenging, fewer children will be identified as having reading difficulties.

ESTIMATING THE PREVALENCE OF
READING DIFFICULTIES

Classroom practitioners, like the designers of the NAEP, are more likely to make criterion-referenced decisions, such as "she doesn't read well enough to understand the fourth-grade history text." Potential employers share this preference; they are looking for high school graduates who can read technical manuals, understand and fill out order forms, and process memos. Educational administrators prefer norm-referencing—"90 percent of the third graders in my school read above third-grade level" or "70 percent of the children in this school district are below average in reading." Of course, each of these various approaches leads to a different set of conclusions and implications concerning the incidence of reading difficulties.

In the absence of a widely accepted basis for a national estimate of reading problems, the NAEP results give a limited but useful view. Although the NAEP does not include assessments of decoding, nor of oral reading, and it is not taken by the age range that is the focus of this study, it provides assessment of some comprehension skills of children over age 9. On these limited assessments, average reading achievement has not changed markedly over the last 20 years (NAEP,

TABLE 3-1 Mean Reading Achievement of 9-Year-Olds on the
National Assessment of Educational Progress, 1971-1996[a]

Group/Subgroup	1971	1980	1990	1992	1994	1996
National average	208	215	209	211	211	212
White	214	221	217	218	218	220
Black	170	189	182	185	185	190
Hispanic		190	189	192	186	194

[a]All scores are scale scores ranging from 0 to 500. A conservative standard error
for the scales is 1.5: since 2 standard errors are most often used to indicate significant differences, a difference of ±3 would be used for this purpose.

1997). And following a gain in scores by black children from 1970
to 1980, the white-black gap has remained roughly constant for the
last 16 years (see Table 3-1).

NAEP provides estimates of the percentage of children at each
grade who are reading at a basic level or below. "Fourth-grade
students performing at the basic level should demonstrate an understanding of the overall meaning of what they read. . . . [T]hey should
be able to make relatively obvious connections between the text and
their own experiences, and extend the ideas in the text by making
simple inferences" (NAEP, 1994, p. 42). In the most recent NAEP
report (1996), 40 percent of fourth graders, 30 percent of eighth
graders, and 25 percent of twelfth graders were reading below this
level. Among black and Hispanic students, the percentages of fourth
graders reading below the basic level are 69 and 64 percent, respectively—this translates into about 4.5 million black and 3.3 million
Hispanic children reading very poorly in fourth grade.

Data from the Prospects study (Puma et al., 1997; Herman and
Stringfield, 1997) confirm this picture. The mean weighted reading
comprehension score for students in the fall semester of first grade in
the Prospects national sample was at the 50th percentile. By contrast, for students in schools in which more than 75 percent of all
students received free or reduced-price lunches (a measure of high

poverty), the mean score for students in the fall semester of first grade was at approximately the 44th percentile. By the spring of third grade, this difference had expanded significantly. Children living in high-poverty areas tended to fall further behind, regardless of their initial reading skill level. In many regards, this finding replicates those from the Coleman report (Coleman et al., 1966) of 30 years earlier, which highlighted the achievement gap related to low incomes. Yet additional analyses from a subsample of Prospects sites, and from the Special Strategies studies conducted in conjunction with the Prospects study (Stringfield et al., 1997), indicate that such differences were not inevitable.

It is the concentration of poor readers in certain ethnic groups and in poor, urban neighborhoods and rural towns that is most worrisome, rather than the overall level of reading among American schoolchildren. Americans do very well in international comparisons of reading—much better, comparatively speaking, than on math or science. In a 1992 study comparing reading skill levels among 9-year-olds in 18 Western nations, U.S. students scored among the highest levels and were second only to students in Finland (see Figure 3-1) (Elley, 1992) .

Despite these heartening findings, the educational careers of 25 to 40 percent of American children are imperiled because they do not read well enough, quickly enough, or easily enough to ensure comprehension in their content courses in middle and secondary school. Although some men and women with reading disability can and do attain significant levels of academic and occupational achievement, more typically poor readers, unless strategic interventions in reading are afforded them, fare poorly on the educational and, subsequently, the occupational ladder. Although difficult to translate into actual dollar amounts, the costs to society are probably quite high in terms of lower productivity, underemployment, mental health services, and other measures.

CONCLUSION

This chapter has examined various issues in identifying and measuring the population of American children with reading difficulties.

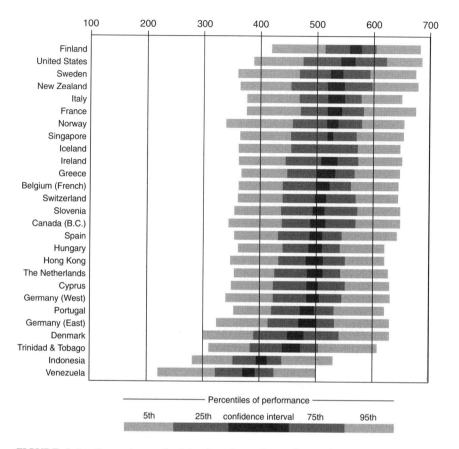

FIGURE 3-1 Countries ranked by fourth-grade reading achievement (narrative score). Note: The center solid bar indicates a confidence interval around the average reading proficiency for a country. The 5th, 25th, 75th, and 95th percentiles are indicated by shaded bars. Source: Elley (1992).

Identifying reading difficulties is essential for young school-age children, to ensure that intervention can be offered early and targeted to the children who need it most. However, this report on the prevention of reading difficulties also addresses prevention efforts that occur before formal instruction in reading. Therefore, we are interested in factors that predict later success and failure in learning to read. These predictors are addressed in the following chapter.

4

Predictors of Success and Failure in Reading

Of the many conditions that appear to contribute to successful reading by schoolchildren, among the more important are each child's (1) intellectual and sensory capacities, (2) positive expectations about and experiences with literacy from an early age, (3) support for reading-related activities and attitudes so that he or she is prepared to benefit from early literacy experiences and subsequent formal instruction in school, and (4) instructional environments conducive to learning.

This chapter reviews the evidence concerning the predictors of reading achievement: some measurable characteristic of a child or the child's home, school, or community that has been associated with poor progress in learning to read.[1] It is critical to distinguish predictors from causes or explanations of reading difficulties—predictors are simply correlates. Nor can predictors be interpreted as suggesting the inevitability of poor reading achievement. To the

---

[1]Some sections of this chapter are based closely on a recent review of prediction research by Scarborough (1998), which provides much more detail about the sources and findings that are the basis for many summary statements presented here.

contrary: the whole point of identifying risk factors is to alert parents, physicians, and teachers to potential obstacles children might face so that effective interventions can be devised and implemented.

In the absence of other (noncorrelational) evidence, therefore, these predictors cannot be considered causes of reading problems but rather as associated conditions implicated in reading difficulty. Nevertheless, the fact that these characteristics correlate with subsequent reading achievement is potentially very useful for identifying children who may be in the greatest need of intervention. Our goal in this chapter is to present ways of identifying who should receive services to prevent reading difficulties.

That an individual or group has been identified as being at risk for reading difficulties has no direct implications for the nature of the appropriate intervention. It is not the case that treating the predictor itself is necessarily the right approach; for instance, if difficulty with letter identification turns out to be a predictor, this does not mean that instruction on letter identification is a sufficient or the best treatment for preventing all reading difficulties (see Adams, 1990). Conversely, the skills that are the focus of treatment may not necessarily be the ones on which the identification of the individual or target group was based. In practice, identification criteria and treatment plans can, and often will, be chosen somewhat independently of each other.

It should be borne in mind while reading this chapter that relationships between effective predictors and reading difficulties are markers only and that other mediating variables, which are not measured in a particular research study, may also correlate with reading difficulties. Again consider letter identification: Scanlon and Vellutino (1996) found a moderately high correlation ($r = .56$) between letter identification and reading achievement. In this same study, the correlation between number identification and reading achievement was .59. Since these results indicate that both poor letter identification and poor number identification predict reading difficulty, they weaken or at least complicate the hypothesis that either of them is a direct cause of reading difficulty. Both may be marker variables for another factor that goes further to explain both letter and number identification.

When deciding which factors to use to identify children who are at risk for reading difficulties, the main determinant should be the strength of the association. (Of course, other practical matters, such as cost and ease of assessment, also affect assessment decisions.) One way to measure the strength of the relationship between a kindergarten predictor and a later reading score is to compute a "correlation" statistic (symbolized by r), which takes a value of zero when there is no predictive relationship at all and takes a value of 1.0 when there is perfect predictability. In between, the higher the correlation, the stronger the tendency for children who did well on the predictor measure to become good readers, and for children who did poorly initially to end up with lower reading achievement scores later. For example, when reading is measured yearly, correlations between scores in one year with scores in the next year are typically in the .60 to .80 range; in other words, they are quite strong but not perfect. As will be seen, correlations between the best kindergarten predictors and later reading scores are not quite as strong (in the .40 to .60 range) but still provide a great deal of useful predictive information. For other predictors, however, the correlations tend to be lower.

Because correlations summarize the strength of the relationship across the full range of children's abilities, their use is consistent with a dimensional account of individual differences in reading discussed in Chapter 3. Another way to look at the strength of prediction instead reflects the categorical model, which continues to predominate in educational practice. In this approach, an at-risk subgroup of kindergartners is designated based on their scores on the predictor measure, and a reading disability subgroup is identified based on later achievement scores. The percentage of children whose outcome classification was correctly predicted is an overall measure of prediction accuracy. Furthermore, a predictor is said to have high sensitivity if most of the disabled readers had been correctly identified as at risk at the outset and to have high specificity if most nondisabled readers had been classified as not at risk. It is also informative to examine errors of prediction, including false positives (children deemed at risk who did not develop reading problems) and false negatives (those who did not meet the risk criterion but nevertheless had difficulty learning to read).

In what follows we attempt to estimate the degree of risk associated with many kinds of predictor measures, alone and in combination. Sometimes the magnitude of risk can be estimated quite closely on the basis of an abundance of longitudinal findings. For other factors, far less information is available regarding the degree of risk they pose. For each predictor, we describe the average strength of its correlation with future reading achievement and, when possible, estimate the probabilities of prediction errors and correct predictions from studies in which risk status has been examined in relation to outcome classifications.

We have organized this chapter by first considering predictors that are intrinsic to the individual and would be identified by assessing the child. We then move to a discussion of factors identified in the household and then to factors associated with the child's larger environment—the neighborhood, the school, and the community.

CHILD-BASED RISK FACTORS

Physical and Clinical Conditions

Some primary organic conditions are associated with the development of learning problems as secondary symptoms. That is, the child's reading and more general learning problems are thought to result from cognitive or sensory limitations that follow from the primary diagnosis. These primary conditions include:

- severe cognitive deficiencies,
- hearing impairment,
- chronic otitis media,
- (specific) early language impairment, and
- attention deficit/hyperactivity disorder.

Cognitive Deficiencies

Children with severe cognitive deficiencies usually develop very low, if any, reading achievement. Other factors that are associated with developmental delays in cognitive abilities include severe nutritional deficiency, very low birthweight, fetal alcohol syndrome, lead poisoning, and severe psychopathological conditions that emerge in early childhood.

Hearing Impairment

Hearing impairment or deafness is another condition well documented to be associated with reading difficulty (Conrad, 1979; Karchmer et al., 1978; Waters and Doehring, 1990). Chronic ear infections (chronic otitis media) often lead to intermittent hearing loss during the early years. Concern has thus been raised regarding the effects of this on language development and, later, on reading. For chronic otitis media and reading difficulties, results are mixed. Wallace and Hooper (1997) reviewed 18 studies examining chronic otitis media and reading and noted a modest association between the two for language-based skills such as reading.

Early Language Impairment

Although there is tremendous variability in the rate with which children acquire language during their first four years of life, some children are so clearly behind by age 3 that it arouses concern on the part of their parents, neighbors, preschool teachers, pediatricians, or others. In many such cases, delayed language development is the first indication of a broader primary condition, such as a general developmental disability, autism, hearing impairment, or neurological condition, which is likely to be associated with reading difficulty.

In other cases, however, an evaluation by a speech-language professional results in a diagnosis of "(specific) early language impairment"(ELI) and usually the initiation of a course of therapy designed to stimulate language growth in one or more domains.

There have been more than a dozen follow-up studies of the later academic achievements of children who were clinically identified as having specific early language impairment. In this work, the sampling criteria, the initial skill levels of the children, and the measures of outcome status have not always been well specified and are rarely comparable from study to study; nevertheless, several general trends are evident. First, between 40 and 75 percent of preschoolers with early language impairment develop reading difficulties later, often in conjunction with broader academic achievement problems (Aram and Hall, 1989; Bashir and Scavuzzo, 1992). Second, the risk for reading problems appears to be lowest among those whose early language weaknesses were relatively mild or were confined to a narrow domain (especially to speech production alone). Nevertheless, some children with only mild-to-moderate language delays, who appear to overcome their spoken-language difficulties by the end of the preschool period, remain at greater risk than other youngsters for the development of a reading difficulty (e.g., Scarborough and Dobrich, 1990; Stark et al., 1984; Stothard et al., in press). Third, regardless of a child's general cognitive abilities or therapeutic history, in general the risk for reading problems is greatest when a child's language impairment is severe in any area, broad in scope, or persistent over the preschool years (e.g., Stark et al., 1984; Bishop and Adams, 1990).

Attention Deficits

Although good evidence indicates that attention deficit/hyperactivity disorder and reading disability are distinct disorders, they frequently co-occur. Longitudinal follow-up indicates that, from the beginning of formal schooling, reading disability is relatively common in children with inattention problems (31 percent in first grade), becoming even more frequent as the child matures (over 50 percent in ninth grade—S.E. Shaywitz et al., 1994; B.A. Shaywitz et al., 1995a).

Other Conditions

A visual impairment is not in itself a predictor of reading difficulty. If not correctable, it makes the reading of printed text impossible, so the visually impaired child must instead learn to read Braille manually. Because Braille notation for English text is alphabetic, and because discovering the alphabetic principle is often the biggest obstacle to children in learning to read, many of the same risk factors that have been identified for sighted children also presumably apply. Unless these or some other Braille-specific processing difficulties (such as poor manual discrimination) are present, there is probably no higher risk for reading difficulties among blind children than among sighted children, provided that early and adequate instruction in reading Braille is provided.

Developmental Differences in Language and Linguistic Development

Children who are developing normally achieve certain milestones of motor, linguistic, and cognitive development at predictable ages. Children who show delays in language development in particular have been studied to determine whether these early language delays relate to literacy problems later on. As described earlier, clinical follow-up studies of preschoolers who had been diagnosed as having ELI indicate that this diagnosis is associated with considerable risk. Even among children who do not receive an ELI diagnosis, there is tremendous variation in language skills. Only a handful of longitudinal prediction studies have initially assessed children from birth through age 4, in part because of the difficulty of testing children accurately in this age range. The main focus of these investigations has been to describe the development of various linguistic and metalinguistic abilities in very young children and then follow them up through their early school years.

To our knowledge, only one study has directly examined the prediction of reading from language and linguistic developmental differences among infants (Shapiro et al., 1990). A composite measure of infant achievement was found to predict reading status (reading disability or not) with .73 sensitivity (i.e., 73 percent of children with reading disability had been classified initially as at risk) and .74 specificity (i.e., 74 percent of nondisabled readers had been classified as not at risk). Individually, the expressive language milestones made a particularly strong contribution to prediction; including IQ in the composite measure did not improve accuracy. Although not sufficiently accurate for practical use, this degree of predictive success is nevertheless remarkably high, particularly in comparison to the results emerging from studies predicting reading difficulty from kindergarten (see section below).

Walker et al. (1994) cumulatively monitored mean utterance length and number of vocabulary words produced, two developmentally sensitive aspects of emerging language. The two early-language measures, which were highly intercorrelated, correlated moderately well with reading scores in grades 1 through 3, as did the preschool IQ scores.

Bryant et al. (1989, 1990) tested young children on several phonological awareness measures, as well as IQ. Performance on reading tests was predicted by receptive vocabulary, expressive language ability, receptive language ability, nursery rhyme recitation, and IQ. Correlations of the rhyme-matching measure with later reading were not reported, and this measure was only weakly related to the tests of phonological awareness at 40-55 months, the last of which were strongly predictive of reading.

Scarborough (1991) considered several language and IQ measures and reading outcomes at the end of grade 2 for a sample of 62 children, about half of whom had parents and/or older siblings with reading problems. IQ scores correlated moderately with later reading, as did scores on receptive language. Expressive vocabulary skill at age 42 months predicted reading a bit more strongly than did receptive vocabulary scores at the same age. In addition, for a subset of 52 children at age 2.5 years (20 from affected families who became reading disabled; 20 similar in sex, socioeconomic status (SES), and IQ; nonreading disability cases from unaffected families; and 12 who became good readers despite a family history of reading disability), measures of expressive phonological (pronunciation accuracy), syntactic (length/complexity of sentences), and lexical (word diversity) abilities were derived from naturalistic observations of children's language during play sessions with their mothers (Scarborough, 1990). The children who became poor readers were much weaker than the other groups on the syntactic and phonological measures. At ages 3, 3.5, and 4 years, however, only the syntactic differences were evident.

What is most striking about the results of the preceding studies is the power of early preschool language to predict reading three to five years later. In fact, the correlations between reading and early pre-school measures are almost as high as those between kindergarten predictors and reading (see next section).

Predictors at School Entry

Acquired Proficiency in Language

Spoken language and reading have much in common. If the printed words can be efficiently recognized, comprehension of connected text depends heavily on the reader's oral-language abilities, particularly with regard to understanding the meanings of words that have been identified and the syntactic and semantic relationships among them. Indeed, many early research reports called attention to the differences between good and poor readers in their comprehension and production of structural relations within spoken sentences.

Given the close relationship between reading and language, we should expect that normally occurring variations in language differences would be related to speed or ease of the acquisition of reading. Earlier, we reviewed the empirical data indicating that language development in the preschool years is indeed related to later reading achievement and that preschoolers with language disabilities are highly likely to show reading problems as well. Here we consider whether variation in language abilities at the time children typically begin to receive formal reading instruction also relates to variability in reading outcomes.

Verbal Memory The ability to retain verbal information in working memory is essential for reading and learning, so it might be expected that verbal memory measures would be effective predictors of future reading achievement. Many prediction studies have included such measures within their predictor batteries. From the results of those studies (Scarborough, 1998), it is clear that, on average, kindergartners' abilities to repeat sentences or to recall a brief story that was just read aloud to them are more strongly related to their future reading achievement than are their scores on digit span, word span, and pseudo-word repetition measures. Sentence or story recall (r = .45), in fact, compares favorably with other predictors of reading (see Table 4-1).

Lexical and Syntactic Skills Several kinds of vocabulary measures have been examined as predictors of future reading achievement. On each trial of a "receptive" vocabulary test, the child must indicate which of several pictures best corresponds to the word (usually a noun, adjective, or gerund) spoken by the examiner. A long series of items of increasing difficulty is available, and testing terminates when the child's vocabulary level is exceeded. As shown in Table 4-1, in 20 prediction studies the mean correlation between receptive vocabulary scores in kindergarten and subsequent reading scores in the first three grades is .36.

With regard to lexical abilities, one can also examine expressive, rather than receptive, vocabulary, which is also sometimes referred to as "confrontation naming" or simply "object naming." On such tests, the child is shown a series of drawings of objects and is asked to name each one. Compared with receptive tests, these measures place greater demands on accurate retrieval of stored phonological representations of lexical items and on the formulation and production of spoken responses.

To our knowledge, only five kindergarten prediction studies have included confrontation naming measures in the predictor battery, but the magnitude and consistency of the results of those studies suggest that naming vocabulary is a reliable predictor of future reading ability. On average, expressive vocabulary measures are associated (r = .45) with a considerable amount of variance in subsequent reading scores, which compares favorably with the effect sizes for receptive vocabulary and IQ.

Not only the accuracy of name production but also its speed can be measured. Rapid serial naming speed has been shown to correlate with concurrent and future reading ability but not with IQ in several dozen studies of schoolchildren (e.g., Ackerman et al., 1990; Bowers and Swanson, 1991; Cornwall, 1992; Denckla and Rudel, 1976b; Felton et al., 1987; Spring and Davis, 1988; Wolf and Obregon, 1992). Rapid serial naming speed has been found to be

TABLE 4-1 Prediction of Reading Difficulties at School Entry

Factors Identified in the Child	Number of Samples	Strength of Relationship
Language		
Verbal memory for stories/sentences	11	Median r = .49 mean r = .45 *(SD* = .14)
Lexical skills		
1. Receptive vocabulary	20	Median r = .33 mean r = .36 *(SD* = .17)
2. Confrontation naming	5	Median r = .49 mean r = .45 *(SD* = .07)
3. Rapid serial naming	14	Median r = .40 mean r = .38 *(SD* = .09)
Receptive language, syntax/ morphology	9	Median r = .38 mean r = .37 *(SD* = na)
Expressive language	11	Median r = .37 mean r = .32 *(SD* = .16)
Overall language	4	Median r = .47 mean r = .46 *(SD* = .15)
Phonological awareness	27	Median r = .42 mean r = .46 *(SD* = .13)
Early Literacy-Related Skills		
Reading "readiness"	21	Median r = .56 mean r = .57 *(SD* = .12)
Letter identification	24	Median r = .53 mean r = .52 *(SD* = .14)
Concepts of print	7	Median r = .49 mean r = .46 *(SD* = .20)

NOTE: Only studies with sample sizes of 30 or more were considered. At least one of the risk factors of interest had to be assessed initially when the children were within about one year of beginning formal schooling in reading, and at least one assessment of reading skills had to be obtained after one, two, or occasionally three years of instruction. If a word recognition measure was used in a prediction study, its correlation(s) with predictors was used; otherwise, a composite reading score or, rarely, a reading comprehension measure was instead accepted as the criterion variable. When more than one correlation value per risk factor was available in a given sample of children (because multiple reading assessments were conducted and/or because multiple measures of the predictor were used), the average correlation for the sample was used for aggregation. To obtain the average correlations across samples, therefore, each contributing sample contributed only one independent observation. SOURCE: adapted from Scarborough (1998).

related to speech production (Kamhi and Catts, 1986; Kamhi et al., 1988). Somewhat weaker associations with reading are obtained when "discrete" naming (response time to name an individual stimulus) rather than "serial" naming is measured, suggesting that the naming speed problems of poor readers involve more than just difficulty in retrieving and producing item names. A full understanding of the relationship between speeded naming and reading remains to be determined.

Studies have also been made of the semantic, morphological, and syntactic skills of kindergartners. Receptive language measures (sentence comprehension) that emphasize the understanding of complex syntactic and morphological forms have been more successful predictors than other (or unspecified) kinds of receptive measures (Table 4-1).

Expressive language (production) measures, which include mean length of utterance, sentence completion, tasks requiring the child to fill in morphological markers, and others, are about equally strongly predictive of reading as receptive language. It should be noted, however, that the goal in these studies has been to predict reading achievement during the first few school grades, when the emphasis is primarily on the acquisition of word recognition and decoding skills rather than on the comprehension of challenging material.

Overall Language In examining the connection between measures of overall language ability and future reading achievement, the highest average correlation has been found when a broad composite index of language abilities has been used. Since only four studies have taken this approach, these findings can be considered promising but not conclusive at this point.

Phonological Awareness Phonological awareness, or phonological sensitivity, is the ability to attend explicitly to the phonological structure of spoken words, rather than just to their meanings and syntactic roles. This metalinguistic skill involves treating language as the object of thought, rather than merely using language for communication.

Given the importance of phoneme-letter mapping in the English alphabetic writing system, phonological awareness would be expected to be an excellent predictor of the future reading skills of kindergartners, particularly when the child's appreciation of the subsyllabic or phonemic structure of words is measured. This predictive correlational relationship has been examined in 27 research samples from 24 studies (Table 4-1). On average, phonological awareness ($r = .46$) has been about as strong a predictor of future reading as memory for sentences and stories, confrontation naming, and general language measures.

When classificatory analyses are conducted, phonological awareness in kindergarten appears to have the tendency to be a more successful predictor of future *superior* reading than of future reading *problems* (Wagner, 1997; Scarborough, 1998). That is, among children who have recently begun or will soon begin kindergarten, few of those with strong phonological awareness skills will stumble in learning to read, but many of those with weak phonological sensitivity will go on to become adequate readers (Bradley and Bryant, 1983, 1985; Catts, 1991a, 1996; Mann, 1994; also see discussion of the reciprocity between phonological awareness and reading presented in Chapter 2).

In sum, despite the theoretical importance of phonological awareness for learning to read, its predictive power is somewhat muted, because, at about the time of the onset of schooling, so many children who will go on to become normally achieving readers have not yet attained much, if any, appreciation of the phonological structure of oral language, making them nearly indistinguishable in this regard from children who will indeed encounter reading difficulties down the road.

Acquired Knowledge of Literacy

Even before children can read in the conventional sense, most have acquired some information about the purposes, mechanics, and component skills of the reading task. For some children, opportunities for acquiring this sort of information abound, whereas others have relatively little relevant exposure (McCormick and Mason,

1986). Therefore, by the time children are about to begin school, they vary considerably in how much they already know about books and reading. Researchers have tested children's reading readiness, letter identification, and concepts of print to determine whether differences in these abilities can predict differences in future reading achievement.

Reading Readiness Reading readiness is a term used by both researchers and educators to mean accomplishment of skills presumed to be prerequisite to benefiting from formal reading instruction. It is measured by comparing the accomplishments of children in kindergarten, where prereading skills are practiced, with their scores on standardized reading tests in the primary grades. Reading readiness has been shown to have a high correlation with reading ability: children who lack reading readiness at school entry have a harder time learning to read in the primary grades. This has been found in prediction studies since 1950 (Hammill and McNutt, 1980; Scarborough, 1998).

Letter Identification Among the readiness skills that are traditionally evaluated, the one that appears to be the strongest predictor on its own is letter identification. Table 4-1 shows a summary of results for longitudinal studies since 1975 that have included this measure. Just measuring how many letters a kindergartner is able to name when shown letters in a random order appears to be nearly as successful at predicting future reading, as is an entire readiness test.

The prediction of future reading by kindergarten measures of letter identification and other early reading skills is quite substantial, accounting on average for nearly one-third of the variance in reading at grades 1-3. Nevertheless, the predictive accuracy derived from using such readiness measures alone may be lower than desirable for practical purposes. For instance, in Scanlon and Vellutino's very large district-wide sample, letter knowledge was highly correlated with reading test scores and with teacher ratings of reading skill at the end of first grade. The results obtained when letter identification was used to classify kindergartners as at risk versus not at risk are shown in Table 4-2.

TABLE 4-2 Accuracy of Prediction of Grade 1 Reading Status from Kindergarten Letter Identification Differences

Classification of Kindergartners According to Their Letter Identification Skills

A. Stricter kindergarten cutoff

		"at risk" (bottom 10 percent)	"not at risk" (top 90 percent)	Total
Grade 1 Reading (Teacher Ratings)	Bottom 20 percent	63 (correctly predicted)	131 "miss" errors	194
	Top 80 percent	37 "false alarm" errors	769 (correctly predicted)	806
		100	900	1,000

B. More lenient kindergarten cutoff

		"at risk" (bottom 25 percent)	"not at risk" (top 75 percent)	Total
Grade 1 Reading (Teacher Ratings)	Bottom 20 percent	118 (correctly predicted)	73 "miss" errors	191
	Top 80 percent	132 "false alarm" errors	677 (correctly predicted)	809
		250	750	1,000

SOURCE: Adapted from Scanlon and Vellutino (1996)

The upper part of the table illustrates the pattern of prediction errors when a rather strict criterion was adopted, that is, when letter identification scores were used to identify the bottom 10 percent of kindergartners as at risk. When approximately the bottom 20 percent of first graders were designated as having reading difficulties, 83.2 percent of the grade 1 outcomes of the approximately 1,000 children would have been correctly predicted on the basis of letter knowledge. This is far better than chance and better than could be achieved using any other single kindergarten measure, but it still means that a considerable number of prediction errors would occur. Of the 100 kindergartners who would have been identified as most at risk (and who would presumably be targeted to receive intervention), 37 would have turned out *not* to have reading difficulties. Furthermore, of the 900 children deemed not to be at risk on the basis of letter knowledge, 131 (14.5 percent) would have developed reading problems by the end of first grade. In other words, only about one-third of the children who became the poorest readers would have been selected initially for early intervention.

Table 4-2B also shows that, when a more lenient criterion was used to classify kindergartners, such that 25 percent rather than 10 percent were considered at risk, the "miss" rate would drop to a more acceptable level (10 percent). However, the overall accuracy of prediction would decrease (to 79.5 percent), and the rate of false positives would increase substantially, such that less than half of the at-risk group would be expected to develop reading difficulties.

To increase the accuracy with which kindergartners at greatest risk can be identified, it may be useful to examine other individual risk factors that may provide additional information about how readily a child is likely to learn to read.

Concepts of Print The term "concepts of print" refers to a general understanding of how print can be used rather than knowledge about specific letters. It has been shown to have a moderate correlation with reading ability in the primary grades. A recent study with even higher correlations used two types of measures related to print: ones related to understanding how print can be used and ones related to the mechanics of the writing system (letter naming or letter-sound correspondences) (Stuart, 1995). It therefore appears promising that this combined approach will be more accurate in identifying children at risk, although more work on developing and validating these test batteries is needed.

Other Factors Measured at School Entry

Researchers have examined a number of other factors to see whether there is a connection between them and future reading achievement. A number of longitudinal studies have examined kindergartners' speech perception or production abilities, as well as visual and motor skills, nonverbal memory, age for grade, and sex. The results suggest that these measures are consistently weak predictors of subsequent reading differences. Likewise, nonverbal IQ scores are poor predictors, but verbal (and overall) IQ is about equivalent in strength to receptive vocabulary and various other language measures.

Prediction Based on Multiple Risk Factors

We have assessed individual child predictors to determine whether any of these factors are sufficiently strongly related to reading difficulties that they can be used to help identify children who should receive prevention, intervention, or remediation. Note that from the research we have different measures that predict more strongly at different ages. Across the age span of birth through grade 3, cognitive deficiencies, hearing impairment, and a diagnosed specific early language impairment have strong associations with future reading difficulties. Low IQ and lack of general language ability in infancy through kindergarten are associated with future reading difficulties. Also, in kindergarten, reading readiness measures, letter identification, concepts of print, verbal memory for stories and sentences, confrontation naming, overall language, phonological awareness, and expressive vocabulary or naming skills are associated with future reading ability.

From our review of child-based factors, it should be clear that many measurable individual differences among children at the outset of schooling are reliably correlated with future reading achievement but that most are not strong enough on their own to provide the level of predictive accuracy that would be desired for practical purposes. For this reason, many researchers have examined the combined effects of several or many predictors (e.g., Badian, 1982, 1994;

Butler et al., 1985; Felton, 1992; Bishop and Adams, 1990; Catts, 1991b, 1993; Horn and O'Donnel, 1984).

Different researchers included very different sets of predictor measures in their kindergarten batteries. Most used are some kinds of index of early print skills, such as letter knowledge, word recognition, concepts of print, teacher ratings, and writing. Unfortunately, the other measures that appear to be the strongest single predictors (phonological awareness, sentence/story recall, confrontation naming, and broad language indices) were rarely assessed in these studies, so their potential contributions to prediction when combined with other variables remain unknown.

In most of the studies, multiple regression analyses yielded measures of the strength of the relationship between kindergarten measures and later reading achievement. On average, 57 percent of the variance in reading scores was accounted for by the analysis. In comparison, the mean effect size for readiness tests alone was considerably lower, indicating that adding other kinds of measures to the traditional readiness tests can effectively strengthen the prediction. Moreover, it is impressive that the average correlation in these studies is about as strong as the year-to-year correlations among reading achievement.

Classificatory analyses were conducted in three studies that had the kindergarten measure as the predictor of second or third grade reading achievement (Badian, 1982; Butler et al., 1985; Felton, 1992). The percentage of children whose reading outcome status (reading disabled or nondisabled) was correctly predicted by kindergarten risk status (based on the predictor battery) ranged from 80 to 92 percent. These prediction analyses tended to achieve specificity (i.e., 80 to 92 percent of nondisabled readers had been classified as not at risk in kindergarten) but somewhat lower sensitivity (i.e., 56 to 92 percent of reading-disabled children had been classified initially as at risk). Negative predictive power ranged from 89 to 99 percent; in other words, on average, the proportion of not-at-risk children who nevertheless developed reading problems was low. Positive predictive power, however, ranged from 31 to 76 percent; that is, the proportion of at-risk children who turned out not to have reading difficulties was substantial and was not markedly lower than when predictions have been based on individual predictors.

In addition, two recent longitudinal studies are particularly informative about the prediction of reading ability for children with early language impairment, based on their observed differences at about the time of school entry (Bishop and Adams, 1990; Catts, 1991, 1993). In both studies, 50 percent of the variance in reading achievement in the sample could be accounted for by a small set of predictors measured at about age 5. In Catts's study, measures of phonological awareness and rapid serial naming of objects permitted 83 percent of the children's outcomes to be correctly predicted, with a false positive rate of 32 percent and a false negative rate of 13 percent. In the Bishop and Adams sample, the predictor set included IQ and a combination of language ability indices. Clearly, the accuracy of prediction in these samples was lower than in the population-representative samples.

The pattern of classification errors is quite similar across these studies and suggests that a fair number of children who will have reading difficulties do not obtain low enough scores to merit an at-risk designation on the basis of the kinds of kindergarten measures that were used (most typically literacy-specific knowledge, phonological awareness, and IQ). Whether the inclusion of sentence/story recall, naming vocabulary, and broader kindergarten batteries would help to pick up these cases is unknown, but it merits investigation on the basis of the strong bivariate results.

Nevertheless, it is clear that batteries consisting of multiple measures are becoming accurate enough to be very useful for identifying individual children who are at greater risk than their classmates. Close monitoring of these children (including follow-up assessments and observations by their kindergarten teachers) would permit them to receive additional assistance (if it turns out to be needed) as soon as possible, a highly desirable objective. Note, however, that individual testing of all kindergartners, which can be costly, probably has less utility in a school in which a large number of entering students are at risk due to economic disadvantage or other group risk factors, discussed below. In that circumstance, the highest priority in allocating resources should address the goal of raising the group's overall level of achievement.

FAMILY-BASED RISK FACTORS

In many circumstances, early identification of children who will have reading difficulties might proceed better by considering target groups rather than by assessing individuals. Demographic data suggest that a majority of reading problems tend to occur in children from poor families with little education, although they may of course occur in families that are neither poor nor undereducated. Also, being a member of a family in which reading difficulties have occurred before may also constitute a risk, whether for biological or environmental reasons. We review here a number of factors identifiable at the level of the family to assess their value in identifying children who should receive prevention and intervention activities.

Family History of Reading Difficulties

Are children whose parents or older siblings have exhibited reading problems at greater risk for reading difficulties than are other children of otherwise similar backgrounds? Decades of research on the familial aggregation of reading problems suggest that this is so. Factors identified as family risk factors include family history of reading problems, home literacy environment, verbal interaction, language other than English, nonstandard dialect, and family-based socioeconomic status (SES). It is important to bear in mind, however, that family patterns of reading problems can be attributed either to shared genetic or to shared environmental factors (see Chapter 1).

If a child is diagnosed with a reading disability, there is a higher than normal probability that other family members will also have difficulties with reading (see Finucci et al., 1976; Hallgren, 1950; Gilger et al., 1991; Vogler et al., 1985). The exact probability seems to depend on a variety of factors, including the severity of the child's reading disability. Furthermore, when the parents' diagnosis for reading disability is based on self-report, the family incidence tends to be lower than when the diagnosis is based on the direct measurement of parents' reading skills (Gilger et al., 1991).

Most studies of familial incidence first diagnose a child with reading disability using a severity criterion that would identify 5 to 10 percent of children who have normal intelligence and have had what for the majority of children is effective education. The investigators then attempt to use a similar severity criterion to diagnose reading disability in the parents. Evidence for the family nature of reading disability is based on parental rates that are substantially above the 5 to 10 percent rate estimated for the population. Scarborough (1998) computed the average rate of reading disability among parents across eight family studies that included a total of 516 families. The rate across studies varied from 25 to 60 percent, with a median value of 37 percent. Thus, all studies found rates for reading disability among parents of reading-disabled children that were considerably higher than expected in the normal population. The median proportion of reading disability among fathers (46 percent) was slightly higher than the median proportion among mothers (33 percent).

A few studies have attempted to estimate the prospective risk to the child when parental disabilities are identified first (Finucci et al., 1985; Fowler and Cross, 1986; Scarborough, 1990). Those prospective studies clearly show that parents' reading disabilities predict a higher than normal rate of reading disabilities in their children (31 to 62 percent versus 5 to 10 percent). Although parental reading disabilities are not completely predictive of their children's reading disabilities, the substantially greater risk at least warrants very close monitoring of their children's progress in early language and literacy development. Results from two predictive studies (Elbro et al., 1996; Scarborough, 1989, 1990, 1991) suggest that whether these children develop reading problems can be predicted from preschool measures of language and literacy skills. If so, it would be potentially affordable to assess that small subset of the population a year or two before kindergarten and to provide intervention to those with the weakest skills. Of course, to do so would require an effective means of persuading parents with a history of reading problems to step forward so that this service could be provided for their offspring.

This sort of recruitment program has never been attempted, so its feasibility is unknown.

Home Literacy Environment

Families differ enormously in the level to which they provide a supportive environment for a child's literacy development. Measures of the home literacy environment itself, therefore, may provide an indication of an individual child's degree of risk for reading difficulties. Hess and Holloway (1984) identified five broad areas of family functioning that may influence reading development. The first four are:

1. *Value placed on literacy:* by reading themselves and encouraging children to read, parents can demonstrate that they value reading.

2. *Press for achievement:* by expressing their expectations for achievement by their children, providing reading instruction, and responding to the children's reading initiations and interest, parents can create a press for achievement.

3. *Availability and instrumental use of reading materials:* literacy experiences are more likely to occur in homes that contain children's books and other reading and writing materials.

4. *Reading with children:* parents can read to preschoolers at bedtime or other times and can listen to schoolchildren's oral reading, providing assistance as needed.

The fifth area, *opportunities for verbal interaction*, is presented in the next section. Although conceptually distinct and perhaps analytically useful to consider separately, in practice these areas may be highly interrelated. In addition, home characteristics and social class covary to a degree.

We review results of longitudinal prediction studies that have examined aspects of the home environment during children's early years (birth to about age 5) in relation to the development of literacy knowledge and skills during the preschool years and especially to the children's subsequent academic achievement during the primary school grades. Few studies have derived overall measures of the quality of the preschool home environment.

Most longitudinal studies have looked at the home environment of children at different ages and have identified contributors to literacy development. Unless otherwise indicated, measures of home variables were derived from parental interviews or questionnaires administered at or shortly before the children entered kindergarten, and reading achievement was measured by standardized tests in the first and/or second grade (e.g., DeBaryshe, 1993; DeBaryshe et al., 1991; Mason, 1980; Mason and Dunning, 1986; Scarborough et al., 1991; Share et al., 1984; Thomas, 1984; Wells, 1985).

In summary, although there is considerable evidence that differences in the home literacy environments of preschoolers are related to subsequent achievement differences, the strength of these correlations has tended to be modest, particularly when measured in large population-representative samples (Bus et al., 1995; Scarborough and Dobrich, 1994). Thus, a preschooler whose home provides fewer opportunities for acquiring knowledge and skills pertaining to books and reading is at somewhat higher risk for reading difficulties than a child whose home affords a richer literacy environment.

Opportunities for Verbal Interaction

The major dimension of variability for measures of verbal interaction in the home is the dimension of quantity. It is now clear that, though poor and uneducated families provide much the same array of language experiences as middle-class educated families, the quantity of verbal interaction they tend to provide is much less (Hart and Risley, 1995). A lower quantity of verbal interaction constitutes a risk factor primarily in that it relates closely to lowered child vocabulary scores, as shown in one large prospective observational study (Hart and Risley, 1995) and in a score of less rigorous studies. Because vocabulary is associated with reading outcomes (see Table 4-1), it seems likely that reduced opportunities for verbal interaction would function as a risk factor. Furthermore, language-rich experiences in the home are typically associated with activities (like book reading, shared dinner table conversations) that themselves show only modest predictive value. It is possible, too, that the effects of differences in verbal interaction may not show up until after the primary grades, that is, when more high-level comprehension is required.

Home Language Other Than English

When a preschool child's home language is not primarily English, the ease of learning to read printed English is likely to be impeded to some extent, particularly if reading instruction in English begins before the child has acquired oral proficiency in English (see August and Hakuta, 1997). One difficulty in trying to evaluate the degree of risk associated with limited English proficiency is that cultural as well as linguistic differences are also involved and may introduce other kinds of risk factors.

Many Hispanic children with limited English proficiency also have in common that their parents are poorly educated, that their family income is low, that they reside in communities in which many families are similarly struggling, and that they attend schools with student bodies that are predominantly minority and low achieving. Not surprisingly, the other factors that have been proposed to explain the typically low levels of academic achievement among Hispanic students include many that have been cited as contributing to the risk factors facing other minority groups, including low SES (and its many concomitant conditions), cultural differences between the home and school (e.g., regarding educational values and expectations), sociopolitical factors (including past and ongoing discrimination and low perceived opportunities for minorities), and school quality.

In summary, low English proficiency in a Hispanic child is a strong indication that the child is at risk for reading difficulty. That low reading achievement is a widespread problem among Hispanic students even when they are instructed and tested in Spanish, however, indicates that linguistic differences are not solely responsible for the high degree of risk faced by these children and that the role of co-occurring group risk factors, particularly school quality, home literacy background, and SES, must be considered.

Use of a Nonstandard Dialect of English in the Home

Dialect differences among English speakers are widely recognized—for example, a Boston accent or a Southern drawl. There is ample evidence that listeners make stereotyped judgments about speakers of particular dialects. Of greater concern here, however, is that some dialect differences are viewed by some not as regional variations but as "incorrect" English, connoting aberrant or delayed language development, poor learning, lazy or sloppy articulation, or even purposeful insolence. Particularly under these conditions, the differences between a young child's dialect and the standard classroom English dialect may become a risk factor for reading difficulties.

With regard to reading instruction in particular, the risk for confusion is considerable. For example, if the teacher is pointing out the letter-sound correspondences within a word that is pronounced quite differently in the child's dialect than in the teacher's, the lesson could confuse more than enlighten. Moreover, teachers who are insensitive to dialect differences may develop negative perceptions of children and low expectations for their achievement, and they may adjust their teaching downward in accord with those judgments.

Although these situations undeniably occur, there are many difficulties in measuring the extent to which they happen and the degree to which their occurrence is correlated with, and may contribute to, poor reading achievement. As is the case for children with limited English proficiency, dialect differences are often confounded with poverty, cultural differences, substandard schooling, and other conditions that may themselves impose very high risks for reading difficulties. Even measuring the phenomena and their relation to achievement is confounded by the risk factor itself (Labov, 1966; Smitherman, 1977; Wolfram, 1991). The knowledge base, therefore, is spotty. Some dialects have been researched more thoroughly than others.

Socioeconomic Status

Socioeconomic differences are conventionally indexed by such demographic variables as household income and parents' education and occupation, alone or in some weighted combination. In educational studies, furthermore, the socioeconomic level of a school or district may be estimated by the percentage of the enrollment qualifying for federal lunch subsidies. (For a critique and a discussion of some recommended modifications of current methods of measuring SES, see Entwisle and Astone, 1994). Families rated low in SES are not only less affluent and less educated than other families but also tend to live in communities in which the average family SES is low and tend to receive less adequate nutrition and health services, including prenatal and pediatric care. In other ways, too, low SES often encompasses a broad array of conditions that may be detrimental to the health, safety, and development of young children, which on their own may serve as risk factors for reading difficulties. Teasing apart the various aspects of the environment associated with low SES is virtually impossible, and this should be borne in mind as we discuss some particular risk factors that are linked to poverty.

As far back as Galton's (1874) studies of English scientists, SES has consistently been shown to predict cognitive and academic outcomes (Hess and Holloway, 1984; White, 1982, Pungello et al., 1996). Although reliable, the relationship between SES and reading achievement is more complex than is generally realized. Consider, for example, how the findings of Alexander and Entwisle (1996)—that low SES students progress at identical rates as middle and high SES students during the school year, but they lose ground during the summer—shed light on the relationship between SES and reading achievement.

The degree of risk associated with the SES of the individual child's family differs considerably from the degree of risk associated with the SES level of the group of students attending a particular school. The evidence for this, and its implications for the prevention of reading difficulties among such students, is reviewed here. In an earlier section, we turned our attention to aspects of the home environment that may be responsible for the degree of risk posed to the individual child from a low SES home.

In principle, low SES could potentially carry risk for reading difficulty for an individual child and for entire groups of children. That is, low SES is an *individual risk factor* to the extent that among children attending the same schools, youngsters from low-income families are more likely to become poorer readers than those from high-income families. Low SES is also a *group risk factor* because children from low-income communities are likely to become poorer readers than children from more affluent communities. Because the former are more likely to attend substandard schools, the correlation between SES and low achievement is probably mediated, in large part, by differences in the quality of school experiences. It is thus not very surprising that the strength of the correlation between SES and achievement is stronger when the unit of analysis is the school than when the unit of analysis is the individual child (Bryk and Raudenbush, 1992, on multilevel measures of school effects).

When the average SES of a school (or district) and the average achievement level of the students attending that school are obtained for a large sample of schools, a correlation between SES and achievement can be calculated using the school as the unit of analysis. In a meta-analytic review of the findings for 93 such samples, White (1982) found that the average size of the correlation was .68, which is substantial and dovetails with the conclusion of the section below that attending a substandard school (which is usually one whose students tend to be low in both SES and achievement) constitutes a risk factor for the entire group of children in that school.

When achievement scores and SES are measured *individually* for all children in a large sample, however, the strength of the association between SES and achievement is *far lower*. In White's (1982) meta-analysis, for instance, the average correlation between reading achievement and SES across 174 such samples was .23. Similarly, the correlation was .22 in a sample of 1,459 9-year-old students whose scores were obtained through the National Assessment of Educational Progress (NAEP) evaluations (Walberg and Tsai, 1985). In a meta-analysis of longitudinal prediction studies, Horn and

O'Donnell (1984) obtained a correlation that was only slightly higher (.31) between SES and early school achievement.

Similar SES findings were found in population-representative studies in the United States and in other English-speaking countries (e.g., Alwin and Thornton, 1984; Estrada et al., 1987; Richman et al., 1982; Rowe, 1991; Share et al., 1984; Wells, 1985). In other words, within a given school or district, or across many districts within a country, SES differences among children are relatively weak predictors of achievement. Thus, all else being equal, coming from a family of low SES (defined according to income, education, and occupation of the parents) does not by itself greatly increase a child's risk for having difficulty in learning to read after school income level has been accounted for.

We are not saying here that SES is not an important risk marker. What we are saying is that its effects are strongest when it is used to indicate the status of a school or a community or a district, not the status of individuals. A low-status child in a generally moderate or upper-status school or community is far less at risk than that same child in a whole school or community of low-status children.

Analysis of Family-Based Risk Factors

Parents' reading disabilities predict a higher than normal rate of reading disabilities in their children (31 to 62 percent versus 5 to 10 percent). Although parental reading disabilities are not completely predictive of their children's reading disabilities, the substantially greater risk at least warrants very close monitoring of their children's progress in early language and literacy development. Lack of English proficiency for a Hispanic child is a strong indication that he or she is at risk for reading difficulty; however, linguistic differences appear to be less responsible than other co-occurring group risk factors, particularly school quality. In a similar manner, the occurrence of family use of nonstandard dialect and individual family SES covary considerably with factors such as school quality, which is discussed in the next major section of this chapter.

The quantity of verbal interaction in families constitutes a risk factor primarily in that it relates closely to child vocabulary scores.

Findings related to home literacy environments are mixed. Many of the large-scale studies (Walberg and Tsai, 1984; White, 1982) of the correlations between home environment and school achievement have focused primarily on samples of children in elementary school (or older). Because the focus of this report is on the prevention of reading difficulties in young children, it is especially important to consider the different roles that home environment may play at different ages. In particular, the opportunities provided in the home for literacy acquisition during the preschool years may contribute primarily to the child's acquisition of attitudes toward literacy, of knowledge about the purpose and mechanics of reading, and of skills (such as vocabulary growth and letter knowledge) that may facilitate learning when school instruction begins. Once the child has begun to attend school and has started to learn to read, the contributions of home and parents may be somewhat different; assistance with homework, listening to the child's efforts at reading aloud, the availability of resources such as a dictionary and an encyclopedia, and so forth may be particularly important for fostering high achievement in school.

NEIGHBORHOOD, COMMUNITY, AND SCHOOL-BASED RISK FACTORS

As is clear from our discussion of the family-based factors that constitute risks, it is extremely difficult to disentangle the effects of family practices from factors such as the neighborhood where the family lives, the cultural and economic community of which the family is a part, and the school the child attends. In this section, we focus on these issues, noting that more research has addressed schooling rather than environmental risks to reading development.

A school in which students are performing at a much higher (or much lower) level than might be predicted using such standard measures as family SES is often described as an "outlier." Studies of outlier schools have overwhelmingly concentrated on positive outlier schools. Variously referred to as studies of "exemplary schools" (Weber, 1971), "unusually effective schools" (Levine and Lezotte, 1990), and "high-flying" schools (Anderson et al., 1992), these positive outlier studies have made important contributions to the field (for a review, see Stringfield, 1994). Of the studies that have examined both positive and negative outlier schools, the largest and longest running has been the Louisiana School Effectiveness Study (Stringfield and Teddlie, 1988, 1991; Teddlie and Stringfield, 1993). Classroom practices in ineffective schools (regardless of community SES) were characterized by significantly lower rates of student time on task, less teacher presentation of new material, lower rates of teacher communication of high academic expectations, fewer instances of positive reinforcement, more classroom interruptions, more discipline problems, and a classroom ambiance generally rated as less friendly (Teddlie et al., 1989).

Stringfield and Teddlie (1991) also conducted detailed qualitative analyses of the 16 case studies. Those analyses added significantly to the quantitative findings. Qualitative differentiations were made at three levels: the student, the classroom, and the school.

At the level of *student activities*, ineffective schools were found to be different from more effective, demographically matched schools in two ways. First, students' time-on-task rates were either uniformly low or markedly uneven. Time on task is a good predictor of achievement gain (Stallings, 1980). In some schools, very few academic tasks were put before any students, and in other schools there were marked differences in the demands made of students, with only some students being required to make a concerted academic effort. Students in positive outlier schools were more uniformly engaged in academic work.

The second student-level variable was whether tasks were put before the students in what appeared to the students to be an organized and goal-oriented fashion. When interviewed, students at ineffective schools were much less likely to be aware of *why* they were being asked to do a task, how the task built on prior schoolwork, and how it might be expected to lay a foundation for future work.

At the classroom *level*, ineffective schools were characterized by a leisurely pace, minimal moderate-to-long-term planning, low or uneven rates of interactive teaching, and a preponderance of "ditto sheets" and other relatively unengaging tasks. One of the most readily observable of the classroom differences was that teachers in ineffective schools simply failed to cover all of the district-mandated materials by year's end. These students were not being provided equal "opportunity to learn." (For a discussion of the power of opportunity to learn, see Muthen et al., 1991). Finally, ineffective schools were structured such that teachers almost invariably taught in isolation from one another; there was little focus on building a professional knowledge base within the school. An additional factor, class size, is related to achievement (Mosteller et al., 1996).

During the kindergarten year, there is evidence that teacher-child relationships are important for later school achievement. Studies have defined the significant qualities of these relationships (Howes and Hamilton, 1992; Howes and Matheson, 1992). One study used a scale based on these findings that describes teachers' perceptions of different qualities of their relationships with their students (Pianta and Steinberg, 1992). Another study compared results on this scale and readiness tests and found that two global qualities of the teacher-child relationship, dependency or conflict, were related to poor performance (Birch and Ladd, 1997). Dependency is an index of the child's overdependence on the teacher; conflict is an index of friction in the teacher-child relationship. Closeness in the teacher-child relationship was associated with better readiness performance. Closeness is an index of warmth and open communication in the teacher-child relationship.

At the *school level,* ineffective schools were observed to be different from their demographically matched peers along seven dimensions: (1) they were not academically focused; (2) the school's daily schedule was not an accurate guide to academic time usage; (3) resources often worked at cross-purposes instructionally; (4) principals seemed uninterested in curricula; (5) principals were relatively passive in the recruitment of new teachers, in the selection of professional development topics and opportunities for the teachers, and in the performance of teacher evaluations; (6) libraries and other media resources were rarely used to their full potential; and (7) there were few systems of public reward for students' academic excellence. Similar descriptions of a smaller set of negative outlier schools have been provided by Venezky and Winfield (1979).

SUMMARY

In this chapter we have examined information about risk factors to determine what kinds of risk are so strongly related to reading difficulties that they can potentially be used to identify children in need of prevention and early intervention. It is clear that the relationships between risk factors and reading achievement are continuous and probabilistic, not categorical or deterministic. Misleading conclusions can be reached if risk factors are not interpreted in this light. It must always be borne in mind that many children whose language and literacy skills are weak at the outset of schooling become successful readers. A majority, however, do not, giving rise to the correlational evidence we have reviewed. It bears repeating, also, that a causal relationship to reading has been shown for only some, but not all, of the measures that best predict future reading ability. Our review of prediction studies indicates clearly that no single risk factor, on its own, is sufficiently accurate to be of practical use for predicting reading difficulties. In combination, however, measures of various kinds of risk—individual, familial, and demographic—can provide useful estimates of future achievement levels. Although prediction accuracy is far from perfect, errors of prediction can be tolerated as long as children's progress is carefully monitored during kindergarten and beyond. As discussed below, how different school systems can best use the available information about risk indicators must be tailored to their particular needs, goals, and resources.

Group Risk Factors

It is abundantly clear that some groups of children are at risk for reading difficulties because they are affected by any or all of the following conditions:

1. They are expected to attend schools in which achievement is chronically low,
2. they reside in low-income families and live in poor neighborhoods,
3. they have limited proficiency in spoken English, and

4. they speak a dialect of English that differs substantially from the one used in school.

Individual Risk Factors

The evidence also indicates that *individual children,* whether or not faced with the adverse conditions just mentioned, may be at greater risk than other otherwise-comparable children for reading difficulties for any or all of the following reasons:

1. They are children of parents with histories of reading difficulty;

2. they have acquired less knowledge and skill pertaining to literacy during the preschool years, either through lack of appropriate home literacy experiences and/or as a result of some inherent cognitive limitations;

3. they lack age-appropriate skills in literacy-related cognitive-linguistic processing, especially phonological awareness, confrontational naming, sentence/story recall, and general language ability;

4. they have been diagnosed as having specific early language impairment;

5. they have a hearing impairment; and

6. they have a primary medical diagnosis with which reading problems tend to occur as a secondary symptom.

Practical Use of This Information

Detecting problems early, in order to avoid other problems later on, is the most practical course. The ease, cost, and reliability with which various risk factors can be measured are therefore a central concern.

Many of the group factors named above (e.g., a child is expected to attend a school in which achievement is chronically low, the child lives in a low-income family and neighborhood) are easily accessible measures. When they are present, effective preventions and early interventions can be provided throughout the age span we are addressing in this report—birth through grade 3.

Pediatric screening tools are effective in identifying children who have severe sensory or developmental impairments (hearing impairment, specific language impairment). When these are present, preventions and early interventions can be provided.

There is less practical utility in conducting population-wide individual screening of infants, toddlers, and preschoolers who have acquired less knowledge and skills pertaining to literacy during the preschool years, either through lack of appropriate home literacy experiences or as a result of some inherent cognitive limitations, or of those who lack age-appropriate skill in literacy-related cognitive-linguistic processing, for the purpose of identifying those who are at greatest risk for reading difficulties. Some screening (i.e., language milestones) is already part of regular well-baby visits; in this case the information could help to define risk, especially when aggregated with other risk factors.

Kindergarten screening, in contrast, has become reasonably accurate when a combination of skills is measured (although the optimal combination is not yet identified). Ideally, screening procedures should be quick and inexpensive; they should identify all or most children who have the specific problem; and they should mistakenly detect none or few children who do not have the problem.

To achieve the goal of preventing reading difficulties, it will not be feasible or appropriate to provide the same sort of intervention to all of these groups and individuals, although some kinds of programs may be of benefit to all. In the next chapter, we review and evaluate the possible approaches that can be taken toward addressing the problems of groups and individuals who have been identified as being at risk.

Part III

Prevention and Intervention

What is currently known about preventing reading difficulties? The committee members' expertise and judgment were central in selecting the material and practices presented in Part III. Converging evidence from experimental investigations, qualitative studies, correlational studies, and various quasi-experimental designs, presented here and in other parts of the report, led us to focus on particular practices and programs.

In addition, a number of challenges are inherent in examining prevention efforts:

- The heterogeneity of children and the vagueness and inconsistency of the definitions used to characterize the reading problems of children;
- the complexities of providing rich descriptions of the interventions (within the space constraints of journal articles), especially given the trend toward multifaceted multicomponent interventions;
- inconsistencies across studies with regard to the measures that are employed, rendering comparisons risky;
- the constrained nature of the measures selected that impede the ability to determine more fully the impact of interventions;

- the intervals between the administration of measures that preclude the study of rate and degree of change over time;
- how little we learn about concurrent instruction, despite the fact that many interventions are supplementary in nature; and
- the difficulties inherent in characterizing and examining the effects of nonintervention factors that can influence reading growth, including social, cultural, ethnic, environmental, and ecological factors such as socioeconomic status, parent education, dialect, and first language.

Despite these limitations, important findings can be culled from the intervention literature, especially if we examine how the patterns emerging across these studies can contribute to understanding.

In Chapter 5, we present information on prevention efforts for infants, toddlers, and preschoolers to ensure that children arrive at school with the necessary skills and developmental attainments that will enhance their preparedness for, and receptiveness to, early reading instruction. Excellent reading instruction in the early grades is a major prevention strategy. We therefore examine the major literacy goals for kindergarten and each of the primary grades in Chapter 6.

In some situations, organizational change is needed in a school so that effective reading instruction can take place. In Chapter 7, we address interventions targeted to changes in classrooms and entire schools—for example, reduction in class size or school restructuring—and other initiatives such as the hiring of bilingual teachers in order to be responsive to children whose home language is not English.

There are some children for whom good instructional practices and preschool experiences are not enough; children who require extra instructional time because of persistent reading difficulties are discussed in Chapter 8.

5
Preventing Reading Difficulties
Before Kindergarten

Americans want their children to start school ready to learn, a goal that includes preparedness for reading instruction. As we discussed in Chapter 4, among those children who are likely to begin school less prepared to learn to read are (1) children living in low-income communities; (2) children with limited English proficiency; (3) preschool children slated to attend an elementary school where achievement is chronically low; (4) children suffering from specific cognitive deficiencies, hearing impairments, and early language impairments; and (5) children whose parents have a history of reading problems. Children who are particularly likely to have difficulty learning to read in the primary grades are those who begin school with less prior knowledge and skill in certain domains, most notably letter knowledge, phonological sensitivity, familiarity with the basic purposes and mechanisms of reading, and language ability.

In this chapter, we discuss research findings on how the various worlds in which infants and toddlers live affect the development of their ability to learn to read. We begin by discussing the role of parents and caregivers, including both the beliefs they hold concerning reading and literacy and the behaviors they engage in with their children in support of literacy development. We then discuss the literature on preschool environments and their contributions to read-ing skills development.   Next we discuss biological and physical conditions and their effects on reading ability development. We present information on clinic- and pediatrician office-based literacy development efforts. Finally, we examine how children with physi-cal and cognitive impairments have been aided in their efforts to learn to read.

PARENTAL AND FAMILY INFLUENCES

Adults who live and interact regularly with children can pro-foundly influence the quality and quantity of their literacy experi-ences. A wide range of factors in turn affect the nature of these interactions, including the parents' attitudes and beliefs about read-ing and literacy, the children's motivation for reading, the opportu-nities parents provide their children and their actual behaviors with them, and the parents' own reading and literacy ability levels.

Parents' Beliefs and Attitudes

There is increasing evidence that parental beliefs and attitudes regarding literacy and reading in particular influence children's lit-eracy development (DeBaryshe, 1995; Baker et al., 1995; Spiegel, 1994). The values, attitudes, and expectations held by parents and other caregivers with respect to literacy are likely to have a lasting effect on a child's attitude about learning to read. The socioemo-tional context of early literacy experiences relates directly to children's motivation to learn to read later on. Some researchers have found that parents who believe that reading is a source of entertainment have children with a more positive view about reading than do parents who emphasize the skills aspect of reading develop-ment (Baker et al., 1997).   Another study found that children who view school learning as irrelevant to life outside school are less mo-tivated to invest time and effort in learning to read (Purcell-Gates, 1994; Stipek et al., 1995).

Parental Behaviors

Box 5-1 is an example of how some parents interact with their children during literacy activities. Asking and responding to questions is a principal aspect of parent-child interactions about text (Durkin, 1966). The frequency and manner of responding to children's questions is therefore an important parental influence on early reading ability (Teale, 1978). A study of the interactions during parent-child reading revealed that at least a thousand questions about print and books were asked by two children over a period of several years (Yaden et al., 1984). When parents are shown how to become more responsive and "dialogic" during shared reading, gains in their children's skills have been recorded (e.g., Whitehurst et al., 1994).

Aspects of literacy likely to be influenced by the family and home environment include print awareness, concepts, and functions; knowledge of narrative structure; literacy as a source of enjoyment; and vocabulary and discourse patterns (Snow and Tabors, 1996; Baker et al., 1995; Clay, 1975; Burns and Casbergue, 1992; Taylor, 1983; Taylor and Dorsey-Gaines, 1988). Studies of children's early language development indicate that parent-child influences are reciprocal: children influence the ways that adults behave toward them, and adults influence children's learning experiences and opportunities (Lewis and Feinman, 1991; Belsky et al., 1984).

Parents who believe their children are interested in reading are more likely to provide abundant print-related experiences than parents who do not perceive such interest (Hiebert, 1981). Parents' interpretations of children's interest in print, however, are partly a function of their expectations of young children's capabilities in general. For example, one parent may judge a child to be interested only if the child asks to have a story read; another parent may judge a child to be interested if he or she expresses pleasure when the parent offers to read a story. Children's interest may also be a function of the kind of reinforcement received for involvement with print in the past (Hiebert, 1986).

BOX 5-1
An Example of Parent-Child Literacy-Oriented Interactions

A visit to the home of Jaime, 5, and Danny, 3:

Danny has just gotten up from a nap and is lying on the floor, not quite awake yet; Jaime has been watching Mister Rogers and is playing with his blocks and dinosaurs in the living room. In the corner there is a little bookshelf with 20 or so children's books, including three that are due back to the library the next day. (Making sure they are back in time will be Mom's job, since it is her day off from work.) There are also some puzzles, a magnetic board with letters, and a canvas bag filled with plastic farm animals. Dad is sitting on the sofa, reading the newspaper. In a few hours, after the boys' mother comes home from work, he will be leaving for his job as a night guard.

Dad takes the boys into the kitchen for some juice and crackers. As they finish he asks them if they want to hear a story.

"Yes!" they both say.

"Let's read *Tacky the Penguin*," Jaime says.

"No, I want the caterpillar," Danny whines.

"No! We read that last time!" Jaime says.

Before they can continue arguing Dad steps in. "Cut it out you guys; we'll read them both. We read *The Hungry Caterpillar* last time, right? So let's start with Tacky, and then we'll read the caterpillar story, OK?"

The boys seem satisfied with this. They go back to the living room and sit on either side of their father as he begins to read the story of a funny penguin named Tacky. The boys listen intently, sometimes asking questions about something that catches their interest in the pictures. Their father answers; sometimes he says he doesn't know. Danny has apparently forgotten he wanted the caterpillar story; he too is engrossed and recites the rhyming lines and claps the beat as his father reads them. They finish Tacky and then read *The Very Hungry Caterpillar*.

"OK, guys, I've got some stuff to do, then I'm going to start making dinner before Mom comes home. You can play here or in your room. I don't want to hear any fighting, OK?" Dad goes to the kitchen, gets a stack of bills and his checkbook from the drawer, and sits at the table to write checks.

Jaime stays in the living room and plays with his blocks and dinosaurs.

Danny follows Dad into the kitchen. "I want to write!" he says.

"You want to write, too?"

"Yeah," Danny says.

Dad gets a blank piece of paper and a not-too-sharp pencil and puts it next to him. "OK, sit here and write with me."

Danny climbs on a chair and takes up the pencil. He begins to write, intently, and makes a series of squiggles:

"Hey, buddy, that's pretty good," Dad says. "What did you write?"

Danny uses the eraser end of the pencil as a pointer and sweeps slowly across the marks he has made. "Daaa....nnnn....yyy," he says, slowly and deliberately. Danny had seen his brother, who was learning to write his name, do the same thing many times.

"How do you write Daddy?" Danny asks.

His father writes it for him and then continues writing checks.

Danny writes a little longer and then goes to join his brother in the living room, who by this time has tired of blocks and dinosaurs and is looking at a big book of nursery rhymes from around the world. He has heard some of these so many times he has memorized them and is reciting them quietly to himself as he points with his finger in the general vicinity of the words he is saying. Danny listens.

Jaime, suddenly aware of his audience, holds the book up, as his kindergarten teacher does, and "reads" to his younger brother.

Danny listens for a few minutes, then says, "I want to read!"

Jaime, a little impatient, says, "Danny, you can't read yet. Look, this is an A, this is an M . . ." and he points to letters that he can recognize on the page.

Danny listens and watches. He starts to make another plea for a turn to read when they hear the key in the latch.

"Mom's home!" Jaime says. He drops the book, and both boys go running to the front entrance.

In the next few hours, the family will have dinner, talk about how the day went, and then Dad will leave for work. Mom will clean up the dinner dishes, play with the boys, and give them a bath.

Finally, just before bed time, they climb into Jaime's bed and Mom tells the boys to choose a book to read for a bedtime story. The boys again argue over what book she will read, and each boy takes a different one from the shelf they have in their room.

"I know," Mom says, "Let's finish *Frog and Toad*, since we've got to take it back to the library tomorrow."

"Yeah!" both boys say almost in unison, and they run to the living room to get one of the library books.

"Hey, don't run!" Mom calls out. But it's too late; they're already in the living room arguing over who is going to take the book to Mom.

Snow and Tabors (1996) describe four mechanisms of inter-generational transfer of literacy: (1) simple and direct transfer, (2) participation in literacy practice, (3) enjoyment and engagement, and (4) linguistic and cognitive mechanisms. Simple transfer includes activities such as storybook reading and participation in writing shopping lists. Parents reading to and with children—called dyadic book reading—has been widely studied (e.g., Chomsky, 1972; Laosa, 1982; Anderson et al., 1985; Teale and Sulzby, 1986); it has been identified as a source of knowledge about print (Clay, 1979), about letters (Burgess, 1982), and about the characteristics of written language (Feitelson and Goldstein, 1986; Purcell-Gates, 1988). Print-rich environments—which include the presence of such items as magnetic refrigerator letters, posters, writing materials for making lists and memoranda, and newspapers and books in the home, as well as parent-child attention to environmental print—have been linked to children's acquisition of an awareness of print (Goodman, 1986; Harste et al., 1984).

Literacy practice involves children learning the functional uses of literacy as they engage in a variety of purposeful literacy acts in the everyday life of the family. Key to this means of literacy learning is parents' modeling of literacy as useful in solving problems and the establishment of social literacy practices in which children can participate as a functional and important part of their lives. Children learn from parents how to use literacy to engage in problem-solving activities (Goodman, 1986). Edwards (1995) has demonstrated the effectiveness of parent coaching in holding children's attention, asking questions, interacting with text-relevant comments, and providing feedback to their children. Those who view literacy as social practice argue that children learn the purposes of literacy in the family setting, although they may differ from family to family (Leichter, 1974; Taylor and Dorsey-Gaines, 1988).

Enjoyment and engagement are another way that parents transfer literacy skills to their children. Enthusiasm about literacy activities is suggested by many researchers as a route to development of the child's active engagement in literacy tasks (Snow and Tabors, 1996; Baker et al., 1995). Activities such as family storybook reading promote positive feelings about books and literacy (Taylor and

Strickland, 1986). Lancy and Bergin (1992) found that children who are more fluent and positive about reading came from parent-child pairs who viewed reading as fun, kept stories moving with a "semantic" rather than a strict "decoding" orientation, and encouraged questions and humor while reading. Children who learn from their parents that literacy is a source of enjoyment may be more motivated to persist in their efforts to learn to read despite difficulties they may encounter during the early years. Pretend reading sessions, attempting to identify words and letters on t-shirts and cereal boxes, and play with educational toys were reported by parents as important activities in which their children engaged with print. Baker et al. (1995:245) note that "Parents' descriptions of their children's early efforts to engage in literacy activities often reflected amusement but also suggest awareness of the value of such behaviors."

Finally, parents help children to develop oral language precursors to literacy by means of linguistic and cognitive mechanisms. Parents in the Baker et al. (1995) study reported that their children enjoyed singing songs heard on the radio or television and chanting nursery rhymes and other rhyming games. Heath (1983) reported that the children of low-income families are often exposed to elaborate narratives in the course of their everyday lives. She suggested that this experience nurtures a high level of familiarity with the structural organization of stories. Mealtime conversation also provides an opportunity for children to acquire knowledge about narratives when family members recount the day's activities, thus giving children an experience that is of well-documented value in learning about language and communication (Snow and Tabors, 1993).

Teaching Parents to Teach Children

Parent-oriented prevention and early intervention services provide alternatives for improving outcomes in language and literacy development. These programs are for parents of young children, whether or not the children receive early childhood center-based services. In general, the services include regularly scheduled home visits by a parent educator. The curriculum used includes information on child development, guidance in fostering a child's development, and school readiness. Access to resource materials and developmental and sensory screening is often provided.

Parents as Teachers is one such program for parents beginning in the third trimester of pregnancy and continuing until the children are 3 years old (National Diffusion Network, 1996). At age 3, children, in the program performed significantly better than comparison children on tests of cognition and language. Their parents demonstrated more knowledge of the content in the program curriculum. At follow-up in first grade, program children scored significantly better than the comparison group on standardized tests of reading ability. At grade 1, parents who participated in the program were found to be significantly more involved in their children's school experience than were comparison-group parents.

Another program, the Home Instruction Program for Preschool Youngsters (HIPPY), is a home-based instruction program in which parents serve as the child's first teacher. The program provides children with school readiness skills and makes reading one of many activities parents and children do together. In examining four parent education models that included HIPPY, researchers found that they all included effective components addressing cultural awareness, interagency collaboration, and the development of close ties between home and school (Baker and Piotrkowski, 1996). Weaknesses in the programs included lack of theoretical support, insecure funding, and a lack of updated and appropriate curricula.

Although the programs described above assess language or literacy outcomes, their focus is not specific to language and literacy. A number of programs do target language and literacy. A training program on dialogic reading, developed by Whitehurst et al. (1994), in essence reverses the roles between adult and child. When most adults share a book with a preschooler, they read and the child listens. In dialogic reading, the adult helps the child become the teller of the story. Small-group dialogic reading took place in the classroom (e.g., four children to one adult, three to five times per week), and one-on-one dialogic reading took place at home with the same books used in the classroom. The fundamental reading technique is a short interaction between a child and the adult. The adult prompts the child to say something about the book, evaluates the child's response, expands the child's response by rephrasing and adding information to it, and repeats the prompt-evaluate sequence to make sure that the child has learned from the expansion.

Compared with a control group of children not participating in the program at school and at home, children who participated made significant gains in their development of language skills and concepts of print. In addition, parents' participation in the at-home component of the program strongly affected the degree to which individual children profited from the program. Follow-up testing indicated that the program intervention, which took place in preschool, persisted through the end of kindergarten. The program primarily affects language, and no effects were seen on first- and second-grade reading achievement (Whitehurst, 1997). Thorough follow-up testing has not taken place beyond the second grade.

Another researcher studied literacy-specific intervention with parents whose children attended a public school Head Start program (Neuman et al., 1995). Books were provided to families, and parents were taught to engage in storybook reading strategies that enhanced interaction with the child and to extend the reading to include precursors to reading. One part of the intervention included parent groups, and the other part involved parents reading the books to their children. Parents' reading sessions with children were audiotaped so that the children could listen to their parents reading to them on the tape. Results indicated that the storybook reading became more interactive, with children contributing at increasing levels. Children's concept of print scores and receptive language scores increased compared with children who did not receive the intervention.

Family Literacy Programs

Family literacy programs seek to enhance literacy within families. In contrast, an intergenerational literacy program fuses adult literacy with preschool programs to enhance the literacy growth of adults and children who may be unrelated (Daisey, 1991).

The impetus for family-based programs is broad, ranging from (a) research on the positive influence that family literacy experiences can have on subsequent literacy achievement in school (Schickedanz, 1981; Snow and Goldfield, 1983; Teale and Sulzby, 1986), (b) the relationships between parents' expectations and attitudes regarding educational attainment and children's achievement (Fingeret, 1990), and (c) the widely held belief that it is difficult for a classroom or school to make up for the lack of literacy activities in the family. A review of family-based literacy projects quickly reveals the complexities inherent in attempting to describe, much less evaluate, these programs. The variations among them are enormous; in fact, a hallmark of a successful program is that it is tailored to the needs of the specific population it serves.

An example of a family-based literacy program is the Even Start Family Literacy Program, which was established in 1989 with the goal of integrating early childhood education and adult education for parents into a unified program. The program was evaluated over a period of several years in the mid-1990s by means of a large-scale national survey called the National Evaluation Information System and an in-depth study that provided longitudinal information on a few programs through randomized experimental designs. Evaluators examined short-term effects on children, parents, and families. Five of the measures used related to children's reading ability. The Even Start family literacy program had the greatest impact on availability of reading materials in the home, parents' expectations of their children's success in school, and skills related to children's readiness for school, although researchers evaluating the program cautioned that it is difficult to attribute the positive effects to the program alone.

In a review of the literature, as well as firsthand studies of a sample of 11 Even Start[1] family literacy projects, researchers note

---

[1] Even Start refers to legislation that was passed in 1988, appropriating funds to initiate, continue, and evaluate family literacy projects. A total of 75 grants were awarded by the U.S. Department of Education in 1989 to local education agencies, which, in hand with Head-Start, Adult-Basic-Education, and other community based programs, were to provide intergenerational literacy experiences.

four features critical to the success of these programs (DeBruin-Parecki et al., 1997). The first relates to steps taken to ensure participation, which range from the provision of child care and transportation, to addressing emotional barriers such as fear of school and low self-esteem, to recognizing, respecting, and incorporating cultural and familial differences. A second critical feature is the use of a curriculum that is both meaningful and useful—that includes, for example, English-language instruction, workplace preparation, and modeling and coaching of parent-child literacy activities. The third critical feature is the participation of a stable and capable staff who bring diverse expertise to this work. The final critical feature is the necessary funding to ensure that these programs can be sustained over time.

A research synthesis on family literacy programs notes that "documented research consistently supports the finding that participants in family literacy programs are benefited by increased positive literacy interactions in the home between parent and child as a correlate of their participation" (Tracey, 1994). Projects that rely solely on the family to provide intervention for their young children, not working in conjunction with center-based programs, have had only moderate success; the most effective intervention, taking place during infancy, was a well-designed program using professionals (Abt Associates, 1995).

PRESCHOOLS

Preschool Classrooms as Language and Literacy Environments

Having examined family literacy programs in which one component is preschool instruction, we now review the research on preschools more generally. Most studies that examine the quality of preschools use broad-gauge tools that include language and literacy as only one small portion of the assessment. Such studies have found that it is precisely on measures of the language environment that preschool programs serving poor children scored in the inadequate range.

A study of children in North Carolina public preschools found that they had lower ratings on language and reasoning measures than for other aspects of the Early Childhood Environment Rating (Bryant et al., 1993). Scores were particularly low for items involving dramatic play (a context for rich language use), cultural awareness, and professional opportunities, suggesting that the children's language development needs are not being served optimally and that mechanisms for improvement are unavailable. A study of 32 Head Start classrooms similarly found the lowest scores for language and reasoning on the same test (Bryant et al., 1993).

Two other studies have also focused on the language environments in preschool classrooms. The Bermuda Day Care Study showed that quality of conversation in the classroom and amount of one-on-one or small-group interactions that children engaged in were highly related to language measures (Phillips et al., 1987). Also, for low-income children at age 4, the quality of group book reading experiences was found to be correlated with kindergarten language and literacy measures (Dickinson and Smith, 1994). Cognitively challenging conversation and the use of a wide vocabulary by teachers were correlated with the children's subsequent language and literacy development (Dickinson et al., 1993).

The quality of adult-child discourse is important, as is the amount of such interaction. One study found that the amount of cognitively challenging talk that children experience is correlated with the amount of time they talk with adults (Smith and Dickinson, 1994). Another study also found an association between conversational partner and topic (Michell and Stenning, 1983). Given the importance of adult-child interaction, it is disturbing that some children may rarely interact with a preschool teacher, receiving little or no individualized attention (Kontos and Wilcox-Herzog, 1997; Layzer et al., 1993). Modest enhancements of the quality of classroom experiences show positive effects on children's language development and preliteracy skills (Whitehurst et al., 1994).

Finally, Neuman (1996) studied the literacy environment in child care programs. Day care providers were targeted because of their role in providing care for infants, toddlers, and preschoolers; in many situations, the language and literacy needs of these children are not the caretakers' primary concern. Traditional caretaking, such as keeping children safe, fed, and clean, are often the main focus. Yet many of these children are in special need of early language stimulation and literacy learning.

Caretakers were given access to books and training on techniques for (a) book selection for children of different ages, (b) reading aloud, and (c) extending the impact of books. The program was evaluated with a random sample of 400 3- and 4-year-olds who received the intervention, as well as 100 children in a comparison group. Results showed that literacy interaction increased in the intervention classrooms; literacy interactions averaged five per hour before the intervention and increased to 10 per hour after the intervention. Before the intervention, classrooms had few book centers for children; after the intervention, 93 percent of the classrooms had such centers. Children with caretakers who received the intervention performed significantly better on concepts of print (Clay, 1979), narrative competence (Purcell-Gates and Dahl, 1991), concepts of writing (Purcell-Gates, 1996), and letter names (Clay, 1979) than did children in the comparison group. At follow-up in kindergarten, the children were examined on concepts of print (Clay, 1979), receptive vocabulary (Dunn and Dunn, 1981), concepts of writing (Purcell-Gates, 1996), letter names (Clay, 1979), and two phonemic awareness measures based on children's rhyming and alliteration capacity (Maclean et al., 1987). Of these measures, children in the reading-aloud group performed significantly better on letter names, phonemic awareness, and concepts of writing.

Preschool Can Make a Difference

The number of months that children spend in preschool has been found to be related to achievement test scores in second grade, behavior problems in third grade, and school retention in kindergarten through third grade (Pianta and McCoy, 1997). Children with more preschool experience had higher achievement scores and fewer behavior problems and were less likely to be required to repeat a grade. The National Center for Education Statistics (1995) found that preschool experience was associated with children's literacy and numeracy skills. Our review focuses on preschool programs with outcomes on language development and literacy.

Given the pervasive evidence of differences in language and emergent literacy skills associated with class, culture, and linguistic background, it is heartening that preschool has been shown to benefit children's performance in domains that relate to school success (Haskins, 1989; Lee et al., 1988; McKey et al., 1985). A recent comprehensive review of early childhood programs for children from low-income families concludes that preschool programs can produce large effects on IQ during the early childhood years and sizable persistent effects on achievement, grade retention, special education, high school graduation, and socialization (Barnett, 1995).

Head Start is the most widely known early intervention program for economically disadvantaged children, although state and Title I programs provide services for substantial numbers of children. Head Start programs provide or arrange comprehensive services for children and families, including a "developmental" curriculum, psychological and social services, nutrition and health, and parent involvement and education.

Programs designed for children in poverty, including large-scale public programs, were found to produce immediate effects for reading achievement of about 0.5 standard deviation (White and Casto, 1985; McKey et al., 1985; Ramey et al., 1985). On average, these estimated effects declined over time and were negligible several years after children exited the programs. However, some programs produced sizable gains that persisted into the school years. Although a variety of different approaches produced positive effects, the magnitude of initial effects appears to be roughly related to a program's intensity, breadth, and attention to the involvement of the children's parents (Bryant et al., 1994).

An example of a comprehensive preschool program with a randomized design is the Abecedarian Project (Campbell and Ramey, 1994). Infants in the experimental group received enriched day care that stressed language and cognitive development through age 5. At follow-up testing, the children in the experimental group had statistically significant higher reading achievement from age 8 (grade 3) through age 15 (grade 8).

Helping Preschoolers Develop Phonological Awareness

As reviewed earlier in this volume, phonological awareness plays a crucial role in learning to read, and the development of this meta-phonological ability typically begins by about age 3 and improves gradually over many years. Because the wide differences among kindergartners in this skill are predictive of future reading achievement, researchers have begun to investigate the possibility of reducing those differences by enhancing the development of phonological awareness prior to the start of school. The results to date suggest that this is a promising approach to reducing young children's risk for future reading difficulties.

Is phonological awareness training helpful for improving this ability in 4- to 5-year-old preschoolers who are at risk for reading difficulties? The available evidence suggests that it is. For instance, Brady et al. (1994) studied 42 inner-city children aged 4 to 5 years. At the outset, fewer than half could generate rhymes, and none could segment simple words into phonemes or read any words. The 21 children who received training were closely matched to the 21 who did not on receptive vocabulary, age, and initial phonological abilities. Training took place in small groups for a total of 18 hours over four months, with three 20-minute sessions per week.

Exercises first directed the children's attention to rhyme (e.g., "One, two, three. Come to me: Which two words rhyme?"), segmentation of morphemes and syllables (e.g., "Say a little bit of 'butterfly . . . Can you say 'butterfly' without the 'but'?"), categorization of sounds (e.g., "Which word doesn't belong: mop, top, pop, can?"), and identification of syllables (e.g., "Do you hear 'doe' in 'window'? In 'doughnut'? In 'candy'?"). The next phase was devoted to illustrating phonemic contrasts (e.g., /p/ vs. /b/) through exercises designed to allow the children to experience the relevant articulatory gestures (Lindamood and Lindamood, 1975) and through segmentation and identification games at the phoneme level (e.g., "Say a little bit of 'boat'"; "Can you say 'boat' without the 'lip-popper'?"; "Which word starts with a lip-popper: 'pool' or 'light'?"). Last, the phonemes in two- and three-phoneme words were segmented using a "say it and move it" procedure (Blachman, 1987). On the post-tests, 12 of the 21 controls were still unable to generate any rhymes, and only one could segment any words into phonemes. In contrast, all but one of the trained group could generate rhymes, and six succeeded in full phonemic segmentation. As will be reviewed later, methods such as these have produced increases in phonological awareness and in subsequent reading in samples of unselected kindergartners and first graders (Chapter 6) and beginning readers from at-risk groups (Chapter 7).

Somewhat younger at-risk children have also been shown to benefit from training in phonologically oriented instruction. Dorval et al. (1980) selected 22 4-year-olds from one cohort of the Abecedarian Project (described above): 11 from the experimental group (who received the preschool day care intervention) and 11 (matched on familial risk factors) from the control group in that study. The reading readiness component of that program included individual tutoring in phonological awareness and letter-sound knowledge, in brief sessions (3 to 10 minutes) twice per week over 45 weeks. The training method, based on that of Wallach and Wallach (1979), involved several steps, all of which were completed for a single phoneme/letter before proceeding to the next one to be learned. The first steps involved oral exercises in phonological awareness alone: repeating aloud words beginning with the target phoneme, with extra emphasis on enunciating the first phoneme (e.g., /b/-/b/-ball), choosing which of two pictures begins with the target phoneme, and identifying whether or not a picture begins with that phoneme. Next, the letter corresponding to the target phoneme was introduced by having the child trace, and eventually draw, the letter. Additional steps required the child to match letters to pictures or spoken words on the basis of their beginning sounds, differentiating the target item from two other phoneme/letter items that were previously trained.

On the post-test, for each of five phonemes in turn, five picture pairs were shown successively. The child was asked to name the pictures and then to point to the one that began with the phoneme pronounced by the examiner. For the last two blocks of trials, the child was also given two opportunities to identify the target phoneme. At the end of each block, knowledge of letter-phoneme associations was tested by asking the child to select which of three letters represented the phoneme. On the phoneme recognition items, on which chance guessing would yield a score of approximately 50 percent correct, the average for the trained group far exceeded that of the controls (88 versus 58 percent correct); all but one of the tutored children were at least 78 percent correct, and all but one of the untrained children were less than 70 percent correct. The experimental group also outperformed the controls (62 versus 31 percent) on the letter recognition items (chance level = 33 percent). Finally, because the same training program had previously been used with 6-year-olds, a comparison could be made of the rates of progress during training for different age groups. It appeared that the amount of benefit per hour of tutoring was essentially equivalent for the 4- and 6-year-old high-risk samples, indicating that little would be gained by delaying instruction until school age.

Given that 4- and 5-year-olds, even those from high-risk backgrounds, can successfully be trained in phonological awareness and letter-sound associations, is this sufficient to permit a young child to discover the alphabetic principle and use it to read simple words? This question was pursued in a series of clever experiments by Byrne and Fielding-Barnsley (1989). Their criterion for mastery of the alphabetic principle was success by a child in choosing, say, "mow" rather than "sow" as the pronunciation for the printed word "mow" after the child had been taught to read the words "mat" and "sat." (Only children with no prior knowledge of the relevant letters were included.)

First, transfer was not achieved by children who could readily be trained to differentiate compound words (e.g., bus stop vs. door-stop) or pseudowords (bifsek vs. fotsek), indicating that learned associations at the morphemic/syllabic level do not transfer to the phonemic level. Second, neither was the criterion met by children who were trained to the criterion in segmenting the initial phoneme from the last part (rime) of numerous words beginning with the relevant phonemes (e.g., by asking the child to make a frog puppet talk in its funny way, saying "m . . . at," and "s . . . ad"), indicating that segmental awareness alone is not sufficient for discovery of the alphabetic principle. Third, even when these same children were then trained to identify the first sounds (/m/ and /s/) of numerous words, such that they could correctly say which of two words started with the same sound as "mat" (or as "sat"), transfer did not occur. That is, phonemic awareness was not sufficient for the emergence of the alphabetic principle. Finally, after these children were trained to associate the letter M with /m/ and S with /s/, transfer did occur for the children who had succeeded on the prior tasks. However, even if they mastered the letter-sound associations, children who had not succeeded on the phonological awareness training did not meet the criterion for knowing the alphabetic principle. In short, "neither phonemic awareness nor knowledge of the correspondence between letters and phonemes is sufficient for the emergence of initial insights into the alphabetic principle. But both in combination seem . . . to firmly promote its acquisition in otherwise preliterate children" (Byrne and Fielding-Barnsley, 1989:317).

Subsequent experiments of a similar nature demonstrated that both aspects of phonemic awareness segmentation and identity are usually necessary for successful transfer. That is, before children demonstrated mastery of the alphabetic principle, most needed to know that /m/ is a component of /mat/, that words like /mat/ and /mow/ start with the same component, and that /m/ is symbolized by a particular graphic form.

Taken together, the results of these training studies indicate that phonological awareness can be successfully enhanced through training in young children who are not yet very advanced in metaphonological skill. The same techniques and exercises that have been designed for slightly older children (see Chapter 6) can, with little modification, apparently be used with children at least as young as 4 years, and perhaps even earlier. It is also encouraging that substantial effects have been demonstrated with samples who are at risk for future reading difficulties due to economic disadvantage. To increase school preparedness of these children and those from other at-risk groups, however, it is clear that instruction in phonological awareness ought to be accompanied by training in letters and letter-sound associations also. Children who enter school with these competencies will be better prepared to benefit from formal reading instruction.

Program Quality of Preschools

The overall program quality in a child care setting has been found to be an important determinant of positive effects on language and preliteracy skills (see Barnett et al., 1987, for a review). The evaluation of public preschool programs in North Carolina found evidence that participation in the programs reduced the degree of delay of high-risk children in communicative skills (Bryant et al., 1993). The quality of the preschool program attended was related to children's vocabulary scores at kindergarten, as well as to kindergarten reading scores for boys only. These effects were found even though, in general, the preschool programs evaluated were of generally mediocre quality. The analysis of children in Head Start classes by Bryant et al. (1993) showed that classroom quality was related to child outcomes on measures of school readiness, independent of the quality of children's home environments.

Assessments of programs like CARE (Roberts et al., 1989; Wasik et al., 1990), the Infant Health and Development Program (IHDP, 1990; Brooks-Gunn et al., 1994), the Comprehensive Child Development Program (St. Pierre and Lopez, 1994), and Even Start (St. Pierre et al., 1993) have documented the enhanced value of high-quality classroom-based experiences for children in poverty, with bigger effects from more intensive and higher-quality programs, as well as evidence for positive effects on language development in particular.

How Universal Is the Impact of Preschools?

The evidence that preschool can have a beneficial effect on children's early language and literacy development is heartening, but we need to know whether preschool experiences have similarly positive results for all subgroups of children at risk. Low-income African American and Hispanic children, particularly Spanish-speaking Hispanic children, have similar immediate benefits from preschool experiences as European American children; however, those benefits are not maintained as the low-income African American and Hispanic children progress through the early grades. An analysis of data from the National Longitudinal Survey of Youth shows positive effects of Head Start attendance on European American children's vocabulary scores and a reduction in their grade retention, compared with siblings who did not attend preschool or who attended preschools other than Head Start (Currie and Thomas, 1995). In this analysis, positive effects of Head Start or of other preschool experiences were not found for African American children. Barnett and Camilli (1996), however, have presented a critique of these findings.

Important points to consider are that the African American children may be attending Head Start programs of lower quality, may subsequently attend poor schools, or may have less developed vocabulary to begin with and thus need even more intensive interventions than the European American children. They may benefit less from Head Start classrooms in which standard English is used because they are more comfortable with a dialect of English (African American Vernacular English) that their caregivers are reluctant or unable to use, so that optimal adult-child communication is disrupted. Very little is known about the impact of speaking nonstandard dialects like African American Vernacular English on access to learning in preschool or primary classrooms, a question we address in Chapter 9.

Spanish-speaking children attending English-language preschools also may face special problems. A recent study compared children from Spanish-speaking homes who were in English-medium Head Start classrooms to those in a Spanish-medium pilot classroom and to their English-speaking classmates (Bronson, 1996, as cited in Dickinson and Howard, 1997). The social adjustment of Spanish-speaking children in English-medium classrooms lagged behind that of other children in the same classrooms, whereas that of the children in the Spanish-medium classroom was greatly advanced over both groups. Given the power of preschool children's social development to predict long-range outcomes, including literacy (Cohen et al., 1995), these results are striking.

Of further concern is the risk that Spanish-speaking children will lose Spanish while acquiring English in all-English preschools (Fillmore, 1991). After immigration, the shift to English as a first language from generation to generation is a universal and inevitable process (Pedone, 1981). However, Hispanic families are experiencing a very rapid shift toward English monolingualism among children of immigrant parents, leading to difficulties in communication across generations within households.

Many would argue that Head Start is one factor in this shift. Head Start was initiated before the recent upsurge in immigration, and planning within Head Start has not yet articulated specific policies for language-minority children comparable to those, for example, that guide services to non-English speakers in public elementary schools (SocioTechnical Applications Research, 1996). The same report indicates that English is the language of instruction in most Head Start classrooms. Within the Head Start community of educators and parents, developing readiness for school is often equated with learning English, despite the evidence that a strong basis in a first language promotes school achievement in the second language (Cummins, 1979; Lanauze and Snow, 1989). Research is needed to examine whether high-quality preschool experiences are equally beneficial to Spanish-speaking children when offered in English as when offered in Spanish.

It is clearly the case that young children have an amazing capacity for language learning, including learning second or foreign languages. Having a bilingual capability by learning English as a second language can be seen as an asset for anyone. However, the asset may turn into a risk for young Hispanic children getting ready for reading, if learning a foreign language comes at the expense of building on very early home language development in ways that promote the metalinguistic experiences needed for alphabetic reading. When toddlers are stretching their language capacities, putting together their native language expertise in ways that will promote their future success at reading, learning a second language cannot take the place of learning with one's own first language. Pre-schoolers' experiences with their own language allow, for example, phonemic sensitivity to develop; the child can then experience the alphabetic insight and get the idea needed for learning to read. The undeniable asset of a second language need not be provided at a time or in a way that could create a risk to the child's preparation for reading.

HEALTH FACTORS AND PRIMARY PREVENTION

Performance at any age is the result of two categories of interrelated factors: biological integrity and environmental determinants. Recent research demonstrating the brain's susceptibility and responsiveness to changes in its environment has made the distinction between biological and social influences increasingly complex and reciprocal. It has been shown that developmental capacities can be enhanced by positive environmental stimuli, even in cases of early biological deficiencies (such as exposure to drugs or poor nutrition). For instance, Hawley et al. (1993) found that the single most powerful determinant of child outcomes for children who had been exposed to drugs before birth was the quality of their postnatal environment.

Programs have therefore been developed in hospitals, clinics, and community centers to lower prenatal, perinatal, and postnatal risks for mothers and their infants. These programs provide services such as prenatal care, nutritional supplements for pregnant women and children, hospital-based services, and home visits to enhance natural caregiving. Table 5-1 presents information on a selection of prevention and intervention programs aimed at improving the chances of at-risk infants. By enhancing children's health and developmental status, interventions at this early age are effective in improving their chances for success in learning to read later on.

Because of their regular contact with children during early childhood, pediatricians and other health care and human service professionals have the opportunity to promote reading. At routine visits, they can help guide parents and encourage children's literacy development. In the pediatrician's office or well-baby clinic alone there is a wide range of professionals well versed in observing a child's growth, noting needs, and communicating with caretakers for the child's benefit. In many cases, social service agencies and organizations also have opportunities to assist the child and the family. Often because of a referral from medical or social services, speech and language therapists or professionals in reading clinics become involved with a child's development with respect to reading.

There is a growing shift in medical circles from treatment of a condition after it is identified to prevention and health promotion at very early ages (Green, 1994). Prevention efforts fall into three categories: (1) intervention to ameliorate illness and prevent complications when it is known that the child is in difficulty, (2) identifying probable problems with early screening devices, and (3) anticipatory guidance for all families (Osborn, 1996).

For reading problems, the first category affects a small but important number of children who must be referred to specialists beyond the pediatrician or family practitioner (e.g., medical specialties, speech and language therapists, occupational and physical therapists). The acumen of the pediatrician's diagnosis at the earliest possible time is crucial. For example, the early detection of deafness correlates with higher reading scores among profoundly deaf children, regardless of the onset of deafness (congenital versus after birth) (Padden and Tractenberg, 1996).

For the second category of prevention in pediatric settings, there are screening devices related to reading that have focused more on the child's visual functions, although more recent efforts to assess phonological processing deficits as well are being undertaken (Nelson, 1996). There is also a parent screening device that could allow identification of home factors that are likely to impede literacy development, but it has not been systematically studied for effectiveness (Davis et al., 1991, 1993).

The third category, anticipatory guidance, affects the greatest number of children. The pediatrician can give parents guidelines for dealing with different aspects of growth and development (Green, 1994). The time spent in regular pediatric visits is limited, however, and complete coverage of the suggested topics would require more than an hour. Studies of pediatric visits document that less than a minute is given over to anticipatory guidance (Korsch et al., 1971).

A number of pediatric literacy programs are in place in large cities around the country. A good example is Reach Out and Read (ROR), which was first launched in 1989 in Boston City Hospital by

TABLE 5-1 Examples of Intervention Programs for Infants and Young Children

Age Range of Children Targeted	Description of Intervention	Evaluation Findings
Pre/perinatal	Statewide effort (Massachusetts) to provide prenatal care for high-risk mothers through clinics within health centers, high schools, and other community centers.	The number of infants with one or more risks declined from 37 percent in 1990 to 34 percent in 1994 (National Education Goals Panel, 1996).
Pre/perinatal	Provision of nonintrusive, developmentally appropriate care services to preterm and low-birthweight infants in neonatal intensive care units of hospitals aimed at preventing developmental delays.	Faster development with fewer medical problems (Als et al., 1994).
Infants	Nutritional supplementation for pregnant women, mothers, and children from economically disadvantaged families to ensure adequate diets.	Improved academic performance of children (Pollitt et al., 1993).

Infants	Home visits of mothers of low-birthweight infants to enhance quality of care through provision of emotional and social support to mothers and instruction on child development using a developmentally ordered curriculum.	Children of mothers actively engaged in program developed faster than those of passively engaged mothers. Mothers with inadequate housing, health care, child care and social/emotional support were less likely to become actively engaged (Liaw et al., 1995).
Birth to 5	Preschool and day care centers serve children with special needs in the same environment as other children. Community-based child care arrangements provided for children with chronic otitis media.	Children with chronic otitis media who attended day care during the first three years of life were more often alone, had fewer verbal interactions with peers, and were less attentive to story reading (Feagans and Manlove, 1994).

NOTE: These programs were selected based on the expertise of the committee and on the basis that they had been formally evaluated.

pediatricians and early childhood educators. It has three components:

- waiting room volunteers who model reading aloud and book sharing,
- giving a picture book to children at each visit from six to 60 months of age, and
- reading guidance and modeling by pediatrician at each visit.

This program has since been replicated and disseminated across the country, varying in the nature of the waiting room activities, the actual people hired to read in the waiting room, and the sort of advice given to parents to guide them in reading activities with their children.

In a 1991 evaluation of the program in Boston, 79 parents were interviewed about their children's daily routines and favorite activities. Parents who spontaneously mentioned looking at books in response to either question were categorized as having a literacy orientation. Results of the evaluation indicated that parents who had been given a book at the pediatrician's office were more likely to report a literacy orientation (parents mentioning looking at books, reading books as a favorite activity, going to the library, etc.) Having been exposed to waiting room readers or to guidance by the pediatrician had no association with literacy orientation.

In a report on the effectiveness of pediatric literacy programs, Needlman (1997) presents the results of evaluations of four additional programs: (1) the Providence Prospective Study (N = 100) (High et al., 1996), (2) the Atlanta Replication (N = 124) and Extension Study (N = 47) (Hazzard et al., 1996), (3) the Oakland Calfornia Replication Study (N = 96) (Bethke, 1997), and (4) the Pediatrician-Enhanced Early Learning Study (N = 300) (Needlman, 1997). Each of these programs provides similar core experiences for parents and their young children. The results of the four additional evaluations were similar to the findings of the 1991 study presented above. Additional findings were that the program was not consistently effective for parents with higher education, although it was consistently effective for parents with less education, and that the program did not increase children's scores on the preschool language scale (Needlman, 1997).

EARLY INTERVENTION FOR CHILDREN WITH PHYSICAL AND COGNITIVE IMPAIRMENTS

In our discussion in Chapter 4 of risk factors associated with early reading difficulties, we identified children who are deaf or hearing impaired, who have language impairments, and who have cognitive deficits as needing early intervention that may reduce their risk of reading difficulties. Here we review programs to address their early intervention needs as related to reading outcomes when the children are in the primary grades.

Children with Hearing Impairments

Most deaf children begin kindergarten and first grade with very limited English vocabularies and delayed recognition of syntactic structures in English. Deaf children perform as well as hearing children on nonverbal tasks (Furth, 1966; Rittenhouse, 1979) demonstrating that they have the cognitive abilities to learn and achieve in school. They also have the perceptual skills needed to differentiate letters and can learn a finger-spelled alphabet as early as age 3 1/2 (Quigley, 1969).

While having cognitive capacities for learning, deaf children face a serious obstacle in learning to read because they lack the speech foundation on which reading ordinarily rests. Additionally, limitations in the experience of deaf children reduce their opportunities to acquire vocabulary and to master the full set of linguistic structures that hearing children usually acquire by the age of 6 (Andrews and Mason, 1986). In a longitudinal experimental study of 45 deaf children between 5 and 8 years of age, Andrews and Mason found that deaf children's reading abilities are increased through opportunities to match their internalized manual language to printed word. Because deaf children are unable to develop strategies to "sound out" new words, they naturally bypass the phonological system and move through a "holophrastic" system, matching signs and meanings of whole words to print.

The authors identify a three-stage model of reading development according to which deaf children learn: First, the child learns about printed word symbols and can label pictures with manual signs. At the second stage, the child can recognize words on signs and food labels, can recognize the alphabet using finger spelling, and can read and print a first name. Finally, at the third stage, the child learns to actively break down letters into words and makes significant gains in sight word vocabulary, spelling, and printed knowledge. Parents and preschool teachers can enhance deaf children's communicative and reading ability growth by beginning very early to communicate with these children through finger spelling and manual signing.

Although there is evidence suggesting that highly skilled college deaf readers show speech coding during reading (Hanson et al., 1991), other evidence suggests that deaf children can encode print directly with meaning without using auditory decoding or phonological mediation (Ewoldt and Hammermeister, 1986; Stotsky, 1987). Literacy instructional practices that focus on building subskills, such as phonological awareness, rather than on providing opportunities to derive meaning from text are less effective with deaf children. In a case study of three profoundly deaf preschool children, Williams (1994) found that the children's understanding of written language and uses of literacy were appropriate despite their delayed receptive language development. A recent study (Lillo-Martin et al., 1997) found that improvements on segmentation of sounds of English words were made after phonological training but not after semantic training.

Early identification of hearing-impaired children and early intervention to begin teaching them symbolic language can be paramount for later achievement (Robinshaw, 1994). One model of comprehensive services for these children is the SKI-HI Institute's Project Insite (National Diffusion Network, 1996). This comprehensive program provides screening, audiological, diagnostic, and assessment services and complete home intervention programming for children from birth through age 5 and their families. Audiological services, hearing aid evaluation and loaner system, video units and tapes for total communication, hearing aid molds, psychological services, and transition to educational environments are included. Children with hearing impairments who enroll in this program experience increases in language growth, including auditory, communication language, and vocabulary levels.   A recent evaluation revealed that children who took part in the program experienced the greatest amount of growth and development in the domain of cognition, communication, and language.

Children with Language Impairments

Most children who receive a diagnosis of specific language impairment receive treatment during the preschool years. Understandably, the primary goal of such interventions is to address the oral language difficulties of the child, and their efficacy has been evaluated accordingly (Dattilo and Camarata, 1991; Fey, 1990; Friedman and Friedman, 1980). Because it is now recognized that these children are also at risk for later reading problems, it is important to identify what kinds of early interventions, if any, might also be effective in reducing that risk (Fey et al., 1995a; Kirchner, 1991). To date, the kinds of help that these preschoolers currently receive does not appear to affect longer-term literacy outcomes (Fey et al., 1995b; Yancey, 1988; Huntley et al., 1988), nor does the amount of speech-language therapy a child receives reduce the risk for future reading difficulties (Aram and Nation, 1980; Bishop and Edmundson, 1987; Stark et al., 1984).

As described earlier, successful readers ordinarily acquire a great deal of information about print concepts during the preschool years, and children who begin school knowing less about the nature and purposes of books and reading are less likely to be high achievers in reading. Studies have shown that preschoolers with specific language impairment are less knowledgeable about print and about story structure than are other children of the same age (Bishop and Adams, 1990; Weismer, 1985; Gillam and Johnston, 1985). In one study, this weakness was not found to be associated with the child's exposure to and participation in literacy activities; instead, the children with specific language impairment apparently learned less about print concepts than their age mates with better language skills did (Gillam and Johnston, 1985). Moreover, interventions that produced differences in the quality of parental book reading have had inconsistent effects on oral language abilities for children with specific language impairment and have not examined long-term reading achievement outcomes (Dale et al., 1996; Whitehurst et al., 1989).

Second, children with limited phonological awareness at the time of school entry are at risk for reading failure, and training on the phonological structure of spoken words enhances not only awareness but also reading skills. Not surprisingly, given that metalinguistic skills tend to develop in conjunction with basic language abilities (Chaney, 1992), children with specific language impairment tend to be somewhat behind, on average, in attaining the insight that words are composed of smaller component sounds (Catts, 1991a, 1993). To date, one intervention study has produced impressive short- and long-term gains in phonological awareness by children with specific language impairment, compared with untreated samples of preschoolers with specific language impairment and those with normal language abilities (Warrick et al., 1993). A similar program, provided for somewhat lower-functioning language-impaired children, was less successful (O'Connor et al., 1993).

In sum, although some promising results have been obtained in these early intervention studies, no clear-cut means has yet been established for reducing the high degree of risk associated with specific language impairment.

Children with Cognitive Deficits

Research has shown that special education in early childhood has significant effects on young children with cognitive deficits (Carta et al., 1991; Casto and Mastropieri, 1986; Mallory, 1992). These children have apparently intact physical sensory systems but still exhibit significant delays in learning and developing their capacities to remember, think, coordinate, and solve problems. It is not clear whether particular program features have targeted outcomes for young children and whether there are significant effects on reading achievement.

There has been considerable controversy about how best to structure early interventions for young children. For instance, researchers disagree about the extent to which content learning should be presented directly (typically called a didactic or behavioristic approach), as opposed to embedding content in the child's play or self-directed interests (generally called the developmental or constructivist approach). Some research suggests that better overall achievement results from more developmental approaches (Schweinhart et al., 1986), particularly for infants and toddlers (Mintzer et al., 1992).

One preschool program built on a developmental model that had positive follow-up results in reading achievement for children with cognitive deficits is High/Scope model (see Box 5-2). The High/Scope Perry Preschool program is based on the constructivist educational theories of Jean Piaget and John Dewey (Hohmann and Weikart, 1995). It advocates active learning by providing children with opportunities to act according to their personal initiative and engage in direct key experiences with people, materials, events, and ideas. High/Scope's aims are to foster the development of intrinsic motivation and independent thinking and acting, provide a safe environment for social interaction and learning, and build a sense of community among students and staff through teamwork and cooperative group activities. The curriculum is guided by five components, including active learning (as described above), learning environment, adult-child interaction, daily routine, and assessment.

The preschool space is divided into various "interest areas" (e.g., water play, drawing and painting, pretend play, "reading" and "writing") with a wide assortment of materials made available to the children. A daily routine is followed that includes small-group time, large-group time, outside time, transition times, and the "plan-do-review process"—a three-step process aimed at teaching children to take responsibility and make choices, thereby exercising control over their lives. Adults regularly engage children in conversation, soliciting their responses to experiences, offering encouragement and focusing on their strengths, using a problem-solving approach to conflicts that arise, and generally building authentic relationships with them. Finally, teachers meet to plan and share their observations of

---

BOX 5-2
Essential Features of the High/Scope Program

Structured arranging and equipping of classroom
• Rooms divided into centers (e.g., for dramatic play, art, books, blocks, music). Each has an ample supply and variety of needed items (specifics are listed in curriculum). Materials are stored in the areas where they are used. Space is available for storing and displaying children's work and belongings. Adults familiarize children with the names and contents of the areas. Equipment is changed and added throughout the year.
• Environment accommodates children with disabilities.

Daily routine
• General characteristics (e.g., consistent transitions), planning time, work time, clean-up time, recall time, small-group time, outside time, and circle time.

Planning in a team and teaching methods
• Maintain a comfortable, secure environment.
• Support children's actions and language.
• Help children make choices and decisions.
• Help children solve their own problems and do things for themselves.
• Support active learning, enhance language, develop concepts through experiencing and representing different aspects of classification, seriation, number, spatial relations, and time.

---

students on a daily basis, using the High/Scope Child Observation Record and taking daily anecdotal notes to inform their assessments.

The 58 key experiences or skills included in the High/Scope curriculum are distributed among several domains: creative representations, language and literacy, initiative and social relations, movement, music, classification, serration, number, space, and time. For example, in the category of language and literacy are six key experiences that include talking with others about personally meaningful experiences, describing objects, events and relations, writing in various ways (such as drawing, scribbling, and invented spelling) and reading in various ways (such as reading storybooks, signs, symbols, and one's own writing) (Hohmann and Weikart, 1995:345).

Results from the reading subtest of the California Achievement Test for the High/Scope Perry Preschool study indicate that children in the program consistently scored better than those in the control group. Children in the program also had fewer special education placements for mild mental retardation and, when placed in special education, spent fewer years there than did those not in the program. The standardized effect sizes (and, as a result, patterns of statistical significance) in the Perry Preschool study suggest the possibility that effects on reading grew over time. Follow-up studies comparing experimental group children with randomly assigned peers indicated the persistence of social and educational benefits extending into adulthood (Schweinhart et al., 1985).

Other studies compared cognitively oriented programs and academically oriented programs as a means of intervention for preschool children with cognitive deficits. The effect of program features was examined in a randomized design with children who had mild to moderate disabilities (Dale and Cole, 1988). Direct instruction (Becker et al., 1975; Becker, 1977) is a program with academic skills as content. Distar language is the preschool version and includes an extensive analysis of language skills involved and a particular teaching method. Instruction is systematic, teacher directed, and fast paced, with procedures for error correction and reinforcement. Mediated instruction (Haywood et al., 1992) is a program with cognitive processes as content. It teaches generalizable cognitive strategies, with an emphasis on enhancing motivation to want to learn through systems of task-intrinsic reinforcement. Children are taught to identify problems, monitor their responses, and avoid impulsive, rapid responding.

The preschool interventions (children ages 3 to 5) produced differential results that were consistent with the models of the two different programs. The direct instruction group had significantly higher performance on two tests of language development. The mediated instruction group had significantly higher verbal and memory scores and scores on mean length of utterance derived from language samples.

In follow-up studies, significant differential effects were found on two measures of cognitive ability, favoring the mediated instruction group, but none of the measures of academic ability, including reading ability, showed a significant differential effect. By the second year of follow-up, there were no significant differential effects of the two programs, although the overall benefits of the early intervention appeared to continue, including reading achievement (Cole et al., 1989).

The important finding of this study was that, at the end of the first year in the preschool programs and at follow-up when children were 9 years old, there was an interaction between the treatment and aptitude. Children who showed higher general cognitive ability before the preschool intervention gained more from direct instruction; children who had lower general cognitive ability before the intervention gained more from mediated instruction (Cole et al., 1993). This effect was significant at age 9 in tests of reading comprehension (Mills et al., 1995).

In sum, some promising findings indicate the nature of early intervention for children with cognitive deficits that reduce their high degree of risk for reading difficulties. Even with these interventions, children with cognitive deficiencies remain at risk for reading difficulties and need ongoing intensive interventions.

SUMMARY

Children who arrive at school ready to learn have typically had the opportunity to acquire a good deal of knowledge about language and literacy during their preschool years. Well before formal reading instruction is appropriate, many informal opportunities for learning about literacy are available, to varying degrees, in most American homes and child care settings. Ideally, these opportunities mean that children have acquired some level of awareness of print and of the utility of literacy, that they may have some specific knowledge of letters or frequently encountered words, that they have developed some capacity to play with and analyze the sound system of their native language, and that they are motivated to use literacy. Language development during the preschool years, in particular the development of a rich vocabulary and of some familiarity with the language forms used for communication and books, constitutes another equally important domain of preparation for formal reading instruction.

Primary prevention of reading difficulties during the preschool years involves ensuring that families and group care settings for young children offer the experiences and support that make these language and literacy accomplishments possible. Parents and other caregivers should spend time in one-on-one conversation with young children, read books with them, provide writing materials, support dramatic play that might incorporate literacy activities, demonstrate the uses of literacy, and maintain a joyful, playful atmosphere around literacy activities. For most children, these primary prevention efforts will ensure that they are ready for formal reading instruction.

Some children require more intensive secondary prevention efforts, including children in high-risk groups as well as those who have been identified as having language or cognitive delays or other sorts of impairments that may make literacy learning difficult. During this developmental period, secondary prevention does not look very different from primary prevention, differing primarily in intensity, quantity, and maintenance of the highest possible quality of interactions around language and literacy. Family-focused efforts are often designed to remove impediments to the availability of such support at home, through parent education, job training, and the provision of social services. Excellent preschools can also make a difference for at-risk children; excellent in this case implies providing rich opportunities to learn and to practice language and literacy-related skills in a playful and motivating setting. Substantial research confirms the value of such preschools in preventing or reducing reading difficulties for at-risk children.

6

Instructional Strategies for Kindergarten and the Primary Grades

The mission of public schooling is to offer every child full and equal educational opportunity regardless of the background, education, and income of the child's parents. A most fundamental and important issue facing schools is how to teach reading and writing, particularly in the early grades. Children who struggle in vain with reading in the first grade soon decide that they neither like nor want to read (Juel, 1988). Even if they do not fall into any of the recognized at-risk categories, these children soon are at risk of poor literacy outcomes.

The major prevention strategy for them is excellent instruction. The intervention considered in this chapter is therefore schooling itself; we outline the major literacy goals for kindergarten and the first three primary grades, examining evidence concerning effective methods to attain those goals.

INTRODUCTION

Previous Reviews

The issue of what constitutes optimal reading instruction has generated discussion and debate and the investment of research effort over many decades. This report builds on earlier work, yet our scope limits us only to briefly summarizing earlier efforts. We acknowledge the degree to which our report benefits from this work and draw the reader's attention to the long history of thinking about these topics.

First-Grade Studies

Between 1964 and 1967, the U.S. Office of Education conducted the Cooperative Research Program in First Grade Reading Instruction; this was an early and ambitious effort at large-scale evaluation of instructional approaches. The program, coordinated by Guy L. Bond and Robert Dykstra, included classroom approaches that emphasized systematic phonics instruction, meaningful connected reading, and writing; its results surpassed those of mainstream basal programs. Conceived and conducted prior to much of the psycholinguistic research on the subprocesses and factors involved in reading acquisition, these studies were not submitted to the levels of analysis characteristic of later efforts. Nonetheless, they pointed to a consistent advantage for code-emphasis approaches while indicating that one single simple method was not superior for all children and all teachers.

The Great Debate

Among efforts to identify factors associated with more and less effective beginning reading practices, Jeanne S. Chall's (1967) work, *Learning to Read: The Great Debate*, remains a classic. While producing this work, Chall visited classrooms, interviewed experts, and analyzed programs. Yet it was her review and analysis of the then-available research on instructional practices that yielded the most stunning conclusions. Chall found substantial and consistent advantages for programs that included systematic phonics, as measured by outcomes on word recognition, spelling, vocabulary, and reading comprehension at least through the third grade. Moreover, the advantage of systematic phonics was just as great and perhaps greater for children from lower socioeconomic backgrounds or with low-level abilities entering first grade as it was for better prepared or more privileged children. Chall also noted the need to provide children with the practice in reading that would generate reading fluency and the value of providing challenging reading material in addition to texts that enabled children to practice skills they had acquired.

Chall's conclusions regarding beginning instruction were challenged by people who raised questions about the validity of the research studies available for her review and the difficulty of applying a classification system that attempted to divide programs into code- and meaning-emphasis categories (e.g., Rutherford, 1968). Although Chall did not suggest that her findings be used to endorse systematic phonics approaches, her work has been highly influential in support of those who endorse a heavy emphasis on phonics in beginning reading.

Beginning to Read

In 1990, Marilyn J. Adams published *Beginning to Read: Thinking and Learning About Print.* Like Chall, Adams synthesized available research but also included a review of the literature on the psycholinguistic processes involved in reading. She concluded that direct instruction in phonics, focusing on the orthographic regularities of English, was characteristic of good, effective reading instruction, but she noted the need for practice in reading, for exposure to a lot of reading materials as input to vocabulary learning, and for motivating, interesting reading materials. Evidence from classroom research on the advantages of incorporating a code-oriented approach to early reading instruction was interpreted by Adams in light of evidence from basic research on the cognitive processes involved in reading and evidence concerning the nature of the code itself. Adam's research synthesis was highly convergent with that of Chall, both in confirming the importance of teaching children explicitly about the code of English orthography and in noting that good readers must have access to many experiences with literacy that go beyond the specifics of phonics instruction.

Adams's synthesis was especially useful in drawing together research from across several different subdisciplines of psychology, child development, linguistics, and education. Most importantly, perhaps, her review pointed to the critical importance not just of children's learning but also of their basic early understandings of print and how print works, and, in particular, of the scattered but already converging evidence for the key role of basic phonemic awareness in fostering alphabetic understanding.

Follow Through

Provoked by finding that gains made by Head Start students during preschool tended to dissipate with time, in the early 1970s the federal government sponsored another large study comparing the long-term effects of reading instructional methods. The objective of Project Follow Through was to determine which general educational approaches or models worked best in fostering and maintaining the educational progress of disadvantaged children across the primary school years. By design, the 20 models included in the project contrasted broadly in philosophy and approach and included basic skills models, emphasizing basic academic skills; cognitive-conceptual models, emphasizing process over content learning; and affective models, emphasizing self-esteem, curiosity, and persistence.

Analyses of the data revealed major findings (Stebbins et al., 1977): (1) The effectiveness of each Follow Through model varied substantially from site to site. No model was powerful enough to raise test scores everywhere it was implemented. (2) Models that emphasized basic skills (language, math computation, vocabulary, spelling) succeeded better than others in helping children gain these skills. (3) Models that emphasized basic skills produced better results on tests of self-esteem than did other models, including those specifically aimed at self-esteem. (4) No model was notably more successful than the others in raising scores on cognitive conceptual skills. (5) When models emphasized cognitive areas other than basic skills, children tended to score lower on tests of basic skills than they would have without the program.

The researchers concluded that "most Follow Through interventions produced more negative than positive effects on basic skills test scores" (Stebbins et al., 1977). The only notable exception to this trend was the Direct Instruction Model, which promoted the teaching of skills and concepts essential to reading, arithmetic, and language achievement. It emphasized the systematic teaching of phonemic and language skills and promoted academic engagement. Students who participated during four full years (kindergarten through third grade) in the direct instruction program performed close to or at national norms on measures of reading, math, language, and spelling.

The national Follow Through evaluation study has been criticized for many problems of the type often associated with field research in education and social services, including nonrandom assignment of subjects, unclear definition of treatment, problems of assessing implementation, less than ideal instrumentation, misleading classification of models and outcome measures, inadequate research design, questionable statistical analyses, and the use of methodological and statistical strategies that favored some type of model over others (Stebbins et al., 1977; House et al., 1978). Perhaps because of some of these factors, intersite variation among models was larger than between-model differences (House et al., 1978).

In subsequent analyses, however, much of this variation disappeared when demographic factors were properly considered in the designation of control sites and outcome aggregation (Gersten, 1984), adding confidence to Project Follow Through's positive data on the value of the Direct Instruction Model. Moreover, follow-up studies of students suggested lasting effects of direct instruction. (Recall our discussion of direct instruction and cognitively oriented preschool education models, which have some similar results as those findings on direct instruction in kindergarten through grade 3 and also some contrasting findings.)

Although the Follow Through results suggest very positive effects for the program, it has not been as widely embraced as might be expected. It may be that teachers believe that direct instruction in general is only for teaching factual content to students of low ability and not for promoting problem solving or higher-level thinking (see review by Peterson et al., 1982), although confirmatory evidence is not available.

Other Efforts

The classroom observational research of Stallings et al. (1986) and Soar (1973) described and linked critical features of the Follow Through approach to student outcomes. The work of these researchers played a large role in the various syntheses of research on effective teaching written in the late 1970s and the 1980s, such as those by Brophy and Good (1984) and Rosenshine and Stevens (1986). Classroom observation by Stallings and Soar uncovered the strong correlation between children's academic engaged time and growth in achievement and certain patterns of teacher-student interaction. In addition, it indicated the importance of explicit instruction for enhancing the achievement of disadvantaged students, a conclusion reinforced by subsequent observational research (e.g., Brophy and Evertson, 1978; Good and Grouws, 1975).

Given previous efforts to assess instructional practice, the committee sought to examine current research on reading instruction. The next section describes the criteria used in selecting such studies.

Selection Criteria

Building on the previous work on instruction, the committee examined instructional practices that were supported by convergent evidence. We sought evidence about individual differences in response to treatment. Furthermore, we were interested in studies that assessed both short- and long-term reading outcomes, although long-term outcomes were available for only a few programs. Evaluations of instructional programs in kindergarten classrooms are not numerous, yet inferences about what such programs must cover are tightly constrained by the preschool predictors of literacy success on one side and the first-grade requirements on the other. Moreover, the major instructional tension associated with kindergarten literacy objectives is less about what children should learn than how they can be helped to learn it in an appropriate manner.

Similarly, we know from intense research efforts what first-grade children ought to accomplish in reading, yet intense debate continues on what and how they should be taught. Questions of how to organize and support learning in a way that results in the best possible outcomes for the largest number of children are an urgent educational priority. In view of this and because the research base permits, the section on first grade is principally directed to evaluations and comparisons of instructional programs. Beyond first grade, the relevant issues and goals multiply as the relevant research base recedes. In the dual interest of reviewing what is known and pointing toward key unknowns, our discussion of second- and third-grade issues is taken up goal by goal.

Converging evidence from experimental investigations, correlational studies, nonequivalent control-group studies, and various other quasi-experimental designs and multivariate correlational designs presented in this and other chapters led the committee to focus on particular practices and programs. Many of the classroom investigations presented in this chapter have high external validity—that is, their results are generalizable to the children and settings that we are studying—and are less robust in internal validity (i.e., experimental control of variables) because of the logistical difficulties involved in carrying out such investigations. Hence, there is a need to look for a convergence of results—not just consistency from one method. When convergence is obtained, confidence increases that our conclusions have both internal and external validity.

Among the most important ways to prevent reading difficulties is classroom instruction in literacy activities, which begins in kindergarten.

KINDERGARTEN

The Kindergarten Challenge

A kindergarten classroom typically consists of an adult and 20 to 25 students—a very different scenario from a home or preschool. The management demands of the typical kindergarten classroom necessitate a level of conformity and control of comportment that challenges many entering children, regardless of how accommodating the classroom may be to children's individual natures and needs.

A child can no longer demand the attention or assistance of the attendant adult at will; each must learn how to solicit individual attention and to wait patiently while the teacher is attending to others. To a greater or lesser extent depending on the classroom, every kindergartner must learn to sit quietly, to listen considerately to both the teacher and other students, to communicate cooperatively, to restrain behavior to within acceptable limits, to accomplish tasks both independently and with others, to share resources, to treat others respectfully, and to try to learn and do what she or he is asked to learn and do. Meanwhile, preparing children to learn to read is the top priority on the kindergarten teacher's agenda.

Fostering Literacy in the Kindergarten Classroom

The delicate balance for the kindergarten teacher is thus one of realizing means of promoting literacy learning in ways that are at once developmentally sensitive and appropriately foresighted, in order to ensure that as children leave kindergarten they have the capacities needed to function well in the typical first grade. More specifically, two goals are paramount. The first is to ensure that children leave kindergarten familiar with the structural elements and organization of print. By the end of kindergarten, children should be familiar with the forms and format of books and other print resources and be able to recognize and write most of the alphabet; they should also have some basic phonemic awareness, that is, understanding of the segmentability of spoken words into smaller units. The second major goal of kindergarten is to establish perspectives and attitudes on which learning about and from print depend; it includes motivating children to be literate and making them feel like successful learners. In this section, we provide examples of materials and activities that have been used well toward these ends.

Reading aloud with kindergartners has been broadly advocated. By actively engaging children with different aspects of shared books, read-aloud sessions offer an ideal forum for exploring many dimensions of language and literacy. This is especially important for children who have had little storybook experience outside school (Feitelson et al., 1993; Purcell-Gates et al., 1995). Among the goals of interactive storybook reading are developing children's concepts about print, including terms such as "word" and "letter" (Holdaway, 1979; Snow and Tabors, 1993); building familiarity with the vocabulary of book language (Robbins and Ehri, 1994), as well as its syntax and style (Bus et al., 1995; Feitelson, et al., 1993); and developing children's appreciation of text and their motivation to learn to read themselves.

Effective practices for fostering these goals include encouraging children to ask their own questions about the story; to respond to others' questions; to follow the text with movement, mime, or choral reading; and to notice the forms and functions of print features (words, punctuation, letters, etc.). In addition, children's learning from and about storybooks is enhanced by repeated readings (Martinez et al., 1989). Recall from Chapter 4 that many of the outcomes of reading aloud as measured in kindergarten are significantly associated with reading achievement outcomes in first through third grades.

In recent years, parents and teachers have been increasingly encouraged to share nonfiction as well as fiction with youngsters. To explore the educational impact of these recommendations, Mason et al. (1989) asked several kindergarten teachers to read three different types of selections: storybooks, informational texts, and easy-to-read picture books. They found that, depending on the type of text with which they were working, these teachers spontaneously but consistently and dramatically shifted the focus and nature of the accompanying discussion and surrounding activities. Not only the instructional emphases but also the complexity and nature of the language produced by both the teacher and the students appeared to change distinctively across these types of reading situations.

Before reading the storybook aloud, the teachers initiated discussions about its author, central characters, and concepts; during story reading, they clarified vocabulary and engaged the students in making predictions and explaining motives and events; afterward they asked them to reflect on the meaning and message of the story.

Given the science text, in contrast, teachers engaged the children in activities designed to help them relate the text to their everyday experiences. Socratically probing their responses, teachers led students to predict and explain, to deduce and test causes, and to discern necessary from sufficient conditions. In addition, vocabulary tended to be handled through rather elaborate concept development instead of definition.

Finally, given easy-to-read picture books, discussion was more limited but firmly focused on the print and the words on each page. In short, the potential value of reading different genres with children extends well beyond any properties of the texts themselves. Moreover, the kinds of activities and discussion associated with each genre make distinctive contributions toward developing children's appreciation of the nature, purposes, and processes of reading.

The sheer availability of books has been suggested as an important catalyst for children's literacy development (Gambrell, 1995; Gambrell and Morrow 1996; Krashen, 1996). But the impact of books on children's literacy development depends strongly on how their teachers make use of them. Demonstration of the effects of books, augmented with materials, training, and home involvement to stimulate oral interaction around books, with Spanish-speaking kindergartners can be found in Goldenberg (1994).

A good kindergarten program should also prepare children to read by themselves. Few kindergartners are developmentally ready for real reading on their own. However, a variety of print materials have been especially designed to support early ventures into print. By way of example, we describe three: big books, predictable books, and rebus books.

Big books are nothing more than oversized storybooks. As such, they offer opportunity for sharing the print and illustrations with a whole group of children in the ways that one might share a standard-sized book with just a few (Holdaway, 1979). A common classroom activity with big books, for example, is fingerpoint reading: as the teacher points to the words of a familiar text or refrain in sequence, the children are challenged to recite the words in time. Beyond leading children to internalize the language of a story, fingerpoint reading is useful for developing basic concepts about print, such as directionality. Slightly more advanced children can be led to discover the visual differences between one word and two words or between long words and short words. Repeated words may be hunted down with the goal of establishing them as sight words, and rhyming texts may be well suited to introducing a basic notion of letter-sound correspondences.

Patterned or predictable books, as their name suggests, are composed of text that is at least semirepetitive or predictable. The classic in this category is the story by Bill Martin, Jr., *Brown Bear, Brown Bear, What Do You See?* (1992). The first page of the story vividly depicts a red bird along with a printed answer for the bear, "I see a red bird looking at me." The second page restates the initial question as "Red bird, red bird, what do you see?" and answers with reference to a third animal. Each successive page varies only the name of the creature that is pictured and named. By perusing patterned and predictable books, children learn how to use predictions and picture cues to augment or reinforce the text, even as they develop basic book-handling habits.

In *rebus books*, words or syllables of words that are beyond the children's reading ability are represented in the text itself by little pictures, or rebuses, of their referents. An example of a sentence in a rebus book is presented in Box 6-1. Entry-level rebus books are often designed to build a basic sight repertoire of such short and very frequent function words as "the," "of," "is," and "are." As the child's skill in word recognition progresses, the number of different printed words is increased. Several studies have demonstrated that the use of rebus books at entry levels can measurably ease children's movement into real reading (Biemiller and Siegel, in press; MacKinnon, 1959).

Variations of the *language experience* approach offer yet another way to ease children into reading. The objective of this approach is to impart the understanding that anything that can be said can be

BOX 6-1

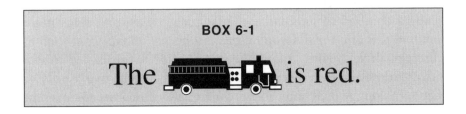

written and vice versa (Allen, 1976). The basic method of the language experience approach thus consists of writing down what children say and then leading them to appreciate that what has been written is what they have said.

The range of opportunities for capturing talk in writing is enormous—from labels or captions on artwork for young children, to illustrated storybooks produced by older ones. The method can be used for cognitively preparing a class activity or, afterward, for summarizing it. The approach provides a natural medium for clarifying such print basics as the idea that individual words are separated by spaces in print and that the end of a line is not always the end of a thought. The children may be led to notice that every time a particular word is written, it is comprised of the same ordered set of letters. From there, the child might be led to notice that "each letter of the alphabet stands for one or more sounds that I make when I talk" (Allen, 1976:54). Research affirms that use of language experience activities in the kindergarten classroom is of general benefit in enhancing reading readiness (Stahl and Miller, 1989).

Play-based instruction, in which children are encouraged to reflect on situations through dramatizations of their own invention, is also appropriate in kindergarten (Galda, 1984; Smilansky, 1968). Settings that provide choice, control, and appropriate levels of challenge appear to facilitate the development of self-regulated, intentional learning (Turner and Paris, 1995). Meanwhile, a major goal of sociodramatic play is to increase oral language use. Children interact and use new language as they plan, negotiate, compose, and carry out the "script" of their play (Crenshaw, 1985; Levy et al., 1992). In addition, children practice verbal and narrative skills that are important to the development of reading comprehension (Gentile and Hoot, 1983).

Researchers have observed that 20- to 30-minute play sessions are necessary for children to create the elaborate scripts that lead to the intentional use of literacy in dramatic play (Christie et al., 1988). Similarly, children write more often when they have ready access to appropriate materials, such as paper, markers, pencils, and stamp pads (Morrow and Rand, 1991; Neuman and Roskos, 1992; Schrader, 1985; Vukelich, 1990). Even so, the teacher's participation and guidance are pivotal in helping children to incorporate literacy materials into their play (Himley, 1986; Isenberg and Jacob, 1983; Morrow and Rand, 1991). For example, one study compared children who played in a print-rich center with or without literacy-related guidance from their teacher (Vukelich, 1994). When later tested on their recognition of print that had been displayed in the play environment, those who had received teacher guidance were better able to recognize the words, even when presented in a list without the graphics and context of the play surround.

Kindergarten teachers can facilitate language and literacy development through play-based literacy instruction if they:

- allow enough time and space for play in the classroom,
- provide the needed material resources,
- develop children's background knowledge for the play setting,
- scaffold the rehearsals of dramatic retellings, and
- become involved in play settings so as to guide the children's attention and learning through modeling and interaction.

Helping Children to Discover the Alphabetic Principle

As discussed in earlier chapters, English is an alphabetic language in which printed letters systematically, but not entirely consistently, represent phonemes (the smallest meaningful phonological elements within spoken words.) In order to grasp this fundamental principle of alphabetic literacy, it is therefore imperative that children first acquire some degree of (a) letter knowledge, including the ability to distinguish and identify the letters of the alphabet, and (b) phonological awareness, an appreciation of the fact that spoken words are made up of smaller units of sound. The training studies of Byrne and Fielding-Barnesley (1989) illustrate dramatically that both letter knowledge and phonological awareness are needed in combination for young children to acquire the alphabetic principle. Several lines of research offer some guidance on how these skills can successfully be promoted through kindergarten activities.

Questions of how much *alphabetic instruction* kindergartners need have been contentious. It seems clear that there is no need to wait until a child knows *all* the letters of the alphabet to start explicit instruction in decoding—knowledge of the sound value of a few consonants and vowels may be enough on which to build phonemic awareness and initial word reading instruction (Fielding-Barnesley, 1997). Yet, until a child can reliably recognize some letters, learning the alphabetic principle and using it to read novel words is precluded.

As reviewed in Chapter 4, children enter school with widely varying degrees of letter knowledge, and how well kindergartners can identify letters is a strong predictor of future achievement in reading. Almost all kindergartners can comfortably learn to recognize and print most of the letters by the end of the year, if they are taught in ways that respond to their developmental needs. Some evidence suggests that an environmental literacy or whole-language orientation in kindergarten is more effective than phonics-oriented instruction, particularly for children with low initial scores on knowledge of literacy conventions, including letter knowledge (Sacks and Mergendoller, 1997), presumably because these children are not yet developmentally prepared to benefit from explicit instruction in letter-sound relationships.

Turning to phonological awareness, there is an extensive research base in support of the effectiveness and practical utility of providing kindergartners with instruction in this skill. As noted in earlier chapters, children begin school with different degrees of insight into the phonological structure of words, with some of them still unaware that words contain smaller speech elements, and other children having already become aware of the existence of syllables, onsets and rimes, and even phonological segments. Research indicates that the latter are very likely to turn out to be successful readers (see Chapter 4) but that the prognosis for entering kindergartners with little or no phonological awareness is less clear. Many can and do begin to attain this sensitivity during the kindergarten year and respond successfully once formal reading initiation begins.

Several studies have documented, furthermore, that young children who receive specific training in phonological awareness are able to learn to read more quickly than children of similar backgrounds who do not receive such training. Lundberg et al. (1988)

provided training in phonological awareness to Danish children before they began formal reading instruction and then measured their achievement at the end of first and second grade. In comparison to children who did not receive the training, the trained group showed stronger word reading skills at the end of second grade (although this difference was not as apparent earlier). Moreover, the benefits were significantly stronger for children whose initial phonological skills were lowest (Lundberg, 1994).

Similar evidence for the effectiveness of training in phonological sensitivity in facilitating early reading acquisition have been obtained in large-scale studies of German (Schneider et al., 1997) and Norwegian (Lie, 1991) beginning readers. Likewise, in Cunningham's (1990) kindergarten sample, post-test reading scores were higher for children who received phonological training than for a comparison group that instead listened to stories and discussed them. In a longitudinal study of Australian youngsters, furthermore, the benefits of phonological awareness training at ages 4 to 5 years have been shown to be maintained through third grade (Byrne and Fielding-Barnsley, 1991, 1995).

These findings are theoretically important in showing the effects of training in phonological awareness *alone*, unaccompanied by instruction in letters or spelling-sound relationships. They tell us that the positive effects in other studies, which have introduced training in phonological awareness in conjunction with lessons about letters and reading, probably did not succeed solely because they included print instruction but rather because the (oral) training in phonological skills also made a contribution to the trained children's superior achievement (e.g., Ball and Blachman, 1991; Cunningham, 1990; Fox and Routh, 1976, 1984; McGuinness et al., 1995; Uhry and Shepherd, 1993). In a similar vein, Scanlon and Vellutino (in press) found that, of all the various foci of language arts instruction observed in the kindergarten classroom, only the proportion of time that was devoted to analyzing the internal structure of spoken and written words reliably predicted differences in reading achievement at the end of first grade. Although the relative contributions of the various components of training cannot be readily estimated, the consistent gains in reading achievement obtained in these studies are of considerable practical significance.

In both classroom-based and experimental interventions to train phonological awareness, the nature of the training has been crafted to be age appropriate and engaging. A variety of games and activities have been designed to direct children's attention to the sounds, rather than just the meanings, of spoken words. These activities can involve, for instance, detecting and producing rhymes and alliterative sequences in songs and speech, identifying objects in the environment whose names begin (or end) with the same sound, clapping to indicate the number of syllables (or phonemes) in a spoken word, and so forth. An English translation of the original Lundberg program has recently been published in the United States (Adams et al., 1998), and other research-tested materials and commercial products (including software) for use in phonological awareness training prior to formal reading instruction are now widely available for kindergarten teachers who wish to strengthen the phonological skills of their students.

Another kindergarten activity that promotes both letter knowledge and phonological awareness is writing. In many kindergarten classrooms, children are encouraged to compose and write independently. Interestingly, in the aforementioned Scanlon and Vellutino (in press) study, writing was the context in which word analysis most often took place, typically as using phonological analysis in the service of "figuring out" the spellings of words. At the earliest stages, writing may consist of scribbling or strings of letter-like forms. If opportunities to write are ample and well complemented by other literacy activities and alphabetic instruction, kindergartners should be using real letters to spell words phonetically before the school year is out.

The practice of encouraging children to spell words as they sound (sometimes called invented or temporary spelling) has been shown to hasten refinement of children's phonemic awareness (Adams, Treiman, and Pressley, in press; Treiman, 1993) and to accelerate their acquisition of conventional spelling when it is taught in first grade and up (Clarke, 1988). Such spellings can be carried out using letter blocks or letter cards, to ease the motor challenge of printing.

Children's independent spellings yield direct evidence of their level of phonological sensitivity and orthographic knowledge, enabling the knowledgeable teacher to tailor instruction and respond to individual difficulties.

Enhancing children's letter knowledge and phonological awareness skills should be a priority goal in the kindergarten classroom. Not only will these abilities be key to the children's success in learning to read in the first grade, but they are also critical to the effectiveness of the prereading activities so important in kindergarten. For example, fingerpoint reading with big books is meant to help children learn to recognize individual words and induce general knowledge about the alphabetic system through repeated, active, and meaning-laden associations of the spoken and printed wording of texts (Holdaway, 1979). Instructional intentions notwithstanding, however, research indicates that children's ability to fingerpoint in phase with recitation depends on their ability to sound the initial consonants of words; it depends, in other words, on prior letter knowledge and phonemic awareness (Ehri and Chun, 1996; Ehri and Sweet, 1991; Morris, 1983, 1992, 1993). Similarly, a major goal of posting meaningful labels and print in play centers and around the classroom is to induce students, by virtue of repeated attention, to learn the letters and words displayed; again, however, children who do not already know some letters tend neither to attend to nor to learn from environmental print (Masonheimer et al., 1984).

Hanson et al. (1987) found positive effects of a kindergarten reading program in which children were given code-oriented instruction and used decodable texts developed by SWRL, the Beginning Reading Program. Small positive effects were found when the children were in their senior year of high school (Hanson and Farrell, 1995). A similar type of program for Spanish-speaking children learning to read in Spanish (Goldenberg, 1994) is presented in Chapter 7.

Activities and materials for supporting appropriate instruction in the kindergarten classroom abound. Examples beyond those already mentioned include books on tape; puppet theater; computer-based reading, writing, and storybook activities; board games; activity sheets; children's magazines; and all manner of individual and group

projects. In large measure, of course, the differences among these
activities and materials are in the strategies chosen to engage the
children's interest and attention. Reanalyzing the various techniques
just reviewed to extract the underlying instructional activities, we
can see that they are relatively few in number:

- oral language activities for fostering growth in receptive and
expressive language and verbal reasoning,
- reading aloud with children to foster their appreciation and
comprehension of text and literary language,
- reading and book exploration by children for developing print
concepts and basic reading knowledge and processes,
- writing activities for developing children's personal appreciation of the communicative dimensions of print and for exercising
printing and spelling abilities,
- thematic activities (e.g., sociodramatic play) for giving children opportunity to integrate and extend their understanding of
stories and new knowledge spaces,
- print-directed activities for establishing children's ability to
recognize and print the letters of the alphabet,
- phonemic analysis activities for developing children's phonological and phonemic awareness, and
- word-directed activities for helping children to acquire a basic sight vocabulary and to understand and appreciate the alphabetic
principle.

Basal Reading Programs in Kindergarten

Basal reading packages provide another view of instructional
priorities for each grade. These commercial packages constitute the
core reading program in many classrooms. They generally include
instructional manuals for teachers, with detailed lesson plans and
activities for the whole school year, and accompanying reading and
lesson materials for students. In addition, the packages typically
include any of a variety of ancillary resources and materials, such as
big books; games, workbooks, and manipulables for students; as-

sessment forms; puppets; pocket charts; wall charts and posters; audiotapes of songs for classroom use; books on tape; etc. To accommodate state adoption and purchasing schedules, basal programs are revised and reissued every two to five years, and publishers' decisions about which objectives to emphasize in each new edition are strongly guided by market research. Because of this, an inventory of basal objectives is a slightly time-lagged profile of modal instructional preferences and practices.

The results of a recent analysis of basal reading programs at the kindergarten level is presented in Table 6-1. The reading curriculum programs analyzed were:

- *The Addison-Wesley Reading Program*, Addison-Wesley;
- *Connections*, Macmillan;
- HBJ Reading Program, *Imagination: An Odyssey Through Language, Impressions, Reading Today and Tomorrow*, Harcourt Bruce Jovanvich;
- *Heath Reading*, D.C. Heath;
- *The Literature Experience*, Houghton Mifflin;
- *Merrill Linguistic Reading Program*, SRA School Group;
- *Open Court Reading and Writing*, Open Court;
- *Reading Mastery*, Science Research Associates;
- *Scott Foresman Reading*, Scott Foresman; and
- *World of Reading*, Silver Burdett and Ginn.

As reported in Table 6-1, six categories of instructional activities were a part of the majority of these programs: reading aloud, oral language, phonemic awareness, letter recognition and phonics, writing, and print awareness. Stein's analysis notes what programs have as a part of their package rather than what teachers actually do with the materials.

The analysis included the major reading curriculum programs on the market in 1993. In the years since Stein's analysis was completed, however, most of the programs have been revised; some have been entirely reconstituted; several have been acquired by other publishers; two have been abandoned; and one new package (by Scho-

TABLE 6-1   Kindergarten Basal Reading Programs

Content Area	Definition	Percentage
Suggestions for reading aloud to students	Any recommendation that the teacher read aloud to the students.	77
Oral language activities	Any activities designed to teach language concepts, vocabulary, and background knowledge, as well as those activities designed to promote listening comprehension.	92
Phonemic awareness activities	Games or activities that focus on words and their phonemic elements, oral segmenting and blending activities, oral syllabication, and rhyming activities. (It should be noted that to discriminate phonemic awareness from decoding strategy instruction, only oral activities are included in this category.)	92
Letter recognition or sound/symbol relationships	Activities that isolate letters and/or sounds.	92
Writing activities	Tracing, copying, printing, and/or composing activities.	100
Print awareness activities	Activities that provide exposure to print in various forms or as represented by different media (e.g., signs, labels, letters in clay or fabric).	77

SOURCE: Based on Stein et al. (1993).

lastic) has joined the ranks of major offerings. The point of including the table, however, is that many of the activities mentioned throughout this kindergarten section are represented in the basal programs. Most but not all of the basal programs accord considerable emphasis to reading aloud, oral language development, and letter-sound fundamentals.

Since recommended activities and emphases are fixed, the instructional progression and materials of any given basal are likely not to match the needs and interests of at least some and possibly all students in a class. Currently, the most popular strategy for accommodating the potential range of student needs and interests is to include in each lesson an ample menu of optional activities. Another widely used tactic is to stretch the effective range of suggested activities by giving students themselves license to choose among activities or to exercise options in the activities' execution. Also, although differing in manner, many programs lay out plans that afford classroom time and means for allowing individuals or small groups to work at their respective instructional levels. Except in the hands of the most competent teachers, each of these strategies carries its own variety of risks to classroom order and instructional coverage. Thus, another approach, although increasingly rare, is to ensure the program's conduct and coverage by adopting the safe assumption that no students know anything that has not been taught and detailing everything to be taught in sequence.

Simmons et al. (1994) recently examined the four best-selling commercial basal reading programs to answer two questions: (1) To what extent have educational publishers incorporated instructional design and pedagogical features supported by current research on beginning reading, in general, and phonological awareness, in particular, in the design of beginning basal reading programs? (2) To what extent are the instructional design and pedagogical features of the beginning basal reading programs likely to accommodate the needs of diverse learners? They have a number of general findings:

1. Phonological awareness activities occur but in limited quantity and scope.

2. The phonological awareness activities of segmenting and blending that are most highly correlated with beginning reading acquisition are simply *not* included in any of the basal reading programs.

3. Strategies for teaching students to manipulate the sounds of language are often not conspicuous and do not appear to provide the necessary scaffolding for students with diverse learning needs.

4. The phonological activities required students to manipulate primarily single-syllable and multisyllable words, instead of phoneme-level phonologic units.

Simmons et al. (1995) argue that these findings are common to the design of all four of the programs analyzed and can be construed as reflecting the architectural or pedagogical framework of mainstream commercial reading programs—basic design features that serve as templates for publishers and developers.

Effective instruction necessarily recognizes that learning builds on prior knowledge. Beyond any collection of compelling objectives and engaging activities, therefore, effective instruction requires a developmental plan that extends across days and weeks of the school year as well as a means for monitoring progress so as to adjust that plan accordingly. Most basal reading programs do provide such a plan, as embodied in its lesson sequence. To the extent that these plans are pedagogically well designed, the basal programs can be seen to offer instructional value that extends beyond the specifics of their activities and materials. To the extent that the programs also provide a rationale for activities, including tips and tools for monitoring student progress, they are of great value for improving student performance in reading (Chall et al., 1990).

The potential benefits of a good basal program would seem especially significant for novice teachers. Research demonstrates that, across fields, experts distinguish themselves from novices not merely in the depth and breadth of their domain-specific knowledge, but also in its organization and integration (see Glaser, 1984), leading to advantages in classroom management, in planning, in clarity of presentation, and in responsiveness to student confusion and questions (Borko and Livingston, 1989; Collins and Stevens, 1982; Leinhardt, 1987; Leinhardt and Greeno, 1986).

There is no reason in principle why existing basal programs should not offer manageable, effective, and classroom-friendly instructional guidance. Do they? Unfortunately, the instructional efficacy of commercial basal programs is rarely evaluated and, at present, we can identify no objective, empirically sound evaluation of major kindergarten offerings. Given the programs' potential for supporting teachers, as well as teachers' widespread use and even dependence on these programs in the classroom, such evaluation should be a priority for public policy.

Conclusion

Kindergarten is offered in nearly every state and is mandatory in many. It thus offers itself as a nearly universal, publicly funded opportunity for providing children the literacy preparation they need. In too many schools, however, that opportunity is not used well. Research consistently points to the importance of ensuring that children enter first grade with the attitudes and knowledge about literacy that will enable them to succeed in learning to read. A strong message of this report is that a priority mission of every school district in the United States should be to provide good kindergarten literacy preparation to all children.

FIRST GRADE

Fostering Reading in the First-Grade Classroom

The primary job of first-grade teachers is to make sure that all of their students become readers. Given the current variability in commitment to kindergarten literacy preparation and the widely varying capacities and needs in any group of first graders, this is a challenge whose importance is exceeded only by its complexity.

First-grade instruction should be designed to provide:

- explicit instruction and practice with sound structures that lead to phonemic awareness;
- familiarity with spelling-sound correspondences and common spelling conventions, and their use in identifying printed words;
- sight recognition of frequent words; and
- independent reading, including reading aloud.

Well-written and engaging texts that include words that children can decipher give them the chance to apply emerging skills with ease and accuracy, thereby teaching themselves new words through their relation to known words. In addition, the instructional program should ensure that children have exposure to the following activities:

• Throughout the early grades, time, materials, and resources should be provided (a) to consolidate independent reading ability through daily reading of texts selected to be of particular interest and beneath the frustration level of individual students and (b) to promote advances in reading through daily assisted or supported reading and rereading of texts that are slightly more difficult in wording or in linguistic, rhetorical, or conceptual structure.

• Beginning in the earliest grades, instruction should promote comprehension by actively building linguistic and conceptual knowledge in a rich variety of domains.

• Throughout the early grades, reading curricula should include explicit instruction on strategies, such as summarizing the main idea, predicting events or information to which the text is leading, drawing inferences, and monitoring for misunderstandings, that are used to comprehend text (either read to the students or that students read themselves).

• Instruction should be designed with the understanding that the use of invented spelling is not in conflict with teaching correct spelling. Beginning writing with invented spelling can be helpful for developing understanding of phoneme identity, phoneme segmentation, and sound-spelling relationships. Conventionally correct spelling should be developed through focused instruction and practice. Primary-grade children should be expected to spell previously studied words and spelling patterns correctly in their final writing products.

As in the case of kindergarten instruction, activities and materials for supporting appropriate instruction in the first-grade classroom abound and include many of the types of materials described earlier. The strategies chosen to engage children's interest and attention in these activities and materials determine their effectiveness. In the sections below we present several types of research on effective first-grade reading instruction. The studies presented are ones that in the committee's judgment best represent the converging evidence from observational studies, from experimental training studies that have taken place in controlled settings, and from studies in classroom settings.

Outstanding Teachers

Outstanding teachers can make a big difference in a child's grasp of reading. Outstanding teachers have been characterized in research studies as effectively and deliberately planning their instruction to meet the diverse needs of children in a number of ways. Techniques include:

* creating a literate environment in which children have access to a variety of reading and writing materials;
* presenting explicit instruction for reading and writing, both in the context of "authentic" and "isolated" practice;
* creating multiple opportunities for sustained reading practice in a variety of formats, such as choral, individual, and partner reading;
* carefully choosing instructional-level text from a variety of materials, with a reliance on literature, big books, and linking reading and writing activities;
* adjusting the mode (grouping) and explicitness of instruction to meet the needs of individual students;
* encouraging self-regulation through cognitive monitoring strategies; and
* "masterful" management of activity, behavior, and resources.

A recent observational and survey study conducted by the National Reading Research Center examined the literacy instruction of 123 outstanding primary teachers (identified by supervisor referrals) in general and special education classes (Pressley et al., 1996). The study suggests that excellent teachers effectively cover the key aspects of literacy (see Box 6-2). Other studies confirm this finding

---

BOX 6-2
High-Quality Teaching: One Classroom

In Ms. Levine's first-grade reading class, each of her students had his or her own basket of books, chosen to match their ability. The bulletin boards offered children word attack strategies. The children's journals were full of writing. The class had only 18 children, 9 of whom have limited English ability and 12 of whom are living in poverty.

For two and a half hours, the children moved at an upbeat and energized pace from one interesting and valuable activity to another. Every time the children started getting restless, it seemed to be time to move to a new activity. The children were:

- reading independently,
- reading in pairs (shoulder to shoulder),
- reading in groups of four,
- spelling, and
- writing and writing some more.

While the children worked individually or in groups by themselves, Ms. Levine taught other children individually or in small groups. She then brought the whole class together to teach a phonics lesson on the *aw* sound in words like dr*aw*ing. Without prompting, children clapped out the sounds in the words. Next she read two books to her students, one fiction and one nonfiction, and talked with them about the content of those books. They reviewed what helped them in understanding the book.

(Korkeamaki and Dreher, 1996; Tyler, 1993). Box 6-3 provides a more detailed example of a good teacher at work with her class on literacy activities.

Although portraits of excellent and highly effective teachers are inspiring, we must recognize that the vast majority of children are taught to read by average rather than exceptional teachers. We need to know more about the typical instruction provided by typical teachers—the sources of knowledge they possess and the range of practice and learning opportunities they provide to their students. We turn in the next section to research carried out with teachers across the full range of abilities.

BOX 6-3
Word Wall and Making Words

Researchers have documented one first-grade teacher's method to meet the diverse literacy needs of her students through whole-class reading instruction (Cunningham and Cunningham, 1992; Cunningham et al., 1991). The daily two-hour language arts period was organized into four distinct half-hour instructional blocks devoted to (1) process writing instruction, (2) basal reading instruction, (3) independent free-choice reading of trade books, and (4) word study instruction.

The word study block is the central focus of this discussion. It consists of two primary activities, *word wall* and *making words.* The word wall serves as a foundation for spelling instruction and practice, using five words selected each week from a basal reading lesson or the children's writing. These words are posted and, as a whole group, the children practice reading and spelling them, with a daily chanting-clapping-writing routine. New words are added weekly, and a subset is practiced daily.

Making words is part of the instruction in phonemic awareness, letter-sound relationships, and spelling patterns. For this activity, each child has a set of 26 letter cards, with corresponding uppercase and lowercase letters printed on either side (vowels in red, consonants in black). The teacher displays one or two vowels and three or more consonants to the whole class. After the children locate the same letters from their own collections, the teacher calls out a word for the children to make. A two-letter word is presented first, with succeeding words using more letters; 12 to 15 additional words are spelled daily in this manner and added to the display.

The highlight of this daily routine is the mystery word—one that requires use of all the selected letters. The teacher does not identify this word; the children are encouraged to discover it on their own. Subsequently, the teacher and the children together explore the new words, sorting by various spelling or phonetic features, such as word families, rhymes, and common vowel and consonant combinations.

The making words activity is an engaging medium for explicit instruction about specific spelling-sound correspondences and the alphabetic principle in general. It also provides opportunities for self-assessment and correction, as each new word is displayed and the children compare their spelling construction with that of the teacher. It supports children who are struggling to recognize letters automatically by limiting the number of letters encountered at once. Meanwhile, the physical manipulation of the letter cards accommodates children who might otherwise have difficulty sustaining their attention in whole-group instruction. Finally, the activity is inherently motivational, since children at all levels of achievement can experience both success and instructional challenge as the lessons proceed from simple to more complex.

Three Approaches to First-Grade Instruction

Three classroom approaches represent three distinct and frequently discussed views on explicitly how to develop beginners' phonics and decoding skills in a print-rich environment:

1. whole language in which the emphasis is on connected text, with alphabetic learning assumed to go on implicitly;
2. embedded phonics in which sound-spelling patterns are systematically embedded in connected text; and
3. direct code, in which letter-sound correspondences and practice take place with various kinds of text.

In Box 6-4, we present brief portraits of these three approaches, which are widely used in first-grade classrooms. These portraits are based on a recent study that evaluated the effects of classroom instruction as practiced by teachers representative of the typical range of ability in a Houston metropolitan area school district (Foorman et al., 1998). In reviewing instructional methods and actual classroom practice, it becomes clear that there is enormous variability in how teachers actually conduct their classes. One whole-language classroom may look nothing like another. Thus, the illustrations of instruction in this box are not assumed to be highly representative but rather possible realizations of the basic approach.

Whole-Language Instruction

As defined in the Foorman study, the principle governing instruction in the classroom using the implicit code or whole-language framework is to give priority in reading and writing activities to the child's construction of meaning. Phonics lessons are conducted opportunistically in the context of meaningful reading and writing. The teacher is conceived as the facilitator rather than the director of learning. Authentic performance-based assessments, such as portfolio entries, are preferred to formal or skill-focused assessments of progress.

BOX 6-4
Three Approaches to First-Grade Instruction

Using Whole-Language Instruction

Ms. A began the language arts block by writing the date on the board and having the children—seated on the floor in front of her—choral read the sentence as she pointed to each word. Then Ms. A pointed to the decorations on the walls, to the trade books visible around the room, and to the big book on the easel and reminded the children that the theme for the week was Thanksgiving.

She asked the children why we celebrate Thanksgiving and, from among the enthusiastic flutter of hands, selected one child, who responded, "To celebrate the good food we eat." The teacher nodded and asked, "And what kind of food do we tend to eat on Thanksgiving?" Again, from among the even more enthusiastic waving of hands, Ms. A selected another child, who proudly announced, "My grandma makes turkey and stuffing." Comments of "Mine too!" and "Pumpkin pie" were offered by other children. Ms. A wrote *turkey* and *pumpkin* on the chalkboard and asked the children to repeat after her as she read these words.

Then she proceeded to introduce the big book, explaining that it was about a Thanksgiving feast. She named the title, author, and illustrator, pointing to each word as she said it. She asked the children to name other books by the same author.

Then Ms. A opened the book and introduced the main character, Pam. She covered up the letters -*am* and asked what the first sound of the girl's name was. A girl in the front row confidently proclaimed "/p/." Ms. A praised this response and proceeded to read the story, pointing to each word.

When Ms. A came to the word *pumpkin*, she pointed to the first letter and asked who remembered which sound that letter made. She ignored hands from the front row and called upon a child in the back who tentatively ventured "/p/?"

Ms. A smiled and announced, "Good job!" Then, underscoring the rest of the word, she pointed to the pictures of pumpkins on the page with her other hand and asked, "Now, what does this word say?" The children chimed in "Pumpkin!" Ms. A continued reading the big book in this manner, periodically drawing their attention to the sounds of initial letters and urging them to use context clues to guess the meaning of words.

Then Ms. A told all but eight children to return to their seats and to draw a picture and/or write about their favorite Thanksgiving food. She gathered the eight children around her and passed out individual copies of the book just shared in the big book format. She had the children choral read the story with her, pointing to each word as they read. At the

BOX 6-4   Continued

end of the story she asked the children if they thought Pam had a good Thanksgiving dinner. Then she passed out pieces of paper that had the prompt "I like to eat ___." She read the stem to the children and then asked them to complete the sentence by writing down what they like to eat. If they wanted help with writing a word, she encouraged them to say the word slowly, syllable by syllable, and to write the letters for each sound they heard.

When one child asked how to write "pie," Ms. A modeled [the sounding out] "/p/ /i/" and accepted the child's spelling of *pi* with "That's very good! Why don't you draw a picture of the kind of pie you like to eat for Thanksgiving and we'll add that to your portfolio."

Next Ms. A planned to read a story about the Pilgrims' first Thanksgiving. Then she would have them act out the story, donning the Pilgrim and Native American hats they had cut out yesterday.

Using Embedded Phonics

Ms. B started the language arts block with a morning message, using yesterday's target spelling pattern, *-am*.

She wrote *"Sam will be 15 years young on tuesday"* Then she asked the children to help her edit the message. They changed *young* to *old* and pointed out that Sam will be 7, not 15. With prompting, they agreed to capitalize the *t* in Tuesday and add a period at the end of the sentence.

Ms. B's target spelling pattern for the day was *-ap*. She introduced this pattern through shared reading of a big book. During this shared reading the teacher pointed to each word in the big book as she read the story, occasionally checking the understanding of the 22 children seated cross-legged in front of her by asking a question about the story. When she came to a word containing the target pattern, *tap*, she stopped reading the story, wrote *tap* on the blackboard and asked the children what word family *tap* belonged to. Then Ms. B asked what other words belonged to the *-ap* word family. Hands shot up in the front row with suggestions of *map*, *rap*, and *slap*. She asked the children to spell these words to her as she wrote them on the board. The children had trouble with the *l* in *slap*, so Ms. B had the children stretch out the sounds so that the letter /l/ was apparent.

After writing these words on the blackboard, Ms. B sent all but eight of the students to their seats. A strip of construction paper and a pile of alphabet letters from a bag of cereal were placed at each seat. Students were instructed to glue the letters *-ap* onto the construction paper and make new words by adding letters to the front. One student made *pay*

continued on next page

BOX 6-4 Continued

and was not corrected because the teacher was busy working with the group of eight. When students were finished with this seat work, they were told to read independently a book of their choice.

Ms. B worked with the group of eight by writing yesterday's spelling pattern, -*am*, on a slate board. She elicited words with this pattern in it—*clam, slam, ram*—and wrote them down. She checked their understanding of *ram* by asking a student to use it in a sentence. Then she passed out copies of a book to each child that had the word family in it. The children were familiar with the story and read along with the teacher in choral reading. When they had finished, she gave them each a laminated tag board mat and laminated letters. She asked them to write some words with the -*am* pattern while she listened to one of the children read the story. As he read, Ms. B took a running record of his reading miscues, prompting him to use context cues to guess the meaning of unknown words. Finally, Ms. B introduced a new book to the children that contained the spelling pattern of the day, -*ap*. She previewed each page, eliciting prior knowledge from the students by asking them to expand on their interpretations of illustrations. Then she put the book in a plastic bag for each child to take home and practice reading with a parent.

With 30 minutes left in the language arts block, Ms. B began a process writing workshop on Thanksgiving activities. Students brainstormed about Thanksgiving activities while the teacher wrote down sentences that expressed their ideas. If previously taught spelling patterns appeared, she pointed that out. Once the brainstorming was complete, students wrote about their favorite Thanksgiving activity.

Using Direct Code Instruction

Ms. C started the language arts block by having the children sit crosslegged in front of her and playing a game that practiced discriminating the previously taught consonants *m* and *h*. After writing these letters on opposite sides of the chalkboard and asking the children to say their sounds, Ms. C explained that she would say words that would have either the /m/ or the /h/ sound at the beginning and that they should point to the corresponding letter on the board when they heard its sound.

Then Ms. C introduced an oral blending activity by explaining that she would tell them a story and might need their help blending some of the words. She started out: "The old brown frog sat in the /s/ /u/ /n/. Where did the frog sit?" After finishing the story, Ms. C brought out the children's favorite puppet, Emmett, and said that they were going to play the game they'd played the day before where the children corrected the puppet when he left out a sound. For example, Ms. C would say "loud" and

INSTRUCTIONAL STRATEGIES203

BOX 6-4   Continued

Emmett would reply "lou!" The children eagerly chimed in: "No, loud! /d/, /d/, loud!"

The phonics part of the lesson consisted of introducing /p/ spelled *p*. Ms. C turned over the Sound/Spelling Card 16, Popcorn, posted above the blackboard with all the other cards. To introduce the /p/ sound and its spelling, Ms. C read the popcorn story, starting with: "Ping and Pong like to pop popcorn. As it cooks, it makes this sound: /p/ /p/ /p/ /p/ /p/ /p/ /p/." In subsequent stanzas, the children joined in, making the /p/ sound very fast. Then Ms. C wrote *p* on the blackboard and asked the children to trace the letter *p* on the rug. After that, she taught them how to hold up a fist and burst open their fingers like a kernel of corn popping whenever (giving her a way to see which children were and were not catching on) she pronounced a word beginning with the /p/ sound (e.g., choosing among the set: popcorn, chair, peanut, pumpkin) and, later, ending with the /p/ sound (e.g., top, dog, snoop). Then she asked the children to suggest some words that begin with /p/. When one child suggested "pumpkin pie," Ms. C nodded and asked how many children had had pumpkin pie for Thanksgiving dinner last week.

The next activity consisted of blending words and sentences. Ms. C built words at the board spelling by spelling, encouraging the children to say each sound with her (/p/ /a/, /pa/ /m/, Pam), then to reread it with a natural intonation. She checked their knowledge of capitalization by asking why *Pam* begins with a capital letter. Then she wrote "I am Pam" on the board, underlining *I* because it was an "outlaw" word that they would not be sounding out.

Then Ms. C read a rhyming story that she had written on chart paper resting on an easel. First, she read the title "Dan the Man and His Fat Cat," and then read the story while pointing to each word. The children were able to chime in because of the predictable rhyme patterns. After finishing the story, Ms. C asked if any children had a cat at home and, if so, did their cat behave like this cat. With about 30 minutes remaining in the language arts block, Ms. C dismissed all but eight children to their seats to work on a worksheet that provided additional practice with /p/ spelled *p* (followed by independent reading in a book of their choice). With the remaining eight children she passed out bags of letter cards, *a, h, m, p,* and *t*, and engaged them in a word-building game to spell *sam, ham, hat,* and *pat*. As the children worked on building words, Ms. C completed an assessment form, noting each child's progress on the skills taught. Later, she shared a big book about animal habitats and diets with the children, developing their vocabulary and language while encouraging them to discuss and wonder about the sometimes strange animal behaviors described and depicted.

Embedded Phonics Instruction

In the classrooms Foorman et al. (1998) examined using embedded phonics, phonics instruction was sequenced according to a list of rhyming word families. At the outset of a phonics lesson, teachers present a word containing the target spelling pattern and, by deleting the word's initial consonant or consonant cluster, direct attention to the spelling and sound of its remainder. By substituting different beginning sounds and spellings, students are led to generalize the pattern to new words. Teachers are also given a list of trade books containing words corresponding to each of the instructed spelling patterns. The spelling patterns are then practiced by the children in context through repeated readings of these books, complemented with writing activities in instruction.

The embedded phonics approach has also been shown to be more effective for disadvantaged students than the whole-language approach in a study conducted by its developers (Hiebert et al., 1992).

Direct Code Instruction

The first phase of direct code instruction focuses on establishing the children's basic knowledge and understandings about how print works through linguistic awareness activities, the use of big books, writing, and language games and rebus activities. The second phase focuses on learning to read and spell words independently. Letter-sound correspondences and spelling conventions are explicitly taught and interactively practiced and extended. Independent reading is introduced through a graduated series of books, methodically designed to review/offer practice with the sight words and phonics lessons to date. The purpose is to secure the strategy: if you don't recognize a word, sound it out. In the third phase, the children use anthologies and trade books to develop reading strategies and practice phonics, spelling, and writing.

Comparison

The Foorman study compared the effects of the three types of instruction for 285 children in eight elementary schools in a Houston metropolitan area school district that serves a high proportion of students at risk for reading failure (Foorman et al., 1998). The students were three to eight economically disadvantaged children in each regular education classroom who received services through Title I (the federal school aid program serving poor, underachieving students); the sample was 60 percent African American, 20 percent Hispanic, and 20 percent white. Although both first- and second-grade classrooms were included, the second graders were being taught using the first-grade sequence of instruction because of their low achievement.

There were 53 volunteer teachers: 19 using whole-language instruction, 20 using embedded phonics, and 14 using direct code instruction. Professional development sessions for all teachers were conducted by members of the research staff who had teaching experience and were strong proponents of the approach for which they were responsible. In addition, an "unseen control" group of 13 teachers using whole-language instruction (the district's standard instruction) was trained and supervised by district personnel. Bimonthly monitoring confirmed that classroom teachers in the study generally complied with their assigned instructional approaches. The instructional groups had similar scores on baseline word reading and phonological processing.

Controlling for differences in age, ethnicity, and verbal IQ, the researchers found that children taught via the direct code approach improved in word reading at a faster rate and had higher word recognition skills than children receiving whole-language instruction (either the research-based or the district's standard version). Furthermore, whereas a relatively large percentage of children in the two whole-language groups and the embedded phonics group exhibited no measurable gains in word reading over the school year, the direct instruction group showed growth in word reading that appeared more or less normally distributed.

Despite lower reading performance, children in the research-based whole-language group had more positive attitudes toward reading, a finding consistent with other research (e.g., Stahl et al., 1994). A positive attitude toward reading, although not associated with higher performance in beginning reading, may enable students to sustain an interest in reading through the upper grades. Some decoding skill is likely to be needed before known orthographic rimes are spontaneously used to read unknown words by analogy, so the embedded phonics approach may have positive effects that take longer to be realized. As with any other intervention study, longer-term follow-up with these children is clearly indicated.

The results of this study indicate that early instructional intervention makes a difference for the development and outcomes of reading skills among first- and second-grade children at risk for reading failure. However, not all interventions are equal. The amount of improvement in word-reading skill appears to be associated with the degree of explicitness in the instructional method. Furthermore, children with higher phonological processing scores at the beginning of the year demonstrated greater improvement in word-reading skills in *all* instructional groups. Explicit instruction in the alphabetic principle was more effective with children who began the year doing poorly in phonological processing.

Basal Programs

The analysis of basal reading programs discussed in the section above on kindergarten covered first-grade versions of the programs as well (Stein et al., 1993). The study summarized the practices supported by the basal programs that dominated the first-grade market just a few years ago, analyzing their content in four major areas. Table 6-2 presents these areas, their definitions, and the percentage of the programs that included each area.

A notable aspect of Stein's first-grade analysis is the variability with which major instructional categories are emphasized by the different basal programs. As the table shows, although the programs unanimously support instruction on reading comprehension, few programs emphasize the development of reading fluency, and the extent to which they support oral reading development is unclear. Moreover, the cells with lowest percentages of support center on two categories of instruction: explicit teaching and application of the alphabetic principle and writing. Ironically, these relatively neglected instructional components are among those whose importance is most strongly supported by research. These are the components that have repeatedly been shown to distinguish programs of exceptional instructional efficacy; they also correspond to the abilities that are found to be differentially underdeveloped in students with reading difficulty.

Programs that ignore necessary instructional components tacitly delegate the pedagogical support on which their sales are predicated to the intervention of teachers, tutors, or parents. Even when a program does address key instructional components, it may or may not do so with clarity or effect. In this vein, a particular problem is the currently popular publishing strategy of accommodating the range of student interests and teacher predilections by providing activities to please everyone in each lesson. By making it impossible for teachers to pursue all suggestions, the basal programs make it necessary for teachers to ignore some of them. A good basal program should clearly distinguish key from optional activities.

Basal programs are used in the majority of first-grade classrooms in the United States and thus have substantial influence on both classroom practice and teacher development. In view of this, guidelines and procedures for aligning their instructional goals and methods with research are urgently needed, as are policies for requiring empirical evaluation of their instructional efficacy.

SECOND AND THIRD GRADES

Fostering Independent and Productive Reading

In first grade, the challenge for children is to learn how to read. In fourth grade and up, it is taken for granted that they are capable—independently and productively—of reading to learn. Written language becomes both the primary and the fallback medium through which they are expected to acquire and demonstrate their

TABLE 6-2   Analysis of First-Grade Basal Reading Programs

Content Area	Subcategories with Definitions	Included at High Levels (%)	Included at Minimal Levels (%)
Decoding Instruction			
Sound/symbol relationships: activities that promote the relationship between letters and sounds	Explicit—students saw letters in isolation and are taught their corresponding sounds.	30	20
	Implicit—letters and their sounds are presented within the context of a word.	70	
Phonemic Awareness: games or activities that focus on words and their phonemic elements, oral segmenting and blending activities, oral syllabication, and rhyming activities	It should be noted that, to discriminate phonemic awareness from decoding strategy instruction, only oral activities are included in this category.	60	40
Decoding strategy	Explicit—students are encouraged to read unknown words by examining the individual letters and sounds.	30	10
	Implicit—students are encouraged to read unknown words by making associations with known letters or words.	70	10
	Explicit blending—students encourages to read unknown words by examining the individual letters and sounds and blending them together.	20	10

TABLE 6-2 *Continued*

Content Area	Subcategories with Definitions	Included at High Levels (%)	Included at Minimal Levels (%)
Reading Text			
Text characteristics	Word lists and/or individual sentences	4	0
	Connected text	10	
	Both	100	
Relationship of instruction to text	Observable relationship: activities designed specifically to help students decode the text selection.	100	
	Observable phonics relationship: text clearly written to provide multiple examples of the phonics instruction in the program.	40	
Mode of reading test	Orally		10
	Silently		10
	Both	100	
Includes activities to promote fluency	Activities explicitly labeled as opportunities for students to build reading fluency.	40	10
Reading Comprehension and Writing			
Activities to promote understanding of the text prior to reading		100	
Activities during reading		100	
Activities after reading	Teacher-directed	100	
	Independent	100	

continued on next page

TABLE 6-2   *Continued*

Content Area	Subcategories with Definitions	Included at High Levels (%)	Included at Minimal Levels (%)
Comprehension skill/ strategy training: activities designed to teach students generalizable and strategic skills such as sequencing or discriminating fact from fiction - these activities need not be directly related to a specific text selection		100	

Composing activities—Activities that require students to compose text

	Related to text selection	20	40
	Independent of text selection	10	5
	Both	30	30

SOURCE: Based on Stein et al. (1993).

understanding of school knowledge.   By the time students enter fourth grade, it is therefore imperative that their ability to read be sufficiently well developed that it not impede their capacity to comprehend and that their ability to comprehend—to analyze, critique, abstract, and reflect on text—be adequate to profit from the learning opportunities ahead.

The second and third grades are critical school years for ensuring that all students can make this transition, by building their capacity to comprehend more difficult and more varied texts. At the same time, the curriculum must be designed with due recognition that students' higher-order comprehension can be limited not only by the presence or absence but also by the automaticity of lower-level skills. Higher-order comprehension processes are necessarily thought intensive. They require analytic, evaluative, and reflective access to local and long-term memory. Yet active attention is limited. To the extent that readers must struggle with recognizing the words of a text, they lose track of meaning (Daneman and Tardiff, 1987; Perfetti, 1985).

Word Recognition, Reading Fluency, and Spelling

By the end of third grade, students should possess the skills, habits, and learning strategies needed for fourth grade success. This means not only that students should be reading on grade level but also that they should be demonstrably prepared to discuss, learn about, and write about the ideas and information encountered in their texts. By the end of second grade, students should have been introduced, with guidance, to representative types of text-based learning and performance to come and should be reading at least simple chapter books and other texts of their choice with comfort and understanding. At the beginning of second grade, however, the reading of many children is too laborious and unsure to admit independent reading or understanding of any but the simplest of texts.

At least in early acquisition, reading ability is a bit like foreign language ability: use it or lose it, and the more tenuous the knowledge, the greater the loss. Thus, the well-documented and substantial losses in reading ability that are associated with summer vacation are especially marked for younger and poorer readers (Hayes and Grether, 1983; Alexander and Entwisle, 1996). On the first day of school, second-grade teachers thus typically find themselves faced with two sets of students. A few are reading independently at relatively advanced levels; typically these are students who read well enough at the end of first grade to read on their own during the summer. Many other students seem not to know how to read at all. Most of the latter have simply forgotten what they learned in the first grade, but some failed to learn to read adequately in the first place. As quickly as possible, the second-grade teacher's job is to figure out which group is which and to ensure that all students gain or regain the first-grade accomplishments and move on.

Second-grade basal reading programs generally provide little help toward this end, as they start where they left off at the end of grade one. Given well-structured review, children who have simply forgotten will generally recover quickly. In contrast, for children who fell or sneaked through the cracks in first grade, identification and assistance are urgent. In school lore, second grade is broadly viewed as children's last chance. Those who are not on track by third grade have little chance of ever catching up (Bloom, 1964; Carter, 1984; Shaywitz et al., 1992).

A major task for the second-grade teacher, then, is to ensure that all students understand the nature and utility of the alphabetic principle. To develop the children's phonemic awareness and knowledge of basic letter-sound correspondences, spelling instruction is important. Beginning with short, regular words, such as pot, pat, and pan, the focus of these instructional activities is gradually extended to more complex spelling patterns and words, including long vowel spellings, inflections, and so on.

In later grades, such instruction should extend to spellings *and* meanings of prefixes, suffixes, and word roots: leading children to notice such patterns across many different examples supports learning the target words and helps children transfer spelling patterns and word analysis strategies beyond the lesson, into their own reading and writing (Calfee and Henry, 1986; Henry, 1989). Several guides for spelling instruction (e.g., Bear et al., 1996; Moats, 1995; Moats and Foorman, 1997) based on research on spelling development (e.g., Templeton and Bear, 1992; Treiman, 1993) are available, although no evaluative data on their effectiveness in ordinary classrooms exists.

When readers cannot recognize a word or a spelling pattern and have no one to ask, they have one of two options. They can use context or pictures to guess or finesse its identity, or they can sound it out. Each of these options produces its own patterns of error and dysfluency. Laboratory research with good and poor readers at second grade and beyond has repeatedly demonstrated that, whereas good readers become as fast and accurate at recognizing words without context as with, poor readers as a group remain differentially dependent on context. An overreliance on context is symptomatic that orthographic processing is proceeding neither quickly nor completely enough to do its job.

For readers who are progressing normally, it is often not before the middle of second grade that the ability to read with expressive fluency and comprehension emerges reliably (Chall, 1983; Gates, 1947; Gray, 1937; Ilg and Ames, 1950). Clinical (Harris and Sipay, 1975) evidence and laboratory (Stanovich, 1984) evidence concur that children who can read second-grade texts accurately can read and learn from text with reasonable efficiency and productivity on their own, provided the text level is appropriate. One of the most important questions for second- and third-grade teachers is therefore how best to help children reach this level. Given that the goal is to help children learn to read the words and understand them too, a promising tactic would seem to be to engage them in more connected reading of appropriate text.

It has long been appreciated that a critical factor in considering the learning impact of time spent reading is the difficulty of the text relative to the student's ability. Common terms to describe differences among text are the following:

• The *independent* reading level is the highest level at which a child can read easily and fluently: without assistance, with few errors in word recognition, and with good comprehension and recall.

• The *instructional* level is the highest level at which the child can do satisfactory reading provided that he or she receives preparation and supervision from a teacher: errors in word recognition are not frequent, and comprehension and recall are satisfactory.

• The *frustration* level is the level at which the child's reading skills break down: fluency disappears, errors in word recognition are numerous, comprehension is faulty, recall is sketchy, and signs of emotional tension and discomfort become evident (cited in Harris and Sipay, 1975).

Regardless of a child's reading ability, if too many of the words of a text are problematic, both comprehension and reading growth itself are impeded. As a general rule, it has been suggested that error rates for younger poorer readers should not exceed 1 word in 20 (Clay, 1985; Wixson and Lipson, 1991). If the goal is to increase reading proficiency as quickly as possible, however, this creates a dilemma: whereas children are capable of learning little from text that is beyond their independent level, there is little new for them to learn from text that is beneath their instructional level.

When the goal is to help students conquer any particular text, one widely validated practice is that of asking students to read it several times over (Samuels et al., 1994). The effect of repeated reading practice generalizes to new texts only if the overlap of occurrence of specific words is high between the texts (Faulkner and Levy, 1994; Rashotte and Torgeson, 1985). Researchers using this approach have recently reported some promising, if small sample, results with poor readers in third and fourth grades (Shany and Biemiller, 1995). Instead of using repeated readings of any single passage, the children read from basal reading series that, in the style of the 1960s, were designed to repeat new words across selections. Each child in the experimental condition began at a level in the series that matched her or his own independent reading level. Each was then asked to read successive selections from these books for 30 minutes a day, four times a week, for 16 weeks. Half the children were assisted by a teacher who helped with word recognition as needed; the other half read in tandem with an audiotape machine whose rate was adjustable from 80 to 120 words per minute.

Over the course of the intervention, the children in the teacher-assisted group read five times more words of text than their ability-matched classroom controls; those in the tape-assisted group covered 10 times more words of text than the controls. Both experimental groups made significantly greater gains than controls in speed and comprehension of connected reading.

Comprehension and Fluency

In a more ambitious intervention, Stahl et al. (1997) reorganized the entire reading program in 14 second-grade classrooms in an effort to accelerate reading growth. The schools were in mixed- to lower-income districts. On testing in October of second grade, the children ranged from virtual nonreaders to those who could read comfortably at the fourth-grade level; of the 230 children in all 14 classrooms, 120 were reading at or above grade level. In these classrooms, the teachers introduced each new basal selection by reading it aloud. The discussion following the reading of the selection was complemented with teacher- and student-generated questions and vocabulary work. In addition, the selection was explored more analytically with the help of a variety of organizational frames such as story maps, plot charts, and Venn diagrams. Children in need of extra help were pulled aside for echo reading: each paragraph was read first by the teacher and then by the students. That evening, each student was to read the selection again at home, preferably aloud to a parent.

The next day, students paired up, taking turns reading each page or paragraph to each other. The partner reading routine was pursued for three reasons. First, reading with another was useful in keeping children engaged and on task. Second, the teacher could easily monitor progress and performance by moving around the classroom and listening. Third, following Chall's (1983) recommendation, the researchers sought to increase students' amount of oral reading.

For further reinforcement, a variety of other options were adopted from time to time, such as having each child practice reading one part of the selection for performance; students still having difficulty were asked to reread the selection at least one more time at home. Each selection was also reviewed by completing journals in pairs or as a class. In addition to this work with the basal selections, children were asked to read books of their own choice, both during each school day for 15-20 minutes and at home. In short, the program was set up to promote comprehension growth while encouraging a great deal of reading and rereading for building reading fluency. Responses to the program were strongly positive from both teachers and students.

Oral reading growth was assessed by asking a subsample of 89 students to read aloud both familiar and previously unseen excerpts from their basal reader in November, January, and May. Growth was most pronounced for children who had been reading at or above the primer level at the start of the year, and it was fastest between November and January. Due to ceiling effects, improvement among the children who began the year above the second-grade level could not be measured. The group that started the year below the primer level never caught up; their readings of the basal passages continued to be slow and error prone.

Impact of the intervention was also measured by using Leslie and Caldwell's (1988) *Qualitative Reading Inventory*. This test consists of graded passages for oral reading, each accompanied by comprehension questions. Growth across the school year averaged 1.88 and 1.77 grade levels for the 4 and 10 classrooms that respectively participated in the first and second years of the study. Of the 190 students who started second grade at the primer level or above, only 5 were still unable to read at the second-grade level by spring. For 20 who could not read even the primer on entry, 9 reached or surpassed the second-grade level by spring, and all but one could read at least at the primer level.

Thus, although about 10 percent of the children were still performing below grade level, and although results are measured against expectable gains rather than against the performance of a control group, the outcomes of the study are impressive. It was also longer in duration and broader in scope than most other second-grade reading interventions. In particular, its scope embraced both fluency and comprehension support; children need both.

Comprehension and Word Knowledge

Mature readers construct meaning at two levels. One level works with the words of the text for a literal understanding of what the author has written. However, superior word recognition abilities do not necessarily translate into superior levels of reading achievement (Chall et al., 1990). Productive reading involves, in addition to literal comprehension, being able to answer such questions as: Why am I reading this and how does this information relate to my reasons for so doing? What is the author's point of view, what are her or his underlying assumptions? Do I understand what the author is saying and why? Do I know where the author is headed? Is the text internally consistent? Is it consistent with what I already know or believe? If not, where does it depart and what do I think about the discrepancy? This sort of reflective, purposive understanding goes beyond the literal to the underlying meaning of the text. For purposes of discussion, the development of productive reading comprehension can be considered in terms of three factors: (1) concept and vocabulary development, (2) command of the linguistic structures of the text, and (3) metacognitive or reflective control of comprehension.

Written text places high demands on vocabulary knowledge. Even the words used in children's books are more rare than those used in adult conversations and prime-time television (Hayes and Ahrens, 1988). Learning new concepts and the words that encode them is essential for comprehension development. People's ability to infer or retain new words in general is strongly dependent on their background knowledge of other words and concepts. Even at the youngest ages, the ability to understand and remember the meanings of new words depends quite strongly on how well developed one's vocabulary already is (Robbins and Ehri, 1994).

Can children's word knowledge and reading comprehension be measurably improved through instruction? The answer is yes, according to a meta-analysis of relevant research studies by Stahl and Fairbanks (1986). First, vocabulary instruction generally does result in measurable increase in students' specific word knowledge. Sometimes and to some degree it also results in better performance on global vocabulary measures, such as standardized tests, indicating that the instruction has evidently enhanced the learning of words beyond those directly taught. Second, pooling across studies, vocabulary instruction also appears to produce increases in children's reading comprehension. Again, although these gains are largest where passages contain explicitly taught words, they are also significant given general standardized measures.

Looking across studies, Stahl and Fairbanks (1986) noted differences in the effectiveness of vocabulary instruction as well. Methods providing repeated drill and practice on word definitions resulted in significant improvement with the particular words that had been taught but no reliable effect on reading comprehension scores. In contrast, methods in which children were given both information about the words' definitions and examples of the words' usages in a variety of contexts resulted in the largest gains in both vocabulary and reading comprehension.

An important source of word knowledge is exposure to print and independent reading. As noted above, books introduce children to more rare words than conversation or television does. So educational approaches that encourage children to read more both in school and out should increase their word knowledge (Nagy and Anderson, 1984) and reading comprehension (Anderson et al., 1988). However, several efforts to increase the breadth of children's reading have produced little measurable effect on their reading ability (Carver and Liebert, 1995; see review in Taylor et al., 1990), perhaps because books selected for free reading tend to be at too easy a level for most children (Carver, 1994). Alternately, perhaps children who are doing poorly are less likely to profit from extensive exposure to print than children who are already progressing quite well.

One group of researchers reviewed interactions among print exposure, word knowledge, and comprehension, teasing apart the relations among prior ability and increased reading (Stanovich et al., 1996). They concluded (p. 29): "In short, exposure to print is efficacious regardless of the level of the child's cognitive and comprehension abilities. Even children with limited comprehension skills will build vocabulary and cognitive structures through immersion in literacy activities. An encouraging message for teachers of low-achieving children is implicit here. We often despair of changing 'abilities,' but there is at least one partially malleable habit that will itself develop 'abilities'—reading."

The relation between print exposure and comprehension need not be limited to the child's own reading in school. Cain (1996) studied the home literacy activities of 7- and 8-year-olds whose word reading accuracy was appropriate for their chronological age but who differed in their comprehension ability. She reports the following contrasts: "The children who were skilled comprehenders reported reading books at home more frequently than the less skilled children, and their parents reported that they were more likely to read story books. The skilled comprehenders also reported that they were read to more frequently at home by their parents than the less skilled group and this was confirmed by their parents' responses. ... The skilled children were significantly more likely to read books with their parents than were the less skilled children and also tended to talk about books and stories more frequently than did the less skilled comprehenders." (Cain, 1996:189)

It might be assumed that reading aloud with a child loses its value once children have attained independent accuracy in reading words, but Cain's findings raise the possibility that being read to promotes skilled comprehension at ages 7 and 8, although she points out that no causal link has yet been demonstrated.

Comprehension and Background Knowledge

The breadth and depth of a child's literacy experiences determine not only how many and what kinds of words she or he will encounter but also the background knowledge with which a child can conceptualize the meaning of any new word and the orthographic knowledge that frees that meaning from the printed page. Every opportunity should be taken to extend and enrich children's background knowledge and understanding in every way possible, for the ultimate significance and memorability of any word or text depends on whether children possess the background knowledge and conceptual sophistication to understand its meaning.

A program designed to enhance background knowledge and conceptual sophistication among third graders is Concept Oriented Reading Instruction (CORI). The emphasis of the program is on the comprehension of interesting texts. The program is designed around broad interdisciplinary themes, exploiting real-world experiences, a range of cognitive strategies, and social groupings to promote self-direction. Designed for third graders in high-poverty schools with a history of low achievement, it has been successfully used at both the classroom and the whole-school level. The third-grade students have ranged in reading levels from first to fourth grade, and students with limited English proficiency are mainstreamed and included in the classroom. The program has effectively increased narrative text comprehension, expository text comprehension, and other language arts skills on standardized tests, as well as increasing students' performance on the Maryland School Performance Assessment Program (MSPAP) (Guthrie et al., 1996). Compared to control students, students in the program improved significantly on reading, writing, science, social studies, and language use but not in math, which was not taught in the program. CORI has also been shown to increase the amount and breadth of independent reading and volitional strategies for maintaining engagement in reading activities.

Structures, Processes, and Meta-Processes in Comprehension Instruction

Research on comprehension among young readers has not resolved questions about the nature and separate identity of the difficulties they encounter as they attempt to understand texts. It is difficult to tease apart the effect of stores of word knowledge and background knowledge from the effect of processes (e.g., identifying words quickly and accurately, constructing mental representations to integrate information from the text) and meta-processes (making inferences, monitoring for inconsistencies) (Cornoldi and Oakhill, 1996). Instruction for comprehension, however, generally focuses on understanding complete connected text in situations in which many of the possible difficulties appear bound together and often can be treated as a bundle to good effect.

Many comprehension instruction techniques used in schools today are described as meta-cognitive. A meta-analysis of 20 meta-cognition instruction programs found a substantial mean effect size of .71 (Haller et al., 1988). Instructional programs focusing on self-questioning and identifying text consistencies were found to be most effective. A meta-analysis of 10 studies related to a technique called reciprocal teaching found a median effect size of .88 (Rosenshine and Meister, 1994).

For most active comprehension instruction, whether considered meta-cognitive or not, two pedagogic processes are intermingled: traditional instruction in basic stores of knowledge (the background for the text and for particular words) and instruction in particular comprehension strategies complemented by the active skilled reading of the text by an expert (the teacher) done in such a way that the ordinarily hidden processes of comprehension are displayed (see Kucan and Beck, 1997; Beck and McKeown, 1996). The children have an opportunity to learn from the joint participation (a form of cognitive apprenticeship) as well as from the particulars in the instructional agenda. As Baker (1996) notes, it is an open question whether direct instruction or observational learning provides the greater contribution to student progress.

Reciprocal teaching is a particularly interesting approach to consider in detail both because of its apparent effectiveness and because it illustrates the mixed instructional agenda and pedagogical strategies. Reciprocal teaching provides guided practice in the use of four strategies (predicting, question generating, summarizing, and clarifying) that are designed to enhance children's ability to construct the meaning of text (Palincsar et al., 1993). To engage in reciprocal teaching dialogues, the children and their teacher read a piece of common text. This reading may be done as a read-along, a silent reading, or an oral reading, depending on the decoding abilities of the children and the level of the text. The children and the teacher take turns leading the discussion of segments of the text, using strategies to support their discussion. The ultimate purpose of the discussion, however, is not practice with the strategies but the application of the strategies for the purpose of coming to a shared sense of the meaning of the text at hand. The tenets of reciprocal teaching include (a) meaningful use of comprehension-monitoring and comprehension-fostering strategies; (b) discussion for the purpose of building the meaning of text; (c) the expectation that, when children are first beginning these dialogues, they will need considerable support provided by the teacher's modeling of the use of the strategies and guiding students' participation in the dialogues; (d) the use of text that offers appropriate challenges to the children (i.e., there is content worth discussing in the text and the text is sufficiently accessible to the children); and, finally, (e) the use of text that is thematically related so that children have the opportunity to build their knowledge of a topic or area over time.

Reciprocal teaching was designed as both an intervention to be used with youngsters who were experiencing language-related difficulties and as a means of prevention given the hypothesis that young children should experience reading as a meaningful activity even before they are reading conventionally. It has been investigated principally with children who come from high-poverty areas, children being served in developmental and remedial reading programs, and children identified as having a language or learning disability. Research on reciprocal teaching with young children in first and second grades indicates statistically significant improvement in listening comprehension (which assessed ability to recall information, summarize information, draw inferences from text, and use information to solve a novel problem) and fewer referrals to special education or remedial reading programs. In addition, teachers reported that, as a result of their experiences in reciprocal teaching dialogues, their expectations regarding these children were raised. In other words, children who appeared to have a disability on the basis of their participation in the conventional classroom dynamic appeared quite able in the context of reciprocal teaching dialogues.

Training studies on inferences and comprehension monitoring with 7- and 8-year-olds show that children identified specifically as poor comprehenders profit differentially from certain kinds of instruction. Yuill and Oakhill (1988) compared the effect on skilled and less skilled comprehenders (matched for age and reading accuracy) of a program that lasted for seven 30-minute sessions spread over about two months. The treatment group worked on lexical inferences, question generation, and prediction. One control group read the same texts and answered questions about them in a group discussion format. A second control group read the same texts and practiced rapid word decoding. There appears to have been an interaction between aptitude and treatment. Analyses of post-test results showed that the less skilled comprehenders benefited more from the experimental treatment than did the more skilled, that the less skilled comprehenders derived more benefit from the comprehension training than they did from the rapid decoding condition, but that the more skilled benefited more from the decoding training than from the comprehension training.

Yuill (1996) worked with a similar set of subjects (matched for age and reading accuracy, differing on comprehension ability) to train for the ability to recognize that texts could have more than a single obvious interpretation by using the genre of riddles, which depend on ambiguity and its resolution. The treatment condition focused the children on alternative interpretations in texts by training them to explain the ambiguity in riddles; the control group children also read amusing texts but focused on sublexical awareness activities rather than on meta-comprehension activities. At the end of the two-month period, the experimental treatment group performed significantly better on the post-test in comprehension than the control group did, but there was no significant interaction between skill group and training.

SUMMARY

The nature and quality of classroom literacy instruction are a pivotal force in preventing reading difficulties in young children. Adequate initial reading instruction requires a focus on using reading to obtain meaning from print; understanding the sublexical structure of spoken words; exposing the nature of the orthographic system; practice in the specifics of frequent, regular spelling-sound relationships; and frequent and intensive opportunities to read. Adequate progress in learning to read English beyond the initial level depends on having established a working understanding of how sounds are represented alphabetically, sufficient practice in reading to achieve fluency with different kinds of texts written for different purposes, instruction focused on concept and vocabulary growth, and control over procedures for monitoring comprehension and repairing misunderstandings.

Activities designed to ensure these opportunities to learn include practice in reading (and rereading), writing as a means of word study and for the purpose of communication, invented spelling as a way to explore letter-sound relationships, and spelling instruction to enhance phonemic awareness and letter-sound/sound-letter relationships.

The context of the instruction varied considerably across the interventions considered in this chapter. Although the materials used ranged widely, a significant shared feature was attention to the use of continuous text. The characteristics of the texts used include predictability, the opportunity the text provides to use spelling patterns that have been studied, what Juel (1991) refers to as "phonologically protected" text.

Effective instruction includes artful teaching, a thing that transcends—and often makes up for the limitations of—specific instructional strategies (see Box 6-5). Although in this report we have not incorporated lessons from exceptional teaching practices with the same comprehensiveness as other topics in the research on reading, we acknowledge their importance in conceptualizing effective reading instruction.

Classroom instruction is not the only method of intervention used to prevent reading difficulties. In Chapter 5, we reviewed efforts that can take place in the preschool years. In the next two chapters on prevention and intervention strategies to preventing reading difficulties, we review organization strategies in kindergarten and the primary grades and research on providing extended time in reading-related instruction. In the next chapter, we review institutional responses to the prevention of reading problems.

BOX 6-5
Teaching Children Versus Teaching a Curriculum

Language Arts: You come down solidly advocating that educators need to teach children rather than to teach a curriculum. And you have also stated that the wars between whole language advocates and phonics advocates "are based more on educator identities than on children's needs." Would you talk about that a bit?

Lisa Delpit: I continue to be astounded that folks seem to put themselves into a political and ideological camp and indicate, "I'm going to stay in this camp come hell or high water." I view teaching a little differently. I don't place myself as a teacher in a camp. I see myself as responder to the needs of children. Some children will need to learn explicitly certain strategies or conventions; some children will not need that because they've gotten it through the discourse that they learned in their homes.

In California I saw a black child who was in a class where the kids were supposed to read a piece of literature and then respond to it. The child clearly couldn't read the selection. When asked about the situation, the teacher said, "Oh, he can't read it, but he'll get it in the discussion." Perhaps it's good that he will be able to get it in the discussion, but at the same time nobody is spending time teaching him what he also needs to learn—how to read for himself. So, we can lose track of the fact that children may need different kinds of instruction, depending on their knowledge and background.

Sometimes we have the best intentions but actually end up holding beliefs that result in lower expectations for certain students. We are content that the students are just becoming fluent in writing, so we don't push them to edit their pieces into final products that can be published. We don't do the kind of pushing necessary to get students to achieve at the level that they might be capable of.

SOURCE: An excerpt from "A Conversation with Lisa Delpit" by *Language Arts* (1991:544-545).

7

Organizational Strategies for Kindergarten and the Primary Grades

For most children, good standard classroom instruction using the strategies, materials, and techniques reviewed in Chapter 6 constitutes an adequate measure to ensure the prevention of reading difficulties. For other children in some circumstances, however, good instruction is possible only in the context of broader institutional reform—by which we mean organizational change at the school level. This kind of change may involve modifying classroom and school structure, for instance by reducing class size or restructuring the instructional program of an entire school. For other children, necessary changes may include the hiring of bilingual teachers who can provide initial literacy training in the children's native language. In still other circumstances, instruction may need to be adapted to children's cultural or linguistic characteristics, or it may need to be designed to address the consequences for children's development of living in impoverished neighborhoods.

In this chapter, we address efforts to prevent reading difficulties that involve designing instructional and institutional approaches for groups of children who share developmental or instructional needs. These efforts attempt to ensure access to good instruction for all children, including those who might otherwise not have such access because of socioeconomic disadvantage, inadequate organization of instruction in the schools they attend, limited proficiency in English and in standard English, and cultural differences.

TEACHING READING TO CHILDREN LIVING IN POVERTY

As noted in Chapter 4, social class differences, especially measured in the aggregate, have long been recognized as creating conditions that lead to reading difficulties (Stubbs, 1980), although there is considerable variability within social strata. The conditions causing the reading difficulties are complex, however, and do not rest solely on home experiences (Baker et al., 1995; Delgado-Gaitan, 1990; Goldenberg et al., 1992). Low income level can be accompanied by other factors that place children at risk, for instance, attending a school that has chronic low academic achievement.

Title I of the Elementary and Secondary Education Act of 1965 was the first major federal aid specifically for children from low-income neighborhoods. There were great expectations that Title I would not only help disadvantaged children but indeed also close the large achievement gap between poor children and others. However, the original Title I was actually a funding mechanism rather than a specific program or policy for assisting students at risk; in fact, Congress mandated that all school districts should be eligible for at least some of the Title I funds. Furthermore, because little was known about which compensatory practices or interventions were effective, these federal funds were not used to fundamentally alter the educational opportunities provided to children in poverty (Mosher and Bailey, 1970).

The results of initial evaluations of Title I were quite discouraging, and national studies suggested that there was little evidence that the program had any impact on eligible children, although state and local evaluations provided some evidence of a significant positive impact (Wargo et al., 1972). There were charges that Title I funds were being misspent. Threatened with the loss of funds, states responded by separating further the education of students eligible for these funds by pulling them from their regular classes and putting them into small group settings, with little coordination between the general and remedial educators.

The most rigorous evaluation of Title I in the 1970s, carried out by the System Development Corporation, followed a cohort of 120,000 students for three years. The study determined that, although Title I recipients did better than matched non-Title I students, the children who were most disadvantaged, and therefore the particular focus of Title I funds, were not helped much (Carter, 1984). Despite persistent and pervasive problems with Title I, it was not until 1988 that any major legislative revision occurred that affected the program. When Title I (reauthorized as Chapter I in 1981) was reauthorized as part of the Hawkins-Stafford Elementary and Secondary School Improvement Act, the legislation mandated that the services be linked to the regular school curriculum; that schools in high-poverty areas develop school-wide programs, rather than focusing on individual students; and that curriculum reform efforts stress higher-order thinking skills.

The results of a large-scale national, longitudinal study entitled "Prospects: The Congressionally Mandated Study of Educational Growth and Opportunity" (Puma et al., 1997) again provided discouraging evidence regarding the effectiveness of Title I in addressing the considerable gap between children in high- and low-poverty schools. However, there was an important caveat offered (Puma et al., 1997:vi): "Our inability to discern a compensatory effect of Chapter I is not necessarily an indication of program failure. Limitations of the Prospects study prevented us from observing directly whether Chapter I students would have been worse off (i.e., whether the gap would have widened over time) in the absence of the services they received; in fact, we might expect the gap to grow over time, absent a special intervention. Chapter I may have helped but [it] was too weak an intervention to bring the participating students up to par with their classmates."

Once again, in 1994, Title I was targeted for reform as part of the Improving America's School Act. The current restructured Title I calls for disadvantaged students to learn to the same challenging state standards as all other students through systemic reform consistent with Goals 2000 (McDonnell et al., 1997). The new standards-based Title I programs are just now being developed and implemented.

The rocky history of Title I efforts highlights the challenges associated with the design, implementation, and evaluation of supplementary intervention efforts. From this history we learn the importance of determining the extent to which interventions lead to different educational experiences for children—in terms of their opportunity to learn—and whether these interventions are indeed making an educational difference in the lives of children.

TEACHING READING TO CHILDREN ATTENDING SCHOOLS WITH CHRONICALLY LOW ACADEMIC ACHIEVEMENT

Schools with chronically low academic achievement are those with lower rates of on-task time, less teacher preparation of new material, lower rates of teacher communication of high expectations, fewer instances of positive reinforcement, more classroom interruptions, more discipline problems, and an unfriendly classroom ambiance. We review two major organizational strategies found to be effective in schools with chronically low academic achievement: class size and school restructuring.

Class Size

The abilities and opportunities of teachers to closely observe and facilitate the literacy learning of diverse groups of children are certainly influenced by the numbers of children they deal with. Although the federal government reports steady decreases in the average size of elementary school classrooms, schools in poor urban areas continue to show higher class sizes than schools in all other areas (NCES, 1994).

The relationship between class size and achievement has been of interest for many years (Smith and Glass, 1980). However, several recent developments have renewed interest in this issue, namely, systematic, state-sponsored studies of reduced class sizes in the early grades (such as those conducted in Tennessee) and the use of Title I funds to decrease the student-to-teacher ratio in high-poverty schools. A synthesis of 11 studies of class size concluded that significantly reducing class size to 21 or fewer students with one teacher had positive effects for reading achievement at the end of first grade, although the effects were both small and short term Slavin (1989). Of the 11 studies, 7 reported positive effects on reading in first grade, 3 found no difference, and 1 determined that there was a small effect favoring the larger classes. Four studies examined the effects of reduced class size throughout the primary grades, and only one reported a sustained effect for reduced class size (also see Mosteller et al., 1996).

To understand these outcomes, it is helpful to turn to observational studies, such as those conducted by Evertson and Randolph (1989), which determined that the differences one might anticipate for reduced class size (increases in time spent on reading, lesson format, the number and nature of student-teacher interactions) generally did not come to pass. In summary, although both the quantity and quality of teacher-student interactions are necessarily limited by large class size, best instructional practices are not guaranteed by small class size. Class size reduction efforts must be accompanied by professional development and planning that supports the desired changes in curriculum, instruction, and assessment.

School-wide Restructuring

The recognition that school-wide poor performance is generally associated with a host of factors has motivated more comprehensive interventions, which address curriculum, pedagogy, assessment, professional development, and relationships with families and the community. Well-known school restructuring efforts include Accelerated Schools (Levin, 1991) and the Coalition of Essential Schools Project (Sizer, 1983). The school restructuring effort that has been the subject of the most research is Success For All (Slavin et al., 1992).

Success For All was designed as a prevention and early intervention for students in kindergarten through third grade who are at risk for early reading failure. Every attempt is made to serve all children, including those with special needs. The key features include individualized tutoring, smaller student-teacher ratios for reading lessons, regroupings across grade levels to create more homogeneous reading groups, assessments and reassignments at eight week intervals, a reading curriculum facilitator on site, and a comprehensive reading program that progresses from specially designed materials to basal readers and trade books. The most helpful description of Success For All is provided by its designers (Slavin et al., 1994:76):

> The idea behind Success For All is to use everything known about effective instruction for students at risk to direct all aspects of school and classroom organization toward the goal of preventing academic deficits from appearing in the first place, recognizing and intensively intervening with any deficits that do appear, and providing students with a rich and full curriculum to enable them to build on their firm foundation in basic skills. The commitment of Success For All is to do whatever it takes to see that every child makes it through third grade at or near grade level in reading and other basic skills, and then goes beyond this in the later grades.

In the reading component of the program, reading tutors are one of the most prominent features. On the basis of earlier research (e.g., Slavin et al., 1989), the designers determined that one of the most effective forms of instruction is the use of tutors. Success For All tutors are certified teachers, many of whom are specialists in reading or special education. Tutors work individually with students who are experiencing difficulty in their reading classes for 20 minutes daily, employing the same curriculum in place in the classroom but providing individually tailored, intensive teaching. The classroom reading periods are 90 minutes long and are generally conducted in groups of 15 to 20, with the classroom teachers and the tutors serving as reading teachers to allow for smaller-sized groups. Teachers and tutors communicate regularly to avoid the problems of discontinuity for the child.

The reading program at every grade level includes reading children's literature and engaging the class in a discussion to jointly construct the meaning of the story, as well as enhancing listening and speaking vocabulary and knowledge of story structure. In kindergarten and first grade, story telling and retelling, in which children retell and dramatize stories, is used to develop language skills. The kinds of big book activities described in Chapter 6 are used as well. More instruction to promote conventional reading begins in the second semester of kindergarten, employing minibooks that contain phonetically regular words in interesting stories that are read and reread to partners as well as to the teacher. Letters and sounds are introduced in a predetermined sequence and integrated into words, sentences, and stories.

When students attain the second-grade reading level, they use a form of the Cooperative Integrated Reading and Composition program, in tandem with the district's basal series or trade books (Stevens and Slavin, 1995). It includes more emphasis on comprehension strategy instruction, such as summarizing and predicting, hand in hand with vocabulary building, decoding practice, and story-related writing.

The evaluation research found significant treatment effects across grade levels and at follow-up. In first through third grades, average performance was maintained at grade level, but from fourth grade on, students in Success For All did not reach grade level, although they continued to progress significantly more rapidly than did comparison-group children. This group difference was also maintained during at least two years of middle school, after leaving the Success For All school (see Figure 7-1). The analysis provides evidence that the intervention benefits even the lowest-achieving students, as well as more able ones.

In addition, over successive years of implementation, the positive effects of the program have been observed to increase, although this trend is not entirely consistent (see Englert and Tarrant, 1995, and Chapter 8). One hypothesis is that schools become more effective with experience. Another is that the children in the second year have had the benefit of already having participated in a Success For All program for a year when they enter first grade.

Evaluations conducted at sites other than the original ones monitored by the designers have not been as strong and consistent (see Smith et al., 1996); nevertheless, close to half of the measures evaluated significantly favored the Success For All sites, and only three comparisons (all within one district) favored the control school. This is remarkable given the broad array of features to be operationalized and the complexities of introducing change into schools

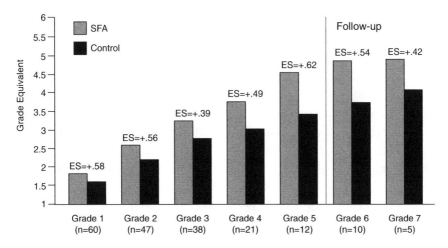

FIGURE 7-1 Comparison of Success For All and control schools in mean reading grade equivalents and effect sizes, 1988-1996. Note: n = number of cohorts. Only includes cohorts in Success For All or control schools since first grade. SOURCES: Adapted from Slavin et al. (1996a, b).

with high reliability (Stringfield, 1995, 1997), but it also sounds a cautionary note about the transportability of even the most success-ful and well-specified programs.

TEACHING READING TO
LANGUAGE-MINORITY CHILDREN

There is no doubt that it is possible to learn to read at a high level of proficiency in a second language, just as it is possible to become a proficient speaker of a second language. Furthermore, as scholars of ancient Hebrew, Greek, and Latin demonstrate, it is possible to become a high-level reader in a language one does not speak at all. These clear cases, though, are generally cases of second-language literacy acquisition after the establishment of proficiency, both oral and written, in a first language. The major question that concerns us is whether it is possible to learn to read for the first time in a second language. Disagreements concerning second-language literacy arise concerning considerably more specific questions about acquisition and ultimate attainment. Is initial literacy instruction in a second language effective? If so, is it effective for all children? Does initial literacy instruction in a second language slow or limit ultimate literacy attainment in the second language? If initial literacy instruction in a second language is contraindicated, what level of first-language literacy should be considered prerequisite to initiation of second-language literacy teaching?

Surprisingly, given the many millions of initially non-English-speaking children who have acquired literacy in English in the United States, and given the many millions of dollars expended on efforts to evaluate bilingual education programs, straightforward, data-based answers to these questions are not available. The accumulated wisdom of research in the field of bilingualism and literacy tends to converge on the conclusion that initial literacy instruction in a second language can be successful, that it carries with it a higher risk of reading problems and of lower ultimate literacy attainment than initial literacy instruction in a first language, and that this risk may compound the risks associated with poverty, low levels of parental education, poor schooling, and other such factors.

In this section we outline sources of evidence supporting these conclusions, conceding, however, that the definitive study has not been carried out. The evidence presented here relates to findings concerning effects of language of initial literacy instruction and effects of longer-term support for first-language literacy; in many specific cases, it is impossible to tell whether positive or negative consequences for patterns of achievement relate to initial or to ongoing support or lack thereof in the native language.

1. *Demographic patterns.* The higher risk of reading problems associated with lack of proficiency in English on school entry is widely documented (NAEP, 1994). Also, rates of school failure, early dropout, and limited literacy attainment are very high in countries in which second-language literacy instruction is widespread, for instance, the African countries that use formerly colonial languages in schooling (Postlethwaite and Ross, 1992) and in European settings in which immigrant children are given exclusively second-language schooling (Tosi, 1979). Of course, such patterns in the

United States and elsewhere are only suggestive and do not indicate causes for reading problems.

2. *Role of social class in limiting risk.* Many children learn to read adequately after initial instruction in a second language, both in the United States and in other multilingual settings in which school and home languages are different. A major challenge is to determine which children manage to thrive under these circumstances and which initial reading instruction in the home language is of particular importance.

One clue in answering this question comes from accounts suggesting that English speakers in French immersion programs in Canada acquire literacy in French first with little difficulty, subsequently transferring their literacy skills successfully to English (cited in August and Hakuta, 1997). French immersion is a magnet program in Canada, generally selected by middle-class, academically motivated families for their children. These same families support literacy acquisition in English in many ways, both prior to their children's exposure to formal instruction and thereafter. It may be that for children in families with many academic and literacy resources, initial instruction in literacy in a second language is unproblematic.

3. *Long-term deficits.* Even Canadian children in French immersion programs, however, may perform better on literacy tasks administered in their first, stronger language (Carey and Cummins, 1983) after as many as 10 years of consistent instruction in the second language. Better performance in the first language is equivalent, of course, to worse than expected performance in the second (although it is not obvious for Canadians because native English speakers tested in French are never directly compared with native French speakers tested in French).

One large study of test scores from initially non-English-speaking children in a school district that had adopted an English-only education policy found that bilingual children caught up with monolingual English-speaking peers in all areas tested within a couple of years after arrival, on average, unless those children had entered U.S. schools in kindergarten or first grade (Collier and Thomas, 1989). In other words, children who had presumably established basic literacy skills in a native language achieved academic parity with peers as soon as they had acquired proficiency in English, but younger arrivals showed long-lasting negative effects on academic achievement associated with initial literacy instruction in English. Similar findings for Finnish speakers in Sweden have been reported by Skutnabb-Kangas and Toukomaa (1979). These results, again, are limited in that they are retrospective and somewhat speculative, but at the very least they show as perhaps questionable the widespread assumptions that earlier exposure and more exposure to the second language are advantageous.

4. *Evaluations of bilingual programs.* While methodologically rigorous evaluations of bilingual education programs are rare (see August and Hakuto, 1997, Chapter 2), and most such evaluations are too small or too flawed to be at all helpful, the most careful met-analysis of studies comparing bilingual to English-only educational programs for language-minority children, carried out by Willig (1985), shows better literacy outcomes in English for children who received transitional bilingual education.

5. *Late-exit programs.* Further support for the position that having later and less total exposure to English literacy may in fact promote achievement in English if the time is spent in developing native-language literacy skills comes from the findings of a large-scale comparison of educational programs for language-minority children (Ramirez et al., 1991). Although they could not compare early- and late-exit bilingual programs within school districts (the ideal match), they did report that children in late-exit bilingual programs had higher levels of achievement than children in early-exit bilingual or in English as a second language programs. Such a pattern of achievement is consistent with a model in which first-language literacy contributes to second language literacy.

6. *Transfer.* Several studies have documented the transfer of literacy skills from a first to a second language. These studies are important in that they suggest a mechanism explaining the positive effects of time spent on first-language literacy for second-language literacy. One study in the Netherlands found that word recognition and reading comprehension levels in the language in which literacy instruction had occurred correlated with the same measures in the

other language for Turkish-Dutch bilinguals (Verhoeven and Gillijns, 1994). Studies that show high interlanguage correlations on literacy and literacy-related language tasks were reviewed by Cummins (1979). Cummins carried out research demonstrating transfer even for such orthographically and typologically distant language pairs as English and Japanese and English and Vietnamese (Cummins, 1984). Researchers have consistently found stronger relationships between literacy tasks than between oral-language tasks across the bilingual person's two languages (e.g., Lanauze and Snow, 1989), again suggesting that time invested in developing first-language literacy works to the advantage of second language literacy achievement.

7. *Theory.* As emphasized throughout this report, the successful reader must have skills in analyzing language in order to understand how the alphabetic code represents meaningful messages. Knowledge available for analysis and access to meaning are thus two crucial factors in successful early reading (Bialystok and Ryan, 1985). Typical English-speaking children have considerable knowledge available for analysis at the time they enter school—several thousand words in their vocabularies, some exposure to rhymes and alliterations, practice writing their own names and "reading" environmental print, and other sources of information about the nature of the analysis they will be expected to engage in. Non-English speakers are confronted with the task of analyzing knowledge they have not yet acquired.

Furthermore, English speakers making initial attempts at reading understand, if they are successful, the products of their efforts. They read words they know and sentences they understand. They can use context and probabilities effectively, and they can self-correct efficiently. Non-English speakers have much less basis for knowing whether their reading is correct because the crucial meaning-making process is short circuited by lack of language knowledge. Giving a child initial reading instruction in a language that he or she does not yet speak thus can undermine the child's chance to see literacy as a powerful form of communication, by knocking the support of meaning out from underneath the process of learning.

It would be highly desirable to be able to cite a study in which children had been randomly assigned to conditions of reading instruction that systematically varied the length of time that instruction was provided in the first language, as well as how early and how intensively instruction was provided in the second language. We lack such a study, so we must draw conclusions from studies that are flawed in design and somewhat equivocal in their findings. It is clear that initial reading instruction in the first language does no harm, and it seems likely both from research findings and from theories about literacy development that initial reading instruction in the second language can have negative consequences for immediate and long-term achievement. This conclusion leads us to urge initial literacy instruction in a child's native language whenever possible and to suggest that literacy instruction should not be introduced in any language before some reasonable level of oral proficiency in that language has been attained.

Examples of successful reading programs in Spanish for Spanish speakers in the United States can be found in Goldenberg and Gallimore (1991), Goldenberg and Sullivan (1994), and Slavin and Madden (1995). In all three cases, early elementary students in targeted schools attained higher levels of reading proficiency in Spanish than students in comparable schools. Although the programs were different, each emphasized structured phonological instruction combined with meaningful uses of print.

TEACHING READING TO CHILDREN SPEAKING NONSTANDARD DIALECTS

Users of nonstandard dialects learning to read in English face challenges analogous to those faced by speakers of other languages. In both cases, children are expected to learn to read a language (standard English) that they use in a limited way. A sizable body of findings has documented differences between mainstream and minority dialects that may bear directly on a mechanism that is central to reading development—the development of sound-symbol links. Learning English spelling is challenging enough for speakers of standard mainstream English; these challenges are heightened by a number of phonological and grammatical features of minority dialects that make the relation of sound to spelling even more indirect.

An important example is African American Vernacular English (AAVE). Many of the approximately 8 million African American students in U.S. schools are also speakers of AAVE. The most characteristic form of the vernacular is spoken by a majority, both youth and adults, in inner cities where there is a high concentration of African Americans. Modified forms of AAVE are spoken by others who have more extensive contact with speakers of other dialects.

For speakers of this dialect, there is a great deal of divergence between spoken and written forms of English (Labov, 1966; Wolfram, 1969). AAVE is characterized by extreme reduction of final consonants, which affects clusters ("so" for "sold," "fin'" for "find"), liquids ("so'd" for "sold," "he'p" for "help," and "fo'" for "four"), and even final stop consonants ("ba'" for "bad," "spea'" for "speak").

In addition, some phonological contrasts are absent for speakers of AAVE, such as -th versus -f at the ends of words. The lack of contrast of /i/ and /e/ before /n/, widespread throughout the South, is an identifying feature of AAVE speakers in the North. Syllable structure is also often radically different from that shown in word spellings, or orthography, that is, in translating the units of the spoken language into letters of the alphabet or letter-like forms. When the medial /r/ is deleted, for example, "parents" (a two-syllable word) might be indistinguishable from "pants," with one syllable only.

Addressing Dialect in Reading Instruction

In order to reduce the gap between what children speak and what they are expected to read, many nations use the vernacular for early reading instruction and introduce the language of wider communication only in higher grades (Feitelson, 1988). Research in regions where children speak a nonstandard dialect has shown an advantage for children who have learned to read in their home language or dialect (Bull, 1994).

As early as 1969, Stewart advocated that African American youth who speak AAVE be provided opportunities to read text that is consistent with their oral language. In his argument, he pointed to

the systematic structure of AAVE and the extensive difference (especially when compared with other American dialects) between AAVE
and the standard English reflected in texts for beginning readers. He
suggested that providing AAVE-speaking youth the opportunity to
read AAVE versions of text would be consistent with the innovations for second-language learners proposing that children first be
taught to read in their native language and then transfer these skills
to whatever language was the goal of the literacy program. In the
1960s, Baratz and Stewart prepared primary text materials and provided some pilot demonstrations of their effectiveness (as cited in
Baratz and Shuy, 1969). A full experimental test of these materials
was not undertaken.

One outcome of Stewart's efforts with his colleagues was the
production of a set of several texts for older children, entitled *Bridge*,
that were written in AAVE. Bridge developers Simpkins and
Simpkins (1981) described their program thus: "The Bridge program
attempts to start where the students are and take them to where their
teachers would like them to be by using the language and culture the
children bring to school as a foundation upon which to build."

Materials are sequenced according to associative bridging; reading in the mainstream dialect is taught as an extension of reading in
the students' familiar dialect. AAVE serves as a springboard from
which to move to the presentation of standard mainstream English.
Accordingly, materials are written in three dialect versions: AAVE,
transition, and standard English (Simpkins and Simpkins, 1981, cited
in Rickford and Rickford, 1995:113).

Simpkins and Simpkins (1981) field tested this program over a
period of 4 months with 540 students from seventh through twelfth
grades. They reported that the experimental students showed significantly greater gains on the Iowa Test of Basic Skills in reading
comprehension than did 123 comparison students who were engaged in remedial reading activities. Specifically, the Bridge students
showed because of 6.2 months of growth for 4 months of instruction, compared with 1.6 months of growth for the comparison students. These reports do not indicate specific applications of dialect
differences to the problems of developing phonemic awareness and
decoding skills. The evaluated interventions appear to have relied

on the overall effect of a given cultural and linguistic style as reading materials rather than focusing on specific linguistic differences that affect sound-to-spelling correspondence.

Objections about the program from parents and teachers led its publishers to discontinue promotion of Bridge. Since the early 1980s, there have been no published studies of new data on the use of AAVE texts. Rickford and Rickford (1995) have recently made a strong case for reopening the issue of whether African American students' reading attainment would be enhanced by using AAVE materials. They obtained mixed results on several pilot studies, however, with some outcomes being actually negative for the AAVE readers.

Teacher Knowledge Across Reading Programs

Recent research has suggested that, across reading programs, teachers should attend to the following principles when providing instruction with dialect speakers, including children who use AAVE, Latino-influenced English, and other nonstandard dialects: (a) distinguish between mistakes in reading and mistakes in pronunciation, (b) give more attention to the ends of words (where much dialect variation is most apparent) in initial reading instruction, (c) present words to students in phonological contexts that preserve underlying forms, (d) avoid contractions, and (e) teach grammar explicitly (Labov, 1995). Clearly there is a rich research agenda represented in the thoughtful application of these principles in literacy instruction; to date, this work has not been undertaken, although research by Craig and her colleagues is providing a rich base from which to evaluate children's use of AAVE (Craig and Washington, 1995).

These principles address only the linguistic aspects of AAVE, as Labov (1995) points out. There are many opposing cultural patterns surrounding the use of language in the classroom, patterns for dealing with authority, and cultural definitions of dignity and respect that create hidden obstacles for the majority of African American children in their dealings with the school system. The linguistic principles must be embedded in a larger perspective that recognizes these children as intelligent, well-adjusted products of their own culture, still full of aspiration and promise. It is only in such a perspective that the standard language can be presented as an avenue toward educational advancement and the improvement of economic opportunity.

TEACHING READING TO CHILDREN WITH CULTURAL DIFFERENCES

Although there is widespread agreement that minority groups differ from each other and from mainstream cultures in several respects, less certain is how and whether cultural differences contribute to reading achievement. A persistent and troubling aspect of reading difficulties is the differential in reading success between mainstream and minority children—African American, Hispanic, Native American, and some Asian and Pacific Islander groups. For example, the reading achievement gap between African American and white students increases as the students progress through school (Entwisle and Alexander, 1988; Phillips et al., in press). In Chapter 6 and earlier sections of this one, we have alluded to the role of cultural differences but have not addressed the topic directly.

Considerable work has suggested that minority groups have specific cultural perspectives on literacy and on academic learning more generally that differ from those of mainstream groups (e.g., Jacob and Jordan, 1987; Tharp, 1989). Several researchers have noted that instruction in reading skills and other informal opportunities for learning about literacy are found in the homes of African American and Hispanic families, suggesting at least one area of potential commonality between home and school. Others have found that instruction in aspects of literacy, such as letter names, simple words, and phonics, was often observed in the homes of minority families (Baker et al., 1995) . Other researchers suggest that minority groups consider direct teaching of this type to be both culturally appropriate and effective (Delpit, 1986, 1988; Goldenberg, 1995).

But even if the research was able to isolate specific cultural configurations that interfere with reading, there is the question of whether we have the ability to adjust cultural factors in the classroom. Cultural differences are entrenched in history and social institutions and are not easily amenable to educators' manipulations. One researcher, for example, argues that high rates of low performance of African American students persist even when they are equal to others on all objective measures of skill and preparation (Steele, 1992). He isolates a complex of psychological and cultural factors, which he refers to as "misidentification with school," that are the product of a long history of racial vulnerability and response to racism. The work of John Ogbu, which addresses the institutionalized racism of school systems and other institutions, also implies the need for massive social change if the minority differential is to be erased (Ogbu, 1982).

Cultural Accommodation

Demonstrations of the benefits of culturally accommodated instruction, whereby educators make certain accommodations to features of students' cultural backgrounds, have empirically documented direct connections between cultural accommodation and student participation (Goldenberg and Gallimore, 1989). When classrooms are compatible with students' home cultures—in such areas as motivation strategies (individualistic versus group or family based) and speaking or participation styles (direct versus indirect, turn-taking rules)—the students are more likely to participate more and in ways that appear to be conducive to effective learning.

A limitation of the cultural accommodation research base is that it has left largely untested the proposition that culturally accommodated instruction has beneficial effects on measured student achievement. For example, Au and Mason (1981), in one of the most widely cited studies in this area, found that when a teacher engaged Native Hawaiian children in reading lessons congruent with sociolinguistic patterns from the children's native culture ("talk-story," a Native Hawaiian discourse style), students participated more in academically productive interactions than when taught by a teacher who was unaware of these interaction styles.

This study is frequently cited as showing a direct connection between culturally accommodated instruction and student achievement, but in reality Au and Mason included no measures of student learning, only indices of children's participation and engagement during actual lessons. That talk-story-like reading instruction produced higher rates of engagement in academic discourse is very important, but participation—although a desirable key to learning—is not the same as achievement, and the two should not be treated as synonymous (see Karweit, 1989).

It is often suggested that early school difficulties are reduced by culturally adapting instruction to children on the basis of their home cultures. For instance, one study concluded that "compatibilities between school and culture have felicitous effects on student achievement and school satisfaction" (Tharp, 1989:349-350) and that "there is evidence that when cultural differences in social organization, sociolinguistics, cognition, and motivation are reflected in compatible classroom practices, such compatibility makes for classrooms that are associated with greater child participation and enjoyment and better school achievement" (p. 355). Other scholars have reached similar conclusions (Au, 1995; California State Department of Education, 1986; Cazden, 1986; Trueba, 1988).

Kamehameha Early Education Project

The Kamehameha Early Education Project (KEEP) is often cited as support for this notion (Tharp, 1982; Tharp and Gallimore, 1988). KEEP is a 20-year research and development effort that succeeded in substantially improving the early reading achievement of Native Hawaiian children. Its researchers and teachers developed instruction guides and curricula on reading that significantly improved early reading achievement among Native Hawaiian children, at the original laboratory site on Oahu and in other sites around the state.

It is uncertain, however, what role culturally accommodated instruction played in the results (Goldenberg and Gallimore, 1989). The KEEP reading program included many components, many of which seemed to have little to do with any particular cultural group, instead illustrating more general principles of effective teaching and classroom organization. Although it is certainly plausible that culturally based factors and more general or universal factors combined to create the effectiveness of the program for Native Hawaiian children, it is impossible to know exactly which dimensions of the program were responsible for the positive effects on student achievement. In the absence of more finely detailed comparisons and data sets on the many dimensions of the program, it is difficult to rule out competing explanations for the program's effects.

The cultural compatibility hypothesis may be an important avenue for helping to improve the early reading achievement of large numbers of children currently not well served by early reading programs. However, evidence for its robust effects on reading achievement or any other dimension of learning is still missing. Tharp is undoubtedly correct when he argues that *"experimental work in actual classrooms is of the highest priority. . . . We need more systematic and evaluated classroom variation. Cultural compatibility must be put to practical use in order to test this simple, commonsensical, and humane proposition"* (1989:357, emphasis in the original).

CONCLUSIONS

The discussion in this chapter leads to several important conclusions. First, there are circumstances that place groups of young children at risk for reading difficulties. A number of efforts have been made to provide reading instruction for these groups of children regardless of their individual status on child-based predictors of reading achievement (see Chapter 4). In addition, however, particular children may also need extra instruction based on child-based predictors of reading achievement—which is the subject of Chapter 8.

Second, to be effective, interventions must take account of existing external factors or characteristics. Consideration should be given to improving existing instructional practices before deciding to implement any intervention.

Third, the process of determining appropriate interventions must take into account the characteristics of students who are at risk for failure. For example, if an entire school is at risk, it might be wiser to begin an intervention that includes school-wide restructuring than to devote resources to any new tutoring technique. Research has shown the effectiveness of school-wide efforts that integrate restructuring focused on organizational issues and coherent classroom reading instruction. To date, such school-wide efforts, when they have included solid and coherent regular classroom reading instruction, have generally proven more effective than disconnected strategies or restructuring focused on organizational issues that have not included classroom-level and curricula changes.

Fourth, hurrying young non-English-speaking children into reading in English without ensuring adequate preparation is counterproductive. The abilities to hear and reflect on the sublexical structure of spoken English words, as required for learning how the alphabetic principle works, depends on oral familiarity with the words being read. Similarly, learning to read for meaning depends on understanding the language and referents of the text to be read. To the extent possible, non-English-speaking children should have opportunities to develop literacy skills in their home language as well as in English.

Fifth, a major challenge to society is the persistent disparity in reading outcomes between African American and European American youth. Although it has long been suggested that the dialect features of African American Vernacular English (AAVE) create an additional challenge to acquiring mainstream literacy for its speakers, few efforts that directly test this hypothesis have been undertaken.

Finally, the positive effects of cultural accommodation are important, as shown by Au and Mason's (1981) finding that students receiving talk-story instruction participated in academically productive interactions, but the research is not conclusive.

8
Helping Children with Reading Difficulties in Grades 1 to 3

As indicated in Chapters 6 and 7, many children learn to read with good instruction, but some do not. And many children have problems learning to read because of poor instruction. In all cases, the question is what kinds of additional instruction (usually called "interventions" because they are not part of the regular school reading instruction) are likely to help.

The purpose of providing extra instructional time is to help children achieve levels of literacy that will enable them to be successful through their school careers and beyond. It is not simply to boost early literacy achievement. Given the focus of this volume, we restrict our discussion to the primary grades; however, it is likely that children who have had interventions in the primary grades will need additional supplementary experiences in the upper grades as well. We know that the literacy demands are of a different nature for older children; as children proceed through the grades, they are expected to learn from informational text with which they may have had few experiences in the primary grades (see Fisher and Hiebert, 1990); they are expected to use text independently; and they are expected to use text for the purpose of thinking and reasoning.

Long-term follow-up studies reveal that even very powerful early interventions often require "booster" sessions.

We begin by discussing some interventions that are specific to reading, targeting the training of phonological skills. We then proceed to discuss individual tutoring and supplementary small-group efforts provided by professionals with specialties in reading that have been designed to provide comprehensive supplementary literacy instruction. We continue with information on computer support for reading instruction, retention in grade, and special education for children with learning disabilities. Although the latter two are not specific to reading, they have often been introduced in response to reading failure. The chapter ends with a brief mention of some controversial therapies for reading problems.

TRAINING IN PHONOLOGICAL AWARENESS

Phonological awareness, the appreciation of speech sounds without regard for their meaning, is critical to discovering the alphabetic principle (the idea that letters generally represent the small speech segments called phonemes). The theoretical importance and strong empirical relationship of phonological awareness to success in learning to read was discussed in Chapters 2 and 4, and the demonstrated benefits of phonological awareness training for children who have not yet begun formal reading instruction were reviewed in Chapters 5 and 6. Here we examine evidence of the effectiveness of such training for two groups of children: beginning students at risk for reading difficulties and schoolchildren with existing reading difficulties (whose achievement is unacceptably low after two or more years of instruction).

Phonological Awareness Training for Kindergartners at Risk

Many children at risk for reading difficulties enter school with little or no phonological awareness. Does explicit instruction and practice in attending to and manipulating the sounds within spoken words facilitate these children's reading acquisition? Evidence is accruing that indeed such training can be of particular benefit to youngsters at risk due to socioeconomic disadvantage and/or weak initial preparedness in reading-related skills.

As was the case in the kindergarten research reviewed in Chapter 6, some training and intervention programs for at-risk youngsters have emphasized phonological awareness exclusively (Bentin and Leshem, 1993; Hurford et al., 1994), whereas others have combined phonological awareness activities with instruction in letter identification and letter-sound correspondences (e.g., Ball and Blachman, 1991; Felton, 1993; Smith et al., 1993; Torgesen et al., 1992, 1997). It is therefore important to point out that even those with the more narrowly focused programs have observed gains in reading skills (word recognition), as well as in phonological awareness itself, relative to control groups. This suggests that the effectiveness of the more broadly focused studies does not rest solely on the inclusion of early reading instruction, but also benefits from lessons that draw the child's attention to the sounds within spoken words.

How effectively has phonological awareness training (alone) benefited word identification? In a sample of 431 children who had not yet received formal reading instruction, 99 had been designated as at risk on the basis of a screening battery (Hurford et al., 1994). Half of the at-risk group received individual tutoring in phonological awareness for a total of about 10 to 15 hours over a 20-week period, during which time regular classroom reading instruction also commenced for all participants. Prior to training, there was a substantial difference (13 to 14 points) between mean standard scores of the not-at-risk children and each at-risk group on the word identification measure. After the training period, this large gap remained for the untrained at-risk group, but the trained group's post-test mean was 7 points below that of the controls who were not at risk.

Another study compared the effects of phonological awareness training with an alternative kind of language training (in vocabulary and sentence skills) as well as with a no-training condition for children at risk on the basis of their initial skill levels (Bentin and Leshem, 1993). Compared with the performance of not-at-risk classmates, the at-risk groups who received no training or alternative language training scored about 40 points lower on two post-tests. In contrast, those who had received training in phonological segmentation scored

30 to 34 points higher, on average, than the other at-risk groups, and within 10 or fewer points of the not-at-risk group's mean.

In the studies in which training has also included instruction in letters and letter-sound relationships, similar patterns of results have generally been found (e.g., Ball and Blachman, 1991; Felton, 1993; Smith et al., 1993; Torgesen et al., 1992, 1997). Modification of the standard Reading Recovery program (described in a later section) so as to include an additional phonologically oriented component has also been shown to be effective; when researchers compared a group of at-risk first graders who participated in the standard program with a matched group in the modified Reading Recovery training, the latter group reached criterion for successful completion significantly faster (Iverson and Tunmer, 1993).

Torgesen and his colleagues (1992, 1997) have also explored the question as to what degree of explicitness in such instruction is most effective for kindergartners with weak letter knowledge and phonological awareness skills when they begin school. At-risk kindergartners were assigned to one of four conditions: a highly explicit and intensive phonologically oriented instruction; a less explicit phonologically oriented instruction delivered in the context of meaningful experiences with reading and writing text; regular classroom support; or no treatment. The group receiving explicit phonologically oriented instruction scored highest on word identification, but only the 12-point difference with the no-treatment group was statistically significant. A similar pattern of means favoring the explicit phonologically oriented instruction group was obtained for reading comprehension, but these smaller group differences were not significant. These data are consistent with those of Foorman et al. (1998, discussed in Chapter 6), suggesting that greater intensity and explicitness of early phonological training may reap greater gains in reading acquisition for at-risk youngsters.

One reason that statistical significance has sometimes been difficult to achieve in these training and intervention studies (with their relatively small sample sizes) has been the considerable variability among children within groups in their responses to treatment. It is clear that a majority of at-risk children who receive training in phonological awareness show strong gains in awareness itself, but a minority—perhaps a quarter (Torgesen et al., 1997)—gain little or no insight into the structure of spoken words, much less into reading, by the end of training. Typically, these children are among the very weakest at the outset in their phonological awareness (and other linguistic) abilities. For these children to reap the benefits of training, it is likely that many more hours of or a different type of special instruction are needed than have typically been provided in studies to date.

The fact that the effects of phonological awareness training have not been found to include gains in reading comprehension in the early grades is not particularly surprising. As discussed previously, reading comprehension depends not just on mastery of word recognition skills but also on a host of other factors, including vocabulary, background knowledge, memory skills, and so forth. Children assigned to the at-risk groups have typically been weaker than classmates in their overall cognitive and linguistic preparedness, and training in phonological awareness is not designed to strengthen other skills that contribute to comprehension. In short, the goal of phonological training is limited to facilitating the acquisition of word-decoding abilities, which are necessary but not sufficient for the development of skilled comprehension.

Taken together, these studies indicate that training in phonological awareness, particularly in association with instruction in letters and letter-sound relationships, makes a contribution to assisting at-risk children in learning to read. The effects of training, although quite consistent, are only moderate in strength, and have so far not been shown to extend to comprehension. Typically, a majority of the trained children narrow the gap between themselves and initially more advanced students in phonological awareness and word reading skills, but few are brought completely up to speed through training, and a few fail to show any gains at all. Hence, it is unrealistic to think of phonological awareness training as a one-shot inoculation against reading difficulties for children at risk. Rather, its greater demonstrated value is as the first of many aggressive steps that can be taken in an ongoing effort to intensify all facets of reading instruction for schoolchildren who need it.

Training for Children with Reading Disabilities

Because most children who are identified as being poor readers are also weaker than their classmates in phonological awareness skills, providing training in awareness has been thought to be helpful for ameliorating these children's reading difficulties. To date, several studies have examined the efficacy of this approach to remediation, with somewhat mixed results.

One of the earliest studies of phonological awareness training for disabled readers focused on phoneme analysis, blending, and phonological decoding of text for students ages 7 to 12 with serious reading difficulties (Williams, 1980). Compared with similarly low-achieving children who did not receive training, the trained group earned significantly higher scores on several measures of phoneme awareness, reading of nonsense words, and reading of regular three-letter words that had not been used in the training materials.

A computer-based training program provided supplemental small-group phonological instruction for children in grades 2 to 5 who were in the bottom 10 percent in word recognition skills (Wise and Olson, 1995; Olson et al., 1997). One group was first trained in phoneme awareness and phonological training and then progressed to reading stories on the computer. The comparison group's training focused on comprehension strategies, beginning with small-group instruction and then reading stories on the computer. In all, the comparison group spent more than twice as much time reading stories as the other group.

In contrast to untrained control groups in previous research that have consistently shown no improvement, both groups made gains in word recognition over the training period. As would be expected, the first group improved significantly more than the comparison group in phoneme awareness and phonological decoding of pseudo words, and these differences were maintained for a year beyond training. The comparison group, which spent much more time actually reading on the computer, scored higher on speeded word recognition. These findings suggested that the phonologically trained group's better decoding skills worked to their advantage when they had unlimited time to apply them, but that they were not yet sufficiently automatized in decoding to do well under time-limited conditions. Although it was hypothesized that with further reading experience the phonologically trained group's word recognition skills would become more automatized, there was no evidence for this (Olson et al., 1997).

Another study also demonstrated that word recognition skills of severely disabled readers can be substantially improved through intensive supplementary training (Lovett et al., 1994). Training was given to each of three groups in explicit instruction in phoneme awareness and letter-sound mappings, training in using common orthographic patterns and analogies to identify unfamiliar words. and study skills training (the control condition). The phonological program produced greater improvement in phoneme awareness and phonological decoding, but the two trained groups showed similar gains in word recognition compared with the controls. Recent analyses on an expanded sample indicate that the two training conditions are about equally effective for older (grades 5 and 6) and younger (grades 2 and 3) children with reading disabilities (Lovett and Steinbach, 1997).

A final study compared immediate and long-term outcomes for groups of children with severe reading disabilities who had received one of four types of training: phonological awareness training alone; reading instruction alone, based on the Reading Recovery approach, but with no coverage at all of letter-sound relationships; training in both phonological and reading skills in combination; and no treatment controls (Hatcher et al., 1994). Performance of the group that received the combined training consistently exceeded that of the control group on both immediate and delayed post-tests, but scores of the other trained groups did not differ significantly from those of the controls. This pattern of results was seen for word recognition, nonword reading, text reading accuracy, and reading comprehension. Immediately after training, the combined training group was six months ahead of the control group, on average, in both accuracy and comprehension of text reading; nine months after the cessation of training they remained four months ahead in accuracy and eight months ahead in comprehension. Despite these considerable gains relative to the progress of other severely disabled readers, their reading levels remained one to two years below age norms.

These studies indicate, first, that intensive training, even over relatively short periods of time, can substantially improve the word-reading skills of children with serious reading disabilities and that these positive outcomes are maintained over months or years after the cessation of training. Whether a continuation of such training over longer periods would lead to a fuller remediation of these children's difficulties remains unknown, however. In particular, fluency and automaticity of word recognition, which may be required for skilled reading comprehension, may require much more or different types of training and extensive practice.

Second, it is clear that phonologically oriented training programs are not the only type of intervention that can facilitate word recognition, although this approach produces the strongest gain in phonemic awareness and phonological decoding when combined with training in other reading skills. Other, more orthographically oriented approaches have been of equivalent benefit for improving word reading in this population, many of whom have already acquired some decoding skills (although these may be minimal) before training. Finally, although most children with reading disabilities are characteristically deficient in phonological abilities (both oral and written), they may also have, in part due to limited print exposure, deficits in oral vocabulary, language comprehension, and background knowledge (Stanovich and West, 1989). Dealing with these problems is clearly beyond the scope and aims of the training programs we have reviewed in this section.

LITERACY TUTORING

In this section, we describe supplementary interventions that take the form of tutoring. They were selected for review because they have received more sustained research attention than other tutoring programs. Like the training studies in phonological awareness reviewed above, they approach the provision of extra time in reading instruction by tutoring children individually.

Reading Recovery

Reading Recovery, which is singled out for a relatively extensive review, has garnered significant attention in the United States. It requires extensive training of teachers, as well as intensive one-on-one instruction with children, rendering it quite costly. The program was designed by Marie Clay for the purpose of intervening with young children in New Zealand identified as having reading problems. For complete descriptions of the instructional program, the reader is referred to Clay (1985) and Pinnell et al. (1988).

The program has a particular framework for providing instruction to the tutees. For the initial 10 days of a child's participation in Reading Recovery, the teacher gathers information about the child's current literacy strategies and knowledge. Following this period, referred to as "roaming the known," each lesson includes (a) engaging the child in rereadings of previously read books; (b) independent reading of the book introduced during the previous lesson (during which the teacher takes a running record to assess fluency); (c) letter identification exercises, if necessary; (d) writing and reading his or her own sentences, during which the child's attention is called to hearing the sounds in words; (e) reassembling the child's sentence which is not cut up into individual words; (f) introduction to a new book; and (g) supported reading of the new book. These activities occur in a 30-minute block of time on a daily basis. One feature of Reading Recovery is time on reading of familiar books—sheer on-task, engaged learning time for students.

Teacher support provided during each of these activities is designed to enhance what are referred to as children's self-extending systems; that is, children are encouraged to use multiple sources of information while reading and writing and to engage in literacy activity using a problem-solving approach, monitoring for the effectiveness with which they are making sense of the text. The short books used by the children have been sequenced on the basis of teacher judgment of difficulty.

Once the child has achieved the level of functioning that matches (within a .5 standard deviation) the competence demonstrated by a randomly selected group of first graders drawn from the child's school on the same tasks, the child is discontinued from the program. Typically, this translates into 60 30-minute sessions over a 12- to 16-week period. Typically, teachers conduct Reading Recovery lessons with four children a day and spend the remainder of their day as first-grade teachers. During the course of a school year, about 8 to 11 children per Reading Recovery teacher generally complete the program successfully and another 27 percent of children are dismissed from the program without having successfully reached criterion performance.

By most professional development standards, the preparation of Reading Recovery teachers is quite extensive. Following 30 hours of training before the beginning of the school year, Reading Recovery teachers participate in weekly sessions in which the central activity is the observation and discussion of two lessons that are conducted by Reading Recovery teachers (working behind one-way viewing windows) with one of their students. The observations are guided by a teacher-leader, who focuses the group's attention on the activity of both the teacher and the child.

There are now a number of publications asking the question, "Does Reading Recovery work?" These include publications by the implementers of Reading Recovery in the United States, including DeFord et al. (1987), Pinnell et al. (1994), and Pinnell et al. (1995). In addition, a number of thoughtful syntheses and reviews have been reported by others, including Center et al. (1995), who also report an empirical study of their own using Reading Recovery, Hiebert (1994a), Rasinski (1995), and Shanahan and Barr (1995). In fact, it appears that the data available through these reviews exceed the data available through firsthand published investigations of Reading Recovery; that is, the reviewers have included in their syntheses technical reports and unpublished documents that have not been disseminated by the Reading Recovery organization.

Clay's own research regarding Reading Recovery in New Zealand (Clay, 1985) has been criticized, in particular by Nicholson (1989) and Robinson (1989). These authors point out that, although Clay provides clear evidence that children improve on measures that she has designed, there is no evaluation for transfer to other reading measures. Perhaps more troubling is their finding that the results reported by Reading Recovery are only for children who have successfully been discontinued from the program, excluding about 30 percent of the participants. Because children are not randomly assigned to Reading Recovery or an appropriate control group, the question is raised whether the growth demonstrated in Reading Recovery might not be explained simply in terms of normal development. Finally, maintenance measures comparing the performance of students successfully graduated from Reading Recovery with other low-progress students who did not receive Reading Recovery tutoring indicate that 12 months after the intervention there are very small differences between the reading achievement of Reading Recovery children and the other low-progress children (Glynn et al., 1992). This finding regarding the failure of the low-progress children to respond to Reading Recovery in the long run was replicated in a reanalysis of Pinnell et al.'s (1988) data on U.S. participants in Reading Recovery, once again indicating that 30 percent of the original sample of low-progress children who were enrolled in Reading Recovery failed to benefit from the program (Center et al., 1995). Similar analyses and conclusions have been presented by Hiebert (1994a) and Shanahan and Barr (1995).

In a study of Reading Recovery conducted by Pinnell et al. (1994), including random assignment of participants to one of five groups—Reading Recovery, three other early intervention programs (differing from one another in group size, amount of teacher training, and whether or not they adhered to Reading Recovery instructional plans), and a control group—the results indicated that following 70 days of program intervention the students in the Reading Recovery clearly outperformed the students in the other three intervention programs on an array of measures of reading achievement. The study being described here contained high amounts of familiar book reading time for the reading recovery group and for one additional intervention group compared to much less time for the other groups. The group that equaled Reading Recovery method in time spent reading familiar books equaled Reading Recovery in outcome data. However, after three months, post-tests using standardized measures did not reveal any statistical differences among the treatment groups, although the Reading Recovery group continued to maintain its gains—12 months later—on those measures that are specific to Reading Recovery (Clay's concepts of print and dictation tasks).

In their own research investigating Reading Recovery, Center et al. (1995) included an analysis of the individual cases of three groups of students participating in Reading Recovery and reported an important finding. They divided their Reading Recovery instructional groups into children who were totally "recovered" versus those who were unsuccessful and examined the profiles of these children in terms of their pretest measures. They reported that the recovered group was markedly superior to the unrecovered group in terms of their pretest metalinguistic knowledge, as determined by assessment of phonemic awareness, word attack, and cloze comprehension (that is, a method of systematically deleting words from a prose selection and then evaluating the success a reader has in accurately supplying the words deleted—McKenna, 1980). Center et al. conclude that children with poor metalinguistic knowledge are less likely to be successful in Reading Recovery. This hypothesis received support from the instructional research of Iverson and Tunmer (1993), who conducted a study including a condition in which they modified Reading Recovery to include explicit code instruction involving phonograms (common elements in word families, such as the letter sequence, "at" in "bat, cat, sat"). Children who were assigned to the modified condition achieved criterion performance more quickly than children in the standard condition.

Despite the controversies regarding the efficacy of Reading Recovery, a number of intervention programs owe their design features to it, and it offers two important lessons. First, the program demonstrates that, in order to approach reading instruction with a deep and principled understanding of the reading process and its implications for instruction, teachers need opportunities for sustained professional development. Second, it is nothing short of foolhardy to make enormous investments in remedial instruction and then return children to classroom instruction that will not serve to maintain the gains they made in the remedial program.

Book Buddies

Book Buddies is a supplementary intervention in which selected children received one-on-one tutorials twice a week in addition to classroom reading instruction, using highly qualified community volunteers as tutors (Invernizzi et al., 1997). These tutors received continuous on-site training and supervision in the delivery of a four-step lesson designed by reading specialists. The four-part plan consists of repeated reading of familiar text to enhance reading fluency, word study (phonics), writing for sounds, and reading a new book. The word study portion of Book Buddies lessons is derived principally from research on developmental spelling; hence instruction initially focuses on beginning consonants, proceeds to beginning and ending consonants, and finally goes to full phoneme representation of consonant-vowel-consonant words, at which point the child has stable speech-to-print concepts and the beginnings of a sight vocabulary.

Although not all Book Buddy children start at the same point, the basic program proceeds through alliteration in whole words to onset-rime segments to individual phonemes. Children are explicitly taught basic letter-sound correspondences and how to segment and manipulate beginning consonants in the onset position of simple words. As they achieve a stable concept of words and begin to acquire a sight word vocabulary, they are encouraged to segment and manipulate the rime unit. Finally, when the corpus of known words is larger and the child begins to read, medial short vowel sounds are examined. The use of known words, gathered from context and then analyzed in isolation (for instance, with the use of word bank cards), provides an opportunity to transfer phonological awareness training and grapheme-phoneme practice from text to automatic reading of sight words.

The third component is writing for sounds. Children are allowed to write in invented spelling, but they are held accountable for those phonics features already taught. The rationale for this activity is that the act of segmenting speech and matching letters to sounds is a rigorous exercise in phonemic awareness. Furthermore, there is substantial research demonstrating that invented spelling can enhance children's memory for words, at least in the beginning stages (Ehri and Wilce, 1987).

The fourth component of each lesson is the introduction of a new book, which includes focusing the child's attention on the sequence of events and assessing the child's related background knowledge. Finally, reading comprehension is fostered throughout the reading of the new book through predictions, discussions, and opportunities to write about the new story.

In summary, this supplementary intervention has four driving principles: children learn to read by reading in meaningful contexts; reading instruction should be differentiated based on the diagnosis of learner need; phonics instruction should be systematic and paced according to a child's developing hypotheses about how words work; and reading, writing, and spelling develop in synchrony as children interact with others who assist their learning and development.

Evaluations of Book Buddies included three cohorts of 358 first and second graders. The first graders were in the bottom quartile of each school's Title I referral list. There were 15 tutors, each of whom was supervised by a university faculty member who made assessments and wrote lesson plans. The cost was estimated to be one-sixth that of Reading Recovery. The effect size was 1.29 for word recognition, which is considerably higher than effect sizes reported for other tutorial programs and is indeed comparable to that found with professionally trained teachers. However, it is important to note that the tutors were carefully prepared, were supervised on a daily basis, and were provided guidance, feedback, and support.

Reading One-One

Reading One-One uses trained and managed paraprofessionals (college students, community residents, teacher aides) to deliver three to five one-on-one tutoring sessions to low-performing readers on a weekly basis throughout the school year (Farkas and Vicknair, 1996). The program aims to serve the lowest-performing readers in elementary school grades 1 to 6, including children with limited English proficiency and children living in poverty. Teachers recommend students who "need help the most" or "could most profit from help."

Prospective tutors are tested on their English-language skills and interviewed. If they pass this stage, they are trained and tested again on the tutor manual used in the program. Each school has an on-site coordinator. Expert staff sit with each tutor during actual tutoring sessions and fill out an appraisal form, which is then used to provide feedback to the tutor. This continues until the tutor has met the program's standard, at which point they are certified.

The curriculum combines explicit instruction on decoding skills with the use of small books that are ranked by difficulty level (see descriptions of these types of books in Chapter 6). They include fiction and nonfiction and range in level from emergent literacy through fluency. After assessment, each child is placed into one of three curricula: alphabet, word-family, or reading-ready. The first of these is for children who are still learning their letters and sounds, the second is for children still learning the most basic decoding skills, and the third is for children who are able to read at least the easiest-level books on their own. Each tutoring session allows for about 30 minutes of instruction.

For all three curricula, the session involves both book reading and explicit instruction on skills related to reading. This is organized as follows:

• for alphabet students—review of previous letters/sounds, new letter/sound instruction, reading (reading to the student and/or assisted reading), assisted creative writing;
• for word-family students—review of previous word families, new word family instruction, reading (reading to the student and/or assisted reading), and creative writing; and
• for reading-ready students—rereading, new reading, high-frequency words practice, and creative writing.

In general, children are assessed every fifth session. For reading-ready children, a running record is taken every session. The child also creates and maintains letter and/or word banks, a copy of which goes home with them.

An evaluation of the Reading One-One program examined the amount of improvement in relation to the number of sessions of tutoring received, which varied unsystematically as a result of varying logistical circumstances (Farkas and Vicknair, 1996). Another evaluation showed that 70 Reading One-One sessions (taking about four to six months) typically raised a child's grade-equivalent score by about half a year (Farkas and Vicknair, 1996).

COMPREHENSIVE LITERACY-ORIENTED EFFORTS WITH SMALL GROUPS OF CHILDREN

Early Intervention in Reading

Early Intervention in Reading is an intervention that took place in regular first-grade classrooms and was directed at improving the reading achievement of the lowest-performing five to seven readers in each class (Taylor et al., 1994). This research was conducted over a four-year period in diverse school settings (rural to inner city). Selection for the intervention was made by identifying the children with the lowest scores on tasks that require them to produce individual sounds in words and to blend sounds together to form words. The lessons were planned in three-day cycles and began with the reading of a picture book to the whole first-grade class. The teacher engaged the class in a retelling of the story, which was printed on large chart paper so that children could read the retelling together over the three days. Also included in the instructional cycle was a writing activity in which the teacher selected three short phonetically regular words, which the children were asked to write. Also, the children engaged in assisted sentence writing about the story. A final component of each instructional cycle was individual reading by each child, using either the retelling or an appropriate book. Throughout the course of the school year, longer trade books were introduced. Although the majority of children participating in this early intervention program were indeed reading by the end of first grade, only one-third to one-half of them were reading at grade level.

Restructured Chapter I

In Chapter 7 we discussed congressional efforts to help disadvantaged children through Title I of the Elementary and Secondary Education Act of 1965, which was reauthorized as Chapter I. Here we have selected an intervention to restructure Chapter I services to illustrate an alternative model for using these resources (Hiebert et al., 1992). The restructuring began by reducing the numbers of students the teacher instructed at any one time from eight to three. This was made possible through the use of teacher aides who were funded by Chapter I. The second step was to work closely with the Chapter I teachers in the design of curriculum and instruction that would enable first graders to achieve grade-appropriate reading skills. Toward this end, there were three activities around which each lesson was organized: reading, writing, and word study (phonemic awareness).

To ensure that the children were engaged in sufficient reading of text, repeated reading of predictable text was selected as the primary oral reading activity, during which children were taught to track the print as they read aloud. Selected books were also brought home, and parents were asked to verify that their children had read at home. The reading of 10 books at home resulted in the award of a trade book. Writing activity included maintaining a personal journal (during which children received guidance in the use of phonetically plausible invented spellings) and constructing sentences around word patterns to which the children had been exposed in the reading activity. Finally, the word study (phonemic awareness) portion of each lesson consisted of two activities: one, designed to heighten awareness of phonemic identity, engaged the child in selecting rhyming words from among a list read aloud, and the other, designed to heighten awareness of phonemic segmentation, called for the child to listen carefully as a word was pronounced with elongated sounds and to move a chip as she or he heard each new sound in the word.

The effectiveness of the restructured program was evaluated in multiple ways. First, the participating students' achievement was compared with an absolute level of achievement (proficient grade-level reading). Second, end-of-year achievement of the participating Chapter I students was compared with nonparticipating students (from district programs that were not enrolled in the restructuring effort.) Finally, the researchers compared the end-of-year performance of the participating Chapter I students with nonidentified classmates who had begun the year with higher performance on reading assessments. All three forms of assessment revealed significant differences in favor of participation in the restructured program, in terms of primer-level fluency, first-grade text fluency, and performance on a standardized reading assessment.

COMPUTER SUPPORT FOR READING INSTRUCTION

Recent advances in computer technology offer new support for reading instruction. Digitized and high-quality synthetic speech has been incorporated into programs focusing on phonological awareness and issues related to emergent literacy, letter-name and letter-sound knowledge, phonological decoding, spelling, and support for word decoding and comprehension while reading and writing stories. Computer speech, along with interesting graphics, animation, and speech recording, has supported the development of programs that are entertaining and motivating for both prereaders and beginning readers.

Talking books, widely distributed on CD-ROM, are among the most popular programs that claim to improve children's reading. Book pages are presented on the computer screen, and children can select the whole text or specific words and phrases to be read aloud by the computer. The most popular books include many clever animations that are highly entertaining to children, perhaps so much so that they distract from the task of reading; children can often access the animations without paying any attention to the print.

Storybook software displays storybooks on the screen. The programs come not only with software but also with ordinary printed material available for use without a computer. Some are stand-alone titles, such as *Living Books* and *Discus* books. Others are parts of larger sets, such as IBM's *Stories and More* and Josten's *Dragontales*.

Multimedia writing tools engage children in oral language about their composing acts and final compositions. Children integrate previously prepared background illustrations, their own drawings, and writing into either stand-alone "papers" or multimedia slide shows.

The development of *comprehensive literacy software* for pre-primary and primary-grade literacy has been accelerating, together with the more recent surge in the power/cost ratio of desktop computers. IBM's *Writing to Read* program set the stage for classroom use of comprehensive literacy software programs for use in beginning reading instruction. Comprehensive literacy software programs that have been developed more recently and for which systematic evaluation has begun include *Foundations in Learning* by Breakthrough, *Early Reading Program* by Waterford, and the *Little Planet Literacy Series* by Young Children's Literacy Project.

Although the promise of new computer technology is real, it is still only a promise by any large-scale measure of effectiveness to address reading instruction. First, the availability of serviceable technology in U.S. schools remains unevenly distributed across school districts and is generally low. Second, for schools that have or are given hardware and software, studies repeatedly report implementation difficulties (Cuban, 1986; Sandholtz et al., 1997; Schofield, 1995).

Finally, even if current computing and networking resources were universally and easily available and practitioners were universally prepared to use them in their classrooms, their potential educational value depends on the quality of the software itself. Software can promote learning only to the extent that it engages students' attention—yet software that engages students' attention may or may not promote learning. The features and dynamics of software that determine its educational efficacy are subtle and, despite developers' best intentions, are often absent or mismanaged (Papert, 1996). As computing resources become more available, software that is well marketed, adequately engaging, and superficially appropriate may be purchased and used for educational purposes regardless of its real educational value in improving students' reading performance. To date, a great deal of educational software design is a commercial art rather than an instructional science: it needs to be both. An analytic base is urgently needed for properly guiding and evaluating future educational software offerings.

In summary, with the availability of technology, quality software, and well-prepared practitioners, there is the potential for students to benefit. The materials described in this section were designed to offer distinct instructional strategies for learning to read; evaluation of each has revealed successful literacy growth and development in children (Sharp et al, 1995; Heuston, 1997; Zimmerman, 1997). Yet the use of educational technology and software is not available for all children; low and uneven distribution of technology places low-income and minority school districts at a disadvantage. Many schools do not have enough computers or have outdated nonfunctioning equipment. They may even lack the technical support and knowledge needed to maintain the use of computers in classrooms. Ultimately, constant evaluation and development of these resources will increase the value of technology in education.

RETENTION IN GRADE

In recent years, some schools have raised their kindergarten entrance age and have adopted the use of screening tests to determine school readiness (Cannella and Reiff, 1989). Some parents, hoping to avoid early school failure—or to increase the likelihood of having a child who excels in comparison to classmates—have responded to the increased academic demands of kindergarten by holding their young children out of school for an extra year before kindergarten. This practice is sometimes referred to as "buy a year" or BAY (May and Welch, 1984). One effect of this growing practice is that the gap between the most and least advanced children in kindergarten and first grade has widened, making it more likely that children at the low end of their classes initially will appear even less successful when compared with older classmates.

In order to accommodate the perceived needs of at-risk children, schools have turned increasingly to providing them with an extra year of school. In addition to retention, or repetition of a grade, some school districts' extra-year programs, variously known as prekindergarten or transitional first-grade or developmental first-grade classes, serve to extend the school career of many youngsters, as does retention at a grade level. Provisions for extra time in school are also secured through full-day (as opposed to half-day) kindergarten classes and through extending the length of the school year. Generally, the purpose of such options is to allow children the time and appropriate experiences needed for future school success.

Across the nation, the children most likely to be retained in early grades are those who are younger than their classmates, boys, children from low socioeconomic backgrounds, and ethnic or linguistic minorities (Meisels and Liaw, 1993). In the early grades, failure to achieve grade-level expectations in reading is the primary reason for retention. Retention has many supporters among teachers, administrators, and the public, but there is little evidence that retention practices are helpful to children (Shepard and Smith, 1990).

It is also important to note that few of these studies distinguish between children who are merely retained and those who are retained and receive special assistance. One such study found more favorable longitudinal results for achievement for children who did receive special services in the year following a grade retention.

A frequently cited effect of retention is the significantly higher school dropout rate for students who have experienced grade retention (Roderick, 1994). Other research indicates that dropping out is not a one-time, one-moment phenomenon. Students *begin* dropping out long before they are actually considered dropouts for data collection purposes. Clearly, we need to learn more about the social, emotional, and cognitive factors that precede dropping out. Furthermore, in the absence of better research, it is probably unwise to suggest, as some have, that the practice of retention in kindergarten and first grade should be entirely banned. It is certainly possible that for some children repeating a grade with services from a reading specialist or related service provider may produce more positive results than merely repeating the same sequence of instruction without any modifications, or moving on to the next grade with or without support. Nevertheless, the value of retention as a practice for preventing reading difficulties has not yet been amply demonstrated.

SPECIAL EDUCATION FOR LEARNING DISABILITIES

One response to the problems of children with reading difficulties is placement in special education programs, primarily services for children identified as learning disabled. In this section we discuss some factors that have limited the delivery of special education services to children with reading difficulties in the primary grades, as well as ways to maximize the benefits of reading instruction in these programs.

Federal legislation, notably Public Law (P.L.) 94-142 in 1975 and its amendments in 1986, was enacted to ensure the basic right to appropriate education for all children with disabilities, including specific learning disabilities in reading and writing. Congress intended that special education should address the problem of identifying and treating reading disabilities during the early school grades.

However, the law contained a definition of specific reading disability that has often contributed to an unfortunate delay in identification and treatment: to be eligible for special education placement, children must exhibit a severe discrepancy, typically 1.5 standard deviation units, between standardized tests of their reading achievement and their general intellectual ability. Schools are often hesitant to use standardized tests of reading achievement or IQ before the third grade, in the belief that most children with early reading problems will grow out of them. Longitudinal studies have shown, however, that most children who are substantially behind at the end of first grade remain behind in the later grades (Juel, 1988). When the disparity between achievement and IQ is finally noted in the later grades, it may be much more difficult for remedial instruction to counteract the emotional and educational consequences of early reading failure.

A second problem with the aptitude-achievement discrepancy criterion is that basic reading deficits and responsiveness to intervention have not been shown to be significantly different in children who meet or do not meet this criterion (discussed in Chapter 3). For example, a child with a standard reading score of 75 and an IQ of 90 is likely to show similar benefits from remedial instruction when compared with a child who has a reading score of 75 and an IQ of

100, but only the latter child would have a sufficient aptitude-achievement discrepancy to be eligible for special education services in most states. The learning disabilities field is acutely aware of the problems created by an arbitrary discrepancy criterion for special education services (see Lyon, 1995). The 1997 reauthorization of P.L. 94-142, however, still includes the earlier discrepancy criterion for specific learning disabilities.

In addition to the need for earlier intervention with less emphasis on aptitude-achievement discrepancy, there are a number of other complexities involved in considering the role of special education for young children with reading difficulties. The 1997 reauthorization of P.L. 94-142 discussed several concerns that needed to be addressed. These included the assurance of quality instruction in the regular classroom to reduce the number of students needing special education services, the use of proven methods and well-trained teachers in special education programs, greater attention to the effective integration of special education and regular classroom instruction, and the maintenance of high expectations for the achievement of children with learning disabilities.

An important component of the 1997 reauthorization of P.L. 94-142 is its detailed agenda for additional research aimed at improving special education. Specified areas of research include the design of assessment tools to more accurately determine the specific needs of children with reading disabilities, longitudinal studies such as the one by Englert et al. (1995) to determine the optimal methods and intensity of instruction, and studies of effective practices for preparing teachers to provide services to children with learning disabilities. The knowledge gained from this research and its dissemination throughout the nation's teaching colleges and primary schools will help special education programs increase their contribution to the early prevention and remediation of reading disabilities.

Although many current special education programs for children with reading disabilities may fail to address some or all of the above concerns, there are some well-documented examples of successful programs. In one, the Early Literacy Project (ELP), special educators worked in collaboration with university educators to devise an approach that would be meaningful and beneficial for students with mild disabilities in primary special education classrooms (Englert and Tarrant, 1995).

The principles of the Early Literacy Project include embedding literacy instruction in meaningful and integrated activities that span the disparate areas of the literacy curriculum (reading, writing, listening, speaking), guiding students to be self-regulating in their learning activity, and responsively instructing students. Activities involve the reading of connected text (using choral and partner reading to enhance word attack and fluency) and writing connected text (using emergent writing principles as well as strategy instruction in composition), interwoven through the use of a thematically based curriculum and teaching. Students in the Early Literacy Project also continue to receive instruction in Project Read, a systematic approach to phonics instruction that was in place in the participating schools. The comparison children for a study of the effectiveness of the ELP program were students in special education settings who were receiving Project Read instruction only.

The outcomes indicated that the average gain of children in the Project Read condition was .5 years on measures of word reading. The growth on the part of ELP students ranged from .7 years for those students whose teachers were in the project one year to 1.3 years for those students whose teachers were in their second year of the project. Furthermore, of the 23 students who received two or three years of instruction in their original teachers' classrooms, 19 were reading at or above grade level by the end of the second or third year and only four students continued to read below grade level.

This research is significant in several respects. First, it illustrates how curriculum and instruction can be designed and conducted in special education settings to advance children's literacy learning. Second, the finding regarding the more significant gains made by children whose teachers were more experienced in this form of instruction points out the important role that teacher expertise plays in maximizing their effectiveness with students who have significant reading problems. Finally, in the push for the inclusion of all children in the general education classroom, regardless of disability condition, it is important that we not lose sight of the intensive assistance that many of these students need in order to achieve at grade level; assistance that will be very difficult to provide in a classroom context in which there is a ratio of 1 teacher to 25 to 30 children.

CONTROVERSIAL THERAPIES

Perhaps because of the serious consequences that a history of reading difficulties poses for children, or perhaps because of the intractable nature of some of these reading problems, the area of reading and learning disabilities has seen more than its fair share of therapies. These therapies are controversial in the sense that they are not supported by either contemporary theoretical understandings of the causes and nature of reading problems, nor are they supported by an empirical base. The therapies range from psychological to pharmaceutical to neurophysiological interventions—although clearly not all such therapies are controversial.

A number of reviews provide examples of controversial treatments that have garnered the attention, typically of the news media, and in turn, of parents and professionals as well (Hannell et al., 1991; Kavale and Forness; 1987; American Optometric Association, 1988; Worral, 1990; Silver, 1987). Those interventions for which, currently, there are no confirmed or replicated research findings that have nevertheless been touted to address reading and learning disabilities include: (a) neurophysiological retraining, which includes "patterning," optometric visual training, cerebellar-vestibular stimulation, and applied kinesiology; (b) nutritional therapies, such as megavitamin therapy and elimination (of synthetic flavors and colors) diet therapies; (c) the use of tinted lenses to correct for color sensitivity and thereby cure dyslexia; and (d) educational therapies, such as modality testing and teaching.

The consequences of the proliferation of quick fixes have an ethical dimension. As desperate parents cling to the hope for a miracle cure for their child's learning problem, more efficacious solutions are ignored. The disappointments add to the stresses already experienced by the parents of children with reading problems. A number of these therapies are a financial burden. Clearly parents need guidance and children need the best interventions for which we can develop evidence as to their efficacy and feasibility.

SUMMARY

Several important themes have been stressed in this chapter. First, each literacy intervention must be considered in light of available resources, including financial, instructional, cultural, timing, and time required. Second, it is imperative to assess the existing external factors or characteristics before simply adding an intervention. Consideration must be given to the adequacy of existing instructional practices before deciding to implement any intervention. Third, the process of determining appropriate interventions must take into account the characteristics of students who are at risk for failure. For example, if an entire school is at risk, it might be wiser to begin an intervention that includes school-wide restructuring, as presented in Chapter 7, than to devote resources on an isolated tutoring technique.

Furthermore, a close examination of the successful supplementary interventions described in this chapter reveals a number of common features across these studies:

• Duration of the intervention—generally occurring on a daily basis for the duration of a school year or a good portion of the school year.

• The amount of instructional time—all successful interventions involve more time in reading and writing than for children not at risk—but extra time is not sufficient in itself.

• In each case, there is an array of activities that generally consist of some reading (and rereading) of continuous text. In addition, each intervention features some form of word study. In some cases, specific strategies for decoding are incorporated.

• In all cases, writing is an important feature. However, the writing activity is not simply support while engaging in invented spelling; it is typically conducted in a more systematic manner.

• Although materials vary among the interventions, in each case there is careful attention paid to the characteristics of the material used, whether they are characterized as predictable, patterned, sequenced from easy to more difficult, or phonologically protected.

There is a focus on using text that children will find interesting and engaging.

• Each program includes carefully planned assessments that closely monitor the response of each child to the intervention.

Professional development of teachers, teachers aides, and professional or volunteer tutors were integral to each program—there is an important relationship between the skill of the teacher and the response of the children to early intervention. Effective intervention programs pay close attention to the preparation and supervision of the teachers or tutors.

PART IV

Knowledge into Action

Both knowledge about reading and a commitment to improvement are required in order to develop and implement policies and practices that will help prevent reading difficulties among young children. In Part IV we describe the contemporary situation and propose our recommendations for change.

In Chapter 9, we discuss the impact that this report must have on the professionals who have daily interactions with the children in day care centers, preschools, kindergarten, and the early elementary grades and on children's families and other community members. Governmental bodies (including federal, state, and local education agencies), publishers, and the mass media also have an impact on the issues.

The best approach to teaching children to read has for decades been a matter of considerable controversy and passionate confrontation. At this point, the science base has developed sufficiently to permit this synthesis of the research on early reading development with the goal of making recommendations about preventing difficulties in reading. In Chapter 10, we weave the insights of many research traditions into clear guidelines for helping children become successful readers.

9

The Agents of Change

Families and other community members are clearly important in the effort to prevent children's reading difficulties, and many of the strategies described in Chapters 5 and 8 are pursued outside schooling. But to reach the important national goal of preventing reading difficulties among young children, the professionals who have daily interactions with the children in day care centers, preschools, kindergarten, and the early elementary grades are the most essential audience for the information in this report. We therefore give teachers and teacher education the most detailed treatment in this chapter on agents of change. We also consider the ways that federal, state, and local education agencies, publishers, and mass media have an impact on the issues. Each of these groups needs knowledge about reading and a commitment to improvement in order to develop and implement policies and practices that will help prevent reading difficulties among young children. In this chapter, we describe the current situation; in the next, we present our recommendations for change.

In broad outline, the prevention of reading difficulties is not exotic. In school and out, young children can profit from a wide range of experiences. In classrooms in which teachers use effective teaching and organizational strategies and appropriate materials, most children make progress. Throughout their early years, children can consolidate their knowledge and skills as they recite songs and rhymes, play with the sounds of words, interact with the meaning and the print while people read to them and take them to the library, play *at* reading and writing, and get engaged with activities through television programs such as *Sesame Street*.

To prevent reading difficulties, children should be provided with:

- Opportunities to explore the various uses and functions of written language and to develop appreciation and command of them.
- Opportunities to grasp and master the use of the alphabetic principle for reading and writing.
- Opportunities to develop and enhance language and meta-cognitive skills to meet the demands of understanding printed texts.
- Opportunities to experience contexts that promote enthusiasm and success in learning to read and write, as well as learning *by* reading and writing.
- Opportunities for children *likely to experience* difficulties in becoming fluent readers to be identified and to participate in effective prevention programs.
- Opportunities for children *experiencing* difficulties in becoming fluent readers to be identified and to participate in effective intervention and remediation programs, well integrated with ongoing good classroom instruction.

Children need the full variety of opportunities and enough of each so that they are successful readers. Adults in different roles in society have different opportunities and obligations to make changes so that reading difficulties can be prevented.

TEACHER PREPARATION

Teacher preparation is fundamental in order to prevent difficulties in reading among young children. A recent study of more than 1,000 school districts concluded that every additional dollar spent on more highly qualified teachers netted greater improvements in student achievement than did any other use of school resources (Ferguson, 1991).

Today's teachers must understand a great deal about how children develop and learn, what they know, and what they can do. Teachers must know and be able to apply a variety of teaching techniques to meet the individual needs of students. They must be able to identify students' strengths and weaknesses and plan instructional programs that help students make progress. In addition to this expertise in pedagogy, teachers must master and integrate content knowledge that underlies the various subjects in the children's curriculum.

Pre-service and in-service teacher education is intended to develop teacher expertise for teaching reading and preventing reading difficulties, but it encounters many obstacles. Programs for teachers' professional development often flounder, lacking a strong apprenticeship system and hobbled by the course-by-course approach in college education. They cannot meet the challenge inherent in trying to prepare teachers for highly complex and increasingly diverse schools and classrooms; the challenge of keeping abreast of current developments in research and practice once teachers begin to teach; the complexity of the knowledge base itself, which often appears to support conflicting positions and recommendations; and the difficulty of learning many of the skills required to enact the knowledge base, particularly to work with those children having the most difficulties.

Early Childhood Education

The field of early childhood education has traditionally offered professional training at prebaccalaureate levels in both pre-service and in-service programs. Some colleges of education have baccalaureate and master's degrees for early childhood teacher education programs, but often they are add-on programs to an elementary teaching certification. Sometimes training in early childhood education is divorced from the schools of education, housed instead in departments of home economics, for example. Given the cognitive complexity and practical importance of development in early childhood, preschool education could be a very demanding and interesting major course of study, but it is seldom presented as such.

In many states, certification requirements for early childhood education are nonexistent. Preschool teachers have a generally low rate of pay (compared, for example, with elementary school teachers); they are generally seen to have lower status than elementary school teachers both in practice settings and in universities and other practitioner preparation settings.

Little systematic attention has been paid to in-service education and other options for professional development for preschool teachers. There are, however, some thought-provoking programs for preparing people to focus on literacy with preschool children, and they raise interesting problems. Box 9-1 is an example of one such program.

Preschool teachers are an important resource in promoting literacy. In view of the power with which language and literacy skills at elementary school entry predict children's responsiveness to early reading instruction, the ability and commitment of early childhood professionals to support the skills that provide a foundation for reading need to be taken seriously. Programs that educate early childhood professionals should include in their curricula information about:

- how to provide rich conceptual experiences that promote growth in vocabulary and reasoning skills;
- lexical development, from early referential (naming) abilities to relational and abstract terms and finer-shaded meanings;
- the early development of listening comprehension skills, and the kinds of syntactic and prose structures that preschool children may not yet have mastered;
- young children's sense of story;
- young children's sensitivity to the sounds of language;
- developmental conceptions of written language (print awareness);
- development of concepts of space, including directionality;
- fine motor development; and
- means for inspiring motivation to read.

BOX 9-1
Preparing Preschool Teachers to Promote Literacy

A 15-year partnership between the Erikson Institute and Head Start staff in Chicago has evolved into professional development that spans 10 months of the year and includes seminars as well as work in preschool centers. Preschool practitioners have durable preconceptions of what activities are appropriate and productive for the children they work with, as McLane and McNamee (1990, 1997) point out. When the Institute staff introduces the Head Start teachers to new activities, strategies, or concepts that can foster literacy, the effort can be undermined unless attention is paid to the adaptations practitioners make to the new activities, strategies, and concepts when they take them into their classrooms.

The institute researchers found it especially important to grapple with Head Start teachers' preference for oral over written communication. When the in-service curriculum focused on shared storybook reading, it tended to be realized as storytelling by the Head Start teachers in their work with the children; emergent group writing tended also to turn into storytelling; dramatic play that once had a literacy focus would turn into play devoid of reference to written language (McLane and McNamee, 1997). When the teachers transformed the activities, the results might be enjoyable and valuable for the children, but the part of the activity that was intended to foster literacy often disappeared.

Only given more extended collaborative work between the institute staff and the Head Start teachers were such problems ironed out and the new approaches refined for maximum value for literacy support. McLane and McNamee came to recognize that the teachers valued oral language artistry and creatively provided occasions for children to develop it. Some of the teachers, though, as they grew up in the same communities that the children currently in their care are being reared in, had developed no fondness for reading and writing. It was easy, then, for the teachers to de-emphasize and eventually lose the literacy aspect of new activities when doing them with the children. With continued effort to address the literacy purpose of the new activities in seminars and in the context of the specific preschool classrooms, the in-service education was more complete and the literacy aspects of the new activities appeared more reliably.

A critical component in the preparation of preschool teachers is supervised, relevant, clinical experience in which pre-service teachers receive ongoing guidance and feedback. A principal goal of this experience is the ability to integrate and apply the knowledge base in practice. Collaborative support by both the teacher preparation institution and the field placement is essential.

Each state has developed and published minimal standards for group child care settings (public or private), addressing such issues as adult-child ratio, safety, and health. In general, however, these standards do not adequately address cognitive, linguistic, and literacy supports. Professional standards for early childhood classrooms have been elaborated by the National Association for the Education of Young Children. Head Start has identified performance standards, which are reviewed and evaluated every three years during site visits to every Head Start program. It is notable that relatively few of the evaluation items are related to issues of the quality of the language or literacy environment.

Although public education does not extend to preschools, movements in many states have given children access to preschool regardless of their parents' ability to pay. The National Governors Association has adopted the following objective: "All disadvantaged and disabled children will have access to high-quality and developmentally appropriate preschool programs that help prepare children for school" (National Governors Association, 1992). Subgoals are listed for states to use to assess progress toward this objective. One subgoal is to track the percentage of programs that are accredited by the National Association for the Education of Young Children or the National Association of Family Day Care and the programs that employ a majority of staff with a child development associate credential. The governors' programs have a good track record with elementary school systemic reforms. Given this record and the interest in early childhood programs stimulated by publicity about brain and behavior developments in the early years, activism by the National Governors Association about preschools can serve as leverage points for change in preschool programs and the preparation of adults working in them.

There is a widespread lack of specificity about literacy and language development in preschool reform efforts. In contrast, in a position paper on teacher preparation the Orton Dyslexia Society takes the following position on requirements for preschool teachers (1997:16):

In addition to stimulating oral expressive language, language comprehension, and print awareness, nursery school and kindergarten teachers should know how best to foster phonological awareness and to link recognition of sounds with letters. Teachers of young children should know how to identify the language problems of children at risk for reading difficulty.

Elementary School Education

In the typical pre-service course of study, very little time is allocated to preparing to teach reading. Virtually all states require that K-3 teacher credential candidates do at least some course work in the teaching of reading (National Association of State Directors of Teacher Education, 1996). In some cases, reading is embedded in a course for teaching English language arts, diluting the focus on reading. The amount of time is insufficient to provide beginning teachers with the knowledge and skills necessary to enable them to help all children become successful readers. As Goodlad (1997:36) notes:

> Most teachers of the primary grades take one course in the teaching of reading. Some take two, so that the average is about 1.3 courses per teacher. This is about enough to enable teachers to accelerate a little the reading prowess of children who learn to read quite readily. It is enough to enable teachers to become quite facile in sorting the children into three groups—one of good, one of fair, and the other of poor readers. . . . Diagnosis and remediation of the nonreaders lie largely outside the repertoire of teachers whose brief pedagogical preparation provided little more than an overview. . . . [M]any first grade children are taught by successive waves of neophytes, large numbers of whom drop out after three or four years of teaching.

Given the severe constraints on the amount of time that can be dedicated to any one topic in a teacher education program, teacher preparation must be seen as a career-long *continuum of development*. In other words, learning to become a successful teacher—of reading or any other subject—cannot be seen as the consummate function of an undergraduate program or a fifth-year credential program. Indeed, what needs to be learned cannot be learned in the limited time available in formal education. Instead, teacher preparation must be seen as a long-term developmental process, beginning with undergraduate preparation, continuing with professional schooling in upper-division and fifth-year courses and field practica, and continuing further once teachers are technically credentialed or licensed and working in classrooms but are still serving apprenticeships before becoming fully expert teachers.

Beginning teachers, particularly for children who are learning to read, cannot be expected to rely on the little preparation their preservice courses provide; no teachers, beginning or experienced, can be expected to grow professionally if isolated. Professional development includes not only formal meetings and courses but also opportunities for teachers to work with each other and to visit classrooms. The National Commission on Teaching and America's Future (1996) has called for support for beginning and for more experienced teachers. Beginning teachers must be successfully inducted into the profession and be provided with additional support, opportunities, and incentives for further education to ensure their early and continued success. More experienced teachers must continue receiving substantive and effective in-service education opportunities, with highly effective teachers receiving rewards and acknowledgments for their skills and demonstrated effectiveness.

What Elementary Teachers Need to Know

In Table 9-1, we align teacher preparation with the opportunities that should be provided to young children in order to best prevent reading difficulties, listing what teachers need to know to be able to provide adequately for their students. Some of the knowledge base can be acquired in general college education, before a concentration in teacher preparation. Other aspects are the more specific knowledge and skills that should be organized as course work and practicum experiences for teacher education.

Take, for example, the first set of studies in Table 9-1, related to giving children the opportunity to explore the various uses and functions of written language and to develop appreciation and command of them. Teachers must have a deep understanding of the what, the how, and the why of language and literacy. To know enough to teach children, they must acquire an understanding of the nature of language that is firmly based on linguistic research about phonologi-

TABLE 9-1 Teacher Preparation Needed to Provide Opportunities for Children to Become Readers

Teacher Study	For Child Opportunity
Linguistic and psycholinguistic studies: • distinctive and contrasting features of written and oral language, the relation between phonological units and alphabetic writing • ontogeny of oral and written language including bilingual development	(1) to explore the various uses and functions of written language and to develop appreciation and command of them.
Rhetorical, sociological, sociolinguistic, and anthropological studies: • genres, registers, and functions of texts, social and cultural contexts of texts and literacy activities, varied theoretical accounts of processing meaning, social and regional dialect variations	
Pedagogy of reading (teaching and assessing): • activities with a variety of texts for young children • integration of school experience with written language out of school	
Psychology of reading: • studies of oral language, phoneme identity and manipulation, letter-sound association, working memory • ontogeny of alphabetic reading and writing	(2) to grasp and master use of the alphabetic principle in reading and writing.
Pedagogy of reading (teaching and assessing): • activities with sublexical structure of spoken language • activities associating letters with sounds • activities to automate word identification processes	

continued on next page

TABLE 9-1 Continued

Teacher study	For Child Opportunity
Linguistic and psychological studies: • ontogeny of oral and written language abilities, including relations among meta-cognitive abilities, print processing abilities, and comprehension abilities	(3) to develop and enhance language and meta-cognitive skills to meet the demands of understanding printed texts.
Pedagogy of reading (teaching and assessing): • activities to develop and practice comprehension and meta-cognition strategies on oral language, on written text read aloud, and as the child reads independently • activities to develop concepts and words (oral and written)	
Psychological, sociological, and anthropological studies: • variations in social and cultural contexts associated with print and oral language and achievement motivation	(4) to experience contexts that promote enthusiasm and success in learning to read and write and in learning by reading and writing.
Pedagogy of reading (teaching and assessing): • activities to serve and expand the literacy goals of the learner, cultivate a variety of interests, and access the affective aspects of written and oral language • activities to enlist the active cooperation of families and community institutions to support the child learning to read	
Psychological and sociological studies: • studies of risk factors for reading difficulties, assessment procedures, diagnostic measures and systems for monitoring progress in reading • studies of prevention programs in schools and out	(5) for children likely to experience difficulties to be identified and to participate in effective prevention programs.

Pedagogy of reading:
- coordination with school and community resources for preventing difficulties
- assessing child's needs and matching to prevention strategies
- activities to build on prevention strategies

Psychological and sociological studies:
- studies of assessment procedures and diagnostic measures
- studies of intervention programs in schools and out

Pedagogy of reading:
- identifying intervention strategies available in school and community
- assessing child's needs in reading and matching with intervention strategy
- managing continuous assessment and placement cycles, and two-way information flow with school and community resources, including reading specialists, tutors, and family
- activities that intervene for children in need, including explicit instruction and enrichment experiences that will provide the context for self-teaching, and instruction to complement and build on intervention strategies that take place out of the classroom

(6) for children experiencing difficulties to be identified and to participate in effective intervention and remediation programs, well-integrated with classroom instruction.

cal, syntactic, semantic, pragmatic, rhetorical structures, as well as the social and linguistic diversity in all of these. From psychological research, they must understand the processes of producing and understanding spoken and written language and the courses of individual development among bilinguals as well as monolinguals. From the humanities and other social sciences, they must understand the variations in structures, contexts, and motives that underlie the concrete instances of written and oral language in society.

That is an information base that may be acquired before a teacher preparation program begins. Teacher candidates must also acquire an understanding of the alphabetic principle and the ways in which oral and written language contrast and support each other as children emerge into literacy and begin to process written language to read and write. The future teacher's child development study must focus on oral language development, emergent literacy development, and the interaction of development and instruction affecting the processing of alphabetic print and getting meaning from it.

Course work and practica to take pedagogical advantage of this knowledge base should teach future teachers how to choose among, create, and work with texts and activities so as to best support children's learning and monitor their progress, providing additional activities that challenge or assist individual children as needed. The texts should include not only the fictional and expository text that appears in school books to be read and discussed, but also children's own writings, with attention to the texts important to the lives of the children out of school, like menus and magazines, notes to and from home, and written versions of songs they enjoy.

Six addenda should be kept in mind while reading Table 9-1. First, there is not a unique relationship between the items on the teacher study list and the different opportunities that should be provided for children; a course or practicum experience may serve more than one purpose. Second, each part is necessary to the whole construction of good teaching that can prevent reading difficulties. Third, teacher study should include preparation for keeping abreast of new developments in the field of teaching reading to young children and for separating the wheat from the chaff therein, as well as practice in translating new information about literacy development and difficulties into instructional and assessment activities for children. The knowledge base will continue to grow and teachers need to be informed consumers of research. Fourth, making schools and staff accountable for improved results must go hand in hand with support for staff and for staff development. Fifth, the responsibility for continuous improvement is shared by a community in the school; there should be pre-service preparation and continuing opportunity for teachers to work with colleagues to increase their collective ability to meet the needs of the children. Sixth, teaching beginning reading and preparing teachers to do so should be the top priority in schools with a record of widespread poor reading performance.

Teacher Education

Teacher education has been under attack for a number of years. The National Commission on Teaching and America's Future (1996) recently issued yet another scathing indictment, calling the state of teacher preparation "a great national shame." In a review of the literature on professional growth among pre-service and beginning teachers, Kagan (1992:162) concludes that "almost every one of the 40 studies reviewed [here] indicates that university courses fail to provide novices with adequate procedural knowledge of classrooms, adequate knowledge of pupils or the extended practica needed to acquire that knowledge, or a realistic view of teaching in its full classroom/school context." Kagan's review has been criticized (Grossman, 1992; Dunkin, 1996), but many teachers seem to agree with her dark appraisal of the state of teacher education (Lyon et al., 1989; Rigden, 1997).

Several commentators note that teacher preparation for the teaching of reading has not been adequate to bring about the research-based changes in classroom practices that result in success (Corlett, 1988; Nolen et al., 1990; Moats and Lyon, 1996; Moats, 1994). Even if sufficient course work with the needed content were available, the problem of transferring the knowledge to the future teacher's practice must be addressed. Case-based instruction with interactive video could be a powerful tool in reaching this goal (see Box 9-2); as with early childhood education, however, the critical

---

BOX 9-2
Case-Based Instruction

Case-based instruction is the norm in business education, and it is becoming more common in teacher pre-service education. One set of materials has been produced to assist in case-based pre-service teacher education related to reading (Risko and Kinzer, 1997; Risko, 1991). Like other case-based instruction, it includes lesson plans, students' reading scores and records, descriptions of the activities undertaken, and background information. The cases are available to be more fully explored than most, because videodiscs are included; the instructor and students can view and review actual classroom footage as well as superimpose different audio tracks onto the teaching events so that the perspectives of parents, administrators, and expert discussants can be linked to the teaching-learning interactions. Of the eight cases, four focus on ordinary development in reading and four on remedial treatment, reflecting a range of situations (urban, suburban, rural, advantaged and disadvantaged populations, ethnic and language diversity), and half of the cases deal with children under grade 4. Evaluations during the five-year development period have shown differences in the courses in which the cases are used as well as in practicum experiences that the students encountered later (Risko, 1992, 1996; Risko et al., 1996).

The patterns of participation in the pre-service courses that used the materials were different and led to increased student ability to integrate sources of information in order to identify problems and resources for solution. In the subsequent practicum, the student teachers who had learned from the videodisc cases were more persistent in problem solving, more likely to identify problems that arose, and more adept at seeking help to solve them. It appears that a pre-service teacher education program can find case-based instruction useful as a bridge between the course-based and practicum-based elements of a program of studies.

---

component in the preparation of pre-service teachers is supervised, relevant, clinical experience in which pre-service teachers receive ongoing guidance and feedback. A principal goal of this experience is the ability to integrate and apply the knowledge base productively and reflectively in practice.

Continuing professional development should build on the pre-service education of teachers, strengthen teaching skills, increase teacher knowledge of the reading process, and facilitate the integration of newer research on reading into the teaching practices of the classroom teacher. Professional development efforts, however, are often poorly implemented and fail to assist teachers to learn complex conceptualizations and make needed changes in their teaching practice (Little et al., 1987).

There are severe structural constraints on in-service teacher education: in the United States, teachers teach all day, have very few pupil-free days as part of their working year, and have very few opportunities to develop new knowledge and skills on the job. Administrative and political commitment to in-service education is lacking, as evidenced by the limited time and financial resources made available. On average, districts spend less than one-half of 1 percent of their resources on staff development (Darling-Hammond, 1996).

A 1978 study reported that the average teacher in the United States engaged in the formal study of teaching and schooling, including new content and curriculum, for only about three days per year (Howey et al., 1978). Professional development in the United States is still characterized by one-shot workshops rather than more effective problem-based approaches that are built into teachers' ongoing work with colleagues (Darling-Hammond, 1996). Considering the broad knowledge that the elementary school teacher needs to teach in all content areas, as well as knowledge of classroom management techniques and appropriate discipline approaches, the percentage of staff development time dedicated to reading must be relatively small.

The content, context, and quality of in-service professional development vary greatly from school district to school district; Calfee and Drum, in *The Handbook of Research on Teaching* (third edition, 1986) describe the situation as chaotic. There is no consistency with respect to content or to the qualifications of providers. There is little doubt that teachers can learn powerful and complex strategies for teaching, provided that they are presented properly (Joyce and Showers, 1988; Lanier and Little, 1986).

Much of the literature on in-service education for the teaching of reading focuses on the development of effective models for presentation (e.g., Collins et al., 1989; Hollingsworth, 1989; Joyce and Showers, 1988; Monroe and Smith, 1985; Winn and Mitchell, 1991). A common theme is the importance of modeling, coaching, and explicit feedback for the learner. Other components of staff development models include teacher involvement in the planning and development of the sessions, a relationship between the goals of the in-service sessions and the goals of the school, the opportunity for teachers to discuss and reflect on the content of the sessions, consideration of the individual differences in the background knowledge and preparation of the participants, and a commitment on the part of the learner to apply the information from the in-service sessions to classroom practice. Reviewing the effects of different components, including theory, demonstration, practice, and feedback, one study found consistent effect size increases when components were combined, with the largest effect size for both knowledge and transfer to practice when in-class coaching was added to theory, demonstration, practice, and feedback (Bennett, 1987).

Professional development is most satisfactory to the individuals involved when it is based on the needs of the professionals in the school and when it is delivered in the school (Futrell et al., 1995). Quality professional development integrates knowledge and skill development: meaningful intellectual substance explicating theories from sources both inside and outside teaching can be tailored effectively to the context, experience, and needs of the particular teachers by providing demonstrations and opportunities for practice and feedback (Little, 1993; Monroe and Smith, 1985; Joyce and Showers, 1988).

Researchers point to a shift in the focus of staff development from specificity, practicality, and intensity in technical support to a cognitive-conceptual framework combined with demonstration and practice (Gersten and Brengelman, 1996). Fundamental understanding of the psychological as well as the social nature of reading and writing on the teacher's part enhances classroom practice (Nolen et al., 1990; Tharp and Gallimore, 1988), mediated by the way the deepening concepts influence instructional decisions (Nolen et al., 1990).

Simply providing teachers with information about new instructional strategies does not necessarily result in changes in existing teaching behaviors (Goldenberg and Gallimore, 1991a). Instead of lectures, staff development can involve teacher research, discussion

---

BOX 9-3
Teacher-Researcher Partnerships

Hamilton and Richardson (1995) developed and implemented a practical argument model of staff development as part of a reading improvement study. The practical argument, a framework for engaging in a dialogue between teachers and researchers, is used to have teachers explain why a teaching practice works or does not work. As the justifications for a practice are identified, alternative practices from the work of colleagues and related recent research are discussed. A study of the process led them to conclude that staff development programs should be interactive, should address teachers' beliefs and practical knowledge about the teaching and learning process, and should examine alternative practices that instantiate both teachers' beliefs and research knowledge.

---

groups, school-university partnership study groups, and activities associated with preparation for certification by the National Board for Professional Teacher Standards. These forms of staff development have the potential for bringing cohesion to a school staff and enhancing the collective responsibility for student learning. Collaborative teacher-researcher partnerships can result in deeper, more long-lasting changes than do the more common one-shot workshops. Box 9-3 presents an example.

Guidelines and Standards for Teacher Education

To prevent reading difficulties among children, professional development for teachers should attend to all the elements of teacher knowledge presented in Table 9-1. Efforts have been made to delineate the preferred content of teacher education with respect to reading at both the pre-service and the in-service stages, but none are complete models; the best way to develop and use them for maximum effect on children's learning has not been studied.

Pre-service Guidelines There are two routes for addressing quality assurance in pre-service education for teachers: (1) accreditation of the institutions that prepare teachers and (2) certification or licensing of the individual beginning teachers. In the United States, these are state functions, but the federal government has a small role in the first process. For accreditation, it recognizes (most recently in 1995) the National Council for the Accreditation of Teacher Education (NCATE) as an accrediting body for schools, departments, and colleges of education. So that state approval processes do not require a duplication of effort by the institution seeking accreditation, 36 states have a partnership agreement with NCATE.

NCATE accreditation is voluntary, and less than half of the approximately 1,200 institutions that prepare teachers apply for accreditation. NCATE expects the accreditation process to provide the teacher education community with opportunities to improve programs and to identify good programs to serve as models for improvement. NCATE has about 30 constituent members, organizations that represent stakeholders, like the American Association of Colleges for Teacher Education, the National Education Association, and the American Federation of Teachers, as well as a variety of subject area organizations (such as the International Reading Association and the National Council of Teachers of English) and specialist organizations (such as the Council of Chief State School Officers and associations of members of boards of education).

In essence, NCATE develops and revises standards and indicators for teacher education units, and programs within them, to meet. With respect to early reading, NCATE has curriculum guidelines for early childhood education, elementary education, and advanced programs for reading education.

While there is nothing in the guidelines contrary to the needs for teacher preparation listed in Table 9-1, it is worrisome to note the lack of specification about the details of knowledge of written and oral language and ways to teach reading. The elementary education guidelines omit important matters for teacher preparation. In contrast to the standards for mathematics, which mention "the development of number sense" (NCATE, 1989:69), nothing about "sound sense" or "letter sense" is mentioned in the 13 guidelines related to reading, writing, and oral language (NCATE, 1989:69-70), and there is no mention about the important relation between the sound structure of language and the alphabet used in reading and writing. Even in the advanced programs for reading education (NCATE 1992:199-215), the use of letters and the relation of sound units to alphabet elements go unnoted.

A second route for considering the quality of pre-service teacher preparation involves the licensing of teachers. As with accreditation, the only way to address licensing criteria nationally is through voluntary collaboration among states. The Interstate New Teacher Assessment and Support Consortium (INTASC) provides a way for states to work cooperatively to formulate policies to reform teacher preparation and licensing. It has developed a draft set of model core standards, expressed as principles elaborated in terms of knowledge, dispositions, and performances (Interstate New Teacher Assessment and Support Consortium, 1992). INTASC has begun developing discipline-specific standards that elaborate on the core standards.

Reading appears in the INTASC English-language arts documents, now available in draft form. The guidelines show clearly an impact of some recent research. Current and sophisticated rhetorical theory is reflected in several places. With respect to early reading and preventing reading difficulties, research related to emergent literacy has had an impact, and sociolinguistic and ethnographic findings have influenced the treatment of student diversity. Just as with the NCATE guidelines, however, the current INTASC draft standards fail when it comes to specificity about learning related to the alphabetic principle.

In-Service Professional Development Guidelines As this report has demonstrated, there are important recent developments in the understanding about learning to read, its developmental progress, and instruction to support it. Teachers who are already licensed must have opportunities to keep up with the changes in the knowledge base and to develop improved instructional strategies. Several groups are developing standards and guidelines for in-service teacher education.

Some are state-level initiatives coordinated with other reforms related to reading instruction. An example is the blueprint for professional development for teachers of early reading instruction produced by the California County Superintendents Educational Services Association under the auspices of the California State Board of Education (1997). The blueprint lays out what teachers need to do and know in nine categories: phoneme awareness; systematic explicit phonics instruction; spelling; diagnosis; research; structure of the English language; relationships between reading, writing, and spelling; improving reading comprehension; and student independent reading of good books. Although this is a full plate, a few of the topics on teacher knowledge listed in Table 9-1 are missing from the blueprint, for example, matters related to emergent literacy development during what the blueprint calls the "pre-alphabetic stage."

Another approach to standards is related to the National Board for Professional Teaching Standards (NBPTS). This is a nationwide effort that experienced teachers volunteer to participate in. NBPTS has developed standards for national board certification for expert teachers with different specialties (e.g., for early childhood generalists, middle childhood generalists, and middle childhood English language arts). The standards address the content of professional development indirectly by describing the outcome achievements for teachers considered accomplished members of their profession. In a more direct way, the standards have become a curriculum for some local professional development efforts (such as the Minnesota High Success Consortium described in Buday and Kelly, 1996). With respect to reading in early childhood, however, the NBPTS standards pay insufficient attention to some aspects of teacher knowledge that are listed in Table 9-1, for example, the alphabetic principle.

Teachers Providing Special Services

An important part of a school's program for preventing reading difficulties is the teachers who have responsibilities and specific expertise for supporting and teaching children identified for special services. This includes not only special education teachers but also those who work with children identified on the basis of limited English proficiency or economic background, as well as those taking a specialist role with respect to reading instruction and the prevention of, or intervention in, reading difficulties.

These teachers need to know what other primary-grade teachers know, but they also need continuing access to detailed research, effective practices, and modes of working with quality materials that address the particular challenges they and their students face. The more in depth and varied their professional resources, the more likely they are to be able to find a way to work effectively with each child. The etiology of a specific child's difficulty may be unknown or the subject of dispute; the validity of a measurement instrument or the effectiveness of a technique may be untested on certain subgroups; and information about a child's prior and concurrent home and community life may be particularly difficult to obtain, interpret, and use wisely. It is particularly crucial that these teachers have continuing access to professional development related to children likely to or already experiencing reading difficulties. They need:

• knowledge of ways to access and evaluate ongoing research regarding typical development and the prevention of reading difficulties;
• knowledge and techniques for helping other professionals (classroom teachers, administrators) learn new skills relevant for preventing or identifying and ameliorating reading difficulties; and
• knowledge and techniques for promoting home support (by parents and other household members) to encourage emergent and conventional literacy and to prevent or ameliorate reading difficulties.

The Orton Dyslexia Society (1997) has produced a position paper on teacher education relevant to special services teachers. Box 9-4 includes the relevant excerpts.

Teachers of language-minority students need additional professional development services:

• If students are in a bilingual education program where they are learning to read in a non-English language, teachers must have an understanding, accompanied by strategies and techniques, for teaching children to read in that language. For alphabetic languages, such as Spanish, many of the same principles that are valid in English

---

BOX 9-4
What Teachers Need to Know to Be
Effective Teachers of Reading

Core Requirements:
1. Conceptual foundations—the reading process. "Teachers must be provided with a solid foundation regarding the theoretical and scientific underpinnings for understanding literacy development"(p. 12).
2. Knowledge of the structure of language, including knowledge of (a) the English speech sound system and its production, (b) the structure of English orthography and its relationship to sounds and meaning, and (c) grammatical structure.
3. Supervised practice in teaching reading

Training Requirements for Reading Specialists, Resource Room/Special Education Personnel
[The above 3 areas plus]
"because these specialists are likely to be working with children with more severe reading problems, they need to know how to pinpoint specific areas of weakness in reading performance for children experiencing difficulty learning to read. They must have expertise in effective remedial strategies targeting structured language methods that have been developed to address the needs of children with reading disabilities" (p. 17).

Speech-Language Specialists
"should know how to assess the phonological abilities of children and other aspects of the structure of language relevant to reading and writing. Expertise in techniques that employ guided discovery of how phonemes are articulated (e.g., Lindamood, 1994) is a valuable skill for enhancing phoneme awareness in children who are not benefiting from strictly auditory activities" (p. 17).

---

are also valid for the other languages; still, there will certainly be differences in instructional materials and some differences in instructional approaches, due to specific structural features of different languages (August and Hakuta, 1997).

• If non- or limited-English-speaking students are in an English as a second language program, where they are learning to read in English, teachers must be skilled in helping these students confront a double challenge: learning to read while learning English as a second language. At a minimum, their teachers should be aware of the pertinent linguistic and cultural differences. Beyond that, they should be especially skilled and knowledgeable about helping these students succeed in an inherently very challenging situation.

GOVERNMENT BODIES

The activities of teachers and students are influenced and constrained by the policies and resources of state and local education agencies, which in turn are influenced by governors, state legislatures, and local school boards. The federal government provides leadership, resources, and incentives, but in the United States, jurisdiction over education is a state and local matter.

States

Any current effort to prevent reading difficulties occurs in the context of *systemic reform*, the term used to describe state initiatives begun in the last decade to improve education. Systemic reform involves the interaction of (a) high standards for all children, (b) assessments to measure the achievement of the standards, and (c) the capacity of teachers and schools to ensure that children achieve the standards. A review of progress in nine states noted a "disjuncture between change oriented political rhetoric and steady incremental progress . . . [of] policies that have evolved over the past five to ten years" (Massell et al., 1997:2). Despite political changes in leadership, some public criticism, and financial problems, the continuation of effort is quite remarkable (p. 7):

> As criticisms and expert reviews of these more unconventional approaches to standards and assessments mounted, policy makers listened and made numerous modifications but, importantly, did not completely toss out the new practices.

The progress is credited to support from the business community within a state and to external support and stimulus from national organizations and projects like the National Governors Association exchange strategies, the National Science Foundation school reform projects, the Goals 2000 initiative promulgated by the federal government, and private foundation funding (Massell et al., 1997:6).

In general, if states pursue systemic reform and focus on preventing reading difficulties informed by the issues covered in this report, there is a good probability that they will supply the needed leadership to districts and schools. State actions on many fronts may have an effect on reading education. Among other things, states can affect the availability and quality of preschool and day care environments available to all children, the days and length of days available for instruction, the support for services like libraries and new technologies during the school year and over the summer, the allocation of additional resources to schools and neighborhoods in great need, norms for salaries and benefits seen for preschool and early elementary teachers, and information clearinghouses for pedagogical techniques and evaluation of materials. In this section, we focus on three primary areas in which states are especially pivotal for providing both support and pressure to raise achievement and to minimize reading problems: curriculum standards, teaching capacity, and textbook approval procedures.

Curriculum Standards

Ideally, standards are an important step to ensuring educational equity within and across schools, school districts, and states and for communicating with publishers and teacher education institutions about what the state wants. It is important to note that assessments from districts that adopted high standards earlier than most indicate that "standards do not damage the academic chances of the least advantaged students. Rather, all students appear to benefit from higher expectations" (Education Commission of the States, 1996:17). Standards can serve as the common reference point for developing curricula, instructional materials, tests, accountability systems, and professional development. Standards can protect school systems from downward drifts in educational expectations and attainment.

For most states, curriculum standards documents relevant to reading are widely available, providing information on assessment, benchmarks, and sometimes even a specification of curriculum material and activities. Only a few, however, have separate standards for reading. Reading is frequently found within the English language arts standards, but for some states it is part of the communication standards. Most state standards documents start at kindergarten; only a few have prekindergarten standards. Many states have standards for a range of grades (K-3 or K-4), providing little detail for separate grades.

None of the available standards provides a model that is complete and consistent with the knowledge base reflected in this report, but the movement of many states appears promising.

It is not yet clear how effective any of the standards-setting movements will be with respect to preventing reading difficulties. Most states do not include research on the effects of their standards as a prominent part of their effort. Oregon, however, has certain districts designated as laboratories to evaluate reforms as they are being developed. Only Kentucky has an independent nonprofit institute charged with evaluating the impact of reform on students and schools (Education Commission of the States, 1996). Research is needed on the effectiveness of standards and benchmarks overall, as well as on the comparative advantages of different approaches to developing and using them.

Building Teaching Capacity

States have traditionally had the responsibility for overseeing institutions that organize pre-service teacher education as well as for licensing individual teachers. Changes are under way in several states on both fronts, but few have developed sufficiently to be evaluated. Ohio, for example, is revising its standards for teacher education and licensing, building on the work of INTASC and NCATE, and is conducting pilot programs for performance assessment linked to the beginning teacher license. California, for another example, is beginning to link high standards for children with accreditation for institutions based on assessments of the performance of the institution's graduates.

Many states encourage teachers to meet the professional standards represented by the NBPTS certification. A total of 33 states

---

BOX 9-5
California's Language Arts Framework

In the late 1980s, California promulgated its English language arts framework advocating literacy instruction that was heavily literature based while de-emphasizing basic, discrete skills—including phonics and decoding (California State Department of Education, 1987a and b).

Dissatisfaction with the literature-based framework began to surface in the early 1990s, but the move away from literature-based programs became a stampede following publication of the 1994 National Assessment of Educational Progress results in reading. California's performance was among the lowest in the nation, and it was one of a handful of states that had significantly declined in the reading proficiency of its students. Although there continues to be disagreement over the role played by the 1987 language arts framework in California's reading score decline, public and political pressure to change the direction of reading instruction mounted. In 1996, the California state legislature passed a bill (AB 3075) which required that teachers be prepared to undertake . . . comprehensive reading instruction that is research-based and includes all of the following:

(i)   The study of organized, systematic, explicit skills including phonemic awareness, direct, systematic, explicit phonics, and decoding skills.
(ii)   A strong literature, language, and comprehension component with a balance of oral and written language.
(iii) Ongoing diagnostic techniques that inform teaching and assessment.
(iv)   Early intervention techniques.
(v)   Guided practice in a clinical setting.

---

encourage teachers to apply for the board certificate by paying the fee and/or providing some released time for preparation and examination. Some states (North Carolina, Ohio, Mississippi) provide salary increases or bonuses for teachers who become board certified. The current California reading reform effort is notable for its very detailed legislation involving teacher preparation (see Box 9-5).

Textbook Purchasing

Books used in elementary schools are provided free to students in most states; a few require a rental fee. In about half the states, textbook choice is controlled at the state level. In many cases, the state approves a list of alternatives, and districts or schools or teachers must choose among them. There is usually a cycle of five to seven years before a new approved textbook list is drawn up.

Laws and customs vary about the process of textbook approval, its accountability to public scrutiny, selector ethics, safeguards, the composition of selection committees, and the provision of training for selectors. In some cases, there are special cycles or special selection committees for subject matter for which the recency and accuracy of information is seen as particularly important, for instance mathematics, science, and computer science. Books for the teaching of reading are too seldom given the special attention that the developments in understanding about it require. Without special provisions, a reform curriculum for children or teacher preparation can flounder in the face of inappropriate books in classrooms.

State approval or failure to approve books influences their production as well. Textbook publishers produce a product for a profit and are driven by market factors. One enormous influence is the texts approved by the most populous states engaged in statewide adoption—California, Texas, and Florida. These are critical markets for the textbook industry, and a reading series that is not on the approved list in these states is unlikely to be sufficiently profitable for the publisher to maintain it.

Guidance for selection committees needs to be well thought out and carefully carried out. Many "scoring rubrics" are not useful or are out of date; also, the information publishers are required to provide is often an inadequate base for rational choice; sometimes members of selection committees lack the expertise to judge content beyond the labels used in promotional materials. There is no denying the level of difficulty, amount of time, and cost of adequate procedures for approving books for use in early reading classes.

The burden is on states to conduct full appraisal of programs for early reading based on more than the main textbooks. Most series have optional parts and, especially recently, add-on kits. It is very important that such supplementary material be tied into the teacher guides and that the guides give assistance about scheduling to ensure that there is ample opportunity for children to explore and practice the content covered in the supplementary and basic materials.

States can play a critical role in making sure that effective and useful information and practices are made available to teachers by insisting that books and materials adhere to the principles about preventing reading difficulties identified in this report. Ideally, state curriculum standards and textbook adoption would be synchronized. Texas recently required publishers to develop textbooks that meet the state standards if they wish to have their materials adopted by the state, and this requirement will apply to its reading language arts standards.

Most important, however, complete appraisal requires examination of the texts in use in ordinary school settings. At a minimum, states should acquire and use efficacy data. This can be done prospectively by requiring textbook publishers to provide evidence of effectiveness based on controlled third-party studies of prototype materials. It can be done retrospectively by querying about curriculum when gathering assessment data. Either approach is rare at present. In New Jersey, local districts choose their own books, but the state is charged with evaluating the effectiveness of what they have used and indicating approval or disapproval, after the fact. Only one state, Nevada, mandates classroom testing of the textbook materials (with mandated evaluation criteria) prior to adoption.

Efficacy testing related to textbook adoption procedures requires different technical expertise than currently used by state adoption committees and publishing houses. But it could contribute to eliminating the periodic politically and ideologically driven convulsions in reading education and thus to preventing reading difficulties among children.

Local Education Agencies

State initiatives do not fully determine district and school changes in curriculum and instruction. Local districts provide the structures and resources that interpret policy initiatives for school and classroom practice (Spillane, 1996). Thus, the local district-level involvement in school reform efforts is key to their progress. The 25 local school districts that Massell et al. (1997) studied have been persistent in their drive to school reform.

Local districts must provide teachers with sufficient support and assistance to ensure effective teaching of reading. Districts need to monitor the implementation of changes in instruction, not assume that once a policy is adopted it will appear intact in the complexity of schools and classrooms. Once a policy is implemented, the district must continue to monitor to ensure that the results are as expected and to support changes needed to ensure continuous improvement. Unless elected and professional district personnel adopt sound policies and practices consistent with the principles in this report, the chances of large-scale prevention of reading difficulties among young children are small.

The Federal Government

The federal government's role in making the kind of changes needed to prevent reading difficulties is complex. Each of its functions needs to be informed by the principles in this report.

First, federal authority and laws that provide for equitable educational opportunities for young citizens in need throughout the country are well known—Head Start, Title I, the Individuals with Disabilities Education Act. Continuing assessment of the results of these policies by the U.S. Department of Education and the design of necessary changes are important government roles.

Second, the federal government coordinates with education reform initiatives among the states, as in the education summits and the recent America Reads/Reading Excellence challenge. Special programs in the U.S. Department of Education undergird these efforts. The various state standards and benchmarks related to reading, for example, can each be available for other states to learn from because of the coordinating efforts of a regional education laboratory.

A third role of the federal government, with respect to preventing reading difficulties, is the stimulation and support of research not only by the U.S. Department of Education through its institutes and programs and the centers, laboratories, and institutes that it works with throughout the country but also by such agencies as the

National Science Foundation and National Institutes of Health. There is a clear need for the design of research agendas for basic and applied research in long-term federal research centers and institutes as well as for the support of promising ideas from field-initiated studies.

A fourth important role is the action initiatives of the U.S. Department of Education, which disseminate information and reward good practices. National clearinghouses provide an infrastructure for researchers; the research summaries and the ASK ERIC service provided through the clearinghouses make the information accessible to practitioners and policy makers. Programs that identify and reward outstanding teachers, schools, and districts provide motivation for the excellence to continue and models for others to follow.

Government-sponsored projects that produce brochures, posters, and public service announcements make information about reading available in a variety of venues. Recent notable efforts include Learning to Read/Reading to Learn (Office of Special Education Programs and the National Center to Improve the Tools of Educators) and Ready Set Read (U.S. Department of Education, the Corporation for National Service, and the U.S. Department of Health and Human Services). These are sophisticated campaigns. Take, for example, the Learning to Read/Reading to Learn campaign. After developing a research synthesis, the producers made the results accessible in a series of tip sheets for parents and teachers. The sheets included specific teaching strategies as well as ways to take advantage of games and ordinary daily activities to promote reading development. The campaign also produced a bibliography and a resource book of professionals who could help communities to address the improvement of reading teaching in their schools. Distribution was facilitated by partnerships with government and private groups and endorsements from influential people.

PUBLISHERS

Publishers are an influential part of the educational enterprise in any domain of elementary education; the instructional materials they produce and market strongly influence how reading is taught in schools (Anderson et al., 1989:35). Some innovations that could help to prevent reading difficulties may suffer because they lack a strategy for wide-scale implementation, but classroom textbooks are one of the few already "scaled-up" parts of educational activities.

States can influence what publishers will include in their reading textbooks through the textbook adoption processes (discussed above), but the influence also works the other way. Researchers have pointed out that published materials are so embedded in the concrete and daily aspects of teaching that they can influence teachers more than state standards or frameworks (Ball and Cohen, 1996). Publishers therefore have a serious responsibility, but the question of interest is how published materials can contribute to needed improvements in instruction.

Having the right principles embodied in the textbooks is not sufficient. Education reforms that rely on innovative materials as the main component can fade or fail to achieve wide-scale impact. On one hand, teachers may not know or have adequate opportunity to learn what they need to know to use the materials adequately; on the other hand, curriculum designers may not know or have the opportunity to learn about the ways that curriculum materials fit into the complex concrete situation that teachers face every day. It is the interplay between professional development and materials development that holds the key.

"Developers' designs thus turn out to be ingredients in—not determinants of—the actual curriculum," Ball and Cohen (1996:6-7) argue. They continue:

> When the gap between the materials and teaching is very wide—leaving to each practitioner to figure out how to deal with student thinking, how to probe the content at hand, and how to map the instruction against the temporal rhythms of classroom life—teachers must invent or ignore a great deal. If they do try to invent and thus learn, they must often learn alone with few resources to help them. Curriculum guides could offer some help in depth while still being humble about the complexities they cannot address. . . . A teacher's guide cannot judge whether a teacher should meet with an individual student or move on, but it can offer concrete illustrations of the nature of student understanding important at a given point, and how other teachers have reached this level.

Research on the effectiveness of an educational program often includes complaints that the classrooms observed are not faithful replications of the designer's ideal or an original experimental version of the program. Taking Ball and Cohen's perspective lets us reframe the issue.

Think of the teacher as a customer of innovative research and materials, rather than a patient who may or may not "take as directed" the medicine prescribed. Industries other than textbook publishing design their products with complicated theories of the user in mind. One study describes different approaches to mass customization embodied in successful cases from various industries Gilmore and Pine (1997). These strategies depend on making changes in the production and marketing process as well as considerable research and experimentation. "Collaborative customization," for example, requires a reanalysis of the parts that make up a product as well as the technology, personnel, and delivery system that allow coconstruction by the customer and the business of the actual product that is bought and used effectively by the customer. There is a striking resemblance between collaborative customization and the use of research partnerships in professional development (discussed above).

Currently, in many cases for elementary education, state or local systems, intending to ensure that public monies are spent on effective materials, offer incentives that make mass production, not mass customization, a sufficient strategy for publishers to pursue. In some states, a state book depository is the end of the delivery system for publishers; contact with the teacher-user of the materials is via a representative on a state or district book adoption committee and perhaps one or two one-shot workshops on a minimal in-service education schedule. Under such circumstances, mass customization of education materials is unlikely to develop naturally and needs an impetus from policy makers, practitioners, and researchers.

Publishers making a productive connection between materials development and professional development would have to *do* research on teachers and students (i.e., support or at least use it), as Ball and Cohen (1996) point out. They particularly indicate the "vast unprobed areas" in students' thinking about language, but also note the need for research on teacher knowledge and teacher learning, especially how materials can support teacher learning and better contribute to the enacted curriculum. The development process for materials would have as a by-product something analogous to the clinical trials run by producers of products that make claims about effectiveness for health. Technical reports on the process of developing and evaluating educational materials should be available, describing research methods, results, and so forth.

Ball and Cohen (1996) provide pointers to the content of published material that should be customized:

- Assistance with expected student approaches to the material—examples of common sequences of approximations to attaining concepts and skills and common misunderstandings, as well as information about what other teachers have done to make progress in the face of obstacles.
- Support for developing the teacher's knowledge of the content and the pedagogical strategies—revealing alternative representations and strategies considered during development and pilot testing of the materials and explaining the relations among them and the rationale for final choice.
- Support for decisions the teacher makes to fit the material into the practical context of schools—the intellectual, social, and political processes; the rhythm of the day and the year; the connection to concurrent academic and nonacademic activities.

Materials developed with attention to these issues would produce a closer correspondence between the designers' understanding of what goes on in the classroom and the reality of what actually takes place there. By giving up the fiction that the published materials are the only influence on the curriculum actually delivered in classrooms, published materials could have a more productive effect on it. If states and districts insist that the content of reading textbooks for children correspond to standards based on the principles in this report, and if publishers develop materials with more interaction with the customers, the fact that the text materials influence the classroom activities more than state frameworks would be no problem; in fact, there would be a partnership for improvement.

MEDIA

There are many ways that the media can be harnessed in the prevention of reading difficulties. We focus on four areas as illustrations: news, public service announcements, special activities for educators, and special activities for children.

News about reading and preventing reading difficulties can contribute to the public dialogue that is an important part of restructuring schools for high-quality student learning (Newmann and Wehlage, 1995). Public dialogue about specific contents of high standards is a crucial part of sustaining school reform. The news media have a social responsibility to provide information about the ways that literacy develops among children and the ways that reading difficulties can be prevented. Recently, differences among experts about beginning reading have been widely covered by print and broadcast media. Continuing the coverage to inform the public about the processes and what it can do to help is the next challenge.

Information on strategies and methods that are useful for caretakers of very young children can take the form of public service announcements, a kind of video or audio brochure. Some public service announcements have appeared advising that parents read to young children, for example; that may be enough for a family that just needs a reminder, but a sample of the kind of interactions that are productive might be more useful for caretakers who are less experienced or who have a limited or unproductive style when they read to children. There is a broad range of other informal activities that can be undertaken that could fit the public service announcement format—from play with internal sound structure of spoken words to the ways a family can encourage a child's emergent writing. Risk factors, too, could be explained in public service announcements (see Chapter 4).

Television directed specifically toward teachers can be found on commercial cable networks (e.g., *Teacher TV* on the Discovery channel) as well as on stations operated by school districts. The current offerings go far beyond the low production value programs of "distance learning" a decade ago. Now lively debates, discussions of concepts, and extensive demonstrations of live classroom experiences are offered, sometimes even with a call-in segment. The information in this report could inform such programming.

Television designed for children is often seen as a competition for the kind of reading practice that helps to prevent reading difficulties or as a source of values incompatible with success at learning. Parents have been advised to watch along with their children to limit the problems that might otherwise arise. In fact, it is also important for children and adults to watch television programs like *Sesame Street* together, even though they may not be a source of worry. Parents and day care teachers who play along with the activities and highlight the productive practices make the most of the good programs for the children's benefit.

Sesame Street is among the most well-known television programs for children. For 25 years preschoolers have watched it in homes and in preschools. Early studies of the impact of *Sesame Street* viewing on academic outcomes were criticized because of the confounding effects of parent education and other home characteristics. Recent studies, however, have controlled for these factors. A large national survey showed that 4-year-olds who are frequent viewers are more likely than less frequent viewers to identify colors, count to 20, recognize letters, and tell connected stories when pretending to read (Zill et al., 1994). Longitudinal studies confirm the positive effects of viewing television programs like *Sesame Street* that are designed with specific principles of child learning in mind. One study, for example, showed that vocabulary gains at age 5 are related to more frequent viewing of *Sesame Street* at age 3 (Huston et al., 1990). Another study followed children for three years and found that those who viewed *Sesame Street* frequently at an early age had an advantage in vocabulary, letter and word recognition, and school readiness, even when the child's language skill and home background factors were controlled for; furthermore, 6- and 7-year-olds who had viewed *Sesame Street* more frequently when they were younger had better reading comprehension scores in first or second grade than children who had been less frequent viewers when they were younger (Wright and Huston, 1995).

CONCLUSION

Central among the implementation issues we raise is teacher preparation and continuing professional development, but we cannot ignore the fact that many parts of society, from parents and community to the federal government, publishers, and the media should also take responsibility for bringing about change in the state of reading education. Many aspects of the existing situation call for researchers in fields that can contribute to the prevention of reading difficulties among young children to be active and aware. If there is variation and change, there is opportunity and need for involvement and analysis by those who know the specifics of literacy learning and development. From choices about teacher preparation and in-service development, to the development of curriculum guidelines and standards, to relations with publishers and media, researchers need to contribute their expertise to understanding what is, developing what can be, analyzing the consequences of the innovations, and trying for improvement again, as needed.

Professional and government leaders concerned about the reading problems in our society need to develop campaigns to help decrease their incidence and prevalence. Previous experiences, both successful and not, to disseminate knowledge and change behaviors—such as smoking cessation, the use of seat belts, childhood immunization, promoting healthy eating—provide starting points for thinking about how we could bring about broad-based changes in literacy practices with young children.

"Dissemination tends to be nobody's job," Weiss (1978) observed somewhat pessimistically. Our view is that, in matters of urgent national importance, such as the prevention of reading difficulties, dissemination of what we know and, more important still, implementation of effective practices and policies based on what we know, are everybody's obligation.

10
Recommendations for Practice and Research

As the committee began its study, it was well aware of the history of controversies that have enveloped reading instruction in the United States, and it assumed that the science base had developed sufficiently to finally put recommendations regarding reading instruction on sound scientific footing. The process of conducting this study, of examining the research on reading, has confirmed this assumption. We have found many informative literatures to draw upon and hope, with this chapter, to weave the insights of many research traditions into clear guidelines for helping children become successful readers.

Our main emphasis has been on the development of reading and on factors that relate to reading outcomes. We have conceptualized our task as cutting through the detail of mostly convergent, sometimes discrepant research findings to provide an integrated picture of how reading develops and thus how its development should be promoted.

CONCEPTUALIZING READING AND READING INSTRUCTION

Effective reading instruction is built on a foundation that recognizes that reading outcomes are determined by complex and multifaceted factors. On the assumption that understanding can move public discussion beyond the polemics of the past, we have made it an important goal of this report to make the complexities known: many factors that correlate with reading fail to explain it; many experiences contribute to reading development without being pre-requisite to it; and although there are many prerequisites, none by itself appears to be sufficient. Our review of the research literature makes clear, nevertheless, the general requirements of effective reading instruction.

Adequate initial reading instruction requires a focus on:

- using reading to obtain meaning from print;
- the sublexical[1] structure of spoken words;
- the nature of the orthographic[2] system;
- the specifics of frequent, regular spelling-sound relationships;
- frequent opportunities to read; and
- opportunities to write.

Adequate progress in learning to read English beyond the initial level depends on:

- having established a working understanding of how sounds are represented alphabetically;
- sufficient practice in reading to achieve fluency with different kinds of texts written for different purposes; and
- control over procedures for monitoring comprehension and repairing misunderstandings.

Effective instruction includes artful teaching that transcends—and often makes up for—the constraints and limitations of specific instructional programs. Although we have not incorporated lessons from artful teaching practices with the same comprehensiveness as

---

[1]Sublexical means concerning the phonological and morphological components of words, such as the sounds of individual and groups of letters.

[2]Orthographic means features of the writing system, particularly letters and their sequences in words.

other topics in the conventional research on reading, we acknowledge their importance in conceptualizing effective reading instruction.

Reading is typically acquired relatively predictably by children who:

- have normal or above average language skills;
- have had experiences in early childhood that fostered motivation and provided exposure to literacy in use;
- are given information about the nature of print via opportunities to learn letters and to recognize the sublexical structure of spoken words, as well as about the contrasting nature of spoken and written language; and
- attend schools that provide coherent reading instruction and opportunities to practice reading.

Disruption of any of these factors increases the risk that reading will be delayed or impeded, a phenomenon particularly prevalent in impoverished urban and rural neighborhoods and among disadvantaged minority populations. Within all demographic groups, children with speech or language impairments, cognitive deficits, hearing impairments or who have a biological parent with a reading disability are at risk for reading difficulties. There are also a number of children, evidently without any of these risk factors, who nonetheless develop reading difficulties. Such children may require intensive intervention and may continue to benefit from extra help in reading and accommodations for their disability throughout their lives. An additional very small population of children with severe cognitive disabilities that limit literacy learning will for a variety of reasons have difficulty ever achieving high levels of literacy.

Three main stumbling blocks are known to throw children off course on the journey to skilled reading. One obstacle is difficulty in understanding and using the alphabetic principle. Failure to grasp that written spellings systematically represent the sounds of spoken words makes it difficult not only to recognize printed words but also to understand how to learn and to profit from instruction. If a child cannot rely on the alphabetic principle, word recognition is inaccurate or laborious and comprehension of connected text will be impeded. A second obstacle is the failure to acquire and use comprehension skills and strategies. A third obstacle involves motivation. Although most children begin school with positive attitudes and expectations for success, by the end of the primary grades, and increasingly thereafter, some children become disaffected. Difficulties mastering sound-letter relationships or comprehension skills can easily stifle motivation, which can in turn hamper instructional efforts.

Levels of literacy adequate for high school completion, employability, and responsible citizenship in a democracy are feasible for all but a very small number of individuals. Yet a substantial percentage of American youth graduate from high school with very low levels of literacy. These youth are particularly likely to be from subgroups in our population that traditionally have done poorly in school (African Americans, Hispanics, and Native Americans) or to be from poor urban neighborhoods. However, low literacy at the high school level characterizes many students from all subgroups, including students who do not belong to identified risk groups. Most of the reading problems faced by today's adolescents and adults are the result of problems that might have been avoided or resolved in their early childhood years.

In this chapter, we present our major findings, conclusions, and recommendations. We begin with primary and secondary prevention[3] during the preschool years. We then move to primary and secondary prevention through educational practice from kindergarten through third grade, with particular attention to the provision of high-quality classroom instruction in early reading to all children. Next we address teacher preparation and professional support. The final section provides a research agenda that includes attention to assessment and its role in identifying effective prevention strategies. Although assessment is not at the core of the committee's expertise, we became convinced in the process of the study that the importance

---

[3]Primary prevention is concerned with reducing the number of new cases (incidence) of an identified condition or problem in the population. Secondary prevention is concerned with reducing the number of existing cases (prevalence) of an identified condition or problem in the population.

of assessment warranted the attention of the field and of our project sponsors.

LITERACY DEVELOPMENT DURING
THE PRESCHOOL YEARS

Public Understanding of Early Literacy Development

Findings: There is abundant empirical and observational evidence that the children who are particularly likely to have difficulty with learning to read in the primary grades are those who begin school with less prior knowledge and skill in certain domains, most notably, general verbal abilities, phonological sensitivity, familiarity with the basic purposes and mechanisms of reading, and letter knowledge. Children from poor neighborhoods, children with limited proficiency in English, children with hearing impairments, children with preschool language impairments or cognitive deficiencies, and children whose parents had difficulty learning to read are particularly at risk of arriving at school with weaknesses in these areas and, as a result, of falling behind from the outset.

Conclusion: It is clear from the research on emergent literacy that important experiences related to reading begin very early in life. Primary prevention steps designed to reduce the number of children with inadequate literacy-related knowledge (e.g., concepts of print,[4] phonemic awareness, receptive vocabulary) at the onset of formal schooling would considerably reduce the number of children with reading difficulties and, thereby, the magnitude of the problem currently facing schools.

Recommendation: We recommend that organizations and government bodies concerned with the education of young children (e.g., the National Association for the Education of Young Children, the National Education Association, the American Federation of Teachers, the International Reading Association, state departments of edu-

---

[4]Concepts of print are a set of understandings about the conventions of literacy, e.g., directionality, intentionality, stability, use of blank spaces and letters, and multiple genres and uses.

cation, the U.S. Department of Education) promote public understanding of early literacy development. Systematic and widespread public education and marketing efforts should be undertaken to increase public awareness of the importance of providing stimulating literacy experiences in the lives of all very young children. Parents and other caregivers, as well as the public, should be the targets of such efforts, which should address ways of using books and opportunities for building language and literacy growth through everyday activities both at home and in group care settings.

Identification of Preschool Children with Special Language and Literacy Needs

Findings: Cognitive and educational research demonstrates the negative effects of deferring identification of, and intervention for, children who need additional support for early language and literacy development. They include those who have a hearing impairment, are diagnosed as having a specific early language impairment, are offspring of parents with histories of reading difficulty, or lack age-appropriate skills in literacy-related cognitive-linguistic processing. There is growing evidence that less supportive early environments for acquiring literacy tend to be associated with several known risk groups, and that some individual risk factors can be identified prior to kindergarten.

Conclusions: Children who are at risk for reading difficulties should be identified as early as possible. Pediatricians, social workers, speech and language therapists, and other preschool practitioners need to be alert for signs that children are having difficulties acquiring early language and literacy skills. Parents and other adults (relatives, neighbors, friends) also play a crucial role in identifying children who need assistance.

Research-derived indicators for potential problems include:

- in infancy or during the preschool period, significant delays in expressive language, receptive vocabulary, or IQ;

- at school entry, delays in a combination of measures of readiness, including
    - —letter identification,
    - —understanding the functions of print,
    - —verbal memory for stories and sentences,
    - —phonological awareness,[5]
    - —lexical skills such as naming vocabulary,
    - —receptive language skills in the areas of syntax and morphology,
    - —expressive language, and
    - —overall language development.

Through adult education programs, public service media, instructional videos provided by pediatricians, and other means, parents can be informed about the skills and knowledge children should be acquiring at young ages and about what to do and where to turn if there is concern that a child's development may be lagging in some respect.

Recommendation: Public authorities and education professionals should provide research-derived guidelines for parents, pediatricians, and preschool professionals so that children who have a hearing or language impairment or who lack age-appropriate skills in literacy-related cognitive-linguistic processing are identified as early as possible and given intervention to support language and literacy development.

Promoting Language and Literacy Growth

Findings: Research with preschoolers has demonstrated that (a) adult-child shared book reading that stimulates verbal interaction can enhance language (especially vocabulary) development and knowledge about concepts of print, and (b) activities that direct

---

[5]Phonological awareness means sensitivity to the fact that there are patterns of spoken language that recur and can be manipulated without respect to the meaning that the language patterns ordinarily convey.

young children's attention to the sound structure within spoken words (e.g., play with songs and poems that emphasize rhyming, jokes, and games that depend on switching sounds within words), and to the relations between print and speech can facilitate learning to read. These findings are buttressed by others showing that knowledge of word meanings, an understanding that print conveys meaning, phonological awareness, and some understanding of how printed letters code the sounds of language contribute directly to successful reading. Other preschool abilities, such as identifying letters, numbers, shapes, and colors, may correlate with future reading achievement, but neither research findings nor theories of reading are available to support the notion that they have a causal link to learning to read.

Failure to develop an adequate vocabulary, understanding of print concepts, or phonological awareness during the preschool years constitutes some risk for reading difficulties. Hence, we recommend interventions designed to promote their growth. At the same time, however, we caution that the focus of intervention should not be limited to overcoming these risk factors in isolation but should be more broadly designed to provide a rich language and literacy environment that methodically includes the promotion of vocabulary, the understanding of print concepts, and phonological awareness. Preschools and other group care settings for young children, including those at risk for reading difficulties, too often constitute poor language and literacy environments. Targeted interventions indicate that literacy and language environments can be improved.

Conclusions: Research provides ample evidence of the importance of cultivating cognitive, language, and social development during children's early years. As ever more young children are entering group care settings pursuant to expectations that their mothers will join the work force, it becomes critical that the preschool opportunities available to lower-income families be designed in ways that fully support language and literacy development. This is perhaps one of the more important public policy issues raised by welfare reform.

Recommendations: All children, especially those at risk for reading difficulties, should have access to early childhood environments that promote language and literacy growth and that address reading risk factors in an integrated rather than isolated fashion. Specifically, we recommend that the following be included in home and preschool activities:

- adult-child shared book reading that stimulates verbal interaction to enhance language (especially vocabulary) development and knowledge about print concepts,
- activities that direct young children's attention to the phonological structure of spoken words (e.g., games, songs and poems that emphasize rhyming or manipulation of sounds), and
- activities that highlight the relations between print and speech.

ENSURING THAT CHILDREN HAVE THE OPPORTUNITY TO LEARN TO READ

Reading Instruction in Kindergarten Through Third Grade

Findings on the mechanics of reading: There is converging research support for the proposition that getting started in reading depends critically on mapping the letters and the spellings of words onto the sounds and speech units that they represent. Failure to master word recognition impedes text comprehension.

There is evidence that explicit instruction that directs children's attention to the phonological structure of oral language and to the connections between phonemes and spellings helps children who have not grasped the alphabetic principle or who do not apply it productively when they encounter unfamiliar printed words. Of course, intensity of instruction should be matched to children's needs. Children who lack these understandings should be helped to acquire them; those who have grasped the alphabetic principle and can apply it productively should move on to more advanced learning opportunities.

Findings on comprehension: Several factors have been shown to promote comprehension: vocabulary, including full and precise understanding of the meanings of words; background knowledge about the subject matter; familiarity with semantic and syntactic structures that signal meaningful relationships among the words; appreciation of the writing conventions used to achieve different communicative purposes (e.g., irony, humor); verbal reasoning ability, which permits inferences to be made by reading between the lines; and verbal memory capacity.

Comprehension can be enhanced through instruction that is focused on concept and vocabulary growth and the syntax and rhetorical structures of written language, as well as through experience gained by reading both independently and interactively in dyads or groups.

Explicit instruction in comprehension strategies has been shown to lead to improvement (e.g., summarizing the main idea, predicting what text will follow, drawing inferences, discussing the author's communicative intent and choice of wording, and monitoring for misunderstandings).

Conclusions: Our analysis of the research literature in reading acquisition leads us to conclude that, in order to prevent reading difficulties, formal instruction in reading needs to focus on the development of two sorts of mastery: word recognition skills and comprehension skills.

Recommendations on the mechanics of reading:

• Kindergarten instruction should be designed to provide practice with the sound structure of words, the recognition and production of letters, knowledge about print concepts, and familiarity with the basic purposes and mechanisms of reading and writing.

• First-grade instruction should be designed to provide explicit instruction and practice with sound structures that lead to phonemic awareness, familiarity with spelling-sound correspondences and common spelling conventions and their use in identifying printed words, "sight" recognition of frequent words, and independent reading, including reading aloud. A wide variety of well-written and engaging texts below the children's frustration level should be provided.

• Instruction for children who have started to read independently, typically second graders and above, should be designed to encourage children to sound out and confirm the identities of visually unfamiliar words they encounter in the course of reading meaningful text, recognizing words primarily through attention to their letter-sound relationships. Although context and pictures can be used as a tool to monitor word recognition, children should not be taught to use them to substitute for information provided by the letters in the word.

• Because the ability to obtain meaning from print depends so strongly on the development of word recognition accuracy and reading fluency, both of the latter should be regularly assessed in the classroom, permitting timely and effective instructional response where difficulty or delay is apparent.

Recommendations on comprehension:

• Kindergarten instruction should be designed to stimulate verbal interaction to instruct vocabulary and encourage talk about books.

• Beginning in the earliest grades, instruction should promote comprehension by actively building linguistic and conceptual knowledge in a rich variety of domains.

• Throughout the early grades, reading curricula should include explicit instruction on strategies such as summarizing the main idea, predicting events and outcomes of upcoming text, drawing inferences, and monitoring for coherence and misunderstandings. This instruction can take place while adults read to students or when students read themselves.

• Conceptual knowledge and comprehension strategies should be regularly assessed in the classroom, permitting timely and effective instructional response where difficulty or delay is apparent.

Recommendations on writing:

• Once children learn to write letters, they should be encouraged to write them, to use them to begin writing words or parts of words, and to use words to begin writing sentences. Instruction should be designed with the understanding that the use of invented spelling is not in conflict with teaching correct spelling. Beginning writing with invented spelling can be helpful for developing understanding of phoneme identity, phoneme segmentation, and sound-spelling relationships. Conventionally correct spelling should be developed through focused instruction and practice. Primary-grade children should be expected to spell previously studied words and spelling patterns correctly in their final writing products. Writing should take place on a daily basis to encourage children to become more comfortable and familiar with it.

Recommendations on reading practices and motivation:
• Throughout the early grades, time, materials, and resources should be provided (a) to support daily independent reading of texts selected to be of particular interest for the individual student, and also beneath the individual student's frustration level, in order to consolidate the student's capacity for independent reading and (b) to support daily assisted or supported reading and rereading of texts that are slightly more difficult in wording or in linguistic, rhetorical, or conceptual structure in order to promote advances in the student's capacities.
• Throughout the early grades, schools should promote independent reading outside of school by such means as daily at-home reading assignments and expectations, summer reading lists, encouraging parental involvement, and by working with community groups, including public librarians, who share this same goal.

Students with Limited Proficiency in English

Findings: Hurrying young non-English-speaking children into reading in English without ensuring adequate preparation is counterproductive. Learning to speak English first contributes to children's eventual fluency in English reading, because it provides a foundation to support subsequent learning about the alphabetic principle through an understanding of the sublexical structure of spoken English words and of the language and content of the material they are reading. The abilities to hear and reflect on the sublexical structure of spoken English words, as required for learning how the alphabetic principle works, depend on oral familiarity with the words being read. Similarly, learning to read for meaning depends on understanding the language and referents of the text to be read. Moreover, because being able to read and write in two languages confers numerous intellectual, cultural, economic, and social benefits, bilingualism and biliteracy should be supported whenever possible. To the extent possible, non-English-speaking children should have opportunities to develop literacy skills in their home language as well as in English.

Recommendations:

• If language-minority children arrive at school with no proficiency in English but speaking a language for which there are instructional guides, learning materials, and locally available proficient teachers, these children should be taught how to read in their native language while acquiring oral proficiency in English and subsequently taught to extend their skills to reading in English.

• If language-minority children arrive at school with no proficiency in English but speak a language for which the above conditions cannot be met and for which there are insufficient numbers of children to justify the development of the local capacity to meet such conditions, the initial instructional priority should be developing the children's oral proficiency in English. Although print materials may be used to support the development of English phonology, vocabulary, and syntax, the postponement of formal reading instruction is appropriate until an adequate level of oral proficiency in English has been achieved.

School-wide Restructuring

Findings: When a large percentage of a school's students are from disadvantaged homes, it is often the case that median student reading achievements in that school will be low. Research has shown the effectiveness of clearly articulated, well-implemented, school-wide efforts that build from coherent classroom reading instruction. Such school-wide efforts, when they have included coherent regular classroom reading instruction consistent with the principles articulated in this report, have often proven substantially more effective than disconnected strategies or restructuring focused on organizational issues that have not included school-wide curricular reform.

Conclusion: The local adaptation of national models is often a more efficient route to meaningful reform than are numerous local efforts to "reinvent the wheel."

Recommendation: In situations of school-wide poor performance, school restructuring designs that include dual foci on organizational issues and coherent classroom reading instruction should be seriously considered.

Extended Time in Reading-Related Instruction for Children with Persistent Reading Difficulties

Thus far, we have emphasized quality instruction and an appropriate curriculum, keyed to high standards, as the primary route to preventing most reading difficulties. However, additional efforts will still be necessary for some children, including supplementary tutoring provided by professionals with specialities in reading and special education support and services.

Findings: At present, many interventions for children in the primary grades are aimed at helping those most at risk of failure, but they are too often implemented as late as third grade, after a child is well behind his or her classmates.

Supplementary instruction has merit if the intervention is time limited and is planned and delivered in a way that makes connections to the daily experiences that the child has during reading instruction. Supplementary instruction can be a significant and targeted enhancement of classroom instruction. In Chapter 8 we presented a number of programs that have supplementary components, but the empirical bases for judging their results are often weak.

Conclusions: Consistent with the view that reading develops under the influence of many early experiences, it is the committee's judgment that deferring intervention until third or fourth grade should be avoided at all costs.

Supplementary programs can neither substitute nor compensate for poor-quality classroom reading instruction. Supplementary instruction is a secondary response to learning difficulties. Although supplementary instruction has demonstrated merit, its impact is insufficient unless it is planned and delivered in ways that make clear connections to the child's daily experiences and needs during reading instruction in the classroom.

Recommendation: If a student is receiving high-quality classroom instruction in first grade but is still having reading related difficulties, we recommend the following:

• Additional instructional services in supplementary reading programs should be provided in the first grade.

• Instruction should be provided by a well-qualified reading specialist who has demonstrated the ability to produce high levels of student achievement in reading.

• Materials and instructional techniques should be provided that are well integrated with ongoing excellent classroom instruction and that are consistent with the findings, conclusions, and recommendations identified above in "Reading Instruction in Kindergarten Through Third Grade." Children who are having difficulty learning to read do not, as a rule, require qualitatively different instruction from children who are "getting it." Instead, they more often need application of the same principles by someone who can apply them expertly to individual children who are having difficulty for one reason or another.

Resources to Meet Needs

Findings: The interventions described in this report require manageable class size and student-teacher ratios, ongoing teacher preparation, qualified specialists, and quality instructional materials in sufficient quantity. School libraries and media resources need to be used effectively. Nationally, there are steady reductions in the average size of elementary classrooms; however, schools in poor urban areas continue to show higher class sizes than schools in all other areas.

Conclusions: To meet the goal of preventing reading difficulties, a greater burden will fall on schools whose entering students are least prepared in the requisite skills (e.g., schools in poor urban areas, schools with high numbers of children who have limited English proficiency). The resources provided for kindergarten and primary-grade classrooms should be proportional to the amount of instructional support needed, as gauged by the entry abilities of the school's population. This type of resource planning contrasts with the practice of giving schools bonuses for high test scores as well as practices directed toward equating per-pupil resources across schools.

Recommendations: To be effective, schools with greater numbers of children at risk for reading difficulties must have extra resources. These resources should be used to ensure that class size, student-teacher ratios, teacher preparation and experience, availability and qualifications of specialists, quality and quantity of instructional materials, school libraries and physical environments will be at least equal to those of schools whose students are less likely to have difficulties learning to read.

Volunteer Tutors

Findings: Although volunteer tutors can provide very valuable practice and motivational support for children learning to read, the committee did not find evidence confirming that they are able to deal effectively with children who have serious reading problems. Effective tutoring programs require comprehensive screening procedures for selecting volunteers, training tutors, and supervising their ongoing work with children.

Conclusions: Volunteer tutors are effective in reading to children, for giving children supervised practice in oral reading, and for allowing opportunities for enriching conversation but not usually in providing instruction per se, particularly for children having difficulties.

Recommendation: The role of well-trained and supervised volunteer tutors should be to expand children's opportunities for practicing reading and for motivational support but not to provide primary or remedial instruction.

PREPARATION AND PROFESSIONAL SUPPORT OF PRESCHOOL AND PRIMARY TEACHERS

Beginning Teachers

Findings: Some beginning teachers do not have sufficient education to enable them to help all children become successful readers. Virtually all states require that candidates for a K-3 teacher credential do at least some course work in the teaching of reading. Too often, however, such course work is insufficient to provide beginning teachers with sufficient knowledge and skills to enable them to help all children become successful readers. One major factor is that very little time is allocated for preparing teachers to teach reading. A second is that teacher training programs are highly variable in their inclusion of the foundations of reading.

Conclusions: A critical element for preventing reading difficulties in young children is the teacher. Central to achieving the goal of primary prevention of reading difficulties is the teacher's knowledge base and experience, as well as the support provided to the teacher; each of these may vary according to where the teacher is in his or her professional development and his or her role in the school.

Teachers need to be knowledgeable about the research foundations of reading. Beyond this, a critical component in the pre-service preparation of primary-grade teachers is supervised, relevant, clinical experience in which they receive ongoing guidance and feedback. A principal goal of this experience is the ability to integrate and apply the knowledge base in practice. Collaborative support by the teacher preparation institution and the field placement supervising teacher is essential. A critical component for novice teachers is the support of mentor teachers with excellent records of success in teaching reading that results in improved student outcomes.

Recommendations: It is absolutely essential that teachers at all grade levels understand the course of literacy development and the role of instruction in optimizing literacy development. State certification requirements and teacher education curricula should be

changed to incorporate this knowledge base, including at a minimum:

- information about language development as it relates to literacy;
- information about the relationship between early literacy behavior and conventional reading;
- information about the features of an alphabetic writing system
and other writing systems;
- information about both phonology and morphology in relation to spelling;
- information about comprehension and its dependence on other
aspects of reading and on language skills;
- information about phonological awareness, orthographic
awareness, and writing development;
- procedures for ongoing, in-class assessment of children's reading abilities;
- information on how to interpret and modify instruction according to norm-referenced and individually referenced assessment
outcomes, including in-class assessments and progress monitoring
measures used by specialists;
- information about the learning and curricular needs of diverse
learners (students with disabilities, with limited English proficiency,
with English-language dialect differences);
- in settings in which children are learning to read in a language
other than English, an understanding of—as well as strategies and
techniques for—teaching children to read in that language and information about bilingual language and literacy development;
- in settings in which non-English-speaking or limited-English-
speaking students are in an English as a second language program
and learn to read in English, information and skill to help these
students confront a double challenge: learning to read and learning a
new language;
- information on the design features and requirements of a reading curriculum;
- information about how teachers apply research judiciously to
their practice, how to update their research knowledge, and how to

influence research agendas, including teacher-researcher collaborations; and

* information about how to maintain and promote motivation to read and positive attitudes toward reading.

Ongoing Staff Development

Findings: Staff development efforts are often inadequate for a number of reasons, including the lack of substantive and research-based content, the lack of systematic follow-up necessary for sustainability, and the one-shot character of many staff development sessions.

Conclusions: Teachers require ongoing in-service staff development support to absorb the information about reading and reading instruction outlined above. Professional development should not be conceived as something that ends with graduation from a teacher preparation program, nor as something that happens primarily in graduate classrooms or even during in-service activities. Rather, ongoing support from colleagues and specialists as well as regular opportunities for self-examination and reflection are critical components of the career-long development of excellent teachers.

Recommendation: Local education authorities and teacher education programs should give teachers support and skills throughout their careers, especially during their early entry into the profession, to ensure that they are well prepared to carry out their mission in preventing reading difficulties in young children.

Early Childhood Educators

Findings: Many preschool programs do not focus on language and literacy experiences that provide a foundation for early reading instruction.

Conclusions: Preschool teachers represent an important—and largely underutilized—resource in promoting literacy through the acquisition of rich language and emergent literacy skills. Early childhood educators should not try to replicate the formal reading instruction provided in schools. Central to achieving the goal of primary prevention of reading difficulties is the preschool teacher's knowledge base and experience and the support provided to the teacher; each of these may vary according to where the teacher is in his or her professional development.

As with primary-grade teachers, a critical component in the preservice preparation of teachers is supervised, relevant, clinical experience in which they receive ongoing guidance and feedback. A principal goal of this experience is the ability to integrate and apply the knowledge base in practice. Collaborative support by the teacher preparation institution and the field placement is essential.

Recommendations: Programs that educate early childhood professionals should require mastery of information about the many kinds of knowledge and skills that can be acquired in the preschool years in preparation for reading achievement in school. Their knowledge base should include at least the following:

- information about how to provide rich conceptual experiences that promote growth in vocabulary and reasoning skills;
- knowledge about lexical development, from early referential (naming) abilities to relational and abstract terms and finer-shaded meanings;
- knowledge of the early development of listening comprehension skills, and the kinds of syntactic and prose structures that preschool children may not yet have mastered;
- information on young children's sense of story;
- information on young children's sensitivity to the sounds of language;
- information on young children's understanding of concepts of print, and the developmental patterns of emergent reading and writing;
- information on young children's development of concepts of space, including directionality;
- knowledge of fine motor development; and
- knowledge about how to instill motivation to read.

Professional Reading Specialists

Findings: Special educators, speech and language clinicians, English as a second language teachers, resource room teachers, and other individuals are available in many schools to support the work of the classroom teacher to prevent reading difficulties. Too often, though, these professionals lack specialized knowledge about the typical and atypical development of reading and of their role in supporting reading instruction.

Conclusions: Schools that lack or have abandoned reading specialist positions need to reexamine their needs for specialists and provide the functional equivalent of such well-trained staff members. Reading specialists and other specialist roles need to be defined so that two-way communication is between specialists and classroom teachers about the needs of all children at risk of and experiencing reading difficulties. Coordination is needed at the instructional level so that children are taught with methodologies that are synergistic and not fragmented. Schools that have reading specialists as well as special educators need to coordinate these roles. Schools need to ensure that all the specialists engaged in child study or individualized educational program (IEP) meetings for special education placement, early childhood intervention, out-of-classroom interventions, or in-classroom support are well informed about research in reading development and the prevention of reading difficulties.

Recommendations: Every school should have access to specialists, including speech and language clinicians, English as a second language teachers, resource room teachers, and reading specialists who have specialized training related to addressing reading difficulties and who can give guidance to classroom teachers.

Educational Products and In-Service Development

Findings: There is currently no requirement and little incentive for publishers or adopting schools to evaluate reading-related materials and in-service programs in terms of their efficacy.

Conclusions: Given the significant expenditures on commercially distributed educational products as well as the widespread reliance on the instructional plans and activities they present, critical attention to the instructional quality of textbooks, basal reading series, curriculum kits, education software, and "promising programs" is both distressingly absent and urgently needed.

Recommendation: Local education agencies should set specific standards of evidence of efficacy for reading-related materials and in-service programs. Materials purveyors that currently do not provide adequate evidence to support data-based decision making about their products should be required to do so. These standards should be used when states, districts, schools, and teachers are choosing materials.

RESEARCH AGENDA

The process of study and discussion on what is known about the effective prevention of reading difficulties in young children has led us to recognize a number of issues that are in special need of attention from researchers. In particular, we have identified two newly emerging areas for research, several related to assessment, and several related to research on interventions.

Emerging Areas for Research

Benchmarks and Standards

Findings: Many state and local school districts have recently developed benchmarks or standards specifying what reading skills children should have acquired at successive points during their school careers. These efforts vary substantively not only in their content, structure, and specificity but also in proposals for their dissemination and use.

Research affirms that such benchmarks or standards can effectively improve reading outcomes but only to the extent that they are valid, specific, meaningful to teachers, and actually influence instructional conduct on a day-to-day basis. Moreover, such benchmarks and standards potentially afford invaluable guidance to school personnel, curriculum planners, publishers, software developers, test designers, and educational researchers for purposes of designing and evaluating instructional plans and materials, designing and evaluating intervention efforts, monitoring progress over time against a constant standard, and developing more sensitive and informative assessments. However, the broader realization of all such benefits will depend on establishing within the educational system new methods and modes for evaluating and iteratively improving, not only the benchmarks themselves but also the various options for their application.

Recommendation: Toward promoting high standards of achievement for all students in all schools, state and local education departments should sponsor research to evaluate and improve the utility and uses of their benchmarks or standards of reading achievement for purposes of informing instruction, evaluation, and allocation of resources and effort, including staffing and staff development as well as student service options.

Basic Research

Findings: As documented in this report, recent progress in understanding reading and its difficulties is largely the product, direct and indirect, of findings from basic research. Key contributions have ensued from a number of disciplines, including the neurosciences, linguistics, computer science, statistics, and the psychologies of memory, perception, cognition, and development. Significant contributions from basic research have clustered under funding programs that have emphasized the study of reading and its difficulties, and they have often been enabled by emerging technologies and computational and analytical techniques.

Recommendation: Government agencies and private foundations should ensure strong and continuing support of basic research and associated instrumentation in conjunction with active emphasis on the pursuit of knowledge relevant to reading and its difficulties.

Research Related to Assessment

Screening and Identification

Findings: Much has been learned about which particular differences among preschoolers and kindergartners are most prognostic of early reading outcomes, and these findings, in turn, have enabled more effective programs of early intervention. However, the array of instruments currently used to measure such differences are time consuming and costly to administer, even as they are mutually redundant and collectively incomplete with respect to the range of knowledge and sensitivities on which reading growth, including longer-term reading growth, depends. Such measures need to be refined, extended, and, as appropriate, combined into screening batteries that are maximally informative and efficient.

Recommendation: Appropriate government agencies and private foundations should sponsor research and development directed toward improving the efficiency, scope, and sensitivity of screening instruments for identifying children at risk of experiencing difficulties in learning to read so as best to ensure early, effective intervention. Such efforts should address factors that influence the development of the knowledge and capabilities that constrain literacy growth in the middle and later grades, as well as those related to initial reading acquisition.

Informal and Curriculum-Based Assessment

Findings: Given that effective instruction consists of responding to children's needs while building on their strengths, it necessarily depends on a sensitive and continual capacity for monitoring student progress. Toward this end, classroom teachers and tutors are in need of a richer and more serviceable inventory of assessment tools and strategies for day-to-day use in verifying that children are reaching curricular goals on schedule, in identifying children in need of extra help or opportunity, in specifying the particular nature of their needs, and in recognizing when difficulties have been adequately overcome to move on. Currently, the availability, quality, and best use of such assessment options vary greatly across classrooms and districts.

Recommendation: Toward the goal of assisting teachers in day-to-day monitoring of student progress along the array of dimensions on which reading growth depends, the appropriate government agencies and private foundations should sponsor evaluation, synthesis, and, as necessary, further development of informal and curriculum-based assessment tools and strategies. In complement, state and local school districts should undertake concerted effort to assist teachers and reading specialists in understanding how best to administer, interpret, and instructionally respond to such assessments.

Decision Making at the School and District Levels

Findings: Schools and school districts are constantly confronted with proposals for curricular or organizational change. Whether gauged in terms of time and money or opportunity and hope, the costs of implementing and even considering such change are substantial. Nevertheless, adequate evaluation of the value added by such efforts is rare in prospect or outcome. Decisions about whether to adopt a new basal program, and if so which one, are an obvious case in point. Concern extends to the range of systemic changes, including, for example, implementation of new student services, such as tutoring programs or after-school instruction, new professional development initiatives, and even new evaluation strategies.

Recommendation: The appropriate government agencies and private foundations should sponsor research to help school systems develop and use data-based decision making. This effort should include methods and means for:

- analysis of the system's strengths and weaknesses so as to identify and prioritize needs;
- evaluation the costs and benefits of proposed solutions to targeted problems so as to guide selection of—or, as necessary, the adaptation or design of—the most promising candidate;
- articulation of an implementation schedule and requirements so as to enable adequate planning;
- collection of data and feedback as necessary for monitoring implementation and measuring results;

• specification of desired outcome criteria and time lines for their attainment;

• public documentation of the effort, including implementation conditions and outcomes, so as to share lessons learned with other systems.

Research on Interventions

Effectiveness of Preschool Interventions

Findings: Increasingly, children at risk of experiencing difficulties in learning to read can be identified with a fair degree of accuracy several years prior to schooling. In complement, there is need for more rigorous and long-term research on how to assist such children most powerfully and efficiently. Although research affirms that some early language and literacy intervention programs have produced substantial and long-term benefits, many other such attempts have not. The more and less effective attributes of such programs cannot be adequately identified on the basis of existing data.

Recommendations: Toward developing more efficient and effective programs of early intervention, appropriate government agencies and private foundations are urged to:

• coordinate early screening and intervention research so as to identify causal difficulties and their most effective redress;

• recognize and study the systemic nature of organizational structures in order to offer useful interventions at the preschool level with ties to family, communities, cultural groups, etc.;

• evaluate how promising interventions can be delivered and sustained with greatest efficacy through Head Start programs, home-based programs, day care centers, software, television, and other media and social institutions;

• sponsor long-term prospective studies of early intervention strategies to assess the impact and longevity of different intervention strategies and their components and to determine how those factors interact with later instruction and experience, in school and out.

Reading Among Children for Whom English Is the Second Language

Findings: The large and growing number of children for whom English is a second language has thrust upon the educational community—practitioners no less than researchers—extremely important questions and challenges not traditionally addressed within the domain of reading science. By far the most controversial of these is whether it is more desirable to promote literacy in a first or second language for limited-English-speaking children. Although far from conclusive, there is evidence that initial reading instruction in a child's home language (e.g., Spanish) makes a positive contribution to literacy attainment (both in the home language and in English) and, presumably, to the prevention of reading difficulties. The question of how best to promote literacy learning in either or both languages is just as important but overshadowed by the politically more volatile issues of which language should be used and for how long. Researchers and educators possess scant empirical guidance on how best to design literacy instruction for such children in either their primary language or English, much less in both.

Recommendations: Appropriate government agencies and private foundations are urged to sponsor research on the factors that influence the literacy acquisition of children for whom English is not the primary language. For various primary languages (e.g., Spanish, Khmer, Chinese) and along key language dimensions such as alphabetic and nonalphabetic writing systems and traditionally literate versus nonliterate languages, issues that need to be addressed include:

- What are the principal difficulties involved in literacy acquisition in the primary language? What methods of primary language reading instruction are effective?
- What can we learn from successful reading instruction practices in countries where the children's primary language is not written? To what extent are these practices applicable in a North American context?

- In what ways might successful methods for teaching primary language literacy be adjusted to anticipate English language literacy acquisition and facilitate the transition to successful English literacy?

- How does the timing of the transition to English influence literacy prospects in each language? What are the optimal instructional strategies for such programs and how do they differ as a function of when the transition is introduced? Once a child makes a transition to English literacy, what are the advantages and disadvantages of continuing primary language academic instruction?

- Are there threshold levels of oral English proficiency and primary language literacy that are required for successful transition to, and satisfactory achievement in, English literacy? If so, are there adequate instruments for assessing these levels?

- How do similarities and differences in the syntax, semantics, phonology, and orthography of the first language ease or impede the challenge of learning to read in English? What are the instructional implications of these similarities and differences?

- To what extent should absolute level of oral English proficiency and relative proficiency in English and the primary language determine whether a limited-English-proficient child receives beginning and early literacy instruction in English?

- Where initial reading instruction is provided only in English, what are the best instructional strategies for developing literacy in English?

- What are the long-term literacy consequences of being taught to read only in a second language (i.e., English)?

- What are the advantages and disadvantages of learning to read in two languages? In particular, what are the cognitive costs and benefits? Is there an optimal timing and sequencing of instruction?

- Can children learn to read in two languages simultaneously, just as they can learn to speak in two or more languages simultaneously? What are the advantages and disadvantages of learning to read in two languages simultaneously?

- How do cultural issues in how text is used and regarded overlap with linguistic issues among children for whom English is a second language?

Role of Dialect in Reading Achievement

Findings: Although it has long been suggested that the dialect features of African American Vernacular English (AAVE) and its phonology create additional challenges for learning to read English, few efforts to test this hypothesis have been undertaken directly. Demonstration studies of linguistically informed instructional programs for African American youth have yielded promising results, but more analytic and longer-term research is required to gauge these benefits and to understand the factors on which they depend.

Recommendations: Studies of the long-term effects of linguistically informed instructional programs on literacy outcomes for speakers of AAVE could include:

- modifications of phonemic awareness and phonics instruction that are sensitive to differences in the phonological characteristics of AAVE and those presumed by English orthography;
- exploration of morphemic and word analysis strategies for reinforcing the structure and significance of English orthography; and
- research on the role of other linguistic factors, such as syntax, in the reading acquisition of AAVE speakers.

Role of Retention and Extra-Year Programs

Findings: Despite mixed research support, schools continue to offer as potential solutions the retention of specific children in a given grade or providing classes of "extra-year" preparation prior to kindergarten or between kindergarten and first grade for groups of children deemed to be at risk. However, there is some evidence to indicate that extra instructional support rather than just the extended time makes a difference in reading outcomes for students who are retained in the primary grades. It is unclear whether delivering the extra support during the first year could be more effective than offering it the second time around. Furthermore, the differences are not clear between the children who thrive in the long run after an extra year and those who do not.

Information is needed about the nature of the specific interventions for literacy available to children in extra-year programs. More sophisticated research is needed to specify common factors, if any, that are found for children who are successful following retention or an extra-year program.

Recommendations: Appropriate government agencies and private foundations should increase research efforts on the role of retention and extra-year programs in the prevention of reading difficulties. Research should be addressed specifically to the provision for appropriate reading instruction and outcomes. Studies of the long-term effects on literacy outcomes from curriculum variations could address the following questions:

- Can we make screening measures sensitive enough to identify children who would benefit from these types of programs?
- Does one type of program work better than another (e.g., outcomes at the end of first grade for children attending transitional K-1 programs versus those who are retained in kindergarten for an additional year)?
- What are the types of literacy instruction offered by such programs and how do they provide for the needed literacy growth of individual children?
- What evidence is there that children given such additional time or instruction profit more than they would have by proceeding with their age-level peers?

Software Focused on Literacy

Findings: Preliminary evaluations indicate that well-designed software programs for supporting early literacy development can produce gains in student performance. Such software can reinforce, motivate, and extend early literacy instruction.

Recommendations: Appropriate government agencies and private foundations should increase research efforts addressing appropriate technology that can support reading instruction. Issues that need to be addressed are whether the software programs are:

- consistent with the recommendations made above for "Reading Instruction in Kindergarten Through Third Grade,"
- consistent with classroom curricular goals as well as the specific needs of individual children, and
- used as a complement to—not as a substitute for—effective teaching or a good curriculum.

Effectiveness of Primary-Grade Interventions

Findings: Research affirms that quality classroom instruction in kindergarten and the primary grades is the single best weapon against reading failure. Indeed, when done well, classroom instruction has been shown to overwhelm the effects of student background and supplementary tutoring. Although research has made great strides in identifying the attributes of effective classroom instruction, many questions have been inadequately addressed.

Recommendations: Toward improving reading outcomes for all children, research toward increasing the efficacy of classroom reading instruction in kindergarten and the primary grades should be the number one funding priority. Beyond issues addressed in other sections of this chapter, questions in need of answers include:

- How best can the development of decoding automaticity be hastened?
- What factors govern children's induction and generalization of spelling-sound knowledge and how can they best be fostered?
- What are the roles and dynamics of syntactic and semantic factors in beginning readers? How do they influence the growth of decoding and fluency?
- Through what means can word recognition and comprehension development be coordinated so that they develop most efficiently and synergistically?
- What kinds of reading and writing activities and instruction serve to maximize the leverage of each on the other?

- How do syntactic competence and awareness influence reading growth? What aspects of syntax warrant instruction?
- What are the best strategies for building vocabulary growth?
- What are the keys to improving content-area reading?
- Can spelling and vocabulary growth be accelerated by learning about derivational morphology and, toward that end, what are the best strategies for its instruction?
- What kinds of instructional practices and activities serve best to develop children's habits of self-monitoring for coherence and comprehension?
- What is the impact of early childhood and primary-grade instructional practices on reading and literacy growth in the middle and upper grades of school? How should the curriculum be changed to maximize such benefit?
- What is the actual incidence and nature of the "fourth-grade slump"? Its prevalence and presenting symptoms should be documented and, if so indicated, research on its underlying causes and best prevention should follow.
- What kinds of curriculum materials (including basal readers) are useful for what purposes, and how can published materials and the reading/writing curriculum be integrated?
- What kinds of knowledge and material support do classroom teachers need for greatest effectiveness?
- How can in-service opportunities be used most effectively?
- What are the best strategies for monitoring and managing the range of student progress and difficulties in any given classroom or building?
- What kinds of classroom, grouping, and staffing options would significantly improve instructional delivery in the primary grades?
- What are the best strategies for maintaining constructive communication and collaboration between parents and teachers in support of children's reading development?

References

Abt Associates
  1995 National Evaluation of the Even Start Family Literacy Program: Final Report. U.S. Dept. of Education, Office of the Undersecretary for Planning and Evaluation Service.
Ackerman, P.T., R.A. Dykman, and M.Y. Gardner
  1990 ADD students with and without dyslexia differ in sensitivity to rhyme and alliteration. *Journal of Learning Disabilities* 23:279-283.
Adams, B.C., L.C. Bell, and C.A. Perfetti
  1995 A trading relationship between reading skill and domain knowledge in children's text comprehension. *Discourse Processes* 20:307-323.
Adams, M., B. Foorman, I. Lundberg, and T. Beeler
  1996 *Phonemic Awareness in Young Children.* Baltimore: Brookes Publishing Co.
Adams, M.J.
  1990 *Beginning to Read: Thinking and Learning About Print.* Cambridge, MA: MIT Press.
  In   Word recognition and reading. To appear in *Elementary Reading Instruction:*
  press *Process and Practice,* C.J. Gordon and G.D. Labercane, eds.
Adams, M.J., R. Treiman, and M. Pressley
  1998 Reading, writing, and literacy. Pp. 275-355 in *Handbook of Child Psychology, Fifth Edition, Vol. 4: Child Psychology in Practice,* I.E. Sigel and K.A. Renninger, eds. New York: Wiley.
Afflerbach, P.P.
  1990 The influence of prior knowledge and text genre on readers' prediction strategies. *Journal of Reading Behavior* 22(2):131-148.
Alexander, K., and D. Entwisle
  1996 Schools and children at risk. Pp. 67-88 in *Family-School Links: How Do They Affect Educational Outcomes?,* A. Booth and J. Dunn, eds. Hillsdale, NJ: Erlbaum.

Allen, R.V.
1976 *Language Experiences in Communication.* Boston: Houghton Mifflin.
Als, H., G. Lawhon, F. Duffy, G. McAnulty, R. Gives-Grossman, and J. Blickman
1994 Individualized developmental care for the very low birthweight preterm infant: Medical and neurofunctional effects. *Journal of the American Medical Association* 272: 853-858.
Alwin, D.F., and A. Thornton
1984 Family origins and the schooling process: Early versus late influence of parental characteristics. *American Sociological Review* 49:784-802.
American Optometric Association, The 1986/87 Future of Visual Development/Performance Task Force
1988 The efficacy of optometric vision therapy. *Journal of the American Optometric Association* 59(2):95-105.
Anbar, A.
1986 Reading acquisition of preschool children without systematic instruction. *Early Childhood Research Quarterly* 1:69-83.
Anderson, A., and S. Stokes
1984 Social and institutional influences on the development and practice of literacy. Pp. 24-37 in *Awakening to Literacy,* H. Goelman, A. Oberg, and F. Smith, eds. Portsmouth, NJ: Heinemann.
Anderson, L., J. Sears, L. Pellicer, M. Riddle, C. Gardner, and D. Harwell
1992 A study of the characteristics and qualities of "High-Flying" compensatory programs in South Carolina as examined through the framework of the SERVE model for effective compensatory programs. Columbia: Department of Educational Leadership and Policies, University of South Carolina.
Anderson, R.C., P.T. Wilson, and L.G. Fielding
1988 Growth in reading and how children spend their time outside of school. *Reading Research Quarterly* 23(3):285-303.
Anderson, R., B. Armbruster, and M. Roe
1989 *A Modest Proposal for Improving the Education of Reading Teachers.* Technical Report No. 487. Urbana-Champaign: University of Illinois, Center for the Study of Reading.
Anderson, R.C., E.H. Hiebert, J.A. Scott, and I.A.G. Wilkinson
1985 *Becoming a Nation of Readers: The Report of the Commission on Reading.* Washington, DC: National Academy of Education, Commission on Education and Public Policy.
Anderson, R.C., and P. Freebody
1983 Reading comprehension and the assessment and acquisition of word knowledge. Pp. 231-256 in *Advances in Reading/Language Research,* B. Hutson, ed. Greenwich, CT: JAI Press.
Anderson, R.C., and P.D. Pearson
1984 A schema-thematic view of basic processes in reading comprehension. Pp. 255-291 in *Handbook of Reading Research,* P.D. Pearson, R. Barr, M.L. Kamil, and P. Mosenthal, eds. New York: Longman.
Anderson, R.C., R.E. Reynolds, D.L. Schallert, and E.T. Goetz
1977 Frameworks for comprehending discourse. *American Educational Research Journal* 14(4):367-381.
Andrews, J., and J.M. Mason
1986 How do deaf children learn about prereading? *American Annals of the Deaf* 131:210-217.

Aram, D., and J. Nation
 1980 Preschool language disorders and subsequent language and academic difficulties. *Journal of Communication Disorders* 13:159-179.
Aram, D.M., and N.E. Hall
 1989 Longitudinal follow-up of children with preschool communication disorders: Treatment implications. *School Psychology Review* 18(4):487-501.
Au, K.
 1995 Multicultural perspectives on literacy research. *Journal of Reading Behavior* 27:85-100.
Au, K., and J.M. Mason
 1981 Social organizational factors in learning to read: The balance of rights hypothesis. *Reading Research Quarterly* 17:115-152.
August, D., and K. Hakuta, eds.
 1997 *Improving Schooling for Language-Minority Children: A Research Agenda.* National Research Council and Institute of Medicine. Washington, DC: National Academy Press.
Backman, J.
 1983 Psycholinguistic skills and reading acquisition: A look at early readers. *Reading Research Quarterly* 18:446-479.
Badian, N.A.
 1982 The prediction of good and poor reading before kindergarten entry: A 4-year follow-up. *Journal of Special Education* 16(3):309-318.
 1984 Reading disability in an epidemiological context: Incidence and environmental correlates. *Journal of Learning Disabilities* 17:129-136.
Baker, L.
 1996 Social influences on metacognitive development in reading. Pp. 331-352 in *Reading Comprehension Difficulties: Processes and Intervention,* C. Cornoldi and J. Oakhill, eds. Mahwah, NJ: Lawrence Earlbaum Associates.
Baker, L., D. Scher, and K. Mackler
 1997 Home and family influences on motivations for reading. *Educational Psychologist* 32(2):69-82.
Baker, L., and R.I. Anderson
 1982 Effects of inconsistent information on text processing: Evidence for comprehension monitoring. *Reading Research Quarterly* 27:281-294.
Baker, A.J., and C.S. Piotrkowski
 1996 Parents and Children Through the School Years: The Effects of the Home Instruction Program for Preschool Youngsters. Final Report to the David and Lucile Packard Foundation. Los Altos, CA.
Baker, L., R. Serpell, and S. Sonnenschein
 1995 Opportunities for literacy learning in the homes of urban preschoolers. Pp. 236-252 in *Family Literacy: Connections in Schools and Communities,* L.M. Morrow, ed. Newark, DE: International Reading Association.
Ball, D.L., and D.K. Cohen
 1996 Reform by the book: What is—or might be—the role of curriculum materials in teacher learning and instructional reform? *Educational Researcher* 25(9):6-8.
Ball, E.W., and B.A. Blachman
 1991 Does phoneme awareness training in kindergarten make a difference in early word recognition and developmental spelling? *Reading Research Quarterly* 26(1):49-66.
Baratz, J.C., and R.W. Shuy
 1969 Teaching Black Children to Read. *Urban Language Series, Number 4.* Washington, DC: Center for Applied Linguistics.

Barnett, W.S.
1995   Long-term effects of early childhood programs on cognitive and school outcomes. *The Future of Children* 5(3):25-50.
Barnett, W.S., and G. Camilli
1996   Definite Results from Loose Data: A Response to "Does Head Start Make a Difference?" Updated version of paper presented at the Seminar on Labor and Industrial Relations, Princeton University. Graduate School of Education, Rutgers University, New Brunswick, NJ.
Barnett, W.S., E.C. Frede, H. Mobasher, and P. Mohr
1987   The efficacy of public preschool programs and the relationship of program quality to efficacy. *Educational Evaluation and Policy Analysis* 10(1):37-49.
Bashir, A.S., and A. Scavuzzo
1992   Children with language disorders: Natural history and academic success. *Journal of Learning Disabilities* 25(1):53-65.
Bates, E., I. Bretherton, L. Snyder, M. Beeghly, C. Shore, S. McNew, V. Carlson, C. Williamson, and A. Garrison, et al.
1988   *From First Words to Grammar: Individual Differences and Dissociable Mechanisms.* New York: Cambridge University Press.
Beals, D.
1993   Explanatory talk in low-income families' mealtime conversations. *Applied Psycholinguistics* 14:489-514.
Bear, D.R., M. Invernizzi, S. Templeton, and F. Johnson
1996   *Words Their Way.* Upper Saddle River, NJ: Merrill.
Beck, I.L., and M.G. McKeown
1981   Developing questions that promote comprehension: The story map. *Language Arts* 58(8):913-918.
1991   Social studies texts are hard to understand: Mediating some of the difficulties. *Language Arts* 68:482-490.
Beck, I.L., M.G. McKeown, C. Sandora, L. Kucan, et al.
1996   Questioning the author: A yearlong classroom implementation to engage students with text. *Elementary School Journal* 96(4):385-414.
Becker, W.C.
1977   Teaching reading and language to the disadvantaged: What we have learned from field research. *Harvard Educational Review* 47:518-543.
Becker, W.C., S. Engelmann, and D.R. Thomas
1975   *Teaching 2: Cognitive Learning and Instruction.* Chicago: Science Research Associates.
Bell, L.C., and C.A. Perfeffi
1994   Reading skill: Some adult comparisons. *Journal of Educational Psycholgy* 86(2): 244-255.
Belsky, J., R.M. Lerner, and G.B. Spanier
1984   *The Child in the Family.* Reading, MA: Addison-Wesley Publishing Co., Inc.
Bennet, B.
1987   The Effectiveness of Staff Development Training Practice: A Meta Analysis. Ph.D. thesis, University of Oregon.
Bentin, S., and H. Leshem
1993   On the interaction between phonological awareness and reading acquisition: It's a two-way street. *Annals of Dyslexia* 43:125-148.
Berent, I., and C.A. Perfetti
1995   A rose is a REEZ: The two-cycles model of phonology assembly in reading English. *Psychological Review* 102:146-184.

Berliner, D., and B. Biddle
  1995 *The Manufactured Crisis: Myths, Fraud, and the Attack on America's Public Schools.*
        Redding, MA: Addision-Wesley.
Besner, D.
  1990 Does the reading system need a lexicon? Pp. 73-99 in *Comprehension Processes in
        Reading,* D. Balota, G.B. Flores d'Arcais, and K. Rayner, eds. Hillsdale, NJ:
        Lawrence Erlbaum Associates.
  In   Basic processes in reading: Multiple routines in localist and connectionist models.
  press *Converging Methods for Understanding Reading and Dyslexia,* P.A. McMullen and
         R.M. Klein, eds. Cambridge, MA: MIT Press.
Bethke, H.
  1997 Survey Evaluation of Literacy Promotion Program. Unpublished report.
Bialystok, E.R., and E.B. Ryan
  1985 Toward a definition of metalinguistic skill. *Merrill Palmer Quarterly* 31:229-251.
Biemiller, A., and L.S. Siegel
  1997 A longitudinal study of the effects of the Bridge reading program for children at risk
        for reading failure. *Journal of Learning Disabilities.*
Birch, S.H., and G.W. Ladd
  1997 The teacher-child relationship and children's early school adjustment. *Journal of
        School Psychology* 35(1):61-79.
Bishop, D. V., and A. Edmundson
  1987 Specific language impairment as a maturational lag: Evidence from longitudinal data
        on language and motor development. *Developmental Medicine and Child Neurol-
        ogy* 29(4):442-459.
Bishop, D.V.M., and C. Adams
  1990 A prospective study of the relationship between specific language impairment, pho-
        nological disorders and reading retardation. *Journal of Child Psychology and Psy-
        chiatry* 31:1027-1050.
Bissex, G.L.
  1980 *GYNS AT WRK: A Child Learns to Read and Write.* Cambridge, MA: Harvard
        University Press.
Blachman, B.A.
  1987 An alternative classroom reading program for learning disabled and other low-achiev-
        ing children. Pp. 49-55 in *Intimacy with Language: A Forgotten Basic in Teacher
        Education,* W. Ellis, ed. Baltimore: Orton Dyslexia Society.
Bloom, B.
  1964 *Stability and Change in Human Characteristics.* New York: Wiley.
Bloom, L., L. Rocissano, and L. Hood
  1976 Adult-child discourse: Developmental interaction between information processing
        and linguistic knowledge. *Cognitive Psychology* 8:521-552.
Bloom, P., A. Barss, J. Nicol, and L. Conway
  1994 Children's knowledge of binding and coreference: Evidence from spontaneous speech.
        Language 70(1):53-71.
Blum-Kulka, S.
  1993 "You gotta know how to tell a story": Telling, tales, and tellers in American and
        Israeli narrative events at dinner. *Language in Society* 22:361-402.
Borko, H., and C. Livingston
  1989 Cognition and improvisation: Differences in mathematics instruction by expert and
        novice teachers. *American Educational Research Journal* 26:473-498.

Bowers, P.G., and L.B. Swanson
1991 Naming speed deficits in reading disability: Multiple measures of a singular process. *Journal of Experimental Child Psychology* 51:195-219.
Bradley, L., and P.E. Bryant
1983 Categorizing sounds and learning to read: A causal connection. *Nature* 30:419-421.
Bradley, L., and P.E. Bryant
1985 *Rhyme and Reason in Reading and Spelling.* Ann Arbor: University of Michigan Press.
Brady, S., A. Fowler, B. Stone, and N. Winbury
1994 Training phonological awareness: A study with inner-city kindergarten children. *Annals of Dyslexia* 44:27-59.
Bransford, J.D., and M.K. Johnson
1972 Contextual prerequisites for understanding: Some investigations of comprehension and recall. *Journal of Verbal Learning and Verbal Behavior* 11:717-726.
Bronfenbrenner, U., P. McClelland, E. Wethington, P. Moen, and S.J. Ceci
1996 *The State of Americans.* New York: Free Press.
Bronson, C.
1996 Project Success Enrichment: Language Arts Manual. Introductory Unit & Bibliography. ERIC document: ED404794.
Brooks-Gunn, J., M.C. McCormick, S. Shapiro, A.A. Benasich, and G.W. Black
1994 The effects of early education intervention on maternal employment, public assistance, and health insurance: The Infant Health and Development Program. *American Journal of Public Health* 84(6):924-930.
Brophy, J.E., and C.M. Evertson
1978 Context variables in teaching. *Educational Psychologist* 12(3):310-316.
Brophy, J., and T.L. Good
1984 Teacher behavior and student achievement. Occasional paper, No. 73. Michigan State University, East Lansing, Institute for Research on Teaching.
Brown, A.L., A.S. Palincsar, and B.B. Armbruster
1984 Instructing comprehension-fostering activities in interactive learning situations. Pp. 255-286 in *Learning and Comprehension of Text,* H. Mandl, N.L. Stein, and T. Trabasso, eds. Mahwah, NJ: Lawrence Erlbaum Associates.
Brown, C.J., and J. Zimmermann
1997 Building Effective Early Literacy Environment in Pre-K Through 1st Grade Classrooms: An Introduction to Breakthrough to Literacy. Presentation to National Alliance of Black School Educators, Reno, NV, December 19.
Brown, R.
1973 *A First Language: The Early Stages.* Cambridge, MA: Harvard University Press.
Bruck, M.
1990 Word-recognition skills of adults with childhood diagnoses of dyslexia. *Developmental Psychology* 26(3):439-454.
Bryant, D.M., L.B. Lau, M. Burchinal, and J.J. Sparling
1994 Family and classroom correlates of Head Start children's developmental outcomes. *Early Childhood Research Quarterly* 9(3-4):289-309.
Bryant, D.M., E. Peisner-Feinberg, and R. Clifford
1993 *Evaluation of Public Preschool Programs in North Carolina.* Chapel Hill: Frank Porter Graham Center, University of North Carolina.
Bryant, P.
1974 *Perception and Understanding in Young Children: An Experimental Approach.* New York: Basic Books.

Bryant, P.E., M. MacLean, L.L. Bradley, and J. Crossland
1990   Rhyme and alliteration, phoneme detection, and learning to read. *Developmental Psychology* 26(3):429-438.

Bryant, P.E., L. Bradley, M. Camlean, and J. Crossland
1989   Nursery rhymes, phonological skills and reading. *Journal of Child Language* 16: 407-428.

Bryk, A.S., and S.W. Raudenbush
1987   Application of hierarchical linear models to assessing change. *Psychological Bulletin* 101(1):147-158.

Buday, M.C., and J.A. Kelly
1996   National board certification and the teaching profession's commitment to quality assurance. *Phi Delta Kappan* (November):215-219.

Bull, T.
1984   Teaching School Beginners to Read and Write in the Vernacular. Paper presented at the World Congress of Applied Linguistics (7th, Brussels, Belgium, August 5-10, 1984).

Burgess, J.C.
1982   The effects of a training program for parents of preschoolers on the children's school readiness. *Reading Improvement* 19(4):313-318.

Burns, M.S., and R. Casbergue
1992   Parent-child interaction in a letter-writing context. *Journal of Reading Behavior* 24(3):289-312.

Bus, A.G., M.H. van IJzendoorn, and A.D. Pellegrini
1995   Joint book reading makes for success in learning to read: A meta-analysis on intergenerational transmission of literacy. *Review of Educational Research* 65(1):1-21.

Bus, A.G., and van IJzendoorn, M.H.
1988   Mother-child interactions, attachment, and emergent literacy: A cross-sectional study. *Child Development* 59(5):262-272.
1995   Mothers reading to their 3-year-olds: The role of mother-child attachment security in becoming more literate. *Reading Research Quarterly* 30:998-1015.
1997   Affective dimensions of mother-infant picturebook reading. *Journal of School Psychology* 35:1-14.

Butler, S.R., H.W. Marsh, M.J. Sheppard, and J.L. Sheppard
1985   Seven-year longitudinal study of the early prediction of reading achievement. *Journal of Educational Psychology* 77(3):349-361.

Butterworth, B.
1983   Lexical representation. Pp. 257-294 in *Language Production,* Vol. 1, B. Butterworth, ed. San Diego: Academic Press.

Byrne, B., and R. Fielding-Barnsley
1989   Phonemic awareness and letter knowledge in the child's acquistions of the alphabetic principle. *Journal of Educational Psychology* 81(1):313-321.
1991   Evaluation of a program to teach phonemic awareness to young children. *Journal of Educational Psychology* 83(3):451-455.
1995   Evaluation of a program to teach phonemic awareness to young children. A 2- and 3-year follow up and a new preschool trial. *Journal of Educational Psychology* 87(3): 488-503.

Caffee, R.C., and P. Drum
1986   Research on teaching reading. Pp. 804-849 in *Handbook of Research on Teaching,* M.C. Wittrock, ed. New York: Macmillan.

Cain, K.
  1996 Story knowledge and comprehension skills. Pp. 167-192 in *Reading Comprehension Difficulties: Processes and Intervention*, C. Cornoldi and J. Oakhill, eds. Mahwah, NJ: Lawrence Erlbaum Associates.
Calfee, R.C., and M.K. Henry
  1986 Project READ: An inservice model for training classroom teachers in effective reading instruction. Pp. 199-229 in *The Effective Teaching of Reading: Research into Practice*, J.V. Hoffman, ed. Newark, DE: International Reading Association.
Calfee, R.C., P. Lindamood, and C. Lindamood
  1973 Acoustic-phonetic skills and reading: Kindergarten through twelfth grade. *Journal of Educational Psychology* 64(3):293-298.
California State Board of Education
  1997 *A Blueprint for Professional Development for Teachers of Early Reading Instruction.* Sacramento: Comprehensive Reading Leadership Center, Sacramento County Office of Education.
California State Department of Education
  1986 *Beyond Language: Social and Cultural Factors in Schooling Language Minority Students.* Los Angeles: Evaluation, Dissemination and Assessment Center, California State University.
  1987a *English-Language Arts Framework for California Public Schools.* Sacramento: California State Department of Education.
  1987b *English-Language Arts Model Curriculum Guide, Kindergarten Through Grade Eight.* Sacramento: California State Department of Education.
Campbell, F.A., and C.T. Ramey
  1993 Mid-Adolescent Outcomes for High Risk Students: An Examination of the Continuing Effects of Early Intervention. ERIC document ED358919.
  1994 Effects of early intervention on intellectual and academic achievement: A follow up study of children from low-income families. *Child Development* 65:684-698.
Cannella, G.S., and J.C. Reiff
  1989 Mandating early childhood entrance/retention/assessment: Practices in the United States. *Child Study Journal* 19(2):83-99.
Cardon, L.R., S. Smith, D. Fulker, W. Kimberling, B. Pennington, and J. DeFries
  1994 Quantitative trait locus for reading disability on chromosome 6. *Science* 266:276-279.
Carey, S.T., and J. Cummins
  1983 Achievement, behavioral correlates and teachers' perceptions of francophone and anglophone immersion students. *Alberta Journal of Educational Research* 29(3):159-167.
Carlisle, J.F.
  1989 The use of the sentence verification technique in diagnostic assessment of listening and reading comprehension. *Learning Disabilities Research* 5(1):33-44.
Carroll, J.B.
  1963 A model of school learning. *Teachers College Record* 64:723-733.
Carta, J.J., et al.
  1991 Developmentally appropriate practice: Appraising its usefulness for young children with disabilities. *Topics in Early Childhood Special Education* 11(1):1-20.
Carter, L.F.
  1984 The sustaining effects study of compensatory and elementary education. *Educational Researcher* 13(7):4-13.

Carver, R.
 1994 Percentage of unknown vocabulary words in text as a function of the relative difficulty of the text: Implications for instruction. *Journal of Reading Behavior: A Journal of Literacy* 26:413-438.
Carver, R.P., and R.E. Leibert
 1995 The effect of reading library books at different levels of difficulty upon gain in reading ability. *Reading Research Quarterly* 30(1):26-48.
Casto, G., and M.A. Mastropieri
 1986 The efficacy of early intervention programs: A meta-analysis. *Exceptional Children* 52:417-424.
Catts, H., M. Fey, and B. Tomblin
 1997 *The Language Basis of Reading Disabilities.* Paper presented at the meeting of the Society for Scientific Studies of Reading, Chicago.
Catts, H.W.
 1991a Early identification of reading disabilities. *Topics in Language Disorders* 12(1):1-16.
 1991b Early identification of dyslexia: Evidence from a follow-up study of speech-language impaired children. *Annals of Dyslexia* 41:163.
 1993 The relationship between speech-language impairments and reading disabilities. *Journal of Speech and Hearing Research* 36:948-958.
 1996 Defining dyslexia as a developmental language disorder: An expanded view. *Topics in Language Disorders* 16(2):14-29.
Cazden, D.B.
 1985 Social context of learning to read. Pp. 595-610 in *Theoretical Models and Processes of Reading*, H. Singer and R. Ruddell, eds. Newark, DE: International Reading Association.
Center, Y., K. Wheldall, L. Freeman, L. Outhred, et al.
 1995 An evaluation of reading recovery. *Reading Research Quarterly* 30(2):240-263.
Chall, J.S.
 1967 *Learning to Read: The Great Debate.* New York: McGraw-Hill.
 1983 *Stages of Reading Development.* New York: McGraw-Hill.
Chall, J.S., V. Jacobs, and L. Baldwin
 1990 *The Reading Crisis: Why Poor Children Fall Behind.* Cambridge, MA: Harvard University Press.
Chaney, C.
 1989 I pledge a legiance tothe flag: Three studies in word segmentation. *Applied Psycholinguistics* 10(3):261-282.
 1992 Language development, metalinguistic skills, and print awareness in 3-year-old children. *Applied Psycholinguistics* 13(4):485-514.
Chomsky, C.
 1970 Reading, writing and phonology. *Harvard Educational Review* 40:287-309.
 1971 Write first, read later. *Childhood Education* 41:296-299.
 1972 Stages in language development and reading exposure. *Harvard Educational Review* 42:1-33.
 1975 *The Acquisition of Syntax in Children from 5 to 10.* Cambridge, MA: MIT Press.
 1979 Approaching reading through invented spelling. Pp. 43-65 in *Theory and Practice of Early Reading, Volume 2*, L.B. Resnick and P.A. Weaver, eds. Hillsdale, NJ: Erlbaum.
Christie, J.F., E.P. Johnsen, and R.B. Peckover
 1988 The effects of play period duration on children's play patterns. *Journal of Research in Childhood Education* 3(2):123-131.

Clarke, L.K.
1988 Invented versus traditional spelling in first graders' writings: Effects on learning to spell and read. *Research in the Teaching of English* 22(3):281-309.
Clay, M.M.
1975 *What Did I Write?* Auckland, NZ: Heinemann.
1979 *The Early Detection of Reading Difficulties. Second Edition.* Auckland, NZ: Heinemann.
1985 *The Early Detection of Reading Difficulties, Third Edition.* Portsmouth, NH: Heinemann.
Cognition and Technology Group at Vanderbilt
1998 Designing environments to reveal, support, and expand our children's potentials. Pp. 313-350 in S.A. Soraci and W. McIlvane, Eds., *Perspectives on Fundamental Processes in Intellectual Functioning*, Vol. 1. Greenwich, CT: Ablex.
Cohen, G.N., M.B. Bronson, and M.B. Casey
1995 Planning as a factor in school achievement. *Journal of Applied Developmental Psychology* 16(3):405-428.
Cole, K.N., P. Dale, P. Mills, and J. Jenkins
1993 Interaction between early intervention curricula and student characteristics. *Exceptional Children* 60(1):17-28.
Cole, K.N., P.E. Mills, and P.S. Dale
1989 A comparison of the effects of academic and cognitive curricula for young handicapped children one and two years postprogram. *Topics in Early Childhood Special Education* 9(3):110-127.
Coleman, J.S., E. Campbell, C. Hobson, J. McPartland, A. Mood, F. Weinfeld, and R. York
1966 *Equality of Educational Opportunity.* Washington, DC: U.S. Office of Education, National Center for Educational Statistics.
Collier, V.P., and W.P. Thomas
1989 How quickly can immigrants become proficient in school English? *Journal of Educational Issues of Language Minority Students* 5:26-38.
Collins, A., J. Brown, and S. Newman
1989 Cognitive apprenticeship: Teaching the craft of reading, writing, and mathematics. Pp. 453-494 in *Knowing, Learning, and Instruction: Essays in Honor of Robert Glaser*, Lauren B. Resnick, eds. Hillsdale, NJ: Lawrence Erlbaum Associates.
Collins, A., and A.O. Stevens
1982 Goals and strategies of inquiry teachers. Pp. 65-119 in *Advances in Instructional Psychology II*, R. Glazer, ed. Hillsdale, NJ: Erlbaum.
Coltheart, M., B. Curtis, P. Atkins, and M. Haller
1993 Models of reading aloud: Dual-route and parallel-distributed processing approaches. *Psychological Review* 100:589-608.
Coltheart, M., B. Curtis, P. Atkins, and Z. Schreter
1991 Computational Modeling of Reading: Dual or Single Route? Paper presented at the Psychonomic Society meeting, San Francisco.
Commission on Emotional and Learning Disorders in Children
1970 *One Million Children: A National Study of Canadian Children with Emotional and Learning Disorders.* Toronto: Leonard Crainford.
Conrad, R.
1979 *The Deaf School Child.* London: Harper and Row.
Cook, T.
1991 Clarifying the warrant for generalized causal inferences in quasi-experiments. *Evaluation and Education at Quarter Century, NSSE Yearbook 1991*, M.W. McLaughlin and D. Phillips, eds.

Corlett, D.
1988 Experiences in reading instruction as the road to teaching reading. *Reading Improvement* 25:313-318.

Cornoldi, C., and J. Oakhill, eds.
1996 *Reading Comprehension Difficulties: Processes and Intervention.* Mahwah, NJ: Lawrence Erlbaum Associates.

Cornwall, A.
1992 The relationship of phonological awareness, rapid naming, and verbal memory to severe reading and spelling disability. *Journal of Learning Disabilities* 25:532-538.

Craig, H., and J. Washington
1995 African-American English and linguistic complexity in preschool discourse: A second look. *Language, Speech, and Hearing Services in Schools* 26:87-93.

Crenshaw, S.R.
1985 A Semiotic Look at Kindergarten Writing. ERIC Clearinghouse #ED269765.

Critchley, M.
1970 *The Dyslexic Child.* Springfield, IL: Charles C Thomas.

Cuban, L.
1986 The ways that schools are: Lessons for reformers. *Policy Options for the Future of Compensatory Education: Conference Papers,* D. Doyle, ed. Washington, DC.

Cummins, J.
1970 Cognitive/academic language proficiency, linguistic interdependence, the optimum age question and some other matters. *Working Papers on Bilingualism* 19:197-205.
1979 Linguistic interdependence and the educational development of bilingual children. *Review of Educational Research* 49(2):222-251.
1984 *Bilingualism in Special Education.* San Diego: College Hill Press.

Cunningham, A.E., K.E. Stanovich, and M.R. Wilson
1990 Cognitive variation in adult students differing in reading ability. Pp. 129-159 in *Reading and Its Development: Component Skills Approaches,* T.H. Carr and B.A. Levy, eds. New York: Academic Press.

Cunningham, A.E.
1990 Explicit versus implicit instruction in phonemic awareness. *Journal of Experimental Child Psychology* 50:429-444.

Cunningham, P.M., D.P. Hall, and M. Defee
1991 Non-ability-grouped, multilevel instruction: A year in a first-grade classroom. *The Reading Teacher* 44(8):566-576.

Cunningham, P.M., and J.W. Cunningham
1992 Making words: Enhancing the invented spelling-decoding connection. *The Reading Teacher* 46(2):106-115.

Currie, J., and D. Thomas
1995 Does Head Start make a difference? *American Economic Review* 85(3):341-364.

Curtis, M.E.
1980 Development of components of reading skill. *Journal of Educational Psychology* 72: 656-669.

Daisey, P.
1991 Intergenerational literacy programs: Rationale, description, and effectiveness. *Journal of Clinical Psychology* 20:11-17.

Dale, P.S., C. Crain-Thoreson, A. Notari-Syverson, and K. Cole
1996 Parent-child book reading as an intervention technique for young children with language delays. *Topics in Early Childhood Special Education* 16(2):213-235.

Dale, P.S., and K. Cole
1988 Comparison of academic and cognitive programs for young handicapped children. *Exceptional Children* 54(5):439-447.

Daneman, M., and P.A. Carpenter
1980 Individual differences in working memory and reading. *Journal of Verbal Learning and Verbal Behavior* 19:450-466.
Daneman, M., and T. Tardiff
1987 Working memory and reading skill re-examined. Pp. 491-504 in *Attention and Performance XII: The Psychology of Reading,* M. Coltheart, ed. Hillsdale, NJ: Erlbaum Associates.
Daniels, P.T., and W. Bright
1996 *The World's Writing Systems.* New York: Oxford University Press.

Darling-Hammond, L.
1996 The quiet revolution rethinking teacher development. *Educational Leadership* 53(6): 4-10.
Dattilo, J., and S. Camarata
1991 Facilitating conversation through self-initiated augmentative communication treatment. *Journal of Applied Behavior Analysis* 24(2):369-78.
Davis, F.B.
1944 Fundamental factors of comprehension in reading. *Psychometrika* 9:185-197.
1968 Research in comprehension in reading. *Reading Research Quarterly* 3:499-545.
Davis, T.C., M.A. Crouch, S.W. Long, et al.
1991 Rapid assessment of literacy levels of adult primary care patients. *Family Medicine* 23(6):433-435.
Davis, T.C., S.W. Long, R.H. Jackson, et al.
1993 Rapid estimate of adult literacy in medicine: A shortened screening instrument. *Family Medicine* 25(6):391-395.
de Villiers, P.A., and J.G. de Villiers
1979 *Early Language.* Cambridge, MA: Harvard University Press.
DeBaryshe, B.D.
1993 Joint picture-book reading correlates of early oral language skill. *Journal of Child Language* 20(2):455-461.
1995 Maternal belief systems: Linchpin in the home reading process. *Journal of Applied Developmental Psychology* 16(1):1-20.
DeBaryshe, B.D., M.B. Caulfield, J.P. Witty, J. Sidden, H.E. Holt, and C.E. Reich
1991 The Ecology of Young Children's Home Reading Environments. Paper presented at the biennial meeting of the Society for Research in Child Development, April 18-21, 1991, Seattle.
DeBruin-Parecki, A., S. Paris, and J. Siedenburg
1997 Family literacy: Examining practice and issues of effectiveness (in Michigan). *Journal of Adolescent and Adult Literacy* 40:596-605.
DeFord, D., G. Pinnell, C. Lyons, and P. Young
1987 *Report of the Follow-up Studies: Vol. 7 Columbus Ohio, Ohio Reading Recovery Project 1985-86 and 1986-87.* Columbus: The Ohio State University.
DeFries, J.C., and M. Alarcon
1996 Genetics of specific reading disability. *Mental Retardation and Developmental Disabilities Research Reviews* 2:39-47.
Delgado-Gaitan, C.
1990 *Literacy for Empowerment.* New York: Falmer.
Delpit, L.D.
1986 Skills and other dilemmas of a progressive black educator. *Harvard Educational Review* 56:379-385.

1988 The silenced dialogue: Power and pedagogy in educating other people's children. *Harvard Educational Review* 58(3):280-298.

Denckla, M.B., and R.G. Rudel
1976a Naming of object-drawings by dyslexic and other learning disabled children. *Brain and Language* 3:1-15.
1976b Rapid automatized naming (r.a.n.): Dyslexia differentiated from other learning disabilities. *Neuropsychologia* 14:471-479.

Dickinson, D.K., and C. Howard
1997 Quarterly Report on New England Quality Research Center Activities. Submitted to Agency for Children and Families. EDC, Newton, MA.

Dickinson, D.K., and M.W. Smith
1994 Long-term effects of preschool teachers' book readings on low-income children's vocabulary and story comprehension. *Reading Research Quarterly* 29(2):104-122.

Dickinson, D.K., L. Cote, and M.W. Smith
1993 Learning vocabulary in preschool: Social and discourse contexts affecting vocabulary growth. Pp. 67-78 in *The Development of Literacy Through Social Interaction. New Directions for Child Development, No. 61: The Jossey-Bass Education Series*, C. Daiute, ed. San Francisco: Jossey-Bass.

Donaldson, M.
1986 *Children's Explanations: A Psycholinguistic Study*. London: Cambridge University Press.

Dore, J.
1974 A pragmatic description of early language development. *Journal of Psycholinguistic Research* 3:343-350.
1975 Holophrases, speech acts, and language universals. *Journal of Child Language* 2:21-40.
1976 Children's illocutionary acts. In *Discourse Relations: Comprehension and Production*, R. Freedle, ed. Hillsdale, NJ: Lawrence Erlbaum Associates.

Dorval, B., and C.O. Eckerman
1984 Developmental trends in the quality of conversation achieved by small groups of acquainted peers. *Monographs of the Society for Research in Child Development*, 206 49(2).

Dorval, B., T.H. Joyce, and C.T. Ramey
1980 Teaching Phoneme Identification Skills to Young Children at Risk for School Failure: Implications for Reading Instruction. Unpublished manuscript, University of North Carolina, Chapel Hill.

Downing, J.
1979 *Reading and Reasoning*. New York: Springer-Verlag.

Dunkin, M.
1996 Types of errors in synthesizing research in education. *Review of Educational Research* 66:87-98.

Dunn, L.M., and L.M. Dunn
1981 *Peabody Picture Vocabulary Test, Revised*. Circle Pines, MN: American Guidance Service.

Durkin, D.
1966 *Children Who Read Early*. New York: Teachers College Press.

Education Commission of the States
1996 *The Progress of Education Reform: 1996*. Denver: Education Commission of the States.

Edwards, P.A.
1995 Empowering low-income mothers and fathers to share books with young children. *The Reading Teacher* 48:558-564.

Ehri, L.C., and C. Chun
  1996 How alphabetic/phonemic knowledge facilitates tet processing in emerging readers.
        Pp. 69-93 in *Literacy and Education: Essays in Memory of Dina Feitelson,* J.
        Shimron, ed. Cresskill, NJ: Hampton Press.
Ehri, L.C.
  1980 The development in orthographic images. Pp. 311-388 in *Cognitive Processes in
        Spelling,* U. Frith, ed. London: Academic Press.
  1991 Learning to read and spell words. Pp. 57-73 in *Learning to Read: Basic Research
        and Its Implications,* L. Rieben, and C.A. Perfetti, eds. Hillsdale, NJ: Lawrence
        Erlbaum Associates.
Ehri, L.C., and L.S. Wilce
  1980 The influence of orthography on readers' conceptualization of the phonemic struc-
        ture of words. *Applied Psycholinguistics* 1:371-385.
  1983 Development of word identification speed in skilled and less skilled beginning read-
        ers. *Journal of Educational Psychology* 75:3-18.
  1985 Movement into reading: Is the first stage of printed word learning visual or phonetic?
        Reading Research Quarterly 20:163-179.
  1986 The influence of spellings on speech: Are alveolar flaps /d/ or /t/? Pp. 101-114 in
        Metalinguistic Awareness and Beginning Literacy, D. Yaden and S. Templeton, eds.
        Exeter, NH: Heinemann.
  1987 Does learning to spell help beginners learn to read words? *Reading Research Quar-
        terly* 22:47-65.
Ehri, L.C., and J. Sweet
  1991 Fingerpoint-reading of memorized text: What enables beginners to process the print?
        Reading Research Quarterly 24:442-462.
Elbro, C.
  1990 Sprogpsykologiske arsager til ordblindhed. Psycholinguistic causes of developmental
        dyslexia. 3rd Symposium on Dyslexia (1988, Alborg, Denmark). *Skolepsykologi*
        27(6):427-447
Elbro, C., I. Borstrom, and D.K. Petersen
  1996 Predicting Dyslexia from Kindergarten: The Importance of Distinctness of Phono-
        logical Representations of Lexical Items. Unpublished paper.
Elley, R.
  1992 *How in the World Do Students Read?* Hamburg: The Hague International Associa-
        tion for the Evaluation of Educational Achievement.
Elliot-Faust, D.J., and M. Pressley
  1986 How to teach comparison processing to increase children's short- and long-term
        listening comprehension monitoring. *Journal of Educational Psychology* 78:27-33.
Ellis, A.
  1985 The cognitive neuropsychology of developmental (and acquired) dyslexia: A critical
        survey. *Cognitive Neuropsychology* 2:169-205.
Ellis, N.
  1997 Interactions in the development of reading and spelling: Stages, strategies, and ex-
        change of knowledge. *Learning to Spell: Research, Theory, and Practice Across
        Languages,* C. Perfetti, L. Rieben, and M. Fayol, eds. Hillsdale, NJ: Lawrence
        Erlbaum Associates.
Englert, C., and K. Tarrant
  1995 Creating collaborative cultures for educational change. *Remedial and Special Educa-
        tion* 16:325-336.

Englert, C.S., A. Garmon, T. Mariage, M. Rozendal, et al.
  1995 The Early Literacy Project: Connecting across the literacy curriculum. *Learning Disability Quarterly* 18(4):253-275.
Entwisle, D.R., and K.L. Alexander
  1988 Factors affecting achievement test scores and marks of black and white first graders. *The Elementary School Journal* 88:449-471.
Entwisle, D.R., and N.M. Astone
  1994 Some practical guidelines for measuring youth's race/ethnicity and socioeconomic status. *Child Development* 65(6):1521-1540.
Escamilla, K.
  1994 Descubriendo la lectura: An early intervention literacy program in Spanish. Columbus, OH: Reading Recovery Council of North America. *Literacy, Teaching and Learning* 1(1):57-70.
Estrada, P., W.F. Arsenio, R.D. Hess, and S.D. Holloway
  1987 Affective quality of the mother-child relationship: Longitudinal consequences for children's school-relevant cognitive functioning. *Developmental Psychology* 23(2): 210-215.
Evertson, C.M., and C.H. Randolph
  1989 Teaching practices and class size: A new look at an old issue. *Peabody Journal of Education* 67(1):85-105.
Ewoldt, C., and F. Hammermeister
  1986 The language-experience approach to facilitating reading and writing for hearing-impaired students. *American Annals of the Deaf* 131:271-274.
Farkas, G., and K. Vicknair
  1996 Reading One-One. Pp.151-175 in *Human Capital or Cultural Capital*. New York: Aldine de Gruyter.
Faulkner, H.J., and B. A. Levy
  1994 How text difficulty and reader skill interact to produce differential reliance on word and content overlap in reading transfer. *Journal of Experimental Child Psychology* 58:1-24.
Feagans, L.V., and E.E. Manlove
  1994 Parents, infants, and day-care teachers: Interrelations and Implications for better child care. Special Issue: The Preschool Child: Recent Research and Its Implications for Early Childhood Practice and Policy. *Journal of Applied Developmental Psychology* 15(4):585-602.
Feitelson, D.
  1988 *Facts and Fads in Beginning Reading: A Cross-Language Perspective.* Norwood, NJ: Ablex.
Feitelson, D., et al.
  1993 Effects of listening to story reading on aspects of literacy acquisition in a diglossic situation. *Reading Research Quarterly* 28(1):70-79.
Feitelson, D., and Z. Goldstein
  1986 Patterns of book ownership and reading to young children in Israeli school-oriented and nonschool-oriented families. *Reading Teacher* 39(9):924-930.
Feldman, L.B.
  1994 Beyond orthography and phonology: Differences between inflections and derivations. *Journal of Memory and Language* 33:442-470.
Felton, R.H.
  1992 Early identification of children at risk for reading disabilities. *Topics in Early Childhood Special Education* 12:212-229.
  1993 Effects of instruction on the decoding skills of children with phonological-processing problems. *Journal of Learning Disabilities* 26(9):583-589.

Felton, R.H., F.B. Wood, I.S. Brown, S.K. Campbell, and M.R. Harter
  1987 Separate verbal memory and naming deficits in attention deficit disorder and reading
        disability. *Brain and Language* 31:171-184.
Ferguson, R.
  1991 Paying for public education: New evidence on how and why money matters. *Harvard
        Journal on Legislation* 28(Summer):465-498.
Ferreiro, E., and A. Teberosky
  1982 *Literacy Before Schooling.* (K.G. Castro, trans.) Exeter, NH: Heinemann.
Fey, M.E.
  1990 Understanding and narrowing the gap between treatment research and clinical prac-
        tice with language-impaired children. Future of Science and Services Seminar (1990,
        Rockville, MD). *ASHA Reports Series American Speech Language Hearing Associa-
        tion* 20:31-40.
Fey, M.E., H.W. Catts, and L.S. Larrivee
  1995a Preparing preschoolers for the academic and social challenges of school. Pp. 3-37 in
        *Language Intervention: Preschool Through the Elementary Years. Communication
        and Language Intervention Series, Vol. 5,* M.E. Fey, J. Windsor, and S.F. Warren,
        eds. Baltimore: Paul H. Brookes Publishing Co.
Fey, M.E., J. Windsor, and S.F. Warren, editors
  1995b *Language Intervention: Preschool Through the Elementary Years.* Baltimore: Paul
        H. Brookes Publishing Co.
Fielding-Barnsley, R.
  1997 Explicit instruction in decoding benefits children high in phonemic awareness and
        alphabet knowledge. *Scientific Studies of Reading* 1(1):85-98.
Fillmore, L.W.
  1991 When learning a second language means losing the first. *Early Childhood Research
        Quarterly* 6(3):323-347.
Fingeret, H.A.
  1990 Let Us Gather Blossoms under Fire... Paper presented at a Conference on Literacy
        for a Global Economy: A Multicultural Perspective (El Paso, TX, February 21, 1990).
Finn, S. E.
  1986 Stability of personality self ratings over 30 years: Evidence for an age/cohort interac-
        tion. *Journal of Personality and Social Psychology* 50(4):813-818.
Finucci, J.M., L. Gottfredson, and B. Childs
  1985 A follow-up study of dyslexic boys. *Annals of Dyslexia* 35:117-136.
Finucci, J.M., and B. Childs
  1981 Are there really more dyslexic boys than girls? Pp. 1-9 in *Gender Differences in
        Dyslexia,* A. Ansara, N. Geshwind, A. Galaburda, M. Albert, and N. Gartrell, eds.
        Towson, MD: Orton Dyslexia Society.
Finucci, J.M., J.T. Guthrie, A.L. Childs, H. Abbey, and B. Childs
  1976 The genetics of specific reading disability. *Annals of Human Genetics* 40:1-23.
Fisher, C. W., and E. H. Hiebert
  1990 Characteristics of tasks in two approaches to literacy instruction. *Elementary School
        Journal* 91(1):3-18.
Fletcher, J.M., S.E. Shaywitz, D.P. Shankweiler, L. Katz, I.Y. Liberman, K.K. Stuebing, D.J.
Francis, A.E. Fowler, and B.A. Shaywitz
  1994 Cognitive profiles of reading disability: Comparisons of discrepancy and low achieve-
        ment definitions. *Journal of Educational Psychology* 86(1):6-23.
Flynn, J.M., and M. H. Rahbar
  1994 Prevalence of reading failure in boys compared with girls. *Psychology in the Schools*
        31:66-71.

Foorman, B.R. D.J. Francis, J.M. Fletcher, C. Schatschneider, and P. Mehta
1998 The role of instruction in learning to read: Preventing reading failure in at-risk children. *Journal of Educational Psychology* 90:37-55.
Foorman, B.R., D.J. Francis, S.E. Shaywitz, B.A. Shaywitz, and J.M. Fletcher
In The case for early reading intervention. *Foundations of Reading Acquisitions*, B.
press Blachman, ed. Mahwah, NJ: Erlbaum.
Fowler, A.
1991 How early phonological development might set the stage for phoneme awareness. Pp. 97-117 in *Phonological Processes in Literacy*, S.A. Brady and D.P. Shankweiler, eds. Hillsdale, NJ: Lawrence Erlbaum Associates.
Fowler, A.E., and H. S. Scarborough
1993 *Should Reading-Disabled Adults Be Distinguished from Other Adults Seeking Literacy Instruction?: A Review of Theory and Research.* Technical Report TR93-7. Philadelphia: National Center on Adult Literacy.
Fowler, C.A., S. Napps, and L. Feldman
1985 Relations among regular and irregular morphologically related words in the lexicon as revealed by repetition priming. *Journal of Experimental Psychology: Learning, Memory, and Cognition* 10:241-255.
Fowler, M.G., and A.W. Cross
1986 Preschool risk factors as predictors of early school performance. *Journal of Developmental and Behavioral Pediatrics* 7(4):237-241.
Fox, B., and D.K. Routh
1976 Phonemic analysis and synthesis as word-attack skills. *Journal of Educational Psychology* 68:70-74.
1984 Phonemic analysis and synthesis as word attack skills: Revisited. *Journal of Educational Psychology* 76(6):1059-1064.
Francis, D.J., S.E. Shaywitz, K.K. Stuebing, B.A. Shaywitz, and J.M. Fletcher
1996 Developmental lag versus deficit models of reading disability: A longitudinal, individual growth curves analysis. *Journal of Educational Psychology* 88(1):3-17.
Friedman, P., and K.A. Friedman
1980 Accounting for individual differences when comparing the effectiveness of remedial language teaching methods. *Applied Psycholinguistics* 1(2):151-170.
Frith, U.
1985 Beneath the surface of developmental dyslexia. Pp. 301-330 in *Surface Dyslexia: Neuropsychological and Cognitive Studies of Phonological Reading*, K. Patterson, J. Marshall, and M. Coltheart, eds. London: Lawrence Erlbaum Associates.
Furth, H.
1966 A comparison of reading test norms for deaf and hearing children. *American Annals of the Deaf* 111(5):461-462
Futrell, M.H., D.H. Holmes, J.L. Christie, and E.J. Cushman
1995 *Linking Education Reform and Teachers' Professional Development: The Effects of Nine School Districts.* Washington, DC: The George Washington University, Graduate School of Education and Human Development, Center for Policy Studies, Institute for Curriculum, Standards, and Technology.
Gadsden, V.L.
1993 Literacy, education, and identity among African-Americans: The communal nature of learning. *Urban Education* 27:352-369.
1994 Designing and conducting family literacy programs that account for racial, ethnic, religious, and other cultural differences. Pp. 31-38 in *Motivation: Theory and Research,* H.F. O'Neil Jr. and M. Drillings, eds. Hillsdale, NJ: Erlbaum Associates.

Galda, L.
1984 Narrative competence: Play, storytelling, and story comprehension. In *The Development of Oral and Written Language in Social Contexts*, A.D. Pellegrini and T.D. Yawkey, eds. Norwood, NJ: ABLEX.

Galda, L., B. Cullinan, and D. Strickland
1997 *Language, Literacy and the Child* (second edition). Forth Worth, TX: Harcourt

Galton, F.
1874 *English Men of Science: Their Nature and Nurture.* London: MacMillan.

Gambrell, L.B.
1995 Motivation matters. Pp. 2-24 in *Generations of Literacy: The Seventeenth Yearbook of the College Reading Association*, W.M. Linek, E.G. Sturtevant, and L. Botha, eds. College Reading Association, Harrisonburg, VA.

Gambrell, L.B., and R.J. Bales
1986 Mental imagery and the comprehension-monitoring performance of fourth- and fifth-grade poor readers. *Reading Research Quarterly* 21(4):454-464.

Gambrell, L.B., and L.M. Morrow
1996 Creating motivating contexts for literacy learning. Pp. 115-136 in *Developing Engaged Readers in School and Home Communities*, L. Baker, P. Afflerbach, and D. Reinking, eds. Mahwah, NJ: Lawrence Erlbaum Associates.

Garner, R.
1980 Monitoring of understanding: An investigation of good and poor readers' awareness of induced miscomprehension of text. *Journal of Reading Behavior* 12:55-63.

Gates, A. I.
1947 *The Improvement of Reading.* NY: Macmillan Co.

Gentile, L.M., and J.L. Hoot
1983 Kindergarten play: The foundation of reading. *The Reading Teacher* 36:46-49.

Gerken, L., P.W. Jusczyk, and D.R. Mandel
1994 When prosody fails to cue syntactic structure: 9-month-olds' sensitivity to phonological versus syntactic phrases. *Cognition* 51(3):237-265.

Gernsbacher, M.A.
1993 Less skilled readers have less efficient suppression mechanisms. *Psychological Science* 4(5):294-298.

Gernsbacher, M.A., K.R. Varner, and M.E. Faust
1990 Investigating difference in general comprehension skill. *Journal of Experimental Psychology: Learning, Memory and Cognition* 16:430-445.

Gersten, R.
1984 Follow through revisited: Reflections on the site variability issue. *Educational Evaluation and Policy Analysis* 6(4):411-423.

Gersten, R., and S. Brengelman
1996 The quest to translate research into practice. *Remedial and Special Education* 17(2): 67-74.

Gersten, R., and J. Woodward
1995 A longitudinal study of transitional and immersion bilingual education programs in one district. *Elementary School Journal* 95:223-239.

Gickling, E.E., and V.P. Thompson
1985 A personal view of curriculum-based assessment. Special Issue: Curriculum-Based Assessment. *Exceptional Children* 52(3):205-218.

Gilger, J.W., B.F. Pennington, and J.C. DeFries
1991 Risk for reading disability as a function of family history in three family studies. *Reading and Writing: An Interdisciplinary Journal* 3:205-217.

Gilger, J.W., I.B. Borecki, S.D. Smith, J.C. DeFries, and B.F. Pennington
1996 The etiology of extreme scores for complex phenotypes: An illustration of using reading performance. In *Developmental Dyslexia,* C.H. Chase, G.O. Rosen, and G.F. Sherman, eds. Baltimore: York Press.

Gillam, R.B., and J.R. Johnston
1985 Development of print awareness in language-disordered preschoolers. *Journal of Speech and Hearing Research* 28(4):521-526.

Gilmore, J.H., and B.J. Pine II
1997 The four faces of mass customization. *Harvard Business Review* (January-February): 91-101.

Glaser, R.
1984 Education and thinking: The role of knowledge. *American Psychologist* 39:93-104.

Glynn, T., N. Bethune, T. Crooks, and K. Ballard
1992 Reading Recovery in context: Implementation and outcome. *Educational Psychology* 12(3-4):249-261.

Goldenberg, C.
1994 Promoting early literacy development among Spanish-speaking children: Lessons from two studies. Pp. 171-199 in *Getting Reading Right from the Start: Effective Early Literacy Interventions,* E.H. Heibert and B.M. Taylor, eds. Boston: Allyn and Bacon.
1996 Latin American immigration and U.S. schools. *Social Policy Reports (Society for Research in Child Development)* 10(1).

Goldenberg, C.N., and R. Gallimore
1989 Teaching California's diverse student population: The common ground between educational and cultural research. *California Public Schools Forum* 3: 41-56.
1991a Changing teaching takes more than a one-shot workshop. *Educational Leadership* 49(3):69-72.
1991b Local knowledge, research knowledge, and educational change: A case study of early [first-grade] Spanish reading improvement. *Educational Researcher* 20(8):2-14.
1995 Immigrant Latino parents' values and beliefs about their children's education: Continuities and discontinuities across cultures and generations. Pp. 183-228 in *Advances in Motivation and Achievement: Culture, Ethnicity, and Motivation, Vol. 9,* P.R. Pintrich and M. Maehr, eds. Greenwich, CT: JAI Press.

Goldenberg, C., and J. Sullivan
1994 *Making Change Happen in a Language-Minority School: A Search for Coherence* (EPR #13). Washington, DC: Center for Applied Linguistics.

Goldenberg, C., L. Reese, and R. Gallimore
1992 Effects of school literacy materials on Latino children's home experiences and early reading achievement. *American Journal of Education* 100:497-536.

Golinkoff, R.M., and K. Hirsh-Pasek
1995 Reinterpreting children's sentence comprehension: Toward a new framework. Pp. 430-461 in *Handbook of Child Language,* B. MacWhinney and P. Fletcher, eds. Oxford: Blackwell.

Good, T.L., and D.A. Grouws
1975 Teacher rapport: Some stability data. *Journal of Educational Psychology* 67(2):179-182.

Goodlad, J.
1997 Producing teachers who understand, believe, and care. *Education Week* 16(48):36-37.

Goodman, Y.M.
1986 Children coming to know literacy. In *Emergent Literacy: Writing and Reading,* W.H. Teale and E. Sulzby, eds. Norwood, NJ: Ablex.

Goodman, Y.M., and C.L. Burke
1972 *Reading Miscue Inventory: Procedure for Diagnosis and Evaluation.* Katonah, NY: Richard C. Owen.
Gough, P.B.
1993 The beginning of decoding. *Reading and Writing: An Interdisciplinary Journal* 5: 181-192.
Gough, P.B., and M.L. Hillinger
1980 Learning to read: An unnatural act. *Bulletin of the Orton Society* 20:179-196.
Gough, P.B., and C. Juel
1991 The first stages of word recognition. Pp. 47-56 in *Learning to Read: Basic Research and Its Implications,* L. Rieben and C.A. Perfetti, eds. Hillsdale, NJ: Lawrence Erlbaum Associates.
Graesser, A.C., K.K. Millis, and R.A. Zwaan
1997 Discourse comprehension. *Annual Review of Psychology* 48:163-189.
Graves, M.F., and W.H. Slater
1987 Development of Reading Vocabularies in Rural Disadvantaged Students, Intercity Disadvantaged Students and Middle Class Suburban Students. Paper presented at AERA conference, April 1987, Washington, DC.
Gray, W.S.
1937 *36th Yearbook of the NSSE.* Part I—The Teaching of Reading: A Second Report. Bloomington, IL: Public School Publishing Co.
Green, M.
1994 *Bright Futures: Guidelines for Health Supervision of Infants, Children, and Adolescents.* Arlington, VA: National Center for Education in Maternal and Child Health.
Grigorenko, E.L., F.B. Wood, M.S. Meyer, L.A. Hart, W.C. Speed, B.S. Shuster, and D.L. Pauls
1997 Susceptibility loci for distinct components of developmental dyslexia on chromosomes 6 and 16. *American Journal of Human Genetics* 60(1):27-39.
Grossman, P.
1992 Why models matter: An alternate view on professional growth in teaching. *Review of Educational Research* 62:171-180.
Guthrie, J.T., K. McGough, L. Bennett, and M.E. Rice
1996 Concept-oriented reading instruction: An integrated curriculum to develop motivations and strategies for reading. Pp. 165-190 in *Developing Engaged Readers in School and Home Communities,* L. Baker, P. Afflerbach, and D. Reinking, eds. Mahwah, NJ: Lawrence Erlbaum Associates.
Haenggi, D., and C.A. Perfetti
1992 Individual differences in reprocessing of text. *Journal of Educational Psychology* 84(2):182-192.
1994 Processing components of college-level reading comprehension. *Discourse Processes* 17(1):83-104.
Hakes, D.T., J.S. Evans, and W. Tunmer
1980 *The Development of Metalinguistic Abilities in Children.* Springer Series in Language and Communication, 9. Berlin: Springer-Verlag.
Haller, E.P., D.A. Child, and H.J. Walberg
1988 Can comprehension be taught? *Educational Researcher* 17:5-8.
Hallgren, B.
1950 Specific dyslexia: A clinical and genetic study. *Acta Psychiatr Neuro Scan* 65(Suppl): 179-189.

Halliday, M.A.K.
  1982 Three aspects of children's language development: Learning language, learning through language, and learning about language. Pp. 7-19 in *Oral and Written Language Development Research: Impact on the Schools*, Y. Goodman, M. Haussle, and D.S. Strickland, eds. Urbana, IL: National Council of Teachers of English.
Hamilton, M.L., and V. Richardson
  1995 Effects of the culture in two schools on the process and outcomes of staff development. *Elementary School Journal* 95(4):367-385.
Hammill, D.D., and G. McNutt
  1980 Language Abilities and Reading: A Review of the Literature on Their Relationship. *Elementary School Journal* 80(5):269-277.
Hannell, G., G. A. Gole, S. N. Dibden, K. F. Rooney, et al.
  1991 Reading improvement with tinted lenses: A report of two cases. *Journal of Research in Reading* 14(1):56-71.
Hanson, R.A., and D. Farrell
  1995 The long-term effects on high school seniors of learning to read in kindergarten. *Reading Research Quarterly* 30(4):908-933.
Hanson, R., D. Siegel and D. Broach
  1987 The Effects on High School Seniors of Learning to Read in Kindergarten. Paper presented at the annual meeting of the American Educational Research Association, Washington, DC.
Hanson, V.L., E.W. Goodell, and C.A. Perfetti
  1991 Tongue-twister effects in the silent reading of hearing and deaf college students. *Journal of Memory and Language* 30:319-330.
Harris, A.J., and E.R. Sipay
  1975 *How to Increase Reading Ability. Sixth Edition.* New York: David McKay Company.
Harste, J.E., V.A. Woodward, and C.L. Burke
  1984 *Language Stories and Literacy Lessons.* Portsmouth, NH: Heinemann.
Hart, B., and T.R. Risley
  1995 *Meaningful Differences in the Everyday Experience of Young American Children.* Baltimore: Paul H. Brookes Publishing Co.
Haskins, R.
  1989 Beyond metaphor: The efficacy of early childhood education. *American Psychologist* 44:274-282.
Hatcher, P.J., C. Hulme, and A.W. Ellis
  1994 Ameliorating early reading failure by integrating the teaching of reading and phonological skills: The phonological linkage hypothesis. *Child Development* 65:41-57.
Hawley, T.L.
  1993 Maternal Cocaine Addiction: Correlates and Consequences. Paper presented at the Biennial Meeting of the Society for Research in Child Development (New Orleans, March 25-28).
Hayes, D.P., and J. Grether
  1983 The school year and vacations: When do students learn? *Cornell Journal of Social Relations* 17(1):56-71.
Hayes, D. P., and M.G. Ahrens
  1988 Vocabulary simplification for children: A special case of "motherese"? *Journal of Child Language* 15(2):395-410.
Haywood, H.C., P. Brooks, and M.S. Burns
  1992 *Bright Start: Cognitive Curriculum for Young Children.* Watertown, MA: Charlesbridge Publishing.

Hazzard, A., T. McFadden-Garden, M. Celano, and L.J. Grant
    1996 Evaluation of a Pediatric Program Designed to Encourage Children's Emergent Literacy. Paper presented at the Pediatric Academic Societies Annual Meeting, Washington, DC.
Heath, S.
    1983 *Ways with Words*. Cambridge: Cambridge University Press.
Henderson, E.H.
    1981 *Learning to Read and Spell: The Child's Knowledge of Words*. DeKalb: Northern Illinois University Press.
Henry, M.K.
    1989 Children's word structure knowledge: Implications for decoding and spelling instruction. *Reading and Writing* 2:135-152.
Herman, R., and S. Stringfield
    1997 Ten Promising Programs for Educating Disadvantaged Students: Evidence of Impact. Arlington, VA: Educational Research Service.
Hess, R.D., and S. Holloway
    1984 Family and school as educational institutions. Pp. 179-222 in *Review of Child Development Research, 7: The Family*, R.D. Parke, ed. Chicago: University of Chicago Press.
Heuston, D.H.
    1997 *Waterford Early Reading Program*. Sandy, UT: Waterford Institute.
Hiebert, E.
    1981 Developmental patterns and interrelationships of pre-school children's point awareness. *Reading Research Quarterly* 16:236-260.
    1986 Issues related to home influences in young children's print-related development. Pp. 145-158 in *Metalinguistic Awareness and Beginning Literacy*, D. Yaden and S. Templeton, eds. Portsmouth, NH: Heinemann.
    1994a Reading recovery in the United States: What difference does it make to an age cohort? *Educational Researcher* 23(9):15-25.
    1994b Becoming literate through authentic tasks: Evidence and adaptations. Pp. 391-413 in *Theoretical Models and Processes of Reading*, 4th ed. R.B. Ruddell, M.R. Ruddell, and H. Singer, eds. Newark, DE: International Reading Association.
Hiebert, E.H., J.M. Colt, S.L. Catto, and E.C. Gury
    1992 Reading and writing of first grade students in a restructured Chapter I program. *American Educational Research Journal* 29(3):545-572.
High, P.C., M.R. Hopmann, L. LaGasse, and H. Linn
    1996 Evaluation of a Clinic Based Book Sharing and Bedtime Promoting Program for Low Income Urban Families. Paper presented at the Pediatric Academic Societies Annual Meeting, Washington, DC.
Himley, M.
    1986 Genre as generative: One perspective on one child's early writing growth. In *The Structure of Written Communication: Studies in Reciprocity Between Writers and Readers*, M. Nystrand, ed. Orlando, FL: Academic Press.
Hirsh-Pasek, K., D.G. Kemler-Nelson, P.W. Jusczyk, and K.W. Cassidy
    1987 Clauses are perceptual units for young infants. *Cognition* 26(3):269-286.
Hohmann, M., and D. Weikart
    1995 *Educating Young Children*. Ypsilanti, MI: High/Scope Press.
Holdaway, D.
    1979 *The Foundations of Literacy*. Sydney, Australia: Ashton Scholastic.
Hollingsworth, S.
    1989 Learning to teach reading: Suggestions for preservice and inservice education. *The Reading Teacher* 42(May-June):698-702.

Horn, W.F., and J.P. O'Donnell
  1984 Early identification of learning disabilities: A comparison of two methods. *Journal of Educational Psychology* 76(6):1106-1118.
House, E.R., and others
  1978 No simple answer: Critique of the follow through evaluation. *Harvard Educational Review* 48(2):128-160.
Howes, C., and C.E. Hamilton
  1992 Children's relationships with caregivers: Mothers and child care teachers. *Child Development* 63(4):859-866.
Howes, C., and C.C. Matheson
  1992 Sequences in the development of competent play with peers: Social and social pretend play. *Developmental Psychology* 28(5):961-974.
Howey, K.R., S. J. Yarger, and B. R. Joyce
  1978 *Improving Teacher Education.* Washington, DC: Association of Teacher Educators.
Huntley, R.M., K.S. Holt, A. Butterfill, and C. Latham
  1988 A follow-up study of a language intervention programme. *British Journal of Disorders of Communication* 23(2):127-140.
Hurford, D.P., M. Johnston, P. Nepote, S. Hampton, S. Moore, J. Neal, A. Mueller, K. McGeorge, L. Huff, A. Awad, C. Tatro, C. Juliano, and D. Huffman
  1994 Early identification and remediation of phonological-processing deficits in first-grade children at risk for reading disabilities. *Journal of Learning Disabilities* 27(10):647-659.
Huston, A.C., J.C. Wright, M.L. Rice, D. Kerkman, and M. St. Peters
  1990 Development of television viewing patterns in early childhood: A longitudinal investigation. *Devlopmental Psychology* 26:421-428.
Huttenlocher, J., and P. Smiley
  1987 Early word meanings: The case of object names. *Cognitive Psychology* 19(1):63-89.
Ilg, F.L., and L.B. Ames
  1970 *School Readiness.* New York: Harper & Row.
Infant Health and Development Program
  1990 Enhancing the outcomes of low-birth-weight premature infants. *Journal of the American Medical Association* 263(22):3035-3042.
Interagency Committee on Learning Disabilities
  1987 *Learning Disabilities: A Report to the U.S. Congress.* Washington, DC.
Interstate New Teacher Assessment and Support Consortium
  1992 *Model Standards for Beginning Teacher Licensing and Development: A Resource for State Dialogue.* Washington, DC: Council of Chief State School Officers.
Invernizzi, M., C. Juel, and C.A. Rosemary
  1997 A community volunteer tutorial that works. *The Reading Teacher* 50(4):304-311.
Isenberg, J., and E. Jacob
  1983 Literacy and symbolic play: A review of the literature. *Childhood Education* 59(4):272-276.
Iverson, S., and W.E. Tunmer
  1993 Phonological processing skills and the Reading Recovery Program. *Journal of Educational Psychology* 85(1):112-126.
Jackson, M.D., and J.L. McClelland
  1979 Processing determinants of reading speed. *Journal of Experimental Psychology: General* 108:151-181.
Jackson, N.E.
  1991 Precocious reading of English: Origin, structure and predictive significance. In *To Be Young and Gifted*, A.J. Tannenbaum and P. Klein, eds. Norwood, NJ: Ablex.

Jackson, N.E., G.W. Donaldson, and L.N. Cleland
  1988 The structure of precocious reading ability. *Journal of Educational Psychology* 80: 234-243.
Jacob, E., and C. Jordan
  1987 Eplaining the school performance of minority students (Theme issue). Afterword: Where are we now? *Anthropology and Education Quarterly* 18(4):365-367.
Jenkins, J.R., M.L. Stein, and K. Wysocki
  1984 Learning vocabulary through reading. *American Educational Research Journal* 21(4): 767-787.
Joyce, B., and B. Showers
  1988 *Student Achievement Through Staff Development.* White Plains, NY: Longman.
Juel, C.
  1988 Learning to read and write: A longitudinal study of 54 children from first through fourth grades. *Journal of Educational Psychology* 80(4):437-447.
  1991 Beginning reading. Pp. 759-788 in *Handbook of Reading Research*, Vol. 2, R. Barr, M.L. Kamil, P.B. Mosenthal, and P.D. Pearson, eds. Mahwah, NJ: Lawrence Erlbaum Associates.
Juel, C., P.L. Griffith, and P.B Gough
  1986 Acquisition of literacy: A longitudinal study of children in first and second grade. *Journal of Educational Psychology* 78(4):243-255.
Jusczyk, P.W., A.D. Friederici, J.M.I. Wessels, V.Y. Svenkerud, and A.M. Jusczyk
  1993 Infants' sensitivity to the sound patterns of native language words. *Journal of Memory and Langauge* 32:402-420.
Just, M.A., and P. A. Carpenter
  1987 *The Psychology of Reading and Language Comprehension.* Boston: Allyn and Bacon.
  1992 A capacity theory of comprehension: Individual differences in working memory. *Psychological Review* 99:122-149.
Kaderavek, J., and E. Sulzby
  1998a Emergent literacy issues for children with language impairment. *Handbook of Early Language Impairments in Children: Volume II, Assessment and Treatment,* L.R. Watson, T.L. Layton, and E.R. Crais, eds. New York: Delmar.
  1998b Parent-child joint book reading: An observational protocol for young children. *American Journal of Speech-Language Pathology.*
Kaestle, C.
  1991 *Literacy in the United States.* New Haven, CT: Yale University Press.
Kagan, D.
  1992 Professional growth among preservice and beginning teachers. *Review of Educational Research* 62:129-170.
Kamberelis, G., and E. Sulzby
  1988 Transitional knowledge in emergent literacy. *National Reading Conference Yearbook* 37:95-106.
Kame'enui, E.J., D.W. Carnine, and R. Freshi
  1982 Effects of text construction and instructional procedures for teaching word meanings on comprehension of contrived passages. *Reading Research Quarterly* 17(3):367-388.
Kamhi, A.G., and H.W. Catts
  1986 Toward an understanding of developmental language and reading disorders. *Journal of Speech and Hearing Disorders* 51(4):337-347.
  1989 *Reading Disabilities: A Developmental Language Perspective.* Boston: Allyn and Bacon.

Kamhi, A.G., H.W. Catts, D. Mauer, K. Apel, and B.F. Gentry
1988   Phonological and spatial processing abilities in language- and reading-impaired children. *Journal of Speech and Hearing Disorders* 53(August):316-327.

Kao, G., and M. Tienda
1995   Optimism and achievement: The educational performance of immigrant youth. *Social Science Quarterly* 76:1-19.

Karchmer, M.A., et al.
1978   Early Manual Communication, Parental Hearing Status, and the Academic Achievement of Deaf Students. Paper presented at the American Education Research Association Annual Meeting, March 1978, Toronto, Ontario, Canada.

Karweit, N.
1989   *The Effects of a Story Reading Program on the Vocabulary and Story Comprehension Skills of Disadvantaged Prekindergarten and Kindergarten Students.* Report No. 39. Washington, DC: Office of Educational Research and Improvement.

Kavale, K.A., and S.R. Forness
1987   Substance over style: Assessing the efficacy of modality testing and teaching. *Exceptional Children* 54(3):228-239.

Kintsch, W.
1988   The role of knowledge in discourse processing: A construction-integration model. *Psychological Review* 95:163-182.
1992   How readers construct situation models for stories: The role of syntactic cues and causal inferences. Pp. 261-278 in *From Learning Processes to Cognitive Processes: Essays in Honor of William K. Estes,*Vol. 2, A.F. Healy, S.M. Kosslyn, and R.M. Shiffrin, eds. Hillsdale, NJ: Lawrence Erlbaum Associates.

Kirchner, D.M.
1991   Using verbal scaffolding to facilitate conversational participation and language acquisition in children with pervasive developmental disorders. *Journal of Childhood Communication Disorders* 14(1):81-98.

Klenk, L., and A.S. Palincsar
1996   Enacting responsible pedagogy with students in special education. *Curriculum Trends, Special Education, and Reform: Refocusing the Conversation. Special Education Series,* M.C. Pugach and C.L. Warger, eds. New York: Teachers College Press.

Kontos, S., and S. Wilcox-Herzog
1997   Teachers' interactions with children: Why are they so important? *Young Children* 52:4-12.

Korkeamaki, R., and M.J. Dreher
1996   Trying something new: Meaning-based reading instruction in a Finnish first-grade classroom. *Journal of Literacy Research* 28(1):9-34.

Korsch, B.M., B. Freemon, and V.F. Negrete
1971   Practical implications of doctor-patient interaction analysis for pediatric practice. *American Journal of Diseases of Children* 121:110-114.

Kozol, J.
1991   *Savage Inequalities: Children in America's Schools.* New York: Crown.

Krashen, S.D.
1996   *Every Person a Reader.* Culver City, CA: Language Education Associates.

Kucan, L., and I. Beck
1997   Thinking aloud and reading comprehension research: Inquiry, instruction, and social interaction. *Review of Educational Research* 67:271-99.

LaBerge, D., and S.J. Samuels
1974   Toward a theory of automatic information processing in reading. *Cognitive Psychology* 6:293-323.

Labov, W.
  1966 Some sources of reading problems. Pp. 140-167 in *New Directions in Elementary English*, A. Frazier, ed. Champaign, IL: National Council of Teachers of English.
  1995 Can reading failure be reversed: A linguistic approach to the question. Pp. 39-68 in *Literacy Among African-American Youth: Issues in Learning, Teaching and Schooling*, V. Gadsden and D. Wagner, eds. Cresskill, NJ: Hampton Press.

Labov, W., P. Cohen, C. Robins, and J. Lewis
  1968 A study of the nonstandard English of Negro and Puerto Rican Speakers in New York City. Cooperative Research Report 3288. Vols. I and II. Philadelphia: U.S. Regional Survey, Linguistics Laboratory, University of Pennsylvania.

Lanauze, M., and C.E. Snow
  1989 The relation between first- and second-language skills: Evidence from Puerto Rican elementary school children in bilingual programs. *Linguistics and Education* 1:323-340.

Lancy, D.F., and C. Bergin
  1992 The Role of Parents in Supporting Beginning Reading. Paper presented at the annual meeting of the American Research Association, San Francisco, CA, April 20, 1992.

Landauer, T.K., and S.T. Dumais
  1997 A solution to Plato's problem: The latent semantic analysis theory of acquisition, induction, and representation of knowledge. *Psychological Review* 104:211-240.

Language Arts
  1991 A conversation with Lisa Delpit. *Language Arts* 68:544-545.

Lanier, J., and J. Little
  1986 Research on teacher eduation. Pp. 527-569 in *Handbook of Research on Teaching*, 3rd ed. M.C. Wittrock, eds. New York: Macmillan.

Laosa, L.M.
  1982 School, occupation, culture and family: The impact of parental schooling on the parent-child relationship. *Journal of Educational Psychology* 74:791-827.

Lass, B.
  1982 Portait of my son as an early reader. *Reading Teacher* October:20-28.
  1983 Portait of my son as an early reader II. *Reading Teacher* February:508-515.

Layzer, J.I.
  1993 *Observational Study of Early Childhood Programs*. Final Report. Volume 1 Life in Preschool. Cambridge, MA: Abt Associates.

Lee, V.E., J. Brooks-Gunn, and E. Schnur
  1988 Does Head Start work? A 1-year follow-up comparison of disadvantaged children attending Head Start, no preschool, and other preschool programs. *Developmental Psychology* 24(2):210-222.

Legarreta, D.
  1979 The effects of program models on language acquisition by Spanish-speaking children. *TESOL Quarterly* 13:521-534.

Leinhardt, G.
  1987 Development of an expert explanation: An analysis of a sequence of subtraction lessons. *Cognition and Instruction* 4:225-282.

Leinhardt, G., and J. Greeno
  1986 The cognitive skill of teaching. *Journal of Educational Psychology* 78:75-95.

Leichter, H.
  1974 Families as environments for literacy. Pp. 38-50 in *Awakening to Literacy*, H. Goelman, A. Oberg, and F. Smith, eds. Portsmouth, NH: Heinemann.

Lerner, J.W.
1989 Educational interventions in learning disabilities. *Journal of the American Academy of Child and Adolescent Psychiatry* 28:326-331.

Lesch, M.F., and A. Pollatsek
1993 Automatic access of semantic information by phonological codes in visual word recognition. *Journal of Experimental Psychology: Learning, Memory, and Cognition* 19:285-294.

Leslie, L., and J. Caldwell
1988 *Qualitative Reading Inventory.* New York: Harper Collins.

Levin, H.M.
1991 Educational acceleration for at-risk students. Pp. 222-240 in *Children in Poverty: Child Development and Public Policy*, A.C. Huston, ed. Cambridge, England: Cambridge University Press.

Levine, D., and L. Lezotte
1990 *Unusually Effective Schools.* Madison, WI: National Center for Effective Schools R & D.

Levy, A.K., C.H. Wolfgang, and M.A. Koorland
1992 Sociodramatic play as a method for enhancing the language performance of kindergarten-age students. *Early Childhood Research Quarterly (Special Issue: Research on Kindergarten)* 7(2):245-262.

Lewis, M., and S. Feinman, eds.
1991 *Social Influences and Socialization in Infancy.* New York: Plenum Press.

Liaw, F.R., S. Meisels, and J. Brooks-Gunn
1995 The effects of experience of early intervention on low birth weight, premature children: The infant health and development program. *The Early Childhood Research Quarterly* 10(4):405-432.

Liberman, I.Y., D. Shankweiler, F.W. Fischer, and B. Carter
1974 Explicit syllable and phoneme segmentation in the young child. *Journal of Experimental Child Psychology* 18:201-212.

Lie, A.
1991 Effects of a training program for stimualting skills in word analysis in first-grade children. *Reading Research Quarterly* 26:234-250.

Lillo-Martin, D., V. Hanson, and C. Romano
1997 Effects of Phonological Awareness Training on Deaf Children's Reading and Segmentation Ability. Unpublished paper submitted for publication.

Lindamood, C., and P. Lindamood
1975 *Auditory Discrimination in Depth.* Columbus, OH: Science Research Associates/McGraw-Hill.

Lindamood, P.
1994 Issues in researching the link between phonological awareness, learning disabilities, and spelling. In *Frames of Reference for the Assessment of Learning Disabilities*, G.R. Lyon, ed. Baltimore: Paul H. Brookes Publishing.

Little, J.W.
1993 Teachers' professional development in a climate of educational reform. *Educational Evaluation and Policy Analysis* 15(2):129-151.

Little, J., W. Gerritz, D. Stern, J. Guthrie, M. Kirst, and, D. Marsh
1987 *Staff Development in California.* San Francisco and Berkeley: Far West Laboratory for Educational Research & Policy Analysis for California Education.

Lovett, M.W., and K.A. Steinbach
1997 The effectiveness of remedial programs for reading disabled children of different ages: Does the benefit decrease for older children? *Learning Disability Quarterly* 20(3):189-210.

Lovett, M.W., S.L. Borden, T. DeLuca, L. Lacerenza, N.J. Benson, and D. Brackstone
1994   Treating the core deficits of developmental dyslexia: Evidence of transfer of learning after phonologically- and strategically-based reading training programs. *Developmental Psychology* 30(6):805-822.

Lukatela, G., and M.T. Turvey
1990   Automatic and pre-lexical computation of phonology in visual word identification. *European Journal of Cognitive Psychology* 2:325-344.

Lundberg, I.
1994   Reading difficulties can be predicted and prevented: A Scandinavian perspecitve on phonological awareness and reading. Pp. 180-199 in *Reading Development and Dyslexia*, C. Hulme and M. Snowling, eds. London: Whurr.

Lundberg, I., J. Frost, and O-P. Petersen
1988   Effects of an extensive program for stimulating phonological awareness in preschool children. *Reading Research Quarterly* 23:264-284.

Lyon, G., M. Vaasen, and F. Toomey
1989   Teachers' perceptions of their undergraduate and graduate preparation. *Teacher Education and Special Education* 12:164-169.

Lyon, G.R.
1995   Toward a definition of dyslexia. *Annals of Dyslexia* 45:3-27.

MacKinnon, A.R.
1959   *How Do Children Learn to Read?: An Experimental Investigation of Childrens' Early Growth in Awareness of the Meaning of Printed Text.* Toronto: Copp-Clark.

Maclean, M., P. Bryant, and L. Bradley
1987   Rhymes, nursery rhymes, and reading in early childhood. *Merrill-Palmer Quarterly* 33(3):255-281.

Mallory, B.L
1992   Is it always appropriate to be developmental? Convergent models for early intervention practice. *Topics in Early Childhood Special Education* 11:1-12.

Mann, V.
1994   Phonological skills and the prediction of early reading problems. In *Learning Disabilities: New Directions for Assessment and Intervention*, N.C. Jordan and J. Goldsmith-Phillips, eds. Needham Heights, MA: Allyn and Bacon.

Mannes, S., and M. St. George
1996   Effects of prior knowledge on text comprehension: A simple modeling approach. Pp. 115-139 in *Models of Understanding Text*, B.K. Britton and A.C. Graesser, eds. Mahwah, NJ: Lawrence Erlbaum Associates.

Marks, C.B., M.J. Doctorow, and M.C. Wittrock
1974   Word frequency and reading comprehension. *Journal of Educational Research* 67(6): 259-262.

Martin, B.
1992   *Brown Bear, Brown Bear, What Do You See?* New York: Henry Holt and Company, Inc.

Martinez, M.G., M. Cheyney, C. McBroom, A. Hemmeter, and W.H. Teale
1989   No-risk kindergarten literacy environments for at-risk children. Pp. 93-124 in *Risk Makers, Risk Takers, Risk Breakers: Reducing the Risks for Young Literacy Learners*, J. Allen and J.M. Mason, eds. Portsmouth, NH: Heinemann.

Marzolf, D.P., and J.S. DeLoache
1994   Transfer in young children's understanding of spatial representations. *Child Development* 65:1-15.

Mason, J.
1980   When do children begin to read: An exploration of four year old children's letter and word reading competencies. *Reading Research Quarterly* 15:203-227.

Mason, J., and D. Dunning
1986   Toward a Model Relating Home Literacy with Beginning Reading. Paper presented to the American Educaitonal Research Association, San Francisco.
Mason, J., C.L. Peterman, B.M. Powell, and M.K. Kerr
1989   Reading and writing attempts by kindergarteners after book reading by teachers. Pp. 105-120 in *Reading and Writing Connections*, J. Mason, ed. Old Tappan, NJ: Allyn and Bacon.
Masonheimer, P.E., P.A. Drum, and L.C. Ehri
1984   Does environmental print identification lead children into word reading? *Journal of Reading Behavior* 16:257-271.
Massell, D., M. Kirst, and M. Hoppe
1997   Persistence and change: Standards-based systemic reform in nine states. *Policy Briefs, Consortium for Policy Research in Education* RB-21(March 1997):1-12.
May, D.C., and E.L. Welch
1984   The effects of developmental placement and early retention on children's later scores on standardized tests. *Psychology in the Schools* 21(3):381-385.
McConkie, G.W., and K. Rayner
1975   The span of the effective stimulus during a fixation in reading. *Perception and Psychophysics* 17(6):578-586.
McCormick, C.E., and J.M. Mason
1986   Intervention procedures for increasing preschool children's interest in and knowledge about reading. Pp. 90-115 in *Emergent Literacy: Writing and Reading*, W.H. Teale and E. Sulzby, eds. Norwood, NJ: Ablex.
McDonnell, L.M., M.J. McLaughlin, and P. Morrison
1997   *Educating One and All: Students with Disabilities and Standards-Based Reform.* National Research Council. Washington, DC: National Academy Press.
McGuinness, D., C. McGuinness, and J. Donohue
1995   Phonological training and the alphabet principle: Evidence for reciprocal causality. *Reading Research Quarterly* 30:830-852.
McKenna, M.C.
1980   An Introduction to the Cloze Procedure. Newark, DE: International Reading Association.
McKey, R., L. Condelli, H. Ganson, et al.
1985   *The Impact of Head Start on Children, Families, and Communities. Final Report of the Head Start Evaluation, Synthesis, and Utilization Project.* Washington, DC: U.S. Department of Health and Human Services.
McLane, J.B., and G.D. McNamee
1990   *Early Literacy.* Cambridge, MA: Harvard University Press.
1997   Cultural Transformation and Ownership in Literacy Development: Moving from Community to School Discourse Patterns. Paper presented at American Educational Research Association, March 28, 1997, Chicago.
Meier, J.H.
1971   Prevalence and characteristics of learning disabilities found in second-grade children. *Journal of Learning Disabilities* 4(1):7-19.
Meisels, S.J., and F. Liaw
1993   Failure in grade: Do retained students catch up? *Journal of Educational Research* 87(2):69-77.
Mezynski, K.
1983   Issues concerning the acquisition of knowledge: Effects of vocabulary training on reading comprehension. *Review of Educational Research* 53(2):253-279.

Michaels, S.
1991 Sharing time. *Language in Society* 10:423-447.
Michell, L., and K. Stenning
1983 Explanations in the story-telling of five- to seven-year-olds. *Educational Review (Early Childhood Education)* 35(2):187-194.
Miller, G.A.
1988 The challenge of universal literacy. *Science* 241:1293-1299.
Miller, G.E.
1985 The effects of general and specific self-instruction training on children's comprehension monitoring performances during reading. *Reading Research Quarterly* 20:616-628.
Mills, P., P. Dale, K. Cole and J. Jenkins
1995 Follow-up of children from academic and cognitive preschool curricula at age 9. *Exceptional Children* 61(4):378-393.
Mintzer, D., H. Als, E. Tronick, and T.B. Brazelton
1992 Parenting an infant with a birth defect: The regulation of self-esteem. *Zero to Three Classics: 7 Articles on Infant/Toddler Development*, E. Fenichel, ed. Arlington, VA: National Center for Clinical Infant Programs
Moats, L.C.
1994 The missing foundation in teacher education: Knowledge of the structure of spoken and written language. *Annals of Dyslexia* 44:81-101.
Moats, L.C., and B.R. Foorman
1997 Introduction to the special issue of SSR: Components of efffective reading instruction. *Scientific Studies of Reading* 1(3):187-189.
Moats, L.C., and G.R. Lyon
1996 Wanted: Teachers with knowledge of language. *Topics in Language Disorders* 16(2): 73-86.
Monroe, E., and W. Smith
1985 Guidelines for improving reading education. *Reading Improvement* 22:123-125.
Morais, J., P. Bertelson, L. Cary, and J. Alegria
1986 Literacy training and speech segmentation. *Cognition* 24:45-64.
Morris, D.
1983 Concept of word and phoneme awareness in the beginning reader. *Research in the Teaching of English* 17:359-373.
1992 Concept of word: A pivotal understanding in the learning to read process. Pp. 53-77 in *Development of Orthographic Knowledge: The Foundations of Literacy*, S. Templeton and D. Bear, eds. Hillsdale, NJ: Erlbaum.
1993 The relationship between children's concept of word in text and phoneme awareness in learning to read: A longitidunal study. *Research in the Teaching of English* 27: 133-154.
Morrow, L.M., and M.K. Rand
1991 Promoting literacy during play by designing early childhood classroom environments. *Reading Teacher* 44(6):396-402.
Mosher, E.K., and S.K. Bailey
1970 E.S.E.A.–The Office of Education administers a law. *The Politics of Education at the Local, State and Federal Levels*, M.W. Kirst, ed. Berkeley, CA: McCutchan Publishing Corp.
Mosteller, F., R. Light, and J. Sachs
1996 Sustained inquiry in education: Lessons from skill grouping and class size. *Harvard Educational Review* 66(4):797-842.

Moynihan, D.P.
1965   *The Negro Family: The Case for National Action.* Washington, DC: U.S. Department of Labor.

Murnane, R., and F. Levy
1993   Why today's high-school-educated males earn less than their fathers did: The problem and an assessment of responses. *Harvard Educational Review* 63(1):1-19.

Muthen, B.O., C. Kao, and L. Burstein
1991   Instructionally sensitive psychometrics: Application of a new IRT-based detection technique to mathematics achievement test items. *Journal of Educational Measurement* 28(1):1-22.

Myers, M., and S.G. Paris
1978   Children's metacognitive knowledge about reading. *Journal of Educational Psychology* 70: 680-690.

Myklebust, H.R., and B. Boshes
1969   *Minimal Brain Damage in Children.* Final Report, Contract 108-65-142, Neurological and Sensory Disease Control Program. Washington, DC: U.S. Department of Health, Education, and Welfare.

Nagy, W., P. Herman, and R. Anderson
1985   Learning words from context. *Reading Research Quarterly* 19:304-330.

Nagy, W.E., and R.C. Anderson
1984   How many words are there in printed school English? *Reading Research Quarterly* 19:304-330.

Nagy, W.E., and P.A. Herman
1987   Breadth and depth of vocabulary knowledge: Implications for acquisition and instruction. Pp. 19-35 in *The Nature of Vocabulary Acquisition,* M. McKeown and M. Curtis, eds. Hillsdale, NJ: Erlbaum Associates.

Naiden, N.
1976   Ratio of boys to girls among disabled readers. *Reading Teacher* (February):439-442.

National Academy of Education
1996   *Quality and Utility: The 1994 Trial State Assessment in Reading.* Stanford, CA: Stanford University School of Education.

National Assessment of Educational Progress
1981   *Reading, Thinking, Writing: A Report on the 1979-1980 Assessment.* Denver: NAEP.
1994   *The NAEP 1992 Technical Report.* Princeton, NJ: Educational Testing Service.
1995   *NAEP 1994 Reading: A First Look—Findings from the National Assessment of Educational Progress (Revised Edition).* Washington, DC: U.S. Government Printing Office.
1997   *NAEP 1996 Trends in Academic Progress.* Washington, DC: National Center for Education Statistics.

National Association of State Directors of Teacher Education
1996   *The 1996-1997 NASDTEC Manual on Certification and Preparation of Educational Personnel in the United States and Canada,* T.E. Andrews, L. Andrews, and C. Pape, eds. Dubuque, IA: Kendall/Hunt Publishing Company.

National Center for Education Statistics
1994   *Digest of Education Statistics.* U.S. Department of Education, Office of Educational Research and Improvement.
1995   *Approaching Kindergarten: A Look at Preschoolers in the United States. National Household Education Survey.* U.S. Department of Education, Office of Educational Research and Improvement.

National Commission on Teaching and America's Future
   1996 *What Matters Most: Teaching for America's Future.* Woodbridge, VA: National
         Commission on Teaching and America's Future.
National Council for Accreditation of Teacher Education
   1989 *NCATE Approved Curriculum Guidelines.* Washington, DC: NCATE.
   1992 *NCATE Approved Curriculum Guidelines.* Washington, DC: NCATE.
National Diffusion Network
   1996 *Educational Programs That Work: 22nd Edition.* Longmont, CO: Sopris West.
National Education Goals Panel
   1996 *National Education Goals Report, 1995: Executive Summary.* Washington, DC:
         Government Printing Office.
National Governors Association
   1992 *Every Child Ready for School: Report of the Action Team on School Readiness.*
         Annapolis Junction, MD: NGA Publications.
Natriello, G., E. McDill, and A. Pallas
   1990 *Schooling Disadvantaged Children: Racing Against Catastrophe.* New York: Teach-
         ers College.
Needlman, R.
   1997 Pediatric Interventions to Prevent Reading Problems in Young Children. Paper writ-
         ten for the Committee on the Prevention of Reading Difficulties in Young Children,
         National Research Council.
Nelson, K.
   1973 Structure and strategy in learning to talk. *Monographs of the Society for Research in
         Child Development* 38(1-2, Serial No. 149):136.
Nelson, L.
   1996 Disorders of the eye. In *Nelson Textbook of Pediatrics, 15th ed.,* R.E. Behrman,
         R.M. Kliegman, and A. Arvin, eds. Philadelphia: Saunders.
Nettles, M.T.
   1997 *The African American Education Data Book. Volume II: Preschool Through High
         School Education.* Frederick D. Patterson Research Institute of The College Fund/
         UNCF, Fairfax, VA.
Neuman, S., and K. Roskos
   1992 Literacy objects as cultural tools: Effects on children's literacy behaviors in play.
         Reading Research Quarterly 27(3):203-225.
Neuman, S.B.
   1996 Evaluation of the Books Aloud Project: An Executive Summary. Report to the
         William Penn Foundation from BooksAloud!, Temple University, Philadelphia.
Neuman, S.B., T. Hagedorn, D. Celano, and P. Daly
   1995 Toward a collaborative approach to parent involvement in early education: A study
         of teenage mothers in an African-American community. *American Educational Re-
         search Journal* 32(4):801-827.
Newmann, F.M., and G.G. Wehlage
   1995 *Successful School Restructuring: A Report to the Public and Educators by the Center
         on Organization and Restructuring of Schools.* Madison: Center on Organization
         and Restructuring of Schools, University of Wisconsin-Madison.
Nicholson, T.
   1989 A comment on reading recovery. *New Zealand Journal of Educational Studies* 24:
         95-97.
Ninio, A., and C.E. Snow
   1996 *Pragmatic Development.* Boulder, CO: Westview.

Ninio, A., and J. Bruner
1978   The achievement and antecedents of labeling. *Journal of Child Language* 5:1-15.
Nittrouer, S.
1992   Age-related differences in perceptual effects of formant transitions within syllables
       and across syllables. *Journal of Phonetics* 20(3):351-382.
Nolen, P., D. McCutchen, and V. Berninger
1990   Ensuring tomorrow's literacy: A shared responsibility. *Journal of Teacher Education*
       41(May-June):63-72.
Nunes, T., P. Bryant, and M. Bindman
1997   Spelling and grammar—the necsed move. Pp. 151-170 in *Learning to Spell: Re-
       search, Theory, and Practice Across Languages*, C. Perfetti, L. Rieben, and M. Fayol,
       eds. Mahwah, NJ: Lawrence Erlbaum.
O'Connor, R.E., J.R. Jenkins, N. Leicester, and T.A. Slocum
1993   Teaching phonological awareness to young children with learning disabilities. *Ex-
       ceptional Children* 59(6):532-546.
Ogbu, J.
1974   *The Next Generation: An Ethnography of Education in an Urban Neighborhood.*
       New York: Academic Press.
1982   Cultural discontinuities and schooling. *Anthropology and Education Quarterly* 13:
       290-307.
Olson, D.R.
1977   From utterance to text: The bias of language in speech and writing. *Harvard
       Educational Review* 47:257-281.
1995   *The World on Paper.* London: Cambridge University Press.
Olson, R.K., H. Forsberg, and B. Wise
1994   Genes, environment, and the development of orthographic skills. Pp. 27-71 in *The
       Varieties of Orthographic Knowledge, Vol. I: Theoretical and Developmental Is-
       sues*, V.W. Berninger, ed. Dordrecht, The Netherlands: Kluwer Academic Publish-
       ers.
Olson, R.K., B. Wise, F. Connors, J. Rack, and D. Fulker
1989   Specific deficits in component reading and language skills: Genetic and environmen-
       tal influences. *Journal of Learning Disabilities* 22(6):339-348.
Olson, R.K., B. Wise, J. Ring, and M. Johnson
1997   Computer-based remedial training in phoneme awareness and phonological decod-
       ing: Effects on the post-training development of word recognition. *Scientific Studies
       of Reading* 1:235-253.
Orton Dyslexia Society
1997   *Informed Instruction for Reading Success: Foundations for Teacher Preparation.*
       Baltimore: Orton Dyslexia Society.
Osborn, L.M.
1996   Preventive pediatrics. Pp. 18-22 in *Nelson Textbook of Pediatrics*, R.E. Behrman,
       R.M. Kliegman, and A.M. Arvin, eds. Philadelphia: W.B. Saunders.
Osgood, C.E., and R. Hoosain
1974   Salience of the word as a unit in the perception of language. *Perception and Psycho-
       physics* 15(1):168-192.
Otero, J., and W. Kintsch
1992   Failures to detect contradictions in a text: What readers believe versus what they
       read. *Psychological Science* 3:229-235.

Paap, K.R., and R.W. Noel
1991 Dual-route models of print and sound: Still a good horse race. *Psychological Research* 53:13-24.

Padden, C., and R. Trachtenberg
1996 Intended and Unintended Consequences of Educational Policy for Deaf Children. Unpublished manuscript, University of California, San Diego.

Palincsar, A.S., and A.L. Brown
1984 Reciprocal teaching of comprehension-fostering and comprehension-monitoring activities. *Cognition and Instruction* 1:117-175.

Palincsar, A.S., A.L. Brown, and J.C. Campione
1993 First-grade dialogues for knowledge acquisition and use. *Contexts for Learning: Sociocultural Dynamics in Children's Development,* E. Forman, N. Minick, and C.A. Stone, eds. New York: Oxford University Press.

Palmer, J., C.M. MacLeod, E. Hunt, and J.E. Davidson
1985 Information processing correlates of reading. *Journal of Memory and Language* 24: 59-88.

Papandropoulou, I., and H. Sinclair
1974 What is a word? Experimental study of children's ideas on grammar. *Human Development* 17(4):241-258.

Papert, S.
1996 A word for learning. Pp. 9-24 in *Constructionism in Practice: Designing, Thinking, and Learning in a Digital World,* Y.B. Kafai and M. Resnick, eds. Mahwah, NJ: Lawrence Erlbaum Associates.

Paris, S.G., and J.C. Turner
1994 Situated motivation. Pp. 213-237 in *Student Motivation, Cognition, and Learning: Essays in Honor of Wilbert J. McKeachie,* P.R. Pintrich, D.R. Brown, and C.E. Weinstein, eds. Hillsdale, NJ: Lawrence Erlbaum Associates.

Paris, S.G., and M. Myers
1981 Comprehension monitoring, memory and study strategies of good and poor readers. *Journal of Reading Behavior* 13:5-22.

Paris, S.G., D.R. Cross, and M.Y. Lipson
1984 Informed strategies for learning: A program to improve children's reading awareness and comprehension. *Journal of Educational Psychology* 76:1239-1252.

Pedone, R.J., ed.
1981 *The Retention of Minority Languages in the United States: A Seminar on the Analytic Work of Calvin J. Veltman.* Washington, DC: National Center for Education Statistics.

Pennington, B.F.
1989 Using genetics to understand dyslexia. *Annals of Dyslexia* 39:81-93.

Perfetti, C.A.
1985 *Reading Ability.* New York: Oxford University Press.
1992 The representation problem in reading acquisition. Pp. 145-174 in *Reading Acquisition,* P.B. Gough, L.C. Ehri, and R. Treiman, eds. Hillsdale, NJ: Lawrence Erlbaum.

Perfetti, C.A., and D. McCutchen
1982 Speech processes in reading. Pp. 237-269 in *Speech and Language: Advances in Basic Research and Practice,* N. Lass, ed. New York: Academic Press.

Perfetti, C.A., I. Beck, L. Bell, and C. Hughes
1987 Phonemic knowledge and learning to read are reciprocal: A longitudinal study of first grade children. *Merrill-Palmer Quarterly* 33:283-319.

Perfetti, C.A., S.R. Goldman, and T.W. Hogaboam
1979 Reading skill and the identification of words in discourse context. *Memory and Cognition* 2:273-282.

Perfetti, C.A., and S. Zhang
  1995 The universal word identification reflex. Pp. 159-189 in *The Psychology of Learning and Motivation, Vol. 33*, D.L. Medin, ed. San Diego: Academic Press.
Peterson, C., and A. McCabe
  1983 *Developmental Psycholinguistics: Three Ways of Looking at a Child's Narrative.* New York: Plenum.
Peterson, P.L., and others
  1982 Student's aptitudes and their reports of cognitive processes during direct instruction. *Journal of Educational Psychology* 74(4):535-547.
Peterson, R.W.
  1994 School readiness considered from a neuro-cognitive perspective. *Early Education and Development* 5(2):120-140.
Phillips, D.A., K. McCartney, and S. Scarr
  1987 Child-care quality and children's social development. *Developmental Psychology* 23:537-543.
Phillips, M., J. Crouse, and J. Ralph
  In   Does the black-white test score gap widen after children enter school? In *The Black-*
  press *White Test Score Gap*, C. Jencks and M. Phillips, eds.
Pianta, R.C.
  1990 Widening the debate on educational reform: Prevention as a viable alternative. *Exceptional Children* 56(4):306-313.
Pianta, R.C., and M. Steinberg
  1992 Teacher-child relationships and the process of adjusting to school. Pp. 61-80 in *Beyond the Parent: The Role of Other Adults in Children's Lives. New Directions for Child Development, No. 57*, R.C. Pianta, ed. San Francisco: Jossey-Bass.
Pianta, R.C., and S.J. McCoy
  1997 The first day of school: The predictive validity of early school screening. *Journal of Applied Developmental Psychology* 18:1-22.
Pinker, S.
  1984 *Language Learnability and Language Development.* Cambridge, MA: Harvard University Press.
Pinnell, G.S., D.E. DeFord, C.A. Lyons, A. Bryk, et al.
  1994 Comparing instructional models for the literacy education of high-risk first graders. *Reading Research Quarterly* 29(1):8-39.
Pinnell, G.S., D.E. DeFord, C.A. Lyons, and A. Bryk
  1995 "Comparing instructional models for the literacy education of high-risk first graders": Reply. *Reading Research Quarterly* 30(2):272-275.
Pinnell, G.S., D.E. DeFord, and C.A. Lyons
  1988 *Reading Recovery: Early Intervention for At-Risk First Graders. ERS Monograph.* Arlington, VA: Educational Research Service.
Plaut, D.C., J.L. McClelland, M.S. Seidenberg, and K. Patterson
  1996 Understanding normal and impaired word reading: Computational principles in quasi-regular domains. *Psychological Review* 103:56-115.
Pollitt, E., K. Gorman, P. Engle, M. Reynaldo, and J. Rivera
  1993 Early supplementary feeding and cognition. *Monograph of the Society for Research in Child Development* 58(235):1-85.
Postlethwaite, N.T., and K.N. Ross
  1992 Effective Schools in Reading: Implications for Educational Planners. An Exploratory Study. International Association for the Evaluation of Educational Achievement.
Pratt, C., W.E. Tunmer, and J.A. Bowey
  1984 Children's capacity to correct grammatical violations in sentences. *Journal of Child Language* 11(2):129-141.

Pressley, M., J. Rankin, and L. Yokoi
  1996 A survey of instructional practices of outstanding primary-level literacy teachers. *Elementary School Journal* 96:363-384.
Puma, M., N. Karweit, C. Price, A. Ricciuti, W. Thompson, and M. Vaden-Kiernan
  1997 *Prospects: Final Report on Student Outcomes.* Washington, DC: U.S. Department of Education, Planning and Evaluation Services.
Pungello, E.P., J.B. Kupersmidt, and M.R. Burchinal
  1996 Environmental risk factors and children's achievement from middle childhood to early adolescence. *Developmental Psychology* 32(4):755-767.
Purcell-Gates, V.
  1988 Lexical and syntactic knowledge of written narrative held by well-read-to kindergartners and second graders. *Research in the Teaching of English* 22:128-160.
  1991 Ability of well-read-to kindergartners to decontextualize/recontextualize experience into a written-narrative register. *Language and Education: An International Journal* 5:177-188.
  1993 I ain't never read my 'own' words before. *Journal of Reading* 37:210-219.
  1994 Relationships Between Parental Literacy Skills and Functional Uses of Print and Children's Ability to Learn Literacy Skills. Washington, DC: National Institute for Literacy. Paper under Grant no. X257A20223
  1996 Stories, coupons, and the TV guide: Relationships between home literacy experiences and emergent literacy knowledge. *Reading Research Quarterly* 31:406-428.
Purcell-Gates, V., E. McIntyre, and P.A. Freppon
  1995 Learning written storybook language in school: A comparison of low-SES children in skills-based and whole language classrooms. *American Educational Research Journal* 32(3):659-685.
Purcell-Gates, V., and K. Dahl
  1991 Low-SES children's success and failure at early literacy learning in skills-based classrooms. *JRB: A Journal of Literacy* 23:1-34.
Quigley, S.P.
  1969 The deaf and the hard of hearing. *Rehabilitation Literature* 30(2):103-123.
Ramey, C.T., D.M. Bryant, and T.M. Suarez
  1985 Preschool compensatory education and the modifiabliity of intelligence: A critical review. Pp. 247-296 in *Current Topics in Human Intelligence,* D. Detterman, ed. Norwood, NJ: Ablex.
Ramirez, D., S. Yuen, and D. Ramey
  1991 Final report: Longitudinal study of structured English immersion strategy, early-exit and late-exit transitional bilingual education programs for language-minority children. Executive summary. San Mateo, CA: Aguirre International.
Rashotte, C.A., and J.K. Torgesen
  1985 Repeated reading and reading fluency in learning disabled children. *Reading Research Quarterly* 20(2):180-188.
Rasinski, T.V.
  1995 On the effects of reading recovery: A response to Pinnell, Lyons, DeFord, Bryk, and Seltzer. *Reading Research Quarterly* 30(2):264-270.
Rayner, K., and A. Pollatsek
  1987 Eye movements in reading: A tutorial review. Pp. 327-362 in *Attention and Performance XII: The Psychology of Reading,* M. Coltheart, ed. London: Erlbaum Associates.
  1989 *The Psychology of Reading.* Englewood Cliffs, NJ: Prentice-Hall.

Read, C.
1971 Pre-school children's knowledge of English phonology. *Harvard Educational Review* 41:1-34.
1975 *Children's Categorization of Speech Sounds in English: Research Report No. 17.* Urbana, IL: National Council of Teachers of English.

Read, C., Y. Zhang, H. Nie, and B. Ding
1986 The ability to manipulate speech sounds depends on knowing alphabetic reading. *Cognition* 24:31-44.

Recht, D.R., and L. Leslie
1988 Effect of prior knowledge on good and poor readers' memory of text. *Journal of Educational Psychology* 80(1):16-20.

Richardson, V. (ed.)
1994 *Teacher Change and the Staff Development Process: A Case in Reading Instruction.* New York: Teachers College Press.

Richman, N., J. Stevenson, and P.J. Graham
1982 Pre-school to school: A behavioural study. *Behavioural Development: A Series of Monographs.* London: Hospital for Sick Children.

Rickford, J.R., and A.A. Rickford
1995 Dialect readers revisited. *Linguistics-and-Education* 7:107-128.

Rigden, D.W.
1997 Teachers' view: Changing teacher education. *Schools in the Middle* 6(5):23-27.

Risko, V.J.
1991 Videodisc-based case methodology: A design for enhancing preservice teachers' problem-solving abilities. Pp. 121-137 in *Literacy International, National, State, and Local. Eleventh Yearbook of American Reading Forum*, B.L. Hayes and K. Camperell, eds. Logan: Utah State University Press.
1992 Developing problem solving environments to prepare teachers for instruction of diverse learners. Pp. 1-13 in *Developing Lifelong Readers: Policies, Procedures, and Programs. Twelfth Yearbook of American Reading Forum*, B.L. Hayes and K. Camperell, eds. Logan: Utah State University Press.
1996 Creating a community of thinkers within a preservice literacy education methods course. Pp. 3-15 in *Literacy: The Information Superhighway to Success*, K. Camperell, B. Hayes, and R. Telfer, eds. Logan: Utah State University Press.

Risko, V.J., J.A. Peter, and D. McAllister
1996 Conceptual changes: Preservice teachers' pathways to providing literacy instruction. Pp. 104-119 in *Growing Literacy*, E.G. Sturtevant and W.M. Linek, eds. Commerce, TX: College Reading Association.

Risko, V.J., and C.K. Kinzer
1997 *Videodisc, Case-based Reading Instruction in Preservice Reading Education.* New York: McGraw-Hill.

Rittenhouse, R.K.
1979 Motor Development in Deaf and Normal-Hearing Children: A Review of the Literature. ERIC clearinghouse #ED168276

Robbins, C., and L.C. Ehri
1994 Reading storybooks to kindergartners helps them learn new vocabulary words. *Journal of Educational Psychology* 86(1):54-64.

Roberts, J., S. Rabinowitz, D.M. Bryant, M. Burchinal, M. Koch, and C.T. Ramey
1989 Language skills of children with different preschool experiences. *Journal of Speech and Hearing Research* 32:773-786.

Roberts, T.
1976 "Frustration level" reading in the infant school. *Educational Research* 19(1):41-44.

Robinshaw, H.M.
   1994   Deaf infants, early intervention and language acquisition. *Early Child Development and Care* 99:1-22.
Robinson, V.
   1989   Some limitations of systemic adaptation: The implementation of reading recovery. *New Zealand Journal of Educational Studies* 24:35-45.
Roderick, M.
   1994   Grade retention and school dropout: Investigation of the association. *American Educational Research Journal* 31(4):729-759.
Rodgers, B.
   1983   The identification and prevalence of specific reading retardation. *British Journal of Educational Psychology* 51:369-373.
Rosenshine, B., and C. Meister
   1994   Reciprocal teaching: A review of the research. *Review of Educational Research* 64(4):479-530.
Rosenshine, B., and R. Stevens
   1986   Teaching functions. Pp. 376-391 in *Handbook of Research on Teaching, Third Edition,* M. Wittrock, ed. New York: Macmillan.
Rossell, C., and K. Baker
   1996   The educational effectiveness of bilingual education. *Research in the Teaching of English* 30:1-68.
Rowe, K.J.
   1991   The influence of reading activity at home on students' attitudes towards reading, classroom attentiveness and reading achievement: An application of structural equation modelling. *British Journal of Educational Psychology* 61(1):19-35.
Rubin, A.
   1980   A theoretical taxonomy of the differences between oral and written language. Pp. 411-438 in *Theoretical Issues in Reading Comprehension,* R.J. Spiro, B.C. Bruce, and W.F. Brewer, eds. Hillsdale, NJ: Lawrence Erlbaum Associates.
Rutherford, W.
   1968   Learning to read: A critique. *The Elementary School Journal* 69:72-83.
Rutter, M., and W. Yule
   1975   The concept of specific reading retardation. *Journal of Child Psychology and Psychiatry* 16:181-197.
Sacks, C.H., and J.R. Mergendoller
   1997   The relationship between teachers' theoretical orientation toward reading and student outcomes in kindergarten children with different initial reading abilities. *American Educational Research Journal* 34:721-739.
Samuels, S.J.
   1979   The method of repeated readings. *The Reading Teacher* 32:403-408.
   1994   Toward a theory of automatic information processing in reading, revisited. Pp. 816-837 in *Theoretical Models and Processes of Reading* (4th Edition), R.B. Ruddell, M.R. Ruddell, and H. Singer, eds. Newark, DE: International Reading Association.
Sandholtz, J.H., C. Ringstaff, and D.C. Dwyer
   1997   *Teaching with Technology: Creating Student-Centered Classrooms.* New York: Teachers College Press.
Sarason, S., and J. Doris
   1979   *Educational Handicap, Public Policy, and Social History.* New York: Free Press.
Scanlon, D.M., and F.R. Vellutino
   1996   Prerequisite skills, early instruction, and success in first-grade reading: Selected results from a longitudinal study. *Mental Retardation and Developmental Research Reviews* 2:54-63.

In   A comparison of the instructional backgrounds and cognitive profiles of poor, aver-
press age and good readers who were initially identified as at risk for reading failure.
       Scientific Studies of Reading.
Scarborough, H.S.
  1989 Prediction of reading disability from familial and individual differences. *Journal of Educational Psychology* 81(1):101-108.
  1990 Very early language deficits in dyslexic children. *Child Development* 61:1728-1743.
  1991 Early syntactic development of dyslexic children. *Annals of Dyslexia* 41:207-220.
  1998 Early identification of children at risk for reading disabilities: Phonological aware-
         ness and some other promising predictors. Pp. 77-121 in *Specific Reading Disability: A View of the Spectrum*, B.K. Shapiro, P.J. Accardo, and A.J. Capute, eds. Timonium, MD: York Press.
Scarborough, H.S., and W. Dobrich
  1990 Development of children with early language delays. *Journal of Speech and Hearing Research* 33:70-83.
  1994 On the efficacy of reading to preschoolers. *Developmental Review* 14:245-302.
Scarborough, H.S., W. Dobrich, and M. Hager
  1991 Preschool literacy experience and later reading achievement. *Journal of Learning Disabilities* 24(8):508-511.
Schickedanz, J.A.
  1981 Hey! This Book's Not Working Right. *Young Children* 37(1):18-27.
Schley, S., and C.E. Snow
  1992 The conversational skills of school-aged children. *Social Development* 1:18-35.
Schneider, W., and R.M. Shiffrin
  1977 Controlled and automatic human information processing: I. detection, search, and attention. *Psychological Review* 84:1-66.
Schneider, W., P. Kuspert, H. Roth, V. Mechtild, and H. Marx
  1997 Short- and long-term effects of training phonological awareness in kindergarten: Evidence from two German studies. *Journal of Experimental Child Psychology* 66:311-340.
Schofield, J.W.
  1995 *Computers and Classroom Culture.* New York: Cambridge University Press.
Schrader, C.T.
  1985 Written Language Use Within the Context of Young Children's Symbolic Play. ERIC Document (264 585).
Schweinhart, L.J., et al.
  1985 Effects of the Perry Preschool Program on youths through age 19: A summary. *Topics in Early Childhood Special Education Quarterly* 5(2):26-35.
  1986 Consequences of three preschool curriculum models through age 15. *Early Childhood Research Quarterly* 1(1):15-45.
Schweinhart, L.J., H.V. Barnes, D.P. Weikart, W.S. Barnett, and A.S. Epstein
  1993 Significant benefits: The High/Scope Perry Preschool Study Through Age 27. *Monographs of the High/Scope Educational Research Foundation, No. 10.* Ypsilanti, MI: High/Scope Educational Research Foundation.
Seidenberg, M.S., and J.L. McClelland
  1989 A distributed, developmental model of word recognition and naming. *Psychological Review* 96:523-568.
Shanahan, T., and R. Barr
  1995 Reading recovery: An independent evaluation of the effects of an early instructional intervention for at-risk learners. *Reading Research Quarterly* 30(4):958-996.

Shankweiler, D., S. Crain, L. Katz, A.E. Fowler, et al.
  1995 Cognitive profiles of reading-disabled children: Comparison of language skills in phonology, morphology, and syntax. *Psychological Science* 6(3):149-156.
Shankweiler, D., and S. Crain
  1986 Language mechanisms and reading disorder: A modular approach. *Cognition* 24: 139-168.
Shany, M., and A. Biemiller
  1995 Assisted reading practice: Effects on performance for poor readers in grades 3 and 4. *Reading Research Quarterly* 30:382-395.
Shapiro, B.K., F.B. Palmer, S. Antell, S. Bilker, A. Ross, and A.J. Capute
  1990 Precursors of reading delay: Neurodevelopmental milestones. *Pediatrics* 85:416-420.
Share, D.L.
  1995 Phonological recoding and self-teaching: Sine qua non of reading acquisition. *Cognition* 55:151-218.
  1996 Word recognition and spelling processes on specific reading disabled and garden-variety poor readers. *Dyslexia* 2:167-174.
Share, D.L., R. McGee, D. McKenzie, S. Williams, and P.A. Silva
  1987 Further evidence relating to the distinction between specific reading retardation and general reading backwardness. *British Journal of Developmental Psychology* 5:35-44.
Share, D.L., A.F. Jorm, R. Maclean, and R. Matthews
  1984 Sources of individual differences in reading acquisition. *Journal of Educational Psychology* 76(6):1309-1324.
Sharp, D.L.M., J.D. Bransford, S.R. Goldman, V. Risko, C.K. Kinzer, and N.J. Vye
  1995 Dynamic visual support for story comprehension and mental model building by young, at-risk children. *Educational Technology Research and Development* 43: 25-42.
Shaywitz, B.A.
  1996 The Neurobiology of Reading and Reading Disability. Unpublished paper prepared for the Committee on the Prevention of Reading Difficulties in Young Children.
Shaywitz, B.A., J.M. Fletcher, and S.E. Shaywitz
  1995a Defining and classifying learning disabilities and attention-deficit/hyperactivity disorder. *Journal of Child Neurology* 10(Supplement 1):S50-S57.
Shaywitz, B.A., S.E. Shaywitz, K.R. Pugh, R.T. Constable, P. Skudlarski, R.K. Fulbright, R.A. Bronen, J.M. Fletcher, D.P. Shankweiler, L. Katz, and J.C. Gore
  1995b Sex differences in the functional organization of the brain for language. *Nature* 373: 607-609.
Shaywitz, S.E.
  1996 Dyslexia. *Scientific American* 275(5):98-104.
Shaywitz, S.E., and B.A. Shaywitz
  1996 Unlocking learning disabilities: The neurological basis. Pp. 255-260 in *Learning Disabilities, Lifelong Issues,* S.C. Cramer and W. Ellis, eds. Baltimore: Paul H. Brookes.
Shaywitz, S.E., M. Escobar, B.A. Shaywitz, J.M. Fletcher, and R. Makuch
  1992 Evidence that dyslexia may represent the lower tail of a normal distribution of reading ability. *New England Journal of Medicine* 326:145-150.
Shaywitz, S.E., B.A. Shaywitz, J.M. Fletcher, and M.D. Escobar
  1990 Prevalence of reading disability in boys and girls: Results of the Connecticut Longitudinal Study. *Journal of the American Medical Association* 264:998-1002.

Shaywitz, S.E., J.M. Fletcher, and B.A. Shaywitz
1994 Issues in the definition and classification of attention deficit disorder. *Topics in Language Disorders* 14(4):1-25.

Shaywitz, S.E., B.A. Shaywitz, K.R. Pugh, and others
1998 Functional disruption in the organization of the brain for reading in dyslexia. *Proceedings of the National Academy of Sciences*, 95:2636-2641.

Shepard, L.A., and M.L. Smith
1990 Synthesis of research on grade retention. *Educational Leadership* 47(8):84-88.

Shu, H., R.C. Anderson, and H. Zhang
1995 Incidental learning of word meanings while reading: A Chinese and American cross-cultural study. *Reading Research Quarterly* 30(1):76-95.

Silva, P.A., R. McGee, and S. Williams
1985 Some characteristics of 9-year-old boys with general reading backwardness or specific reading retardation. *Journal of Child Psychology and Psychiatry* 26:407-421.

Silver, L.B.
1987 The "magic cure": A review of the current controversial approaches for treating learning disabilities. *Journal of Learning Disabilities* 20:498-504.

Simeonsson, R.J.
1994 Promoting children's health, education, and well-being. Pp. 3-31 in *Risk, Resilience, and Prevention: Promoting the Well-Being of All Children.* Baltimore: Paul H. Brookes.

Simmons, D.C., and E.J. Kame'enui
In   *What Reading Research Tells Us About Children with Diverse Learning Needs:*
press *Bases and Basics.* Mahwah, NJ: Lawrence Erlbaum Associates.

Simmons, D.C., and others
1994 Translating research into basal reading programs: Applications of curriculum design. *LD Forum* 20(1):9-13.

Simpkins, G.A., and C. Simpkins
1981 Cross cultural approach to curriculum development. Pp. 221-240 in *Black English and the Education of Black Children and Youth: Proceedings of the National Invitational Symposium on the King Decision,* G. Smitherman, ed. Detroit: Center for Black Studies, Wayne State University.

Sizer, T.R.
1983 Essential schools: A first look. *Independent School* 43(2):7-12.

Skutnabb-Kangas, T., and T.P. Toukomaa
1979 *Semilingualism and Middle Class Bias: A Reply to Cora Brent-Palmer. Working Papers on Bilingualism, No. 19.* Ontario Institute, for Studies in Education, Toronto. Bilingual Education Project.

Slavin, R.E.
1989 Class size and student achievement: Small effects of small classes. *Educational Psychologist* 24(1):99-110.
1994 *Preventing Early School Failure: Research, Policy, and Practice.* Needham Heights, MA: Longwood Division, Allyn and Bacon.

Slavin, R.E., and N. Madden
1995 Effects of Success for All on the Achievement of English Language Learners. Paper presented at the annual meeting of the American Educational Research Association, San Francisco, CA., April 1995.

Slavin, R.E., N.L. Karweit, B.A. Wasik, N.A. Madden, and L.J. Dolan
1994 Success For All: A comprehensive approach to prevention and early intervention. Pp. 175-205 in *Preventing Early School Failure,* R.E. Slavin, N.L. Karweit, and B.A. Wasik, eds. Boston: Allyn and Bacon.

Slavin, R.E., N.A. Madden, N.L. Karweit, L. Dolan, and B.A. Wasik
  1992 *Success For All: A Relentless Approach to Prevention and Early Intervention in Elementary Schools.* Arlington, VA: Educational Research Service.
Slavin, R.E., N.A. Madden, L.J. Dolan, B.A. Wasik, S. Ross, L. Smith, and M. Dianda
  1996a Success For All: A summary of research. *Journal of Education for Students Placed At Risk* 1(1):41-76.
Slavin, R.E., N.A. Madden, L.J. Dolan, and B.A. Wasik
  1996b *Every Child, Every School: Success For All.* Newbury Park, CA: Corwin.
Slavin, R.E., N.L. Karweit, and N.A. Madden
  1989 *Effective Programs for Students at Risk.* Boston: Allyn and Bacon.
Slowiaczek, M.L., and C. Clifton
  1980 Subvocalization and reading for meaning. *Journal of Verbal Learning and Verbal Behavior* 19:573-582.
Small, M.Y., and J. Butterworth
  1981 Semantic integration and the development of memory for logical inferences. *Child Development* 52(2):732-735.
Smilansky, S.
  1968 *The Effects of Sociodramatic Play on Disadvantaged Preschool Children.* New York: John Wiley and Sons.
Smiley, S.S., D.D. Oakley, D. Worthen, J.C. Campione, and A.L. Brown
  1977 Recall of thematically relevant material by adolescent good and poor readers as a function of written versus oral presentation. *Journal of Educational Psychology* 69: 381-387.
Smith, C.L., and H. Tager-Flusberg
  1982 Metalinguistic awareness and language development. *Journal of Experimental Child Psychology* 34(3):449-468.
Smith, L.J., S.M. Ross, and J. Casey
  1996 Multi-site comparison of the effects of *Success For All* on reading achievement. *Journal of Literacy Research* 28(3):329-353.
Smith, M.K.
  1941 Measurement of the size of general English vocabulary through the elementary grades and high school. *Genetic Psychological Monograph* 24:311-345.
Smith, M.L., and G.V. Glass
  1980 Meta-analysis of research on class size and its relationship to attitudes and instruction. *American Educational Research Journal* 17(4):419-433.
Smith, M.W., and D.K. Dickinson
  1994 Describing oral language opportunities and environments in Head Start and other preschool classrooms. *Special Issue: Head Start* 9(3-4):345-366.
Smith, S.S., L. Christensen, D. Goodale, S. Ingebrand, and K. Steele
  1993 Effects of Phonemic Awareness Training on Impoverished First and Second Graders. Paper presented at the annual meeting of the National Reading Conference, Charleston, SC.
Smitherman, G.
  1977 *Black English and the Education of Black Children and Youth. Proceedings of the National Invitational Symposium on the KING Decision.* Detroit: Center for Black Studies, Wayne State University.
Snow, C.E., and P.O. Tabors
  1993 Language skills that relate to literacy development. Pp. 1-20 in *Language and Literacy in Early Childhood Education*, B. Spodek and O.N. Saracho, eds. New York: Teachers College Press.

Snow, C., and P. Tabors
1996   Intergenerational transfer of literacy. *Family Literacy: Directions in Research and Implications for Practice,* L.A. Benjamin and J. Lord, eds. Washington, DC: Office of Educational Research and Improvement, U.S. Department of Education.
Snow, C.E.
1977   Development of conversation between mothers and babies. *Journal of Child Language* 4:1-22.
1990   The development of definitional skill. *Journal of Child Language* 17:697-710.
Snow, C.E., and A. Ninio
1986   The contracts of literacy: What children learn from learning to read books. Pp. 116-137 in *Emergent Literacy: Writing and Reading,* W.H. Teale and E. Sulzby, eds. Norwood, NJ: Ablex.
Snow, C.E., and B.A. Goldfield
1982   Building stories: The emergence of information structures from conversation and narrative. Pp 127-141 in *Georgetown University Roundtable on Language and Linguistics 1981, Analyzing Discourse: Text and Talk,* D. Tannen, ed. Washington, DC: Georgetown University Press.
1983   Turn the page please: Situation-specific language acquisition. *Journal of Child Language* 10:551-569.
Snow, C.E., B. Pan, A. Imbens-Bailey, and J. Herman
1996   Learning how to say what one means: A longitudinal study of children's speech act use. *Social Development* 5:56-84.
Soar, R.S.
1973   Accountability: Assessment problems and possibilities. *Journal of Teacher Education* 24(3):205-212.
SocioTechnical Research Applications, Inc.
1996   *Report on the ACYF Bilingual/Multicultural Survey.* Washington, DC: The Head Start Bureau.
Spiegel, D.L.
1994   A portrait of parents of successful readers. In *Fostering the Love of Reading: The Affective Domain in Reading Education.* Newark, DE: International Reading Association.
Spillane, J.P.
1996   School districts matter: Local educational authorities and state instructional policy. *Educational Policy* 10(1):63-87.
Spring, C., and J.M. Davis
1988   Relations of digit naming speed with three components of reading. *Applied Psycholinguistics* 9(4):315-334.
St. Pierre, R., J. Swartz, S. Murray, D. Deck, and P. Nicke
1993   *National Evaluation of the Even Start Family Literacy Program: Report on Effectiveness.* Washington, DC: U.S. Department of Education, Office of Policy and Planning.
St. Pierre, R., and M. Lopez
1994   The Comprehensive Child Development Program. Presentation to the National Research Council, Board on Children and Families, Washington, DC, December 16, 1994.
Stahl, S., and P. Miller
1989   Whole language and language experience approaches for beginning reading: A quantitative research synthesis. *Review of Educational Research* 59:87-116.

Stahl, S.A., and M.M. Fairbanks
  1986 The effects of vocabulary instruction: A model-based meta-analysis. *Review of Educational Research* 56(1):72-110.
Stahl, S.A., K. Heubach, and B. Cramond
  1997 *Fluency-oriented Reading Instruction. Reading Research Report No. 79.* Athens, GA: National Reading Research Center.
Stahl, S.A., M.G. Jacobson, and C.E. Davis
  1989 Prior knowledge and difficult vocabulary in the comprehension of unfamiliar text. *Reading Research Quarterly* 24(Winter):27-43.
Stahl, S.A., M.C. McKenna, and J.R. Pagnucco
  1994 The effects of whole-language instruction: An update and a reappraisal. *Educational Psychologist* 29(4):175-185.
Stallings, J., and E. M. Krasavage
  1986 Program implementation and student achievement in a four-year Madeline Hunter Follow Through Project. *Elementary School Journal* 87(2):117-138.
Stallings, J., P. Robbins, and L. Presbrey
  1986 Effects of instruction based on the Madeline Hunter model on students' achievement: Findings from a follow-through project. *The Elementary School Journal* 86:571-87.
Stallings, J.A.
  1980 Allocated academic reading time revisited, or beyond time on task. *Educational Researcher* 9(11):11-16.
Stanovich, K.E.
  1984 The interactive-compensatory model of reading: A confluence of developmental, experimental and educational psychology. *Remedial and Special Education* 5:11-19.
  1986 Matthew effects in reading: Some consequences of individual differences in the acquisition of literacy. *Reading Research Quarterly* 21:360-407.
Stanovich, K.E., A.E. Cunningham, and B.B. Cramer
  1984 Assessing phonological awareness in kindergarten children: Issues of task comparability. *Journal of Experimental Child Psychology* 38(2):175-190.
Stanovich, K.E., and L.S. Siegel
  1994 Phenotypic performance profiles of children with reading disabilities: A regression-based test of the phonological-core variable-difference model. *Journal of Educational Psychology* 86:24-53.
Stanovich, K.E., and R.F. West
  1989 Exposure to print and orthographic processing. *Reading Research Quarterly* 24: 402-433.
Stanovich, K.E., R.F. West, and D.J. Feeman
  1981 A longitudinal study of sentence context effects in second-grade children: Tests of an interactive-compensatory model. *Journal of Child Psychology* 32:185-199.
Stanovich, K.E., R.F. West, A.E. Cunningham, J. Cipielewski, and S. Siddiqui
  1996 The role of inadequate print exposure as a determinant of reading comprehension problems. Pp. 15-32 in *Reading Comprehension Disabilities*, C. Cornoldi and J. Oakhill, eds. Hillsdale, NJ: Erlbaum.
Stark, R., L. Bernstein, R. Condino, M. Bender, P. Tallal, and H. Catts
  1984 Four year follow-up study of language-impaired children. *Annals of Dyslexia* 34:49-68.
Stebbins, L.B., R.G. St. Pierre, E.C. Proper, R.B. Anderson, and T.R. Cerva
  1977 *Education as Experimentation: A Planned Variation Model (Vol. IV-A), An Evaluation of Project Follow Through.* Cambridge, MA: Abt Associates.
Stedman, L.C., and C.E. Kaestle
  1987 Literacy and reading performance in the United States from 1880 to the present. *Reading Research Quarterly* 22:8-46.

Steele, C.M.
1992 Race and the schooling of black Americans. *Atlantic Monthly* 269:67-78.
Stein, M., and others
1993 *The Beginning Reading Instruction Study.* Washington, DC: Office of Educational Research and Improvement.
Stevens, R.J., and R.E. Slavin
1995 The cooperative elementary school: Effects on students' achievement, attitudes, and social relations. *American Educational Research Journal* 32:321-351.
Stevenson, J.
1988 Which aspects of reading ability show a 'hump' in their distribution? *Applied Cognitive Psychology* 2:77-85.
Sticht, T.G., L. Beck, R. Hauke, G. Kleiman, and J. James
1974 *Auding and Reading: A Developmental Model.* Alexandria, VA: Human Resources Research Organization.
Sticht, T.G., and J.H. James
1984 Listening and reading. Pp. 293-317 in *Handbook of Reading Research,* P.D. Pearson, ed. New York: Longman.
Stipek, D., R. Feller, D. Daniels, and S. Milburn
1995 Effects of different instructional approaches on young children's achievement and motivation. *Child Development* 66:209-221.
Stothard, S., and C. Hulme
1996 A comparison of reading comprehension and decoding difficulties in children. Pp. 93-112 in *Reading Comprehension Difficulties: Processes and Intervention,* C. Cornoldi and J. Oakhill, eds. Mahwah, NJ: Lawrence Earlbaum Associates.
Stothard, S.E., M.J. Snowling, D.V.M. Bishop, B.B. Chipchase, and C.A. Kaplan
In Language impaired pre-schoolers: A follow-up into adolescence. *Journal of Speech*
press *and Hearing Research.*
Stotsky, S.
1987 A comparison of the two theories about development in written language: Implications for pedagogy and research. Pp. 371-395 in *Comprehending Oral and Written Language,* R. Horowitz and S.J. Samuels, eds. San Diego: Academic Press.
Stringfield, S.
1994 Outlier studies of school effectiveness. *Advances in School Effectiveness Research,* D. Reynolds, B. Creemers, P. Nesselrodt, E. Schaffer, S. Stringfield, and C. Teddlie, eds. Oxford: Pergamon.
1995 Attempts to enhance students' learning: A search for valid programs and highly reliable implementation techniques. *School Effectiveness and School Improvement* 6(1):67-96.
1997 Underlying the chaos of factors explaining exemplary U.S. elementary schools: The case for high reliability organizations. Pp. 143-160 in *Restructuring and Quality: Problems and Possibilities for Tomorrow's Schools,* T. Townsend, ed. London: Routledge.
Stringfield, S., and C. Teddlie
1988 A time to summarize: Six years and three phases of the Louisiana School Effectiveness Study. *Educational Leadership* 46(2):43-49.
1991 Observers as predictors of schools' multi-year outlier status. *Elementary School Journal* 91(4):357-376.
Stringfield, S., M. Millsap, R. Herman, N. Yoder, N. Brigham, P. Nesselrdot, E. Schaffer, N. Karweit, M. Levin, and R. Stevens
1997 *Urban and Suburban/Rural Special Strategies for Educating Disadvantaged Children: Final Report.* Prepared for Planning and Evaluation Service, U.S. Department of Education, Washington, DC.

Stuart, M.
  1990 Factors influencing word recognition in pre-reading children. *British Journal of Psychology* 81:135-146.
  1995 Prediction and qualitative assessment of five- and six-year-old children's reading: A longitudinal study. *British Journal of Educational Psychology* 65:287-296.

Stuart, M., and M. Coltheart
  1988 Does reading develop in a sequence of stages? *Cognition* 30:139-181.

Stubbs, M.
  1980 *Language and Literacy.* London: Routledge & Kegan Paul.

Studdert-Kennedy, M.
  1986 Sources of variabiity in early speech development. *Invariance and Variability in Speech Processes*, J.S. Perkell and D.H. Klatt, eds. Hillsdale, NJ: Erlbaum.

Sulzby, E.
  1985a Kindergartners as writers and readers. Pp.127-199 in *Advances in Writing Research, Vol. I: Children's Early Writing Development*, M. Farr, ed. Norwood, NJ: Ablex.
  1985b Children's emergent reading of favorite storybooks: A developmental study. *Reading Research Quarterly* 20(4):458-481.
  1987 Children's development of prosodic distinctions in telling and dictating modes. Pp. 133-160 in *Writing in Real Time: Modeling Production Processes*, A. Matsuhashi, ed. Norwood, NJ: Ablex.
  1994 Children's emergent reading of favorite storybooks: A developmental study. Pp. 244-280 in *Theoretical Models and Processes of Reading, 4th ed.*, R.B. Ruddell, M.R. Ruddell, and H. Singer, eds. Newark, DE: International Reading Association.
  1996 Roles of oral and written language as children approach conventional literacy. Pp. 25-46 in *Early Test Construction in Children*, C. Pontecorvo, M. Orsolini, B. Burge, and L.B. Resnick, eds. Hillsdale, NJ: Erlbaum.

Sulzby, E., and W.H. Teale
  1987 Young Children's Storybook Reading: Longitudinal Study of Parent-Child Interaction and Children's Independent Functioning. Final Report to the Spencer Foundation. University of Michigan, Ann Arbor.
  1991 Emergent literacy. Pp. 727-757 in *Handbook of Reading Research, Vol. 2*, R. Barr, M.L. Kamil, P. Mosenthal, and P.D. Pearson, eds. New York: Longman.

Sulzby, E., J. Barnhart, and J. Hieshima
  1989 Forms of writing and rereading from writing: A preliminary report. Pp. 31-63 in *Reading/Writing Connections*, J. Mason, ed. Needham Heights, MA: Allyn and Bacon.

Sulzby, E., and J. Kaderavek
  1996 Parent-child language during storybook reading and toy play contexts: Case studies of normally developing and specific language impaired (SLI) children. *National Reading Conference Yearbook* 37:95-106.

Taft, M.
  1992 The body of the BOSS: Subsyllabic units in the lexical processing of polysyllabic words. *Journal of Experimental Psychology, Human Perception, and Performance* 18(4):1004-1014.

Taft, M., and K.I. Forster
  1975 Lexical storage and retrieval of prefixed words. *Journal of Verbal Learning and Verbal Behavior* 14(6):638-647.

Tannen, D., ed.
  1982 *Spoken and Written Language: Exploring Orality and Literacy.* Norwood, NJ: Ablex.

Taylor, B.M., B.J. Frye, and G.M. Maruyama
  1990 Time spent reading and reading growth. *American Educational Research Journal* 27(2):351-362.
Taylor, B.M., J. Strait, and M.A. Medo
  1994 Early intervention in reading: Supplemental instruction for groups of low-achieving students provided by first-grade teachers. Pp. 107-121 in *Getting Reading Right from the Start: Effective Early Literacy Interventions,* G.H. Hiebert and B.M. Taylor, eds. Boston: Allyn & Bacon.
Taylor, D.
  1983 *Family Literacy: The Social Context of Learning to Read and Write.* Exeter, NH: Heinemann.
Taylor, D., and D. Strickland
  1986 *Family Storybook Reading.* Portsmouth, NH: Heinemann.
Taylor, D., and C. Dorsey-Gaines
  1988 *Growing Up Literate: Learning from Inner-City Families.* Portsmouth, NH: Heinemann.
Teale, W.H.
  1978 Positive environments for learning to read: What studies of early readers tell us. *Language Arts* 55(8):922-932.
Teale, W.H.
  1986 Home background and young children's literacy development. In *Emergent Literacy: Writing and Reading,* W.H. Teale and E. Sulzby, eds. Norwood, NJ: Ablex.
Teale, W.H., and E. Sulzby
  1986 Emergent literacy as a perspective for examining how young children become readers and writers. Pp. vii-xxv in *Emergent Literacy: Reading and Writing,* W.H. Teale and E. Sulzby, eds. Norwood, NJ: Ablex Publishing.
  1987 Literacy acquisition in early childhood: The roles of access and mediation in storybook reading. Pp. 111-130 in *The Future of Literacy in a Changing World,* D. Wagner, ed. New York: Pergamon Press.
Teddlie, C., and S. Stringfield
  1993 *Schools Make a Difference.* New York: Teachers College Press.
Teddlie, C., P. Kirby, and S. Stringfield
  1989 Effective vs. ineffective schools: Observable differences in the classroom. *American Journal of Education* 97(3):221-236.
Templeton, S., and D.R. Bear, eds.
  1992 *Development of Orthographic Knowledge and the Foundations of Literacy: A Memorial Festschrift for Edmund H. Henderson.* Hillsdale, NJ: Lawrence Erlbaum Associates.
Tharp, R.G.
  1982 The effective instruction of comprehension: Results and description of the Kamehameha Early Education Program. *Reading Research Quarterly* 17(4):503-527.
  1989 Psychocultural variables and constants: Effects on teaching and learning in schools. Special Issue: Children and Their Development: Knowledge Base, Research Agenda, and Social Policy Application. *American Psychologist* 44(2):349-359.
Tharp, R.G., and R. Gallimore
  1988 *Rousing Minds to Life: Teaching, Learning, and Schooling in Social Context.* Cambridge: Cambridge University Press.
Thomas, B.
  1984 Early toy preferences of four-year-old readers and nonreaders. *Child Development* 55:424-430.

Torgesen, J.K., R.K. Wagner, and C.A. Rashotte
  1997 Prevention and remediation of severe reading disabilities: Keeping the end in mind. *Scientific Studies of Reading* 1:217-234.
Torgesen, J.K., S. Morgan, and C. Davis
  1992 Effects of two types of phonological awareness training on word learning in kinder-garten children. *Journal of Educational Psychology* 84:364-370.
Tosi, A.
  1979 Bilinguismo e immigrazione: una nota sociolinguistica al piano europeo di mantenimento delle lingue nazionali nelle comunita di emigrati *(Bilingualism and Immigration: A Sociolinguistic View of the European Plan for the Maintainance of National Languages in Immigrant Communities).* *Rassegna Italiana di Linguistica Applicata* 11:243-263.
Trabasso, T., and P. van den Broek
  1985 Causal thinking and the representation of narrative events. *Journal of Memory and Language* 24:612-630.
Tracey, D.H.
  1994 Family Literacy: Research Synthesis. Paper presented at the Annual Meeting of the National Reading Conference (44th, San Diego, CA, November 30-December 3, 1994).
Treiman, R.
  1993 *Beginning to Spell: A Study of First-Grade Children.* New York: Oxford University Press.
Trueba, H.T.
  1988 Culturally based explanations of minority students' academic achievement. *Anthropology and Education Quarterly* 19:270-287.
Tunmer, W.E., M.L. Herriman, and A.R. Nesdale
  1988 Metalinguistic abilities and beginning reading. *Reading Research Quarterly* 23:134-158.
Tunmer, W.E., C. Pratt, and M.L. Herriman, eds., with contributions by J. Bowey
  1984 *Metalinguistic Awareness in Children: Theory, Research, and Implications.* New York: Springer-Verlag.
Turner, J., and S.G. Paris
  1995 How literacy tasks influence children's motivation for literacy. *Reading Teacher* 48: 662-673.
Tyler, B.
  1993 At Risk Students in Whole Language Classrooms: A Naturalistic Inquiry. ERIC Clearinghouse No. SP034827.
Uhry, J.K., and M.J. Shepherd
  1993 Segmentation/spelling instruction as part of a first grade reading program: Effects on several measures of reading. *Reading Research Quarterly* 28(3):218-233.
van den Broek, P.
  1994 Comprehension and memory of narrative texts: Inferences and coherence. Pp. 539-588 in *Handbook of Psycholinguistics*, M.A. Gernsbacher, ed. San Diego: Academic Press.
van der Wissel, A., and F.E. Zegers
  1985 Reading retardation revisited. *British Journal of Development Psychology* 3:3-9.
van Dijk, T.A., and W. Kintsch
  1983 *Strategies of Discourse Comprehension.* New York: Academic Press.
Van Orden, G.C., B. Pennington, and G. Stone
  1990 Word identification in reading and the promise of subsymbolic psycholinguistics. *Psychological Review* 97:488-522.

Venezky, R.L., and L.F. Winfield
1979 Schools that succeed beyond expectations in reading. In *Studies in Education*. Technical Report No. 1. Newark: University of Delaware.

Verhoeven, L., and P. Gillijns
1994 Ontwikkeling van beginnende lees- en spellingvaardigheid. (Development of early reading and spelling abilities.) Special issue: Inequality in Educational Opportunities. *Tijdschrift voor Onderwijsresearch* 19:259-279.

Vogler, G.P., J.C. DeFries, and S.N. Decker
1985 Family history as an indicator of risk for reading disability. *Journal of Learning Disabilities* 18:419-421.

Vosniadou, S.P., D. Pearson, and T. Rogers
1988 What causes childen's failures to detect inconsistencies in text? Representation versus comparison difficulties. *Journal of Educational Psychology* 80:27-39.

Vukelich, C.
1990 Where's the paper? Literacy during dramatic play. *Childhood Education* 66(4): 205-209.
1991 Materials and modeling: Promoting literacy during play. Pp. 215-231 in *Play and Early Literacy Development*, J.F. Christie, ed. Albany: State University of New York Press.
1994 Effects of play interventions on young children's reading of environmental print. *Early Childhood Research Quarterly* 9:153-170.

Wadsworth, S., J.C. DeFries, J.C. Stevenson, J.W. Gilger, and B.F. Pennington
1992 Gender ratios among reading-disabled children and their siblings as a function of parental impairment. *Journal of Child Psychology and Psychiatry and Allied Disciplines* 33(7):1229-1239.

Wagner, R.K.
1997 Phonological awareness training and reading. Paper presented at American Educational Research Association Conference, March, Chicago, IL.

Wagner, R.K., J.K. Torgeson, and C.A. Roshotte
1994 Development of reading-related phonological processing abilities: New evidence of bidirectional causality from a latent variable longitudinal study. *Developmental Psychology* 30(1):73-87.

Walberg, H.J., and S. Tsai
1984 Reading achievement and diminishing returns to time. *Journal of Educational Psychology* 76(3):442-451.
1985 Correlates of reading achievement and attitude: A national assessment study. *Journal of Educational Research* 78(3):159-167.

Walker, D., C. Greenwood, B. Hart, and J. Carta
1994 Prediction of school outcomes based on socioeconomic status and early language production. *Child Development* 65:606-621.

Wallace, I.F., and S.R. Hooper
1997 Otitis media and its impact on cognitive, academic, and behavioral outcomes: A review and interpretation of the findings. In *Otitis Media in Young Children*, J.E. Roberts, I.F. Wallace, and F.W. Henderson, eds. Baltimore: Brookes Publishing Co.

Wallach, M.A., and L. Wallach
1979 Helping disadvantaged children learn to read by teaching them phoneme identification skills. Pp. 227-259 in *Theory and Practice of Early Reading, Vol. 3*, L.A. Resnick and P.A. Weaver, eds. Hillsdale, NJ: Erlbaum Associates.

Walley, A.C.
1993 The role of vocabulary development in children's spoken word recognition and segmentation ability. Special Issue: Phonological Processes and Learning Disability. *Developmental Review* 13(3):286-350.

Wargo, M.J., G.K. Tallmadge, S. Michaels, D. Lipe, and J. Morris
  1972 *ESEA Title I: A Reanalysis and Synthesis of Evaluation Data from Fiscal Year 1965 Through 1970. Final Report.* Palo Alto, CA: American Institutes for Research in the Behavioral Sciences.

Warrick, N., H. Rubin, and S. Rowe-Walsh
  1993 Phoneme awareness in language-delayed children: Comparative studies and intervention. *Annals of Dyslexia* 43:153-173.

Wasik, B.H., C.T. Ramey, D.M. Bryant, and J.J. Sparling
  1990 A longitudinal study of two early intervention strategies: Project CARE. *Child Development* 61:1682-1696.

Waters, G.S., and M.S. Seidenberg
  1985 Spelling-sound effects in reading: Time-course and decision criteria. *Memory and Cognition* 13:557-572.

Waters, G.S., and D.G. Doehring
  1990 The nature and role of phonological information in reading acquisition: Insights from congenitally deaf children who communicate orally. In *Reading and Its Development: Component Skills Approaches*, T. Carr and B.A. Levy, eds. San Diego: Academic Press.

Weber, G.
  1971 *Inner City Children Can Be Taught to Read: Four Successful Schools. Occasional Paper No. 18.* Washington, DC: Council for Basic Education.

Weber, R.
  1993 Even in the midst of work: Reading among turn-of-the-century farmer's wives. *Reading Research Quarterly* 28(4):292-302.

Weismer, S.E.
  1985 Constructive comprehension abilities exhibited by language-disordered children. *Journal of Speech and Hearing Research* 28(2):175-184.

Weiss, C.
  1978 Improving the linkage between social research and public policy. Pp. 23-81 in *Knowledge and Policy: The Uncertain Connection*, L. Lynn, ed. Washington DC: National Academy of Sciences.

Wells, C.G.
  1985 Preschool literacy-related activities and success in school. In *Literacy, Language, and Learning*, D. Olson, M. Torrance, and A. Hildyard, eds. London: Cambridge University Press.

Werker, J.F., and C.E. Lalonde
  1988 Cross-language speech perception: Initial capabilities and developmental change. *Developmental Psychology* 24:672-683.

White, K., and G. Castro
  1985 An integrative review of early intervention efficacy studies with at-risk children: Implications for the handicapped. *Analysis and Intervention in Developmental Disabilities* 5:7-31.

White, K.R.
  1982 The relation between socioeconomic status and academic achievement. *Psychological Bulletin* 91:461-481.

Whitehurst, G.
  1997 Continuities and Discontinuities in the Move from Emergent Literacy to Reading. Society for Research in Child Development. Paper presented at the Symposium: Developmental Psychologists Contribute to Early Childhood Education, Washington, DC, April 4, 1997.

Whitehurst, G.J., D.S. Arnold, J.N. Epstein, and A.L. Angell
1994 A picture book reading intervention in day care and home for children from low-income families. *Developmental Psychology* 30(5):679-689.

Whitehurst, G.J., J.E. Fischel, M. Caulfield, B.D. DeBaryshe, and M.C. Valdez-Menchaca
1989 Assessment and treatment of early expressive language delay Pp. 113-135 in *Challenges to Developmental Paradigms: Implications for Theory, Assessment and Treatment*, P.R. Zelazo and R.G. Barr, eds. Hillsdale, NJ: Lawrence Erlbaum Associates.

Whitehurst, G.J., F.L. Falco, C.J. Lonigan, J.E. Fischel, B.D. DeBaryshe, M.C. Valdez-Menchaca, and M. Caulfield
1988 Accelerating language development through picture book reading. *Developmental Psychology* 24:552-559.

Williams, C.L.
1994 The language and literacy worlds of three profoundly deaf preschool children. *Reading Research Quarterly* 29:125-155.

Williams, J.P.
1980 Teaching decoding with an emphasis on phoneme analysis and phoneme blending. *Journal of Educational Psychology* 72:1-15.

Willig, A.C.
1985 A meta-analysis of selected studies on the effectiveness of bilingual education. *Review of Educational Research* 55:269-317.

Winn, D., and J. Mitchell
1991 Improving reading instruction through staff development. *Reading Improvement* 28:82-88.

Wise, B.W., and R.K. Olson
1995 Computer-based phonological awareness and reading instruction. *Annals of Dyslexia* 45:99-122.

Wixson, K.K., and M.Y. Lipson
1991 Perspectives on reading disability research. Pp. 539-570 in *Handbook of Reading Research, Vol. 2*, R. Barr, M.L. Kamil, P.B. Mosenthal, and P.D. Pearson, eds. Mahwah, NJ: Lawrence Erlbaum Associates.

Wolf, M., and M. Obregon
1992 Early naming deficits, developmental dyslexia, and a specific deficit hypothesis. *Brain and Language* 42(3):219-247.

Wolfram, W.
1969 *A Linguistic Description of Detroit Negro Speech*. Washington, DC: Center for Applied Linguistics.

Wolfram, W.
1991 Bidialect Literacy in the United States. ERIC Clearinghouse No. FL800344.

Worrall, R.S.
1990 Detecting health fraud in the field of learning disabilities. *Journal of Learning Disabilities* 23:207-212.

Wright, J.C., and A.C. Huston
1995 Effects of Educational TV Viewing of Lower-Income Preschoolers on Academic Skills, School Readiness, and School Adjustment One to Three Years Later. Report presented to Children's Television Workshop by CRITC (Center for Research on the Influences of Television on Children), University of Kansas, May 1995.

Yaden, D.B., L.B. Smolkin, and A. Conlon
1989 Preschoolers' questions about pictures, print conventions, and story text during reading aloud at home. *Reading Research Quarterly* 24(2):188-214.

396 PREVENTING READING DIFFICULTIES IN YOUNG CHILDREN

Yancey, P.S.
1988 Speech- and language-impaired three and four year olds: A five year follow-up study. Pp. 52-77 in *Preschool Prevention of Reading Failure*, R.L. Masland and M.W. Masland, eds. Parkton, MD: York Press.

Yuill, N.
1996 A funny thing happened on the way to the classroom: Jokes, riddles, and meta-linguistic awareness in understanding and improving poor comprehension in children. Pp. 193-220 in *Reading Comprehension Difficulties*, C. Cornoldi and J. Oakhill, eds. Mahwah, NJ: Erlbaum.

Yuill, N., and J. Oakhill
1988 Understanding of anaphoric relations in skilled and less skilled comprehenders. *British Journal of Psychology* 79(2):173-186.

Yuill, N., and J. Oakhill
1991 *Children's Problems in Text Comprehension: An Experimental Investigation.* Cambridge: Cambridge University Press.

Yule, W., M. Rutter, M. Berger, and J. Thompson
1974 Over- and under-achievement in reading: Distribution in the general population. *British Journal of Educational Psychology* 44:1-12.

Yurkowski, P., and C. Ewoldt
1986 A case for the semantic processing of the deaf reader. *American Annals of the Deaf* 131(3):243-247.

Zill, N., E. Davies, and M. Daly
1994 Viewing of *Sesame Street* by Preschool Children in the United States and Its Relationship to School Readiness. Report prepared for Children's Television Workshop by Westat, Inc., Rockville, MD.

Zimmerman, J.
1997 *Foundations in Reading.* Oakvale, IA: Breakthrough, Inc.

Zimmermann, J., and C.J. Brown
1996 Breakthrough to Literacy: Engaging Children and Teachers in Effective Early Literacy Environments. Presentation to the Virginia I.R.A., Norfolk, VA, April.

Biographical Sketches

CATHERINE SNOW *(Chair)* is the Henry Lee Shattuck professor of education at the Harvard Graduate School of Education. Her research involves the areas of language and literacy acquisition, as well as second-language acquisition and bilingualism. She has held teaching or research positions at Erasmus University and the University of Amsterdam in the Netherlands, at the University of Cambridge in England, at Hebrew University in Jerusalem, and at Universidad Autonoma in Madrid. Recent books include *Unfulfilled Expectations: Home and School Influences on Literacy* (with W. Barnes, J. Chandler, I. Goodman, and L. Hemphill) and *Pragmatic Development* (with A. Ninio). She has M.A. and Ph.D. degrees in psychology from McGill University; her doctoral thesis focused on language acquisition and mothers' speech to children.

MARILYN JAGER ADAMS is currently a visiting scholar at the Harvard Graduate School of Education. Previously she was a research scientist at Bolt, Beranek, and Newman Inc., the University of Illinois's Center for the Study of Reading, and the Reading Research Education Center and adjunct professor at Brown University and Stavanger College in Norway. Her research is in the field of literacy acquisition and the development of instructional materials and software, and her publications include the book, *Beginning to Read: Thinking and Learning About Print*. Beyond research, she has been involved in the development of a range of educational technology and materials. She is currently lead literacy advisor for "Between the Lions," a public television program on literacy for children ages 4 to 8. She received the Sylvia Scribner award for outstanding contribution to research in 1995 for her work on reading and cognition. She has a Ph.D. in cognitive and developmental psychology from Brown University.

BARBARA T. BOWMAN is cofounder and president of the Erikson Institute in Chicago, Illinois, a graduate school and research center for advanced study in child development, affiliated with Loyola University Chicago. She is an authority on early education and a national advocate for improved and expanded training for practitioners who teach and care for young children. She has an extensive teaching background, having served on the faculty of the University of Chicago Laboratory School, Colorado Women's College, Nemazee School of Nursing, and the University of Shiraz (Shiraz, Iran), and, since 1966, as a faculty member of Erikson Institute. She is past president of the National Association for the Education of Young Children and has served on numerous national boards and advisory panels. Her most recent appointments include the Great Books Foundation and the National Board for Professional Teaching Standards. She holds a bachelor's degree from Sarah Lawrence College and a master's degree from the University of Chicago.

M. SUSAN BURNS is study director of the Committee on the Prevention of Reading Difficulties in Young Children and of the Committee on Early Childhood Pedagogy at the National Academy of Sciences/National Research Council. She was formerly on the faculty at the University of Pittsburgh, involved in direct service research with young children with emotional and developmental disabilities and their families. Her research interests include literacy development in young children, special and early childhood education, child development, and assessment and implementation of intervention programs for students at risk of academic failure. She has a Ph.D. in psychology from Peabody College, Vanderbilt University.

BARBARA FOORMAN is a professor of pediatrics and director of the Center for Academic and Reading Skills at the University of Texas-Houston Health Science Center. She is also principal investigator of the Early Interventions Project of the National Institute of Child Health and Human Development. From 1978 to 1997 she was professor of educational psychology at the University of Houston. She has extensive research experience in the areas of reading and language development, phonological and orthographic awareness, and assessment of reading disabilities. She is the author of *Acquisition of Reading Skills: Cultural Constraints and Cognitive Universals* and has published widely in academic and professional journals. She is currently a consulting editor for the *Journal of Learning Disabilities* and a member of the New Standards Project. She has a Ph.D. in reading and language development from the University of California at Berkeley.

DOROTHY FOWLER, a national board-certified teacher, teaches first grade at Bailey's Elementary School for the Arts and Sciences in the public school system of Fairfax County, Virginia. She is an expert in the areas of early childhood education and reading acquisition. In addition to teaching graduate courses in beginning reading strategies, she has taught children from diverse backgrounds in public school systems throughout the United States. She was a member of the Fairfax County Language Arts Development Team and is the author of the language arts resource guide, *Primary Purposes*. She has a B.A. in education from the University of Toledo and an M.A. in education from the University of New Mexico.

CLAUDE N. GOLDENBERG is an associate professor in the Department of Teacher Education at California State University, Long Beach, and a research psychologist in the Department of Psychiatry and Biobehavioral Sciences at the University of California, Los Angeles. He has conducted extensive research in the fields of Spanish-speaking children's literacy development, home school connections to support academic achievement, and processes of school change and improvement. He is author or coauthor of numerous publications, including an article on first-grade Spanish reading improvement in *Educational Researcher,* for which he and coauthor Ronald Gallimore received the 1993 Albert J. Harris award from the International Reading Association. He is currently on the editorial boards of *Elementary School Journal* and *Literacy, Teaching and Learning.* He has previously served on the National Research Council/Institute of Medicine's Roundtable on Head Start Research. He has a Ph.D. in early childhood and developmental studies from the University of California at Los Angeles.

PEG GRIFFIN was senior research associate for the Committee on the Prevention of Reading Difficulties in Young Children and study director of the Committee on the Strategic Education Research Program Feasibility Study at the National Academy of Sciences/National Research Council. Her early research at the Center for Applied Linguistics focused on literacy education and teacher talk. With developmental cognitive scientists at the Laboratory of Comparative Human Cognition at the University of California, San Diego, she focused on measurement methodology, teaching and learning of math and science, and the use of new technologies. She has a Ph.D. in linguistics from Georgetown University.

EDWARD J. KAME'ENUI is professor of special education and director of the Institute for the Development of Educational Achievement (IDEA) in the College of Education at the University of Oregon, where he currently directs or codirects six federal research and training grants. He is associate director of the National Center to Improve the Tools of Educators (NCITE), a five-year project engaged in the design of high-quality educational tools. He has published extensively on the topics of the remediation of learning disabilities and the instruction of diverse learners, and he has authored or coauthored numerous college textbooks. He currently serves on the editorial boards of *Reading Research Quarterly, Learning Disabilities Forum,* and *Scientific Study of Reading.* He is a member of the research advisory team for the American Initiative on Reading and Writing sponsored by the U.S. Department of Education. He has a Ph.D. in special education from the University of Oregon.

WILLIAM LABOV is a professor of linguistics and psychology as well as the director of the linguistics laboratory at the University of Pennsylvania. He is a member of the National Academy of Sciences and a fellow of the American Association for the Advancement of Science. His research interests within sociolinguistics include the development of African American Vernacular English, the effects of dialect differences on reading success, and the causes of increasing diversity among American dialects; his recent publications in these areas include *Can Reading Failure Be Reversed? A Linguistic Approach to the Question* and *Principles of Linguistic Change*. He is currently engaged in research for the *Phonological Atlas of North America*, funded by the National Science Foundation and the National Endowment for the Humanities, which maps geographic differences in the sound-to-spelling relationships among mainstream and minority communities. He has a Ph.D. from Columbia University.

RICHARD K. OLSON is a professor in the Psychology Department of the University of Colorado at Boulder and a faculty fellow at the Institute for Behavioral Genetics. He is also the associate director of the Center for the Study of Learning Disabilities funded by the National Institutes of Health. His research focuses on genetic and environmental influences on reading and language skills and on the computer-based remediation of deficits in these skills. He serves on the editorial board of the *Journal of Experimental Child Psychology* and is vice-president of the Society for the Scientific Study of Reading. He has a Ph.D. in psychology from the University of Oregon.

ANNEMARIE SULLIVAN PALINCSAR holds Jean and Charles Walgreen Chair in Literacy at the University of Michigan's School of Education, where she prepares teachers, teacher educators, and researchers to work in heterogeneous classrooms. She has conducted extensive research on peer collaboration in problem-solving activity, instruction to promote self-regulation, the development of literacy among learners with special needs, and the use of literacy across the school day. She is an editor of the books, *Strategic Teaching and Learning* and *Teaching Reading as Thinking*. She received an early contribution award from the American Psychological Association in 1988 and one from the American Educational Research Association in 1991. In 1992 she was elected a fellow by the International Academy for Research in Learning Disabilities. Her cognition and instruction article on reciprocal teaching (coauthored with Ann Brown in 1984) is a citation classic. She has M.A. and Ph.D. degrees in special education from the University of Illinois at Urbana-Champaign.

CHARLES A. PERFETTI is a professor of psychology and linguistics, chairman of the Department of Psychology, and a senior scientist at the Learning Research and Development Center at the University of Pittsburgh. He has published some 100 articles and chapters in the field of psycholinguistics, focusing on the process of reading and basic language processes, including both core psycholinguistics issues and reading ability. He authored the books *Reading Ability* and *Text-Based Learning and Reasoning* and edited the book *Learning to Read: Basic Research and Its Implications*. He has a Ph.D. from the University of Michigan.

HOLLIS S. SCARBOROUGH is currently a visiting associate professor of psychology at Brooklyn College of the City University of New York and a research scientist at Haskins Laboratories in New Haven. She is a developmental psychologist with expertise in reading disabilities, language acquisition, and the cognitive and linguistic underpinnings of literacy development and dyslexia. Her published work includes many articles on the preschool antecedents of reading disabilities, on the prediction of reading achievement, on the assessment of children's language abilities, and on the literacy habits and skills of adolescents and adults. She is associate editor of the *Annals of Dyslexia* and serves on the editorial boards of the *Journal of Learning Disabilities*, *Developmental Psychology*, and *Applied Psycholinguistics*. She has a Ph.D. in psychology from New York University.

SALLY SHAYWITZ is a professor of pediatrics and codirector of the Yale Center for the Study of Learning and Attention. Her research has examined learning and particularly reading from a broad perspective, including epidemiologic, definitional, cognitive, and neurobiological domains. She is principal investigator of the Connecticut Longitudinal Study, a sample survey of schoolchildren being followed from kindergarten (1983) to the present (1998), in addition to coleading the Yale Neurodevelopmental Cognitive Group. She uses functional magnetic resonance imaging to examine the functional organization of the brain for higher cognitive functions, including reading. She has reported on sex differences in brain organization for language in *Nature* and on differences in the functional organization of the brain between dyslexic and nonimpaired readers in *Proceedings of the National Academy of Sciences*. In addition, she has authored reviews of dyslexia for *Scientific American* and the *New England Journal of Medicine*. She currently serves on the editorial boards of the *Journal of Learning Disabilities, Learning Disability Quarterly*, and the *Journal of Women's Health*. She has an M.D. from the Albert Einstein College of Medicine and was the recipient of the 1995 distinguished alumnus award of the Albert Einstein College of Medicine.

KEITH STANOVICH is a professor of applied psychology at the Ontario Institute for Studies in Education at the University of Toronto. His research interests involve the areas of cognitive processes involved in reading and reading disabilities. He is the author of *How to Think Straight About Psychology* (Fifth Edition), and he edited *Children's Reading and the Development of Phonological Awareness*. He has served as the associate editor of *Merrill-Palmer Quarterly* for a decade and is a member of eight other editorial boards, including *Reading Research Quarterly*. He has twice received the Albert J. Harris award from the International Reading Association and in 1995 was elected to the Reading Hall of Fame. In 1996 he received the Oscar Causey Award from the National Reading Conference for contributions to research. In 1997 he was given the Sylvia Scribner Award from the American Association of Educational Research. He is a fellow of both the American Psychological Association and the American Psychological Society. He has a Ph.D. in psychology from the University of Michigan.

DOROTHY STRICKLAND is the state of New Jersey professor of reading at Rutgers University. She was formerly the Arthur I. Gates professor of education at Teachers College, Columbia University. A former classroom teacher, reading consultant, and learning disabilities specialist, she is a past president of the International Reading Association. Her areas of expertise include early literacy and literature-based reading and writing. Included among her publications are *Families: Poems Celebrating the African American Experience*, *The Administration and Supervision of Reading Programs*, *Language Literacy and the Child*, and *Emerging Literacy*. She was the 1994 recipient of the NCTE Rewey Belle Inglis Award for outstanding woman in the teaching of English. Her latest book, *Teaching Phonics Today*, is published by the International Reading Association. She has a Ph.D. from New York University.

SAM STRINGFIELD is principal research scientist at the Johns Hopkins University Center for the Social Organization of Schools. He also codirects there the Systemic and Policy Studies section of the Center for Research on Education of Students Placed at Risk. His work involves the areas of national and international issues in school effects, educational program improvement processes, compensatory education, and systemic and policy effects on students placed at risk. He is a founding coeditor of the *Journal of Education for Students Placed at Risk* and is also an executive committee member at large of the International Congress for School Effectiveness and Improvement. He has a Ph.D. in educational psychology from Temple University.

ELIZABETH SULZBY is a professor in the School of Education at the University of Michigan and recently was a visiting professor at Leiden University in the Netherlands. At Michigan she is affiliated with the Combined Program in Education and Psychology and the Center for Human Growth and Development. In addition to articles in research journals and research summaries in handbooks (*Reading Research*; *English Language Arts*; *Early Childhood*), her numerous publications include the influential book, *Emergent Literacy: Writing and Reading* (with William H. Teale). Her research covers issues of in-home mother-child interaction with books (with A.G. Bus and Marinus H. van IJzendoorn), emergent reading, emergent writing, early language impairment (with Joan Kaderavek), and the transitions into conventional reading and writing. She is currently involved in research with Sally Lubeck looking at parent-teacher-researcher collaboration in Head Start. She is a past president of Literacy Development and Young Children, a special-interest group of the International Reading Association; she is currently on the Primary Literacy Panel of New Standards and is conducting research as part of the Center for the Improvement of Early Reading Achievement. She has a Ph.D. in reading education from the University of Virginia.

Index

R

reading comprehension and,
  general, 63, 67, 216-219, 220
school restructuring, 231, 232
second grade, 215
second-language speakers, 11, 325
semantics and, 48
socioeconomic status, 47
spelling and, 6, 321, 322, 344
teacher education, 280, 332
tests and testing, 109
theoretical issues, 11, 325
see also Naming; Sight words;
  Word games; Word
  recognition
Voluntary reading, 81-83
Volunteer tutors, 12, 162, 273, 328
Vowels
  African American dialect, 239
  first grade, 198
  invented spelling, 59
  second grade, 212
  syllable defined, 22
  tutoring, 259

W

Welfare reform, 320
Whole language instruction, 199-201,
  205-206
Word games, 143, 151-152, 187, 203,
  204, 208
  riddles, 223
  see also Rhymes and rhyming
Word recognition, 4, 6, 7, 15, 220,
  272, 315-316, 322, 343
  automaticity and, 75, 79, 90, 252-
  253; *see also* Sight words
  computer-based interventions, 252-
  253
  curriculum casualties, 25-26
  early childhood development, 50,
  53, 62, 65-67, 70-75, 79, 80,
  111
  first grade, 194, 198, 204, 205-206,
  262
  fourth grade, 214

kindergarten, 180, 181-182, 188,
  189, 249, 251, 322
models of, 214
morphemes and, 73-74, 153
neuroscience, 24
onset-rime, 51, 185, 206, 259
phonics and, 173, 259
reading disabled children, 252-254
rebus books, 182, 204
second grade, 205-206, 212-213,
  322-323
second-language speakers, 236-237
small-group instruction, 262, 263
social development and, 262, 263
special education, 270
teacher education, 285, 330
theoretical issues, 236-237
third-fourth grades, 214
third grade, 211, 214
tutoring, 258, 261
see also Alphabetic principle;
  Automaticity; Frustration
  level; Semantics; Spoken
  words; Word games
Writing, 272, 314, 323
  computer-assisted instruction, 265
  early childhood development, 42,
  57, 59-60, 69-70, 142, 149
  deaf children, 164
  first grade, 81, 196, 197, 198, 200,
  204, 207, 209
  first-third grades, 6, 7, 285, 321-
  322
  Head Start, 281
  kindergarten, 183-184, 188, 189,
  191
  literacy defined, 42
  preventive interventions, 278
  second grade, 82
  small-group instruction, 263
  state action, 302
  teacher education, 280, 285, 296,
  298
  third grade, 83, 211
  tutoring, 259, 260
  see also Alphabetic principle;
  Emergent writing; Spelling